African Initiatives in
Christian Mission 4

UNISA

To Suzy and Peter!
With affection
and thanksgiving for our
shared pilgrimage in
Zimbabwe!

John Bunkur
12.12.99

AFRICAN INITIATIVES IN CHRISTIAN MISSION

This monographic series aims at publishing scholarly works of
high merit and wide interest on various aspects of Christian missions
in Africa. Close attention will be paid to the missionary genius and methods
of African Christians, as well as to interpretations of Christianity.

Series editors
Marthinus L Daneel
Dana L Robert

Editorial board
Greg Cuthbertson
Johannes N J Kritzinger
Tinyiko S Maluleke
Isabel Phiri
Tabona Shoko

Publications in series:

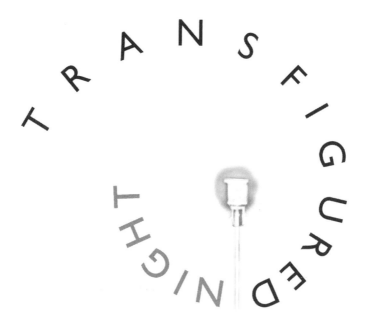

TRANSFIGURED NIGHT

Mission and culture
in Zimbabwe's
vigil movement

TITUS LEONARD PRESLER

FOREWORD BY
JOHN MBITI

UNIVERSITY OF SOUTH AFRICA PRESS
PRETORIA

© 1999 University of South Africa
First edition, first impression

ISBN 1 86888 051 6

Published by Unisa Press
University of South Africa
PO Box 392, 0003 Pretoria

Typeset in 10 on 13 pt Benguiat Book by Pretoria Setters, Pretoria
Printed by Mondipak, Pietermaritzburg

House editors: Liz Stewart, Sarie Moolman
Cover design and layout: Emma Presler, Hetta Vontsteen

CONTENTS

SERIES PREFACE

Literature on Christian mission in Africa has been biased toward the activity of Western-oriented mission. White missionaries, Western mission policies and the relationship of mission to European imperialism have dominated the discussion of African missions. Little or no attention has been paid by scholars to African initiatives in Christian mission, nor have missiological studies been made from the perspective of the so-called 'recipients'. Yet the phenomenal growth of Christianity in Africa has occurred in the twentieth century, much of it after the independence of the continent from outside control. The series African Initiatives in Christian mission represents an attempt to address the reality that the spread of Christianity in Africa, its shape and character, has been the product of African Christians, both in the 'Mission Churches' and the 'African Initiated/Independent Churches (AICs)*.

Mission churches and AICs are the two primary ecclesial contexts in which African initiative has occurred. Mission churches are those that have evolved directly from the outreach of Western denominations, and still represent the collegial traditions concerned. African Initiated Churches are churches begun by Africans in Africa primarily for Africans. AICs have consistently asserted their own leadership autonomy and religio-cultural contextuality free from the immediate control or influence of Western-oriented church leaders. These classificatory terms are somewhat misleading in that AICs are missionary churches *par excellence*, and the mission churches, by virtue of the missionary contributions of their members from the beginnings of their history, could be characterised as

---

* Nomenclature varies on the two groups of African churches. 'Mission churches' have also been called 'Historical or Established Churches'. The acronym 'AICs' originally stood for 'African Independent Churches', a term which is still preferred by many scholars. In recent years, the World Council of Churches has tended to use the term 'African Initiated Churches'. In this series, different authors are free to use any of the three they choose. But in the introduction to the series the editors generally refer to 'African Initiated Churches' because the term resonates with the title 'African Initiatives in Christian Mission'.

African Initiated Churches. Nevertheless the distinction between the two families of churches remains important for historical and sociological reasons.

This series seeks to overcome some of the limitations in previous studies of missions in Africa. Mission churches have been analysed primarily as denominational institutions, with a focus on educational work, or else as participants in political processes such as nation building. Less attention has been paid to mission churches as social movements, as products of indigenous culture and leadership, or as creators of African theologies. In short, the indigenous mission dimension has been weak in many of these studies. Works on mission churches today tend to be generalised rather than based on reliable, representative information gleaned from empirical enquiries. Thus the uniqueness and witness of these churches remains obscure. A predominantly male image of church history, moreover, has resulted in a paucity of literature on the contribution of women to church life and church expansion. The roles of black women pioneers in African churches are of particular interest to the editors of the series.

As regards the African Initiated Churches, the tendency in most of the earlier studies has been to assess AICs in terms of reaction to Western missions, separatism or protest against oppressive colonialism. As a result the missionary genius, missionary methods and missiological significance of AICs have not been studied in depth. However, the contribution of the AICs to the growth and religio-cultural footedness of Christianity in Africa is of vital importance for the development of a relevant mission theology in Africa. It is increasingly evident that in terms of growth rates, indigenised evangelisation, missionary campaigns, and ecclesial contextualisation, the AICs are not peripheral but belong to the mainstream of African Christianity. Their contribution therefore should be evaluated as such, alongside that of the mission churches. Critical, yet open and fair-minded field studies should overcome the bias that has frequently distorted AIC studies in the past.

The ideas behind African Initiatives in Christian Mission originated in an interdisciplinary research project conceived by Professor Marthinus L Daneel. With thirty years of empirical research on AICs in Zimbabwe, Daneel gathered a team of researchers from South Africa, Zimbabwe, and Malawi and received a grant in 1994 from The Pew Charitable Trusts. Assisted by field workers, researchers set out to gather data on different facets of African initiative within various churches in southern Africa. Meeting periodically at the Department of Missiology at the University of South Africa, the researchers reported on the work in progress and received feedback from other team members. The cooperative nature of the project was essential to its success, for the original team included members of mission churches and AICs, academics and practitioners, blacks and whites. The Research Institute for Theology and Religion at Unisa provided administrative support, and Professor Dana Robert participated as the representative of Boston University, the official host institution for the project.

Out of the project meeting emerged a decision to hold an international conference in 1997 on 'African Initiatives in Christian Mission in Southern Africa'. As well as the conference, the group decided to launch a publication series that would make the results of the project available to scholars and church people in Africa. Given the lack of research and its limitations as outlined above, the project participants decided to broaden the focus of the series beyond southern Africa and, by implication, beyond the core group of scholars. The widest possible definition of 'mission' underlies the series. The participant scholars agreed to deal essentially with Christian mission: the outreach of Christian faith and life in the extension of Christ's good news beyond the boundaries of ignorance, cultures, poverty, suffering or whatever obstacles obscure a clear Christian witness in the world. Nevertheless, not all contributors are missiologists and their research methodologies include phenomenological, socio-anthropological, historical and distinctly non-theological approaches, or a combination of these. Yet the team feels that even if the joint venture, against the background of diverse disciplines, runs the risk of controversy and overdiversity within the series, the overall outcome will be both challenging and enriching. The qualification 'African initiative', too, is not subject to narrow definition. Black and white African theologians, for instance, are contributors in this series. And despite the predominant concern with black African initiatives, a number of studies on white missionary endeavour will be included, particularly the attempts of black African scholars to interpret the legacy of white-controlled missions, their impact on African society and the attitudes and response of African communities to such endeavour. In many respects white and black participation in mission in Africa are two sides of the same coin, the implication being that study of one enhances understanding of the other.

On behalf of all participants in this joint research and publishing venture, we express our appreciation to our sponsors, the staff of Unisa's Research Institute for Theology and Religion, and Unisa Press. Their support remains crucial in the realisation of the envisaged goals.

About this publication

Transfigured night is an excellent study of missionary outreach and contextualisation in the contexts of the African Initiated Churches and the mission-founded churches in the eastern regions of Zimbabwe. Titus Presler provides us with a probing and compelling analysis of the manner in which the all-night community gathering, or *pungwe*, of Shona tradition has become a staging platform for mobilisation and empowerment in Zimbabwe's liberation struggle, which culminated in independence in 1980, and in the remarkable renewal and growth of Shona churches in the post-war period.

The *pungwe* is a pivotal nocturnal event of spiritual encounter between family or clan members and their ancestors (*vadzimu*). Through spirit possession, divination, funerals and propitiatory rites the bonds between the living and their forebears are strengthened. Thus, in the deep of the night, so to speak, the protective powers of the ancestors are invoked in order to secure wellbeing for their living descendants, healing for the afflicted, protection for the vulnerable against wizardry attacks, and productive fertility for the land, of which the senior clan *vadzimu* are the custodians. As a focus-point of heightened ritual experience the *pungwe* represents the enacted essence of Shona traditional religions; hence its catalytic significance for spiritual renewal and community solidarity.

xii

Presler draws a convincing picture of the guerrillas' transformation of the *pungwe* during the liberation struggle for the purpose of liberative empowerment. During the all-night *pungwe* rallies of political lectures and rousing *chimurenga* songs, the guerrillas managed – in close collaboration with the spirit mediums – to mobilise and unite peasant society in their quest for the reclamation of the lost lands at the behest of the national ancestral heroes, Chaminuka, Nehanda and Kaguvi, and the regional spirit-guardians of the land. The integration of liberationist objectives with ancestral spirituality brought about a revitalisation of traditional religion, with the intensification of spirit medium and Mwari cult activities. On the other hand, many guerrillas denounced Christianity as an agent of colonialism, with the suppression of services, destruction of churches and martyrdom of individual believers as a result.

A focus on this negative aspect at times obscures the collaborative roles of some of the AICS and individual Christians of virtually all denominations in the war front. In the Masvingo Province, for example, there is ample evidence of Zionist prophets having played prominent roles during *pungwe* meetings, as the Christian counterparts of the spirit mediums, and having at times restrained guerrilla coercion as the underside of *pungwe*'s mission thrust. But the active participation of Christians in the struggle for the lost lands still requires detailed research and publication.

Despite the negative impact of war-time night vigils on church life, the intensity and popularisation of the *pungwe* enable the Christians in eastern Zimbabwe after independence to appropriate and contextualise it as a singularly powerful vehicle of evangelism, community bonding, church growth and theological debate. Presler is at his eloquent best in lucid descriptions of a wide range of innovations in the Christianised *pungwe* ceremonies of virtually all the denominations in Manicaland. The mission-founded churches, for example the Methodists, Anglicans and Presbyterians, have turned their night vigils into revivalist, evangelistic, ecumenical, leadership confirmation and female emancipatory events, with ecstatic manifestations in sermons, song and dance at the time of darkness when spirit possession climaxes in the traditional *pungwe*. Less inhibited by a Christian doctrinal heritage, the AICS in turn have developed their own distinct *pungwe* – patterns of inculturation.

xiii

The Marange Apostles with their fire-walking proclaim the imminent judgment of God and the urgency of conversion. The Pentecostal Apostolic Church of God, led by women, engages in elaborate night ceremonies of fasting, cleansing and confessions as they prepare for the exorcism of vengeful spirits. Ndaza Zionists proclaim the economically liberative presence of God in Zion through their colourful robed dances. The Jekenishen church focuses on a sacred sleep, followed by spiritually inspirational dream narration, and the Unity of the African Apostolic Faith Church arranges nocturnal pilgrimages up wilderness mountains.

Presler's work undoubtedly rates as one of the most significant in-depth studies in recent years on the contextualisation/inculturation of the African church. Its strength derives particularly from extensive fieldwork and participatory observation. This enables the author to unravel with great insight and care not only the rich tapestry of ritual life in the *pungwe* movement, but also the extent to which African grassroots Christians are directing the process whereby the proclamation of the gospel good news and the ritual expressions of worship take root in African cultures.

In view of the phenomenal growth of Christianity in Africa and is increasing significance in the global Christian community, the reading of this study, for academics, church leaders and lay people alike, is a must.

Marthinus Daneel (Project coordinator)
Dana Robert
Series editors

FOREWORD

'When the rain beats the leopard, its fur becomes wet, but its spots do not wash away.' So say the Akan of Ghana.

The introduction of Christianity into Africa through Western missionaries is like rain falling on the leopard. Obviously, the rain makes the fur wet and washes away dust and microbes. It does not intrinsically alter the genetic spots of the leopard, which continue to give it a distinct identity, even if they are not the only features that define what the leopard is. At the same time, the leopard needs the rainwater, and drinks and appropriates it to become part of its own life.

We do not want to push the analogy of this proverb too far, but something similar happened when Christianity came to the Shona people in Zimbabwe. It found Shona Religion standing firmly on its own ground, and it did not wipe it away. Nevertheless, the religious scene could not remain the same thereafter. Titus Presler's book ventures to peer into the arena in which Christianity arrived and settled among the Shona people. He highlights the night dimension of this religious encounter, looking at both its traditional and indigenous heritage and its new and Christian side. For the traditional side, I prefer the use of 'Shona Religion' to the author's 'Shona Spirit Religion', as there is more to people's religion than just one element, however important it may be.

It is a fascinating and informative study, opening up a wealth of insights into the religious life of the Shona, especially around the *pungwe*. As Presler defines it, the *pungwe* is 'a social, political or religious gathering that continues from dusk until dawn'. This glossary definition of the word, however, does not convey the pregnant contents of the term in reality. It is a world of its own, for a *pungwe* is a night vigil full of life – social, religious, spiritual and communal. It is an encounter between the living and the living dead (the departed) or other spirits, and between God and people, who include the sick in search of healing, and those seeking to keep away unwanted spirits and to communicate with other spirits.

Over the generations, *pungwe* became an essential aspect of

Shona life, comparable to the spots of the leopard. Presler explores how the traditional *pungwe* was not washed away by the coming of Christianity, even if some missionaries did advocate that Christians abandon it. Rather than giving it up when they became Christians, the Shona have transformed it into a real asset for church life. During Zimbabwe's fight for independence, *pungwe* was also appropriated to strengthen the political and military struggle. *Pungwe* has now become a positive aspect of the life of most churches, both those stemming directly from missionary work and those founded by local Christians (the Independent Churches).

Presler's study illustrates in a local and specific area how gospel and culture interact. We see Christian life thriving on a scene that has deep roots in Shona religion and culture. An otherwise Western form of Christianity is here being transformed into an appropriate form that speaks the language of the people, the *pungwe* language. The author demonstrates also how the *pungwe* was utilised for the Liberation War which ended with the attainment of independence in 1980.

After that political achievement, the *pungwe* movement (as Presler calls it) was appropriated more and more by the churches, to the degree that it has become an almost indispensable aspect of Christian life. So, appropriately, he writes: 'The pungwe is a flexible but formative ritual phenomenon in Shona life ... The *pungwe* movement is a movement of wilderness nights during which people engage the major spiritual struggles of their lives, gain victory and so make of the wilderness a garden.' The result, he tells us, is that 'Shona Christians have localized Christianity without parochializing it, for they have understood, embraced, and held fast to gospel insights that their fellow Christians in other cultures recognize as universal.'

This study, presented as it is in such a clear, readable and interesting style, gives us important insights into the process of religious change taking place in an African setting, when the Gospel says 'Yes!' to the traditional religious and cultural milieu. A look at local developments elsewhere in Africa makes us realise more clearly that the same process is taking place in other places, modified as it may be by the culture and traditions that reign there. This calls for a theological interpretation of this widespread phenomenon. Presler provides a framework for understanding it, as well as a theological exposition. Among other things, he points out some 'general principles of interaction between old and new. First, the new cannot be apprehended and appropriated except by means of the old, with the result that continuity persists in the midst of change ... Second, as the new is genuinely grasped, it is not merely captured by the old, but it transforms the old, so that elements of continuity experience significant change ... Third, the mutually conditioning encounter of a world religion with a local religion in its cultural context is crucial to the world religion's continuing vitality.'

It is intriguing to see how this study unfolds before reaching these principles, which, in turn, invite discussion and reflection. It enriches our understanding of Africa's explosive Christianity. After the rain the leopard's spots remain, but they are inwardly affected, for the leopard drinks that water to stay alive. The world of the *pungwe* night of the Shona remains, but, we are told, among the Christians it is 'transfigured'.

John Mbiti
Burgdorf, Switzerland

ACKNOWLEDGEMENTS

The journey that produced this study includes many places and many friends, without whose support and assistance it would not have been possible. It is a joy to thank them here.

The congregations of the churches of the Honde Valley welcomed me warmly and gladly to worship and talk with them, and I am especially grateful to these church leaders: Shepstone and Veronica Muzvidzwa of the Anglican Church; many evangelists of the Apostles of Johane Marange, including John Sachikonye of Bonda, who first introduced me to the Apostles in the 1980s; Isaiah Chiwati of the Full Gospel Church; Silas and Lydia Sithole of the Jekenishen Church; Lovemore and Mary Mupinda of the Mugodhi Church; SaMutuhmani of the *Ndaza* Zionists; Evelyn and Ezekiel Mhlambo, and Beulah Johns (Mbuya Maunganidze) of the Pentecostal Apostolic Church of God; and Pearson Chitare, Togarasei Kahlari, and David Mubaira of the United Methodist Church.

Managers, both past and present, of the Eastern Highlands Tea Estates (now Eastern Highlands Plantations) hosted the project and provided generous hospitality and logistical support. I am especially grateful to former personnel manager Lovemore Mbigi, who suggested the Honde Valley as a research site and made initial arrangements at the tea estates; former general manager Anthony Hewgill, who was eager to learn about the beliefs of the plantation workers; personnel manager Webster Zizhou, who coordinated logistical support both when I was on site and when I was out of the country; accountant Shepstone Muzvidzwa, who arranged many meetings and was generous with support; former industrial relations officer Pearson Chitare, who helped with both broad perspectives and daily details; and computer manager John Mufukare, who permitted me to use company computers to write up summaries.

A number of families welcomed me into their homes with care and tenderness. Lovemore and Mary Mupinda and their children received me as an uncle for three months, and Shepstone and Veronica Muzvidzwa and their family welcomed me as a brother for a month. Ezekiel and Evelyn Mhlambo, and Pearson and Veronica Chitare and their children were so hospitable. All my hosts devoted hours to exploring with me the details of Shona religious culture and, in some cases, commenting on drafts. Marthinus Daneel hosted me generously in his home for a long weekend and made available the staff of the Zimbabwe Institute for Religious Research and Ecological Conservation (ZIRRCON) in Masvingo. Nina Barnes helped with logistics from Mutare, and in Harare Anthony and Mim Haggie and Peter and Jane Ivy offered generous hospitality.

In the fieldwork I was blessed with faithful research assistants in Noah Chidhakwa and the late Leon Semu, who accompanied me on fascinating trips and ably transcribed and translated scores of liturgies, sermons and conversations. Violet Matimba made transcriptions and translations in both Massachusetts and Zimbabwe. Michael Mbona of Mandea and Irene Rinopfuka Mahamba, then in Cambridge, commented generously on drafts.

This study of the *pungwe* owes much to members of the Anglican Church in the Diocese of Manicaland who introduced me to the movement in the mid-1980s. Bishop Elijah Masuko invited my family and me to work in the diocese. I am grateful to Gervaise Chidawanyika, Mildred Mbwando, Edward Mangwanda, Sylvester Gorogodo, and other leaders in the Bonda Church District, who were passionate in their commitment to God's movement in the church. Webster and Winnie Simbabure and David and Mary Manyau offered splendid friendship and support as Anglican clergy families.

My wife, Jane Crosby Butterfield, was the first of our family to experience the *pungwe,* and her work with the Mothers' Union built integrally on the *pungwe* movement. I am grateful for her patience and support during the long germination of this project and during two research trips. Our children – Emma, Charlotte, Titus and Amos – treasure their years among the Shona people and were patient and interested during periods of research and writing. Emma has offerred her artistic gifts to the cover design. I am thankful for my parents, Henry Hughes and Marion Anders Presler, whose lifework with Hindus and Muslims in India cultivated in me a perennial interest in the interaction of religion and culture. They supported me in the completion of this project, and my parents-in-law, Charles and Lee Butterfield, offered generous support.

Colleagues in Massachusetts have supported the conception and completion of this work. I am especially grateful to Ian Douglas of the Episcopal Divinity School, who has offered enthusiastic friendship, missiological counsel, and persistent encouragement all along the way. Richard Omohundro believed the project would contribute to God's reign and made copious comments on drafts. Ann Makarias contributed a great deal of fine editing before publication and compiled the comprehensive index. Bishop David Birney, formerly of the Diocese of Massachusetts, encouraged the study. Former wardens Bill Guthrie and Caroline Banks encouraged the project during my pastoral ministry in St Peter's Church, Cambridge, and their successors, Tom Patterson and Lois Bennett, supported, with the Vestry, the sabbatical that produced the book.

I have been blessed with fine teachers who guided the studies that form the background of this study: Dana Robert, Lamin Sanneh and Marthinus Daneel in missiology; Robert Hefner in anthropology; and Paul Sampley and Howard Clark Kee in New Testament. Discussion with students in classes I taught at the Episcopal Divinity School also assisted my thinking. I am grateful to them all.

A number of groups and individuals have been generous in funding: the Episcopal Church Foundation, which granted a three-year graduate fellowship; the Continuing Education Committee of the Diocese of Massachusetts; the Theological Writing Fund of the Episcopal Divinity School; Alan and Louise Rogers of St Andrew's Church in Ayer; Bishop Hays Rockwell; Richard Omohundro; and Henry and Marion Presler.

Funding for field research was provided by the Research Enablement Program, a grant programme for mission scholarship supported by The Pew Charitable Trusts, Philadelphia, and administered by the Overseas Ministries Study Center, New Haven. The colloquium organised in connection with this grant enabled me to receive the encouragement of a number of individuals, especially Gerald Anderson, Kofi Asimpi, David Kerr, Stanley Nussbaum, John Pobee, A Christopher Smith, Yusufu Turaki and Andrew Walls.

Unisa Press has been a delight to work with. Editor Elizabeth Stewart has been patient and painstaking, art director Hetta Vonsteen has offered an attractive design, and publisher Phoebe van der Walt has been very supportive.

I am grateful for the counsel and support offered by all these individuals and many others. Errors of fact and interpretation, however, are my own responsibility. I am sure that in the perennial dynamic of God's mission they will be corrected by the people who are the subjects of this study.

Permission was granted by the Society for Promoting Christian Knowledge to reproduce Hymn 130 ('*Mukristu usnete*') and Hymn 12 ('*Zuva rangu Muponisi*') from the Anglican Shona hymnal, *Ndwiyo Dzomuchechi*.

This work is dedicated to the mission of God, to Jane, to the Anglican congregations of the Bonda Church District, and to the Christian churches of the Honde Valley, Zimbabwe.

ABBREVIATIONS

AACJM	African Apostolic Church of Johane Marange
ABCFM	American Board of Commissioners for Foreign Missions
AC	Anglican Church
AFM	Apostolic Faith Mission
AIC	African Initiated Church
ALS	Autograph letter signed
AMEC	African Methodist Episcopal Church
ATR	African Traditional Religion
BSAC	British South Africa Company
CCAP	Church of Central Africa, Presbyterian
CEB	Christian base community (Spanish, *comunidade eclesiale de base*)
DRC	Dutch Reformed Church
EHTE	Eastern Highlands Tea Estates
FGCG	Full Gospel Church of God
FRELIMO	Front for the Liberation of Mozambique
LAMA	Legal Age of Majority Act
LS	Letter signed
MFC	Mission-founded church
MNR	Mozambique National Resistance
Ms	Manuscript
MU	Mothers' Union
MUMC	Men of the United Methodist Church
PACG	Pentecostal Apostolic Church of God
PV	Protected village
RCC	Roman Catholic Church
RF	Rhodesia Front
RSV	Revised Standard Version
SDAC	Seventh-day Adventist Church
SLAEJC	St Luca's Apostolic Ejuwel Jekenishen Church
SPG	Society for the Propagation of the Gospel in Foreign Parts
SSJE	Society of St John the Evangelist
SSR	Shona Spirit Religion
TD	Typewritten document
TLS	Typewritten letter signed

TMs	Typewritten manuscript
UAAFC	Unity of the African Apostolic Faith Church
UCC	United Church of Christ
UDI	Unilateral Declaration of Independence
UMC	United Methodist Church
US$	United States dollars
ZANLA	Zimbabwe African National Liberation Army
ZANU	Zimbabwe African National Union
ZANU(PF)	Zimbabwe African National Union (Popular Front)
ZAOGA	Zimbabwe Assembly of God, Africa
ZAPU	Zimbabwe African People's Union
ZIPRA	Zimbabwe People's Revolutionary Army
ZIRRCON	Zimbabwe Institute of Religious Research and Ecological Conservation
ZW$	Zimbabwe dollars

Unless otherwise noted, biblical citations are from the New Revised Standard Version with the Apocrypha. Abbreviations of biblical books appear as found in that version.

ILLUSTRATIONS

CHAPTER 1

A night in the valley:
African communities on mission vigil

Evening is approaching in the Honde Valley, a tropical stretch of lowland along Zimbabwe's eastern border with Mozambique. The day has been warm but not hot, for it is April, and winter is approaching. It is Saturday, and for many in the valley the work of the week is done. The farming families scattered throughout the Honde on small holdings bordered by banana and papaya trees have tended to their ripening maize crop, weeded the vegetables, and carefully plucked the leaves from their tea bushes. The shops at Zindi Township and at Hauna, the burgeoning town in the central Honde that the government has designated a 'growth point', are about to close after the main shopping day of the week. Alongside the Pungwe River, hundreds of people are walking along the valley's one tarred road, and the local buses are full. On the Eastern Highlands Tea Estates the vast fields of tea that carpet the lower reaches of the Nyanga Escarpment with a brilliant green are finally quiet. Several thousand tea pluckers, both men and women, have worked the normal Saturday half-day, emptying their cane backbaskets of leaves on the scales, and by now they have received their pay for the week's work. Some board company lorries to return to their hamlets in the valley, from which they came in the pre-dawn darkness. Many walk back to their quarters in the company villages, where they live with their families.

At 5 or 6 o'clock women begin gathering outside the central hall at Village No 3 at Eastern Highlands. They have brought firewood and quantities of *upfu*, the coarse-ground cornmeal with which they plan to make *sadza*, the porridge that is the staple food of people in this part of the world. Fires are kindled, and over them the meal preparation commences, with some women stirring 275-litre barrels of *sadza* while others cut up mounds of cabbage for the relish that they will serve with the *sadza*. The women are members of the United Methodist

1

A typical household kraal in the Honde Valley

Methodist congregation that meets on the tea estate, and they are preparing for a *pungwe* (pronounced poong´-gway), an all-night gathering of singing, preaching, and praying that will conclude at dawn. As dusk falls, people begin to arrive, some in family groups and others individually. Knots of youth drift in. Many of the arrivals are Methodists, but the Methodists have invited all churches to participate in this *mubatanidzwa,* a binding together of various Christian groups. Thus many of the attendees are members of other churches, most of them from other mission-founded churches such as Anglican, Presbyterian, and Salvation Army, with a few Roman Catholics. Some come from the Apostolic, Jekenishen, Full Gospel, and Zion churches.

The Methodists' invitation is broader still, for members have been encouraged to invite friends and relatives who may not be part of any church. Many of the family groups have brought such guests with them – a friend from the next hamlet, an uncle who has never been interested in church, several of the children's friends from school. Members try to make these guests feel at home, inviting the adults into conversation, including the children in games. Then there are the non-church visitors no one invited, but who are simply drawn to the event. Already, popular Shona rock music can be heard from the radio at the beerhall up the lane, but some folks who would ordinarily be there have come here instead. They come by a little awkwardly, loitering at the edges until they see a friend they know. A conversation starts, they are invited to stay for supper, and then for the service. They stay a little while, or maybe long into the night, depending on how they feel about what's going on. Some have no religious affiliation, while others feel fundamentally loyal to the rites of Shona Spirit Religion.

People visit one another, the children running about or playing in the neighbouring crèche, or daycare centre. After dark, the supper is ready, and the mothers serve it on metal plates that groups of five or six people will share, each person dipping in with his or her fingers. Sitting on the edge of the verandah, on benches or on the ground, men eat with men, women with women, boys with boys, girls with girls. The meeting hall is lit by fluorescent lights and equipped with scores of wooden benches for seating. There the youth have begun to sing hymns and choruses loudly, melodiously and, as time goes on, feverishly. The singing is accompanied by the rhythmic clatter of many

3

hosho, dried gourd rattles, and presently several of the youth add drumming to the mix. As people finish their supper they join the youth until almost everyone is in the hall, and the sound becomes massive as the 300 or so people join in the choruses, often clapping or standing to execute a few dance steps. At the front of the hall committee members at a table are checking with one another about the schedule of speakers. Eventually, the lay leader of the local Methodist congregation rises to call the gathering to order. Representatives of other congregations are welcomed, prayers are offered, the theme scripture for the night is read out, and the first speaker is called forward with a hymn. The *pungwe* has begun.

On the other side of the tea estate, at Village No 6, members of the Zion Apostolic Church have likewise gathered at dusk on the level ground near the village's community centre. They have cooked supper on open fires, and all have eaten their fill. During supper, conversation among the men turned to the *mapungwe* (the plural form of *pungwe*) that used to be organised by the *vakomana,* 'the boys' who were the freedom fighters in the *Chimurenga,* Zimbabwe's Liberation War of the 1970s. They recall how the guerrillas came and summoned them to meetings in the night, how they sang liberation songs, and how 'the boys' expounded the conflict between the whites of the Rhodesian Front and the blacks of the Zimbabwe African National Union, or ZANU. One person mentions how someone was tried and shot as a collaborator at a *pungwe* just over the next ridge and how terrifying the experience was. Others recount stories of *mapungwe* they attended, the personalities of particular freedom fighters, how bad the fighting was, and where they moved their families in search of safety. Now, at their own night-time gathering, which continues a long-standing practice in their church, the Zionists have put on their vestments for worship, flowing white veils for the women, brilliantly coloured robes and head coverings for the men. Arches, called 'gates,' of freshly cut poles have been constructed and erected on the bare ground. Designated prophets stand at the gates and hear members confess their sins. Singing has begun, which all join as they finish their confessions. The open ground is essential to the Zionists, for now the men begin their dances, running in an oval about 14 metres long, holding their staffs high, and swirling in their brilliant robes. The occasion is a *dhiri,* the celebration of a young couple who have given birth to their first child. Members' vestments here pose a sharper visual distinction between

4

Spirit medium Mai Makwiana dances while possessed during an all-night vigil at Zindi Township in the Honde Valley

Mothers of infants born since the medium's last possession present their newborns to the medium, who greets them in the name of her guiding spirit, Muzanenhamo

5

members and visitors than among the Methodists, but there are a number of visitors: a few young men, some mothers, quite a few children. They are drawn by the drumming, by the spectacle of costume and dance, and by the preaching. During the night there will be prayers and prophecies, and many will preach, but much of the night will be danced away to the singing and the drumming. Another *pungwe* has begun.

Above the tea estates the terrain ascends more steeply to the west until it meets the Nyanga Escarpment, a 32-kilometre-long face of cliffs that rise up to the 2 816 metre summit of Mount Inyangani, Zimbabwe's highest peak. The *kraal* of Chief Zindi, one of the two main chiefs in this part of the valley, is located in the steeper upland. The time of harvest is not far away, and his household have called the people of the chieftaincy to seek a plentiful harvest from the *vadzimu*, the ancestral spirits of the chief, and especially from the *mhondoro*, the ancient progenitor spirit of the chieftaincy. For many days Chief Zindi's several wives have been brewing ritual beer for the occasion, and on this evening the fast-paced drumming at the kraal can be heard far below in the valley. A bull that for years has been designated as belonging to the *mhondoro* has been slaughtered, and an enormous meal has been prepared for all who will attend. A crowd of about two hundred people are gathering, who include many who are members – some nominal, some committed – of Christian churches. Many have no Christian affiliation; their religion is *Chivanhu*, Shona Spirit Religion. Among the crowd are a number of spirit mediums who will assist the group in meeting the ancestral spirits. The meal concludes after dark. With the help of several assistants presiding over different parts of the liturgy, the chief invokes the spirits, and the first libations of beer are drunk. The mediums dance to the drumming, different dances being performed under the influence of different spirits. The ritual will build toward possession by the spirits in the early hours of the morning. The *pungwe* has begun.

At Pimai, a hamlet just six miles south-west of Eastern Highlands along the main road, members of the Pentecostal Apostolic Church of God are gathering in the thatched shelter that serves as their meeting place until completion of their long-planned structure of brick and mortar. Excitement is high, for the local congregation, designated the Pungwe Branch, after the river that runs nearby, is to be visited by the church's

6

founder, Mbuya Maunganidze of Mutare. Word has been sent to all Pentecostal members in the villages and on the tea plantations, inviting them to attend a *pungwe* at Pimai tonight and encouraging them to bring friends and relatives. Many know about this church's special outreach to women who have been possessed by spirits, and the gathering crowd includes a number of visitors, most of them young women. Supper has been cooked and eaten, and now the folks gather for singing under the thatch. There are about 250 people altogether, and each person is vested according to the subgroup to which she or he belongs – married women, senior men, unmarried women, and so on. The founder arrives with her advisers by car at about 8 o'clock. Singing all the while, many in the shelter move out to greet her, and they dance in the light of lanterns. Mbuya Maunganidze retires to another shelter for supper and consultation with the branch committee and its leader, also a woman. The singing of the congregation is now at fever pitch. Presently the founder is ready. Resplendent in purple robes and an elaborate headdress, she greets the congregation and preaches. Other leaders speak. Later on, the founder will preside over a long session of exorcism as she herself speaks in tongues. The *pungwe* has begun.

At Muparutsa, a hamlet ten miles south of Pimai, perhaps the oldest type of *pungwe* among the Shona people has just begun. It is a vigil at the time of death. Earlier in the day a teenage daughter in the Mvuri family died suddenly and without warning as she was working in the garden in the afternoon. Twelve years old, Nyasha Mvuri was in Grade 7 at the nearby Muparutsa Primary School. The family and the community are shocked, for she seemed the picture of health. Word has been sent to the police at Ruda, near the Hauna Growth Point, but it is hard to know whether they and the medical examiner will arrive today or tomorrow. An uncle is trying to get word to relatives in other parts of the country. The funeral will take place three or four days hence, when distant relatives have had a chance to get here by bus. Meanwhile the community gather at the family's home: all their friends who live nearby; all their neighbours, whether or not they have been especially friendly; all their acquaintances from the shops at Muparutsa, and even co-workers from the tea estates, where Nyasha's parents sometimes work as pluckers. Everyone, or virtually everyone, is here, or will be sometime tonight or tomorrow, for absence is easily interpreted as ill will or even as a sign of having been involved in the death through sorcery.

As each group of visitors arrives, there is the sound of wailing. Dusk approaches, and the neighbours build fires in the Mvuri *kraal* and organise supper for the many people now streaming in. One relative receives contributions of money and records them in a book. People come not simply to offer their condolences and leave; they come to spend the night, and many of them will stay for the several nights that will elapse until the body is buried. Nyasha's body has been placed in one of the sleeping huts, and a blanket has been spread over it. The body cannot be left alone, for that would complicate her spirit's relationship with the family. The Mvuris are Anglican, members of nearby St Peter's Church at Mandea, just yards from the Mozambique border, and Nyasha's mother, Grace, is a member of the Mothers' Union. Many who gather with her are Mothers' Union members. Amidst the weeping, they are also singing church hymns and choruses, mostly from memory, though many have brought their Shona prayerbook hymnals with them. Between songs, one or another of the women and men crowded into the hut offers a prayer, reads a Bible passage or preaches. The preachers offer words of comfort, visions of hope, exhortations to persevere. One preacher breaks down as she recalls the life of Nyasha; someone leads a chorus until she can recover. None of what happens is planned or rehearsed. It will continue through the night, and through tomorrow night, and through the next night. A messenger has been sent to call the Anglican priest; when he arrives, today or tomorrow, he will plan funeral details with the family.

Outside the meeting hut some of the male relatives have gathered around a fire. Nyasha's death was too sudden, they agree. Someone suggests that a *nganga*, a diviner-healer, should be consulted to determine the cause of death. Has some relative engaged in *uroyi*, sorcery, to cause her death? Has the displeasure of the family spirits been incurred somehow? Was she poisoned? Distracted by grief, Nyasha's father, Robert, is unsure of how to proceed. He knows that his wife, Grace, does not want a *nganga* to be involved, for she believes her Christian convictions exclude any involvement in Shona Spirit Religion. He is not so sure, and he fears offending the spirits of his family. In this patrilineal society it is the *vadzimu* of his family who are involved. He agrees to have the *nganga* sent for; maybe the spirit diviner can do his work tomorrow night. Another *pungwe* has begun.

So it goes throughout the valley. From the sacred village of the

Jekenishen Church by the Mtarazi River at Gatsi huge drums can be heard as the Jekenishen faithful gather to dance, pray, sing and preach around the flag they erect for their nocturnal worship. At Chitambo, still further south in the valley, members of the Mugodhi Church gather for a *runyaradzo pungwe*, a time of consolation for the family of a person who died a few months ago. At Buwu, a village up toward the escarpment, a grandfather has died, and the community is gathering for several nights of *pungwe*. At Murara by the Pungwe River, Apostles of Johane Marange are gathering for an all-night celebration, called a *gungano*, as they prepare for the week-long festival their church will hold in July at Macheke near Headlands, about 130 kilometres to the west toward the capital city of Harare. Most of these night gatherings are larger than they were last year or the year before, for visitors attend them, and many of the visitors eventually become church members, who then invite more visitors.

Well beyond the Honde there are other *mapungwe* being held tonight. There may not be quite so many gatherings in any single area as there are here, for the Honde is much more densely populated than other communal lands, and there is an unusual range and number of church groups here. Yet in northern Manicaland west of the Honde, *mapungwe* are just as frequent for any one church group and just as prominent for the communities involved. Someone has heard that at Nyakatsapa, one of the oldest and most prominent Methodist missions, there is a youth *pungwe* being held tonight. The monthly *pungwe* organised by the Bonda Church District, a major Anglican district north of Mutare, is being held tonight at St Theresa's Church at Bvumba in the Manica Communal Area. There is a gathering of Topia, the First Ethiopian Church, near the government's district headquarters at Mutasa. In Mutare, Manicaland's provincial capital of 85 000, *mapungwe* are being held tonight in various churches, especially in such high-density suburbs as Sakubva and Dangamvura, where much of the Shona population are concentrated. And, of course, at any place where someone has died, which is many, many places, the *pungwe* has begun.

CHAPTER 2

The vigil movement in history, culture and research

On the threshold of the third Christian millennium, religion in Africa astonishes and intrigues the world with its vitality, diversity, and complexity.[1] Three interrelated dimensions of religious development in Africa particularly fascinate both general observers and scholars in the wider world. One is the exponential growth of Christianity and Islam in Africa during the twentieth century, so that the entire continent is now a major sphere for two of the great world religions. Second, alongside this growth of world religions is the survival and, indeed, revival of African religions that pre-date world religions' entry upon the scene and which exist in dynamic relationship with Christianity and Islam. Third, it is clear to even the casual traveller that people in Africa have developed forms of religious thought and practice that incorporate both indigenous traditions and distinctive features of the immigrant world religions.

These dimensions bear witness to the power of religious mission in the history and ongoing life of African peoples. Mission consists of the

---

[1]It was not always so. The religious consciousness of western Europe and America has widened steadily but slowly since the Renaissance, and Africa is one of the last regions of religious experience to be included within the circle of serious attention and respect. Even at the Jerusalem Meeting of the International Missionary Council in 1928, there was no paper presented on African religions in the extensive symposium on Christianity's relation to other religions, and only two speakers referred to African religion in the discussion. *The Jerusalem Meeting of the International Missionary Council, 24 March – 8 April, 1928: Vol 1: The Christian life and message in relation to non-Christian systems of thought and life* (New York and London: International Missionary Council, 1928), 297–298. Today, by contrast, the literature on African religion is enormous, and international conferences on religion, mission and church life include it as a matter of course.

spiritual vision and the practical means through which people promote their religious faith and work and invite the adherence and participation of others. In this sense, mission is certainly manifest in the spectacular growth of Christianity and Islam in Africa during the twentieth century. In the case of Islam, the number of Muslims has increased over ninefold between 1900 and the present, from 35 to 330 million, and their proportion of Africa's population has increased substantially, from 32 to 40 per cent. Islam's significant advance in Africa south of the Sahara has been supported by intentional outreach by Muslim organisations as well as by the witness of grassroots Muslim communities.

More dramatic is the twentieth-century story of Christianity in Africa. The nearly fortyfold increase in the number of Christians since 1900, from 10 to 380 million, constitutes more than a fivefold increase in the percentage represented by Christians among the continent's total population, from 9 to 46 per cent.[2] Christians have moved, therefore, from being a small minority to being the largest single religious grouping in Africa. It is well known that Christian mission organisations from Europe and North America played a major role in the initial announcement of the Christian gospel in Africa. What is less well understood is that Africans themselves were the gospel's major propagators, even in the early years of Western mission, and that today the thousands of African Christian churches have powerful and diverse ways in which they share their faith and promote their work.

African Christianity has, during the twentieth century, shifted from being a minor character on the stage of world Christianity, a stage previously dominated by Euro-American actors, to being now a major player as western Europe in particular has become increasingly secular and 'post-Christian'. 'At the end of the century,' Andrew Walls observes, 'Africa is appearing as the Christian heartland.' Increasingly, the global Christian community may need to take its cues from Christians in Africa:

> ... if ... we take the recent accession to Christianity in Africa along with the recent recession from it in the West, African Christianity must be seen as a major component of contemporary *representative* Christianity, the standard Christianity of the present age, a demonstration model of its character. That is, we may need to

---

[2]See table 1, appendix 2.

look at Africa today, in order to understand Christianity itself ... Africa can no longer be taken as peripheral to the study of Christianity; it contains too high a proportion of the world's Christians for that. And Africa may be the theatre in which some of the determinative new directions in Christian thought and activity are being taken.[3]

Mission is a principal area in which African Christians offer models for world Christianity. Among the regions of the world missionised by Euro-American Christians, it is in Africa that the missionised most quickly and most decisively became themselves the principal missioners. This history of mission by Africans among Africans accounts for the extraordinary growth of Christianity on the continent in this century. Extending Walls' comment, today we may need to look at African initiatives in mission in order to understand Christian mission itself.

The all-night vigils practised by many Christian groups in Zimbabwe are an especially striking instance of African Christians developing distinctive modes of mission outreach. Richly resonant with Shona religion, culture and politics, the all-night vigil, or *pungwe,* has become a major catalyst for evangelism and church growth among Shona Christians. This chapter introduces the missiological significance of the vigil movement in relation to African Christianity and discusses the interaction of world religion and local religious culture inherent in the *pungwe.* A review of my own history in the movement introduces the area in eastern Zimbabwe where the vigil movement is strongest and where the bulk of my *pungwe* research took place.

A mission matrix of spirits, war and church

An all-night community gathering among Shona people is called a *pungwe,* a word that combines a reference to continuing through the night with a reference to dawn.[4] Since Zimbabwe's achievement of political independence in 1980, dusk-to-dawn *pungwe* gatherings have become especially popular in most churches, both those founded by

---

[3]Andrew F Walls, 'African Christianity in the history of religions', *Studies in World Christianity* 2.2 (1996),185–186.
[4]See chapter 3 for a detailed discussion of the word's etymology. The plural is *mapungwe.*

Western missionaries and those founded by Africans. The frequency of *pungwe* gatherings and the diversity of churches in which they are held merits calling the phenomenon the *pungwe* movement, or the vigil movement, in Shona Christianity.

After the difficulties churches experienced in maintaining worship and retaining membership during the 1970s War of Liberation, the *pungwe* has been a principal means through which church life has been revived for ordinary Christians. After the war, church membership grew annually by about 10,5 per cent,[5] and, while the causes of this growth are many, the *pungwe* movement has been one of the principal factors. Through the vigils Christians have shared their spiritual vision and invited others to join their communities and participate in their work. This missional thrust catalyses impressive growth among Shona churches and constitutes an important instance of Christianity's growth on the continent. Contributing to the *pungwe* movement's effectiveness for contemporary mission are the *pungwe* tradition in the long-standing religion of the people, Shona Spirit Religion, and the political and military use that guerrillas made of the *pungwe* during Zimbabwe's War of Liberation. These features highlight the second and third aspects of African religion that intrigue the wider world: the revival of ancient African religions and their incorporation and transformation in the African expressions of world religions.

In Shona Spirit Religion (SSR), the dusk-to-dawn gathering is the primary religious event, for in it the family or clan gather to meet the group's ancestral spirits through divination and the experience of possession. All-night vigils are central in spirit possession, in the initiation of spirit mediums, in funerals and in subsequent propitiatory rites, often with the ceremonial climax occurring just before dawn. Among a wide range of Christian churches in Manicaland the *pungwe* is a similarly focal event as the faithful gather for all-night singing, preaching, praying, exorcising and healing, only now the worship is directed to the triune God, rather than to ancestral spirits. Even as Shona Christians oppose the rites of Shona Spirit Religion, participants often

---

[5]Zimbabwe National Evangelism Task Committee, *Target 2000* (Handbook for Target 2000 Congress, held 7–10 September 1992, Harare), B16.
For the decade 1990–2000 demographer David Barrett estimates, in personal correspondence, an annual growth rate of 2,55 per cent for affiliated church membership in Zimbabwe.

carry forward the traditional focus on spirits' presence by emphasising the presence and power of the Holy Spirit.

The spirituality of SSR produced the churches' *pungwe*. The longings and expectations implicit in the traditional all-night gatherings received a Christian focus, and the baptised and transformed *pungwe* flourishes. Among both mission-founded churches (MFCs) and African Initiated Churches (AICs), the night vigils synthesise traditional religion and Christian gospel to meet Shona longings for spiritual encounter, communal solidarity, and liberative empowerment. Where the traditional vigil's focus on the spirits of the family confines its appeal to the members of that group, the Christian vigil's focus on the universal, triune God propels it into an evangelistic mode that reaches out to the unconverted, the unbaptised, and the unchurched. With its roots in Shona religion, the *pungwe* has proved to be a credible setting in which Shona Christians carry on a lively debate about the claims of Christianity and the claims of SSR. Thus the church *pungwe* catalyses public apologetics.

During Zimbabwe's Liberation War, Marxist guerrillas trained in Tanzania and Eastern Europe consistently held all-night rallies during which they instructed rural peasants in the dynamics of colonialism and the goals of liberation, created enthusiasm for the war effort, and organised people to assist in practical ways such as providing food and carrying messages. In building on both the *pungwe* of Shona Spirit Religion and on vigils held in the churches before the war, the guerrillas modelled the adaptability of the *pungwe* and associated the practice with liberative spirituality. The *mapungwe* of the war often featured explicit denunciations of Christianity and strong efforts to advance Shona Spirit Religion as the only legitimate religion of the people. Church operations were often closed down by guerrillas, because some guerrillas associated churches with Rhodesian domination and because the liberation armies sought to demonstrate their power by disrupting the institutions of civil society. The frequent violence against suspected government collaborators during the guerrillas' *mapungwe*, often including executions, left many people with traumatic memories of the wartime night rallies.

Mission was a strong element of the wartime *mapungwe*, for the guerrillas used their rallies to advance the political agenda of the Liberation War and a religious agenda of reviving Shona Spirit Religion.

The two agendas were united by the religious dimension, for the ancestral spirits of SSR were promoted as the ancient custodians of the land which the Rhodesians had taken and which the guerrillas sought to reclaim. The war's eventual culmination in the victory of political independence validated the guerrillas' religious appeal in the eyes of many Zimbabweans. During the early years of independence SSR experienced explicit affirmation in many government pronouncements and ceremonies and a revival of adherence in the populace. Thus, the revival of an ancient African religion has taken place alongside marked Christian growth incorporating specific features of the pre-existing religious tradition.[6]

Despite their adversarial and traumatic associations, the spiritual power and communal intensity of the wartime *mapungwe* so energised the popularisation of Christian versions of the practice that the *pungwe* has become a primary expression of community life, theological development, church growth, and mission outreach among Christians in Manicaland and throughout Zimbabwe. In Zimbabwe's recent history, then, the *pungwe* of Shona tradition has become a crucible of cohesion and empowerment in two diverse contexts: the Liberation War that culminated in political independence in 1980, and the explosive renewal of Shona churches in the post-war period. The *pungwe* movement in the churches since independence is a striking instance of religious incorporation and transformation, with indigenous tradition transformed even as it is incorporated into a world religion. Conversely, the world religion is itself transformed as its theology highlights emphases of indigenous tradition and its practice is influenced by pre-existing rites.

The missional power of the *pungwe* arises largely from this dynamic of incorporation and transformation. The *pungwe* movement is thus a particularly fruitful phenomenon from which to develop a model of the interaction between world religion and local religion in a particular cultural setting. This analysis, in turn, forms a basis for understanding mission initiatives in contemporary African Christianity.

---

[6]See table 1, appendix 2. The influence of 'traditional religions' such as Shona Spirit Religion is much greater than the flat numbers and declining percentages might suggest. Chapter 7 discusses the statistics in greater detail.

Dynamics of religion, culture and mission

All-night vigils among the Shona people catalyse an interaction between immigrant Christianity and indigenous religion and culture. A culturally formed confidence that nocturnal ritual offers spiritual encounter, community solidarity, and liberative empowerment constitutes the formative yet flexible matrix for *pungwe* practice in diverse historical settings. During the war *pungwe* practice prompted freedom fighters to promote Shona Spirit Religion and enabled them to mobilise the rural population for a struggle they otherwise might not have supported so actively. In the churches, the *pungwe* has become a vehicle for expressing and celebrating Christian conviction and community life through Shona idioms with an authenticity that has proved powerful in drawing ever-increasing numbers of people into the life of the churches. *Pungwe* origins in Shona Spirit Religion indicate that a complex religious and cultural practice has enabled the Christian gospel to take deep root in an African culture.

The immigrant and indigenous elements in the *pungwe* movement meet on roughly equal terms in the sense that neither of them enjoys a disproportionate political advantage. The Christian dimension has been so thoroughly appropriated into the indigenous religio-cultural context that it cannot be said that the *pungwe* in the churches represents a foreign Christian intruder masquerading in indigenous religion and culture. Conversely, the *pungwe* in the churches is so authentically Christian that it cannot be said that an indigenous practice has simply absorbed and essentially compromised the immigrant religious impulse. The *pungwe* is a contextual form of African Christianity. In the *pungwe* we see the Zimbabwean church flowering as a Shona religious and cultural phenomenon, for the *pungwe* represents a uniquely African contribution made through African initiative and agency.

Interactions between world religions and local religious cultures are conditioned by a tension between unity and diversity as a nominally unitary world religion is expressed in the particularity of a specific context. The tension is real for both the student of religion and the religionist of any specific context. For the student of religion, variation among religious expressions that share a nominal identification – such as 'Christian', 'Muslim', or 'Buddhist' – highlights the importance of establishing criteria by which relationships of mutual identity and affiliation among these expressions can be posited.[7] For religionists the tension between unity and diversity is experientially urgent. Like crafts, arts, professions, political systems and ideologies, religions have norms of belief and behaviour. It is intrinsic to norms that they introduce criteria of unity and establish boundaries of belief and practice that define group membership. Most simply, the tension is expressed in these questions: 'What must I believe and do to be a member of this group? Once I am a member of the group, how much divergence from stated belief and practice will the group allow before I am no longer considered a member?'[8]

A world religion is one that has made a transition from origins in one particular context to manifold expressions in multiple contexts, a transition that is accomplished through religious mission in some form. Whether by centralised authority or by a much more diffuse consensus, the tension between unity and diversity is generally accommodated through designating certain norms of belief and practice as central and irreducible and allowing for differing views and practices in matters regarded as less important. The criteria by which centre and periphery are established also change over time in response to diverse pressures. Interpretation of the centre or the core of a religion is not static, for the pressure of local interpretation works changes in how people define the core in their context. The cumulative pressures deriving from diverse contexts tend to work changes in the core as defined by the global consensus of a particular religion. The nature and extent of such changes are usually a matter

---

[7]This task is endemic to the study of religion. For an analysis of the relationships among cults and mysteries of the Hellenistic period see Luther Martin, *Hellenistic religions: an introduction* (New York and Oxford: Oxford University Press, 1987), 155–163. For analysis of the relationship between classical Hinduism and tribal religion in the village Hinduism of modern India, see Henry H Presler, *Primitive religions in India: a textbook on the primitive religious type among India's tribals* (Bangalore: Christian Literature Society, for the Senate of Serampore College, 1971), 234–255 and *passim.*

[8]This formulation of questions draws on Howard Clark Kee's analysis of first-century issues of Jewish identity in 'From the Jesus Movement toward Institutional church' in *Conversion to Christianity: historical and anthropological perspectives on a great transformation*, edited by Robert Hefner (Berkeley, Los Angeles, and Oxford: University of California Press, 1993), 47–48. See also the group-grid analysis of social anthropologist Mary Douglas in *Natural symbols: explorations in cosmology*, with a new introduction by the author (New York: Pantheon Books, 1982), 54–64.

of discussion and are often controversial. Typically, divergences regarded as extreme are bracketed as heretical and their associated groups are marginalised or expelled from practical membership in the group.

The interaction between world religion and local context in the *pungwe* movement has four interrelated dimensions, all of them bearing on the missional character of the movement. The first is the specifically interreligious dimension, the encounter between immigrant Christianity and the long-standing religion of the people, Shona Spirit Religion. In this study, religion is understood as the dimension of human individual and social experience concerned with relationships between human beings and reality experienced as supernatural or divine. These relationships are experienced in thought, emotion, and morality, and they are pictured in an idealised way in ritual.[9] The strong resemblance between the church *pungwe* and the all-night ceremonies of SSR forms the basis for this study's claim that the church rite represents an interaction between Christianity and indigenous religion. The interreligious dimension is prominent in the thought of many Manicaland Christians as they discuss the character of God, the operations of the spirit world, the nature of religious experience, the content of moral action, and the relevance of outreach to their non-Christian neighbours. Thus, the interreligious dimension is experienced locally, and it provokes theological reflection that has ontological, ritual, ethical and missional elements. The mutual contextualisation of world religion and local religion in the *pungwe* movement helps to illuminate the character of such interactions on a global basis.

A second dimension of the world-local interaction is culture, understood as the socially patterned media with which people interact to express and organise themselves. The relation between religion and culture is complex, and distinctions are not easy to draw. Religion is not reducible to culture, but it is clear that religious faith, thought and practice are shaped by the wider context of social practice in which they live, producing a religious culture of shared understandings and practices. Similarly, religion itself affects cultural perceptions, practices and norms. This study recognises that the interreligious encounter is shaped in major ways by the cultural dimensions of the religions concerned: in Christianity, the lifeways of incoming British,

---

[9]Detailed discussion of terms such as religion, culture, ritual, SSR and so on is found in appendix 3, Terms of discourse.

18

American and South African missionaries beginning in the late nineteenth century; in SSR, the lifeways of the Shona people. In this cultural dimension the study seeks to illuminate the process by which Christianity as a world religion takes root in human culture.

The interaction of religion and culture leads naturally into the issue of religious change, a third dimension intrinsic to the interaction between immigrant religion and indigenous context. Change of any kind entails newness, but religious change – like ideological, artistic and technological change – rarely involves the sheer replacement of one system by another. Changes in human thought, however radical, always have an incremental and integrative character, for the new cannot be apprehended except by means of the old. The new thus stands in a dialectical relationship with the old, building upon the old at the same time that it challenges the old. The process is thus synthetic as well as creative, eclectic as well as innovative. Religious change is not indiscriminately eclectic, of course, for religious systems have norms and centres of authority, and the distinction between core and periphery tends to be an important one for adherents. Change thus raises questions of identity and authority. In the encounter of Christianity with Shona religion and culture, how are decisions made about the shape of the resulting synthesis? What criteria do people use to determine the acceptability of elements of Shona religion and culture? What criteria are used for accepting elements of Christian tradition and the European form in which it was initially introduced to the Shona people?

Christian mission is the fourth dimension of the encounter of world religion and local context. Christianity arrived among the Shona people through the efforts of Western-origin missionaries whose purpose was to proclaim the Christian gospel, encourage conversion, and gather converts into worshipping congregations. The outward appearance of early Christianity in Zimbabwe was characterised by 'missionary Christianity' in which missionaries dominated the churches politically, and Euro-American forms heavily influenced church life in corporate worship, group organisation, clergy leadership, church finances and sanctuary architecture. Many of these features persist in Shona Christianity under indigenous leadership in the independence period, more so among the MFCs, less so among the AICs. The long history of all-night vigils in the churches, however, undercuts generalisations of missionary dominance, either in the past or the present, and requires recognition of early enculturation and missional outreach by Shona Christian communities, both mission-founded and African Initiated. It becomes clear that Africans moved very quickly from being the missionised to being the principal missioners of the gospel in their own context.

The prominence of the *pungwe* highlights questions in the complex relationship between missionary Christianity and the emergence of the vigil movement as a mission outreach. What link does the *pungwe* have with Protestant revivalism brought by American Methodists? Given the non-missional character of vigils in Shona Spirit Religion, what have been the relative influences of Western missionaries and the wartime rallies in giving the present church *pungwe* such a strong missional character? Much discussion of missionaries' impact has focused on what missionaries failed to do in the past and on what they should resolve to do in the future in being sensitive to culture. The *pungwe* movement suggests that the role of missionaries was more complex than often imagined, encouraging as well as inhibiting indigenous initiatives, and was less central to the cultural debate than often thought.

The missiological dimension of the vigil movement also sheds light on the roles of mission-founded churches and African Initiated Churches in African Christianity. Contemporary discussion sometimes assumes that the vitality and authenticity of African Christianity is to be found chiefly in the AICs and that the MFCs are prominent but relatively inauthentic forms of immigrant Christianity. In fact, the *pungwe* movement began in the MFCs well before the founding of Shona AICs, and the vitality of the movement throughout Shona Christianity demonstrates that the MFCs make distinctive contributions, especially ecumenically, to authentic African Christianity and vital Christian renewal.

Missiology shares religion's general concern for norms and thus puts its particular stamp on global questions of gospel and culture. In the process of Christian diffusion, how is Christ understood through the cultural experience of peoples? In the propagation of the Christian gospel, how are transitions made from one cultural context to another so that religious unity is maintained even as local diversity is honoured? What insights into the Christian gospel are emerging from African communities? In the case of the *pungwe,* how does Shona culture serve both to illuminate and to distort the Christian gospel, and how do Shona Christians go about answering that question? What directions does the *pungwe* movement suggest for mission initiative from within newly evangelised peoples?

The *pungwe* movement among Christians in Manicaland is a phenomenon rich in insight for these questions. The all-night vigils of prayer, preaching and song are a thoroughly contextualised form of Christianity in the African context. They draw enormous numbers of people and are the primary vehicle for religious renewal in most of the churches in eastern Zimbabwe. They are an outstanding example of how the Christian gospel engages culture. The *pungwe* is an event, a praxis, a lived spirituality that brings us to the heart of Christianity as experienced by a people whose life with Christianity began with the Euro-American missions of just a century ago.

Pungwe quest: immersion and research in a movement

Participation as a missioner

The dynamism of the *pungwe* movement became clear to me through a personal engagement with Shona Christians in Manicaland, and research involved intensive fieldwork among a large number of religious groups in a complex and fruitful setting. As a missioner of the Episcopal Church USA in partnership with the Anglican Diocese of Manicaland, I was for three years priest-in-charge of the Bonda Church District in the highlands north of Mutare, the major city of eastern Zimbabwe and see city of the diocese. The period was 1983–1986, a time of political change and social ferment. Independence for Zimbabwe had been won just three years earlier, in April 1980, following sixteen years of confrontation that included seven years of full-scale guerrilla war. The Diocese of Manicaland was likewise young, for in late 1981 it had been constituted from the eastern section of the Diocese of Harare.

St David's Mission, Bonda, commonly known simply as Bonda Mission, was established in 1910 after African evangelists from St Augustine's Mission at Penhalonga gathered a congregation of Christians in the area, and the ministries of the mission have grown over the years. In

1983 the Bonda Church District included three Shona congregations: St David's Church, historically the mother church of all the congregations in the district, St Gabriel's at the village of Chirarwe, and St George's at Dziwa. Later the diocese added to the district five congregations to the south in the Manica Communal Area, in the villages of Bvumba, Manyau, Mapfekera, Njerama, and Zambe.[10] I devoted major attention to the congregations, trekking among them to offer liturgy, preach, and support the local catechists. District-wide events such as lay-training programmes, choir festivals and annual governance meetings were also an emphasis. Such a congregational focus was clearly needed after the suffering of the Liberation War.

Fairly early on, lay leaders approached me with a request that a *pungwe* be held in St David's Church, Bonda. They told me that the *pungwe* would involve people staying up all night in the church, that there would be a good deal of singing and preaching and that this was something people liked to do. My wife, Jane Butterfield, had previously attended an all-night vigil at neighbouring Dziwa and it had been a powerful experience. The request seemed reasonable and I assented with enthusiasm. The event amazed me with the number of people involved, the passion of the preaching, the strength of the singing and, of course, the endurance of several hundred people staying up all night. It was not long before *mapungwe* became quite frequent at Bonda and they were held in connection with youth gatherings, Mothers' Union meetings, stewardship initiatives, men's revivals and major church festivals. Only later did people tell me that previous clergy, both black and white, had generally not permitted such gatherings in church buildings. For decades people had held night vigils more privately in homes in the outlying villages, mainly for spiritual revival. They had called them by such names as *gungano* (meeting) and *rutan-*

---

[10]The mission centre at Bonda itself includes Bonda Hospital, established in 1928, now a well-known medical facility and the only Anglican hospital in the country; St David's Girls High School, a major institution in Zimbabwean secondary education since its founding in 1960; Bonda Primary School, a continuation of the elementary education offered since the founding of the mission; the Bonda Women's Development Centre, established in 1984 for women's economic and social empowerment; and the Community of the Holy Transfiguration, a monastic community of women and men, founded in 1982. Together these institutions make Bonda the largest Anglican mission in the country.

daro (discussion) rather than *pungwe,* the term that became current as a result of the all-night rallies held during the Liberation Struggle, but the nature of the meetings had been similar.

Church people at Bonda and throughout the area north of Mutare preferred the *pungwe* to any other setting when they wished to encourage revival or to launch a major initiative. Seeing the phenomenon as a major factor in the revitalisation of Anglican life in the post-war period, I became an enthusiast of *mapungwe.* I attended many of them at Bonda and at other locations, participated in planning and introduced some innovations such as merging the *pungwe* with the Great Vigil of Easter. The *pungwe* became part of my pastoral strategy, and church members began to celebrate the support that I gave to the practice as a Euro-American priest The same was true of Jane's participation, especially in the frequent *mapungwe* of the Mothers' Union.[11]

Hothouse research in the Honde Valley

In the 1990s I undertook research into the *pungwe* in the Honde Valley, a low-lying and densely populated area along eastern Zimbabwe's border with Mozambique. While contiguous with the highlands area of Bonda west of the valley, this was a fresh context that offered several advantages. The valley and the tea estates are a hothouse of *pungwe* activity among many churches. With people having come from various parts of Zimbabwe and other countries to work and settle in the valley, the *pungwe* can be observed among diverse social groups speaking various Shona dialects and other languages. This diversity includes a large number of church groups, both mission-founded and African Initiated, making for ecumenical breadth. Shona Spirit Religion is strong in the Honde, making the valley ideal for exploring the interaction between gospel and Shona religious culture. Using a secular tea plantation as a base enabled me to avoid direct institutional association with a specific church and facilitated my being accepted as an ecumenical observer by the churches and, to some extent, by traditional religionists.

---

[11]This appreciation was all of a piece with her role as the first white woman in the history of Rhodesian and Zimbabwean Anglicanism to become a member of the Mothers' Union, the organisation of black Anglican women, as distinguished from organisations of white Anglican women.

The Honde Valley boasts a warm and humid climate good for growing tropical fruits and cash crops such as tea, coffee and tobacco. The valley derives its name from the Honde River,[12] which begins in the Mutasa North Communal Land in the highlands and forms the international border for about 15 kilometres before moving on into Mozambique. The term 'valley' was doubtless suggested by the precipitous drop from the 2 000-meter-high Nyanga Escarpment, which runs along the area's western edge as part of the continent's great geological rift. For much of the valley, however, there is no corresponding mountain range or escarpment to the east but rather densely forested lowland stretching into Mozambique. This relatively unimpeded access from Mozambique made the Honde a major battleground in the Liberation War and, more recently, the scene of incursions by rebels during the Mozambican civil war of the 1980s.

The valley's terrain is creased throughout with ridges and genuinely flat areas appear only along the immediate shores of the major rivers. Tea fields form a spectacular vista of rolling green over the hills between the valley floor and the steeper grades of the escarpment. A second major river in the valley is the Pungwe, which descends from the escarpment and moves east, forming, like the Honde River further south, the international border for about 10 kilometres before flowing into Mozambique and, eventually, the Indian Ocean.[13] One tar road descends to the valley from the south and runs about 50 kilometres to the north-east, before ascending as a dirt road up into the remote mountains of Nyafaru. Among scores of villages, Hauna is the one town and the government has designated it a 'growth point'; Gatsi and Zindi are the next largest centres. The three tea plantations at the northern end of the valley represent considerable population centres, with 5 000 to 15 000 residents each.

---

[12]For the Shona word *honde*, Hannan lists no meaning in Chimanyika, although in Chikaranga it denotes smallpox or a pockmark, and in Chizezuru a sable antelope bull. In view of the prominence of sable antelope at low altitudes, especially during the pre-colonial period, the latter meaning may be a more likely source for the name of the river. M Hannan, *Standard Shona dictionary*, 2nd edition with Addendum (Harare: College Press, 1981), sv.

[13]See map 3, appendix 1. The question whether there is an etymological connection between the Pungwe River and the term for all-night vigils is discussed in chapter 3.

Honde Valley vista, looking north-east across the teafields of Eastern
Highlands Tea Estates

Tea pluckers weigh their leaves and load them onto a trailer, where Ndaza
Zionist leader SaMutuhmani receives them

The Bantu peoples living in the 1890s within the bounds of what was becoming Rhodesia and is now Zimbabwe are estimated to have numbered about 500 000.[14] Probably over 80 per cent of the total were members of groups now loosely termed Shona: the Kalanga, Karanga, Korekore, Manyika, Nambya, Ndau, Tawara and Zezuru. The Zulu-related Ndebele in the south-west comprised most of the remainder, with a few smaller groups also represented.[15] The Manyika people inhabit the area east of Rusape and north of Mutambara, which includes the Honde Valley, Bonda and Nyanga. Chimanyika is their dialect and today the eastern districts constitute the government province of Manicaland. In pre-colonial times, the chieftaincy of Mutasa, centred at Watsomba, was a major political influence among the Manyika. Today the seven sub-chiefs and their respective areas found in the Honde Valley are nominally under Chief Mutasa, who is termed *mambo,* which means 'paramount chief' or 'king', although such positions became largely ceremonial in the colonial and independence periods.[16] Chibunji is a sub-dialect of Chimanyika that continues to be spoken in the Honde Valley and westward into the highlands as far as Bonda. While the Honde's population in 1890 was probably not more

---

[14]P E N Tindall, *A history of Central Africa* (Harare: Longmans, 1983), 208.

[15]The social patterns of clans living and interacting in proximity with one another over extended periods of time make strict delineations of ethnic and linguistic groups dubious. It is misleading to call these peoples 'tribes', for the term connotes a distinctive social, religious and cultural identity correlating with a clearly defined distribution of political power in a bounded social group. A satisfactory term for the African context may be 'ethnolinguistic group'. The practice of using 'Shona' as a general designation uniting linguistically affiliated groups is probably European in origin. Nevertheless, 'tribe', 'tribal' and 'tribalism' are used commonly in Zimbabwean political discourse today to characterise current political rivalries. For further discussion, see Aeneas Chigwedere, *From Mutapa to Rhodes: 1000 to 1890 AD* (London, UK, and Salisbury, Zimbabwe: Macmillan, 1980), 153; Leroy Vail, 'Religion, language and the tribal myth: the Tumbuka and Chewa of Malawi', in *Guardians of the land: essays on Central African territorial cults,* ed J Matthew Schoffeleers (Gweru: Mambo Press, 1979), 209; Terence Ranger, *The invention of tribalism in Zimbabwe* (Gweru: Mambo Press, 1985), 4.

[16]Despite the Honde Valley's geographical continuity with Mozambique rather than Zimbabwe, its status as part of Chief Mutasa's realm was what prompted its inclusion in Rhodesia rather than Portuguese East Africa in the Anglo-Portuguese Treaty of 1891.

than 5 000, the 1992 census indicated a population approaching 100 000, close to two-thirds of Mutasa District's 163 812.[17]

The ethnic character, density and lifestyle of people in the Honde Valley in the late twentieth century is conditioned substantially by the area's history under the land management policies of the colonial governments of Rhodesia. For Honde residents, as elsewhere in Zimbabwe, land has always been central to life in its familial, social, economic, political and religious dimensions. Land is the source of economic production, subsistence and prosperity, and the past, present and future of families and clans are linked conceptually to the land on which they have lived and worked. The family's ancestral spirits are the primary custodians of the land and they prefer to be encountered there. Traditional tenure developed in ways designed to preserve these values:

> In African cosmology such an important natural endowment as land does not have a marketable value. Prior to the advent of colonial rule in ... Zimbabwe, the prevailing African land tenure system vested land rights in a corporate group which had overriding rights over those of the individual. The king or chief served as the Trustee who allocated land to newcomers and ensured that its use was in harmony with the traditional land tenure formula. The traditional land tenure system also accepted that land rights were inalienable. Land belonged to the living and to the unborn as well as to the dead. No member of a group could sell or transfer land to an outsider as land was considered a natural endowment in the same category as rain, sunlight and the air we breathe.[18]

The assumptions and intentions of colonial powers about land and its tenure in the late nineteenth century could not have been more different, although the contrast is common to the Western encounter with indigenous societies in Africa, Asia and the Americas. By charter in 1889 the British government gave the British South Africa Company

---

[17] *Zimbabwe Census 1992: preliminary report* (Harare: Central Statistical Office, 1992), 30. Manicaland's population of 1 537 676 made it the largest province, constituting 14,8 per cent of the national population of 10,4 million. Zimbabwe's mid-1997 population was 11,7 million. *Zimbabwe: country profile, 1997–98* (London: Economist Intelligence Unit, 1997), 2.

[18] Henry Moyana, *The political economy of land in Zimbabwe* (Gweru: Mambo Press, 1984), 13.

(BSAC) the right to govern a large area from the Transvaal to the Congo and from Angola to Portuguese East Africa, now Mozambique. From the outset the BSAC interpreted governance as including the right to grant and sell land as well as to occupy and mine it. The relative rights of Europeans and Africans over the land were the principal source of the interracial antagonisms which marked much of Rhodesia's history and which issued in the Ndebele War of 1893, the Ndebele and Shona Rebellions of 1896 and the Liberation War of the 1970s. Colonial administrations assumed that they had authority to determine the use and tenure of land and that immigrant European settlers were entitled to preference in the amount and quality of land for their residence and livelihood. By a succession of land assignments, chiefly the Land Apportionment Act of 1930, a majority of the African peoples were pressed onto limited and poor-quality lands called initially 'Native Reserves', later 'Tribal Trust Lands' and in the independence period 'communal areas'. Even a British official described an early reserve as 'badly watered, sandy and unfit for settlement'.[19]

The Honde Valley remained Crown land until 1950, but the valley's heat and remote location removed it from European interest in settlement. Local land tenure patterns were disrupted in the 1950s when several blocks of land designated as European were used to establish tea plantations. In 1952 William A K Igoe, a London Irish businessman, decided that the Honde had good potential for growing tea, and the first tea was planted in 1954 under the auspices of Aberfoyle Plantations, a Malaysian rubber group of which Igoe was chief executive. The new Eastern Highlands of Rhodesia Plantations consisted of 3 250 hectares of land (about 8 000 acres) at the north-east end of the valley. Several thousand inhabitants who had been living on the land in villages in the sub-chieftaincies of Chikomba and Zindi were removed to other parts of the valley to make room for this major commercial enterprise.

Within a few years Aberfoyle had entered into a partnership with the

---

[19]Moyana, *Land*, 39. Details of the many crosscurrents among rural peasants, African activists, and government policy-making bodies are reviewed by Terence Ranger, *Peasant consciousness and guerrilla war in Zimbabwe: a comparative study* (Harare: Zimbabwe Publishing House, 1985), 19–136; and by Moyana, *Land*, 38–107.

London firm of James Finlay, then the world's largest commercial tea firm. Aberfoyle put up somewhat over half of its holding for sale and started a new estate with the remainder, called Aberfoyle Tea Plantations, on the northern edge of the developed land, leaving what was known as Eastern Highlands Tea Estates (now Eastern Highlands Plantations) on about 1 800 hectares (4 500 acres) just south-west of Aberfoyle. The Rhodesian government established Katiyo Tea Estates as a parastatal enterprise in about 1970 on approximately 1 500 hectares (3 700 acres) of land at the eastern extreme of the valley, and this entailed the relocation of several thousand more residents from the Chikomba and Mandea chieftaincies to other parts of the valley. The tea companies' eviction of Africans from land they considered their own provoked resentment, and initially most Honde residents refused to work on the plantations. Managers hired workers from Mozambique, Zambia and Malawi to supply their labour needs and began contracting with workers from the town of Chipinge and its Chindau-speaking vicinity about 120 kilometres south of Mutare. The resulting cosmopolitan population of the plantations altered the valley's demography as some people who first came to work then acquired plots where they settled and farmed.

In 1950 the entire valley outside the blocks designated European became the Holdenby, Manga and Mutasa North Native Reserves. The Rhodesian authorities found these new reserves a convenient destination for the many Africans they were evicting from the highlands in the late 1940s and early 1950s. Removals to the Honde from the Penhalonga area and Manicaland in general are cited in the biography of Edward Paget, former Anglican bishop of Southern Rhodesia, along with important evidence of the futility of challenging the removals:

> (H)igh regard for African feeling was shown in a different context two years later (in 1944), when he (Bishop Paget) was visiting some of Penhalonga's out-stations. At Muponda's he was told that the land on which the people had lived for generations had been sold by the Government to a European and that they were to be moved to the Hondi (sic) Gorge. This story was to be many times repeated in the next few year, for there was a great belt of Crown land in the Eastern Highlands which had been scheduled for European occupation under the Land Apportionment Act but had, in fact, been occupied by Africans. Legally these were only squatters, for it was

neither Tribal Trust Land nor Native Purchase Area, but their removal was not only a great hardship; it was also a menace to health, for the Hondi Gorge was low-lying, very warm and wet and fever-ridden, whereas the uplands had been fever-free. The Bishop did what he could. 'I promised them that I would present their case to the authorities. It seems to me that a grave injustice threatens these people, whose loyalty has been proved and who as fellow-citizens of this country have a just claim to security and happiness'. No appeals or protests made the slightest difference to the gradual removal of African villages from the hill country ...'[20]

A Select Committee on the Resettlement of Natives that was appointed in 1960 estimated that, between 1936 and 1959, 113 000 Africans were forced to leave lands designated as European areas and resettle elsewhere.[21] It is difficult to estimate how many people moved to the Honde Valley, but 10 000 may not be too high a figure.

The years of the Liberation War, mainly 1972–79, brought major disruptions to the Honde Valley as Rhodesian forces sought to eliminate waves of guerrillas infiltrating from Mozambique. Commercial operations were sometimes shut down, numerous families fled the fighting, and many who remained were forced to live in 'Protected Villages' set up by the government to sequester the local population from contact with the guerrillas. With the coming of peace in 1980, many refugees returned. Valley life in the 1980s was disturbed on a smaller scale by the civil war raging across the border in Mozambique between the governing Front for the Liberation of Mozambique (Frelimo) and the Mozambique National Resistance (MNR or Renamo). Mozambican guerrillas raided the valley periodically, but generally security was impaired only at night and daily life was relatively normal.

The economy of the Honde Valley today is almost entirely agricultural. Most farms consist of five to ten acres of land devoted to maize (the staple crop of southern Africa), vegetables, tropical fruits and coffee and tea, which farmers can sell through the tea plantations. Much of the small-scale farming is subsistence, but farmers who have accumulated 20- to 30-acre holdings through purchase options sell their maize through

---

[20]Geoffrey Gibbon, *Paget of Rhodesia: a memoir of Edward, 5th Bishop of Mashonaland* (Bulawayo: Books of Rhodesia, 1973), 86–87.
[21]Moyana, *Land*, 8.

the national Grain Marketing Board, while fruit is sold in Mutare. As else-where in Manicaland, many men work in cities throughout Zimbabwe, but the tea estates have provided labour for a number of Honde residents who might otherwise have sought urban employment.[22]

Mission research from a tea estate

A tea estate proved an ideal base from which to conduct research into the *pungwe*. The modern, agri-business setting forms an important contrast with the village culture of the Honde Valley's communal areas. Eastern Highlands Tea Estates (EHTE) is a single legal and com-mercial entity, owned since 1988 by the Chillington Group, Ltd, a British transnational corporation, and divided into three units, each with its own divisions and managers accountable to a general manag-er. Production of processed tea in 1991 totalled about 3,5 million kilo-grams, worth about ZW$14 million (about US$4.5 million at the time), most of which was exported. Coffee, tobacco, spices and lumber are also produced on the estates, but tea is the major crop.

The many workers attracted to Eastern Highlands constitute a signifi-cant sub-group of valley society. The labour force averages about 2 500 people, most of them semi-literate labourers, termed 'general workers', who cultivate, harvest and process the crops. These tea-pluckers, called *vakayi* (from the verb *kukaya*, 'to pluck') are the prin-cipal constituency of churches located at EHTE. Most of them are Shona, with significant numbers of Mozambicans and Malawians[23] and women are a significant minority, ranging from 15 to 30 per cent of the workers. In common with agricultural labourers throughout Zimbabwe,

---

[22]The Province of Manicaland as a whole is one of the more rural provinces of Zimbabwe. In 1992 its population was estimated at 1 382 000 and con-stituted 13,9 per cent of the national total. Only 124 400 persons, or 9 per cent of the province, were urban residents. Administratively, the Honde is part of Chitepo District, one of seven districts in the province. Its entirely rural population of 142 600 as of 1992 constituted 10,3 per cent of the provincial total. The Honde's population of about 65,000 thus constituted about 46 per cent of the district total. Zimbabwe National Evangelism Task Committee, Target 2000, handbook for Target 2000 Congress, 7–10 September 1992, Harare: B-5–6, B-29–30.

[23]National and ethnic diversity may be gauged by the nationalities of perma-nent workers listed for the week ending 31 March 1991: 1 086 Zimbabweans, 236 Mozambicans, 80 Malawians, and 7 Zambians. Records of EHTE Personnel Office.

the pluckers occupy the lowest rung on the economic ladder of Zimbabwean society and live in poverty.[24] Clerks, forepersons, school teachers, supervisors and senior managers complete the work force. Their standard of living is much higher than that of the the pluckers, but they were also significant participants in *pungwe* research.[25]

Labour residence on the plantation makes Eastern Highlands a significant social entity beyond its role as an economic enterprise. Some 70–80 per cent of the general workers live in the 13 villages maintained by the company, making for a total resident population, including dependents, of between 10 000 and 15 000 persons.[26] Formerly called 'compounds', the residential groupings are now termed 'villages' in order to stress the company's hope that the workers' way of life will approximate the mutual concern, social cohesion and community celebration found in a Zimbabwean village. Most of the villages, however, are designated by a number, so that there are Villages No 1 through No 11; two additional villages have been named Hilltop and Happy Valley. Village No 3, where much of this project's research took place, is called Zindi, a name it shares with both the Zindi subdivision of EHTE and with the nearby town of Zindi, just outside the EHTE boundary.

The villages vary in size from a few hundred inhabitants to the 5 000 in Village No 6. Some of the villages are decades old, while six have been built and one substantially enlarged since 1980. Accommodation generally consists of one-storey concrete duplexes where each family has one or two rooms for its living. In addition to living quarters, the company sponsors facilities for infant and child care, several

---

[24]The minimum monthly wage of a *mukayi* in 1991 was about ZW$147 (about US$50), and the average earned per worker was about ZW$200, or about US$68 at the time. In 1994 the minimum wage had risen to ZW$223, a 58 per cent increase in three years. A drastic drop in the foreign exchange rate made this equivalent to US$26.50, due largely to inflationary pressures brought on by the 1991 Economic Structural Adjustment Program instituted in response to the International Monetary Fund and the World Bank.

[25]Racial composition of the senior management has undergone a substantial change in the independence period. Of the 12 managers in 1981, 10 were white and 2 were black, but among the 15 managers in 1991, 3 were white and 12 were black. Webster Zizhou, EHTE personnel manager, interview, 17 May 1991, EHTE; Personnel Office records.

[26]Webster Zizhou, EHTE personnel manager, interview, 17 May 1991, EHTE.

primary schools, three clinics, beerhalls, a number of general meeting halls and a variety of events such as soccer matches and holiday celebrations. There are no church buildings on the plantation, but church groups are free to use halls, school classrooms and designated outside grounds for Sunday services, night vigils, Mothers' Union meetings and the like.

Many people on the tea plantation are well integrated into the wider life of the valley as workers visit in surrounding villages and take part in weddings, funerals and other observances. Religion is a prominent source and expression of these connections as congregations on the plantation develop connections with other groups of their own denominations that are located elsewhere in the Honde. Conversely, valley residents frequent the plantations for social occasions and special events. Life on the tea plantations shares the challenges of Zimbabwean society as a whole such as poverty, alcoholism, abuse of women, HIV infection and Aids.

Highlights of the research process

The large number of Christian church groups and night vigils in the Honde made it important to limit attention to few enough groups to ensure in-depth observation and yet include groups both large and small, old and new, mission-founded and African Initiated. Mission-founded churches in the study are the Anglican Church; the United Methodist Church; the Church of Central Africa, Presbyterian; the Full Gospel Church of God; and the Roman Catholic Church. The Anglicans and Methodists have large, predominantly Shona congregations at the plantation and many connections with other congregations in the valley. The Presbyterian congregation is smaller, mostly Malawian and has few related congregations in the valley. There are several Full Gospel congregations in the Honde, and one of them meets at Eastern Highlands. The Roman Catholic Church, which has a strong presence in the valley, appears in the study because its *opposition* to the *pungwe* movement provides a basis of comparison among MFCs.

Five African Initiated Churches received major attention and this study documents three of them in detail: the African Apostolic Church of Johane Marange, the Unity of the African Apostolic Faith Church (also called Mugodhi) and the Pentecostal Apostolic Church of God. Considerable time was spent with two other major AICs with large congregations at EHTE: the Zion Apostolic Church (also called the *Ndaza* Zionists) and St Luca's Apostolic Ejuwel Jekenishen Church, both of them dominated by Chindau-speaking people from Chipinge. Churches of which I was aware but to which I could devote little or no attention were the Apostolic Faith Mission; a Baptist congregation; the Family of God; the (English) Methodist Church (also called Muchakata); the First Ethiopian Church (usually called Topia); the Zimbabwe Assembly of God, Africa (usually called by its acronym Zaoga, pronounced zah-yoh´-jah); Zive Zano ('Know the Plan', a breakaway movement from the United Methodists);[27] and Matenga Zvakazarurwa ('The Heavens Were Opened').

Immersion in the life of the churches was a privilege that evoked in me awe and gratitude as I experienced the depth of people's spiritual life and the open welcome they offered to a stranger in their midst. On any Friday or Saturday night I was aware of six or seven *mapungwe* occurring just within a ten-kilometre radius of the plantation, and I could be confident of an equal number of which I would become aware only after the fact. It was especially gratifying that interest in the project was mutual. Not only was I keen to make contact with groups, but individuals and groups were eager to be involved. A unique expression of such interest was a forum that one plantation official organised to help church leaders discuss inter-church relationships and relations with SSR. Groups often asked me to speak or preach at their gatherings, and the small-group discussions were enthusiastic and stimulating. People attending Christian *mapungwe* were hospitable at their meals and in their homes. Access to the ceremonies of SSR, including ceremonies of divination and possession, was more difficult. The rites' family basis means that information about upcoming rites is not widely circulated beyond the relatives concerned. While access to some rites was arranged, the apparent reluctance of mediums to invite visitors suggested that they distrusted the motives of a Euro-American researcher related to a church that traditionally has been hostile to SSR.

---

[27]Zive Zano has also been translated as 'Self Help'. Terence Ranger, 'Religious pluralism in Zimbabwe: a report on the Britain-Zimbabwe Society Research Day, St Antony's College, Oxford, 23 April 1994', *Journal of Religion in Africa* 25 (3) (August 1995), 245.

CHAPTER 3

Meeting the spirits: the *pungwe* in Shona Spirit Religion

The all-night vigils of the Christian churches arise out of Shona spirituality, for the vigils offer what Shona people expect from religious experience. Shona Spirit Religion has shaped these expectations in the all-night rituals that enact the relationships social groups have with the ancestors who are believed to speak and influence events from beyond the grave. The Christian *pungwe* operates within the spirituality of spirit religion's *pungwe* at the same time that it challenges it theologically and transforms it into a missional vehicle for evangelisation and church growth. The church *pungwe* thus represents an interreligious encounter within the context of culture, and participants at such gatherings intensify that encounter explicitly in their praying and preaching.

On account of their familial source and focus, the night gatherings of Shona Spirit Religion do not typically have a missional dimension. interreligious rivalry sometimes prompts public apologetics on behalf of SSR in ritual settings. In oracular utterances, mediums may exhort all those present to remain faithful to the spirits and their rites and to avoid church groups that spurn SSR. These efforts, however, are directed primarily at retaining the traditional constituency for the ancient ceremonies and are not missional in the sense of promotion and persuasion directed at strangers. It was the guerrillas of the Liberation War who advanced SSR as a mission cause during their night-time rallies, and their efforts have contributed both to the revival of SSR since the war and to the church renewal in which mission has flourished so remarkably.

This chapter discusses the centrality of nocturnal ritual in SSR and highlights the religious perceptions that nurture this prominence. An overview of SSR is offered and the social and religious meaning of the word *pungwe* is discussed. A descriptive section details the role of night vigils in rituals of death, in ceremonies for ancestral spirits and in spirit possession. A discussion of night's role in the malevolent practices of wizards completes the picture of the role of night in the spirituality of Shona Spirit Religion.

Spirits and obligations in Shona Spirit Religion

In 1980, 'tribal religion' was the primary religious profession of over 3 034 300 Zimbabweans, who constituted 40,5 per cent of the nation's population. Because 12 per cent of the population is Ndebele, the traditional religion of that ethnic group in western Zimbabwe accounted for a comparable proportion of the country's 'tribal religionists', but the vast majority of them were adherents of SSR. This proportion was less than half of the proportion of tribal religionists in 1900, who were 96 per cent of the country's 500 000 African inhabitants.

By the year 2000 the number of tribal religionists is expected to rise to 3 700 000, but proportionally they will have declined to 30,1 per cent of the population.[1] The declining proportion suggests that in the future more young people will reach adulthood with little exposure to SSR, and fresh influences from the traditional background may become more infrequent. The dual religious loyalty of many Zimbabweans, however, is not reflected in the statistics, which gauge only the *public* religious profession of respondents. Long exposure to Zimbabwean Christianity and countless conversations suggest that for the majority of Shona Christians the ancestral spirits exercise authority in their lives alongside Christianity. In this perspective it is clear that SSR is now and will be for the foreseeable future a major factor in Zimbabwean religion.

Shona Spirit Religion's influence on the church *pungwe* as a mission movement requires that the religion's main features be understood. Like any religion, SSR is a complex of interdependent convictions and

---

[1] See tables 1 and 2 in appendix 2. 'Tribal religionists' was a designation used by David Barrett throughout the *World Christian encyclopedia: a comparative survey of churches and religions in the modern world, AD 1900–2000* (Nairobi, Oxford, and New York: Oxford University Press, 1982). In the second edition, forthcoming, the term is changed to ethnoreligionists.

practices, but for the sake of overview it is helpful to highlight five principal aspects: spirits, God (known as Mwari), possession experiences, religious functionaries and rituals.[2]

The first aspect is the spirits who constitute much of the supernatural reality in which many Shona people believe they live. A spirit is the immaterial presence that extends a person's individual existence beyond physical death. A person dies to earthly, bodily life, but lives on as a spirit who maintains a personal relationship with those who walk on earth at the same time that he or she enters the company of those who have gone before. Relationship is fundamental to most spirits' existence, for they are defined by their relationship to a social group. Ancestral spirits are the spirits of those who have died from within one's family, understood as the 'extended family'. The individual and the family relate most immediately to the spirits of grandfather and grandmother (*sekuru* and *mbuya*); a family has a principal family spirit (*mudzimu*); and a clan relates to the spirit of the progenitor of the lineage or clan (*mhondoro*). A large ethno-linguistic group has a paramount spirit (*mhondoro*), who is the ancient spirit of the paramount chief's lineage and who operates in a territorial and political context. The generic term for an ancestral or family spirit is *mudzimu*, the plural being *vadzimu* or *midzimu*. The general term for 'spirit' is *mweya*, so that *vadzimu* are a type of *mweya*.[3]

Spirits are all-seeing and all-knowing, Shona people believe. No event, action, relationship or motivation escapes their attention. No secret can be hidden from them and they cannot be deceived. Moreover, they have power over people, events and natural processes. They are able to cause illness and death, good harvests and prosperity, disaster and drought, lightning and flood, friendship and enmity. Realms of

---

[2]For general reviews of Shona Spirit Religion see Marthinus L Daneel, *Old and new in Southern Shona Independent Churches, Vol 1, Background and rise of the major movements* (The Hague and Paris: Mouton, 1971), 79–182; Michael Gelfand, *The spiritual beliefs of the Shona* (Gweru: Mambo Press, 1977); Marshall Murphree, 30–59; and Michael Bourdillon, *The Shona peoples: an ethnography of the contemporary Shona, with special reference to their religion*, 3rd ed (Gweru: Mambo Press, 1987).

[3]*Mudzimu* is defined in the *Standard Shona dictionary* as '1 Spirit elder of family. 2 Soul of a dead relative'. Hannan, sv. In common usage, the term does have a secondary, generic meaning of 'spirit', and so some Christians use it for the Holy Spirit; most commonly, the Holy Spirit is *Mweya Unoyera*.

concern and power widen in concentric circles, depending on the type of spirit: the power and concern of family spirits are limited to the intimate details of close relationships; the spirits of larger groups have more general concerns, but they are equally able to affect intimate details that interest them. As all spirits have power to protect and to harm, people's relationship with them includes both loyalty and fear.

Spirits that are defined chiefly by their coming from *outside* established social groupings are the *mashavi*:

> The *shavi* spirits have in common that they never belong to the *rudzi* (tribe or lineage) of their hosts. They are spirits that come from afar, from under the ground, from the deep pool or merely from distant places. Their names sometimes indicate their (ethnic) origin, such as the *Dzviti* (Matabele), *Changani* (Shangaan), *ChiRozvi* (Rozvi) and *Murungu* (European) *shavi*, or else, as in the case of the *Muvimi* (hunting) *shavi,* the name of the spirit indicates the special kind of skill it confers on its host ... Nearly all the *shavi* spirits are concerned with the art of healing or divination. One spirit may be particularly good at detecting the causes of illness or death, while another specialised in medicine for particular ailments.[4]

Many *mashavi* are conceived as wandering over the country as they search for resting places in people whom they possess. Animal *mashavi* prompt distinctive dances in people they possess, and generally they do not speak through their mediums.

A prominent spirit in the Honde Valley is the *njuzu,* the water spirit, half human and half fish, often called 'mermaid' among English-speaking Shona and generally conceptualised as female. *Njuzu* spirits inhabit pools in rivers, and they are believed to seize people, taking them underwater for days at a time to be initiated as *njuzu* mediums, through whom they speak to the community. At the beginning of the rainy season in the Honde Valley, the high winds that blow in from the Indian Ocean are said to bring an *njuzu* spirit that inhabits a large and exceptionally clear pool of water at the Pungwe Falls that cascade down the escarpment into the Honde.[5]

---

[4]Daneel, *Major movements,* 128.
[5]This particular *njuzu,* called Chirikudzi, plays a prominent role in Sara Maitland's novel *Ancestral truths* (New York: Henry Holt, 1993), 124 and *passim.*

Ngozi are the avenging spirits of deceased people who return to seek recompense for murder, theft, or some other grievance that was not rectified during a person's lifetime. 'Of all the Shona spirits,' Daneel writes, 'the *ngozi* is the most formidable, dangerous and therefore also the most feared.'[6] The most prominent type of avenging spirit in the Honde Valley is the *chikwambo,* which afflicts many women and which has been a major factor in the rise of a new church (discussed in chapter 6) founded and led by women.

God, called Mwari, is the second principal aspect of SSR.[7] Known by various names in different localities, the deity is conceived monotheistically as a personal creator God with responsibility for the people's major concerns such as rain, harvests and war. The most common name is Mwari, the designation of the originally territorial spirit cult located in the Matopo Hills near Bulawayo.[8] The extent of Mwari's involvement in human affairs is ambiguous. Traditional religionists believe that Mwari is ultimately responsible for all things and the deity occupies a supreme and indispensable place in their cosmology. In southern Zimbabwe, the deity's involvement in rain-making, fertility and chieftancy politics continues through a network of annual and seasonal communications between many chiefs and the Mwari cult at

---

[6]Daneel, *Major movements,* 133.

[7]For discussions of the place of a high-God in Shona Spirit Religion, see Daneel, *Major movements,* 80–91; Bourdillon, 2nd ed, 266–271; and Marshall Murphree, *Christianity and the Shona* (New York: Humanities Press, 1969), 48–50.

[8]Vasco Musiwacho suggests that the origin of the name Mwari is the conflation of *mu* and *ari,* 'the one who is'. *'Mavambo ruziyo rwechivanhu'.* (Beginnings of the story of the religion of the people), TD (mimeographed), (Mutare) (1985), 1. In a more historical vein, Daneel writes of the name: 'Its origin, according to Shona tradition, dates back to the time when the Mbire tribe migrated from the Tanzanian lake regions. The name "Muali" is still used in the vicinity of Mt Kilimanjaro and designates God as the "Sower" and therefore the God of fertility.' *Major movements,* 81. Arguing, however, that in Africa 'the great royal cults emerged as the result of the imposition of control by kings over pre-existing high-God or prophetic centres', Ranger and Kimambo conclude that the Mwari cult developed on its own in southwestern Zimbabwe before the rise of Rozvi kingship. *The historical study of African Religion: with special reference to East and Central Africa* (London, Nairobi, and Ibadan: Heinemann, 1972), 6.

Matonjeni in the Matopo Hills near Bulawayo.[9] When it supported the Shona uprising of 1896, the cult legitimised the principle of armed struggle to recover the land, which Mwari regarded as a sacred possession.[10] With similar concern for the land and its just distribution, the spokespersons of Mwari at Matonjeni supported the Liberation War of the 1970s and held before their followers a vision of reconciliation between the black and white races of Rhodesia.[11] The deity thus has substantial involvement in the life of the Shona people, especially at times of national crisis.

A distance between Mwari and daily human affairs, however, pervades the ordinary person's spirituality and concentrates the devotee's attention on the spirits. Several shrines of Mwari (Mwali, among the Ndebele) are active today in the Matopos hills near Bulawayo – Matonjeni, Njelele, Dula and Dzilo – and the shrine in the Mambo Hills in northern Matabeleland was reopened in 1989, after being closed since 1896.[12] Pilgrims do visit the shrines seeking guidance for their personal dilemmas, but the communications with chiefs that in the past were a principal means of expressing Mwari's influence now tend to be limited to the southern region of the country. Highlighting an ambivalence between the immanence and transcendence of God in African religions, John Taylor concludes,

> This is the dichotomy in primal religion. The intimate Presence which is the form in which God belongs to the African world-view has been hidden by man's inner estrangement; the God who is 'outside', whom African man has 'made', is too remote to meet man's needs.[13]

Daneel notes a similar ambivalence among the Shona:

---

[9]Marthinus L Daneel, *The God of the Matopo Hills: an essay on the Mwari Cult in Rhodesia* (The Hague: Mouton, 1970), *passim*.

[10]Terence O Ranger, *Revolt in Southern Rhodesia, 1896–97: a study in African resistance* (Evanston: Northwestern University Press, 1967), 148–160 and *passim*.

[11]Marthinus L Daneel (Mafuranhunzi Gumbo), *Guerrilla snuff* (Harare: Baobab, 1995), 69–80; *Matopo Hills*, 77–85.

[12]Ranger, 'Religious pluralism', 230–237.

[13]John V Taylor, *The primal vision: Christian presence amid African Religion* (London: SCM Press, 1963), 78–79.

Mwari was not totally lost sight of but, in the composite picture of Shona traditional religion, He did become the Personal Being beyond and above the ancestral hierarchies and therefore could only be approached indirectly through the mediation of senior lineage ancestors (*mhondoro* or *varudzi*), or through the messengers who went to distant shrines to hear what Mwari had to say about the community as a whole.[14]

In view of this dominant pattern, I stress that the spirits are the principal reality in SSR.[15]

Spirit possession is the central religious experience of SSR and its third principal aspect. Spirits are not only posited as objects of belief, but they are received as powerful indwelling presences through the experience of possession. It is in possession that the spirits come near and people apprehend the supernatural. In this experience the spirits provide analysis, direction and prediction regarding relations among the living and relations between the living and themselves. The term

---

[14]Daneel, *Major movements*, 83. See Gelfand, *Spiritual beliefs*, 135. John Pobee's description of the place of the ancestors among the Akan in Ghana holds equally for their place among the Shona: 'Perhaps the most potent aspect of Akan religion is the cult of the ancestors ... (F)or all practical purposes the ancestors are treated as ends in themselves, as the real givers of these good things in life.' John Pobee, *Toward an African theology*, (Nashville: Abingdon, 1979), 46, 66.

[15]Do Shona people worship their ancestors or simply venerate them? Is SSR monotheist or polytheist? Mwari occupies a place of unique power and honour, and the worship due to Mwari is qualitatively different from the attention the *vadzimu* receive. Nevertheless, the substantial power and independent volition of ancestral spirits prompt people to address them in ways that are often indistinguishable from prayer to a highest deity. If asked, virtually all adherents of SSR would respond that they worship one God. Therefore, this study maintains that SSR is monotheistic and that adherents venerate their ancestors, although this veneration often appears to be worship. Geoffrey Parrinder offers a helpful analysis: 'Perhaps the African attitude to the different classes of spiritual beings might be expressed approximately in terms used in Roman Catholic theology. *Latria* is used to denote that supreme worship which is due and accorded to God alone. *Dulia* is the reverence and homage that should be paid to saints and angels. *Hyperdulia* is used of the special homage paid to the Virgin Mary. It might be helpful to speak of *Latria* for the Supreme Being alone in Africa, with *Hyperdulia* for the gods and *Dulia* for the ancestors.' *African traditional religion*, 3rd ed (London: Sheldon Press, 1974), 65–66.

people use most often for being possessed by a spirit is *kusvikirwa*, the passive form of a cognate of the verb *kusvika*, 'to arrive'.

The coming near of the spirits requires human vessels and agents, the religious functionaries who are the fourth major aspect of SSR. From the verb denoting ecstatic spirit possession is derived the noun denoting a spirit medium, *svikiro*, the plural of which is *masvikiro*. The term designates all whose ritual role is to be the vessel and voice of the spirit of a deceased person or an alien spirit, and it focuses that work on the ordering of community life, whether in family, clan or territorial group. The authority of family mediums is somewhat limited to their periods of possession, while more institutional authority is accorded to mediums responsible for larger groups and areas. Mediums can be male or female, and they appear to be about evenly divided between the sexes.

Working beyond the confines of family, diviner-healers, or *nganga*, are mediums who divine through possession the causes of misfortunes, give advice about the enterprises of life and heal people of diseases. They prescribe herbs for many illnesses but believe the main causes of misfortune and sickness are spirits who are displeased by people's ritual and ethical lapses. Making a living by servicing the public, they focus on discerning and responding to these personal and spiritual factors. Usually they work locally, but success can prompt people to come from great distances, and a diviner-healer may also travel to other areas of the country when summoned for help. A *nganga* may be known as a *svikiro* if spirit possession leads him or her into addressing community issues.

The fifth aspect of Shona Spirit Religion is ritual, the complex and varied ceremonies by which people invite, receive, hear, propitiate and inquire of the spirits. People hold rituals in connection with events such as illness, death, planting, harvest and marriage. Carrying out ritual obligations to spirits is prominent in many ceremonies. While routine inquiries made through a *nganga* may be pursued individually, most Shona ritual is corporate activity that initiates, articulates and celebrates the community's encounter with the spiritual realm. Because a family, clan or broader ethno-linguistic group is brought together by ritual, the community is defined largely by the ritual obligations of its members. The most important physical elements in ritual are specially brewed beer, tobacco snuff and animals kept and eventually killed for ceremonial purposes. The *pungwe* is a ritual setting that conditions the specific rituals of SSR that take place within it.

The most common Shona designation for the body of belief and practice that constitutes SSR is *Chivanhu,* meaning 'the practice of the people'. Beliefs and practices of *Chivanhu* vary geographically. In the crucial matter of funeral rites, for instance, people in Manicaland and Mashonaland often differ in where they bury their dead. A Manicaland woman was accustomed to collective burial grounds located well away from villages and usually overgrown by weeds because people feared venturing near the sites. When she moved to Mashonaland, she was surprised to find well-kept graves located within the homesteads of families and decorated with flowers on anniversary occasions. In her experience, people in Mashonaland focus on cultivating relationships with their ancestral spirits and therefore work with spirit mediums (*masvikiro*), whereas in Manicaland adherents seem more focused on obtaining healing and therefore work more with diviner-healers (*nganga*).[16] Between Bonda and Nyanga, only an hour's drive apart, people differ about the direction a body should face when placed in a grave. Amid the many variations, however, there are strong themes that provide unity to SSR over geographical diversity and continuity over time.

The term *pungwe* in Shona tradition

The term *pungwe* has been well known among Shona people in many parts of the country for at least several generations. It is a generic term for any gathering that continues through the night until dawn or sunrise. The word does not appear in the dictionary of 'Standard Shona', but, etymologically, each syllable of the word pertains to the practice. In Chimanyika the idiomatic expression *pu pu pu* means 'spending the whole night' and *ngwe-e* means 'dawn'. In addition, *hwe* means 'becoming light at sunrise'.[17] Together these constituent elements of the word *pungwe* do tell the whole story: 'spending the whole night until dawn'.

The word's principal historical connotation for many people is the night meetings that freedom fighters organised during the Liberation

---

[16]Wilma Muzvidzwa, interview, 4 January 1994.
[17]In Chimanyika, the Shona dialect of Manicaland, and Chizezuru, the dialect

43

War, but interviews with people in diverse areas of the country make it clear that the word *pungwe* has a long history in social and ritual usage. *Pungwe* is not the specific name of a *particular* gathering, but it is the generic name for any gathering that lasts the whole night until dawn or sunrise. Various areas have traditional dances that were held in *pasichigare*, or traditional, society and continue to be held frequently.[18] At these social occasions, which have no particular religious association, people begin dancing in the evening, and they continue through the night. Marriage is an event in traditional society that typically prompts a *pungwe*, with all-night dancing occurring when the bride arrives at the groom's village, or *musha*, and when the groom goes to pay his respects at his wife's village.

Pungwe as a name for purely social dances continues in the age of rock bands, which often bill an all-night engagement as a *pungwe* on their posters, whether in Mutare or at Hauna in the Honde Valley. Thomas Mapfumo, the internationally known Shona popular music star, advertised a concert in the national newspaper primarily as a *pungwe*:

---

of Mashonaland, *ngwe-e* is idiomatic of 'beginning to dawn'. In these two dialects and in Chikaranga the word is also an idiom for 'being clear', with reference to the sky. In Chizezuru and Chikaranga, the term is also an idiom for 'being very white', after something has been cleaned. *Pupupu ngwe-e* is idiomatic for 'passing from dark to dawn'. In addition, the verbs *kupupudza* and *kupupudzira* refer to passing the night without sleeping and carrying on activities throughout the night. Hannan, sv. One informant suggests a relationship among these overtones, the Pungwe River, and the general term *pungwe*, namely that there is an exceptionally clear pool at the bottom of the Pungwe Falls, where the river cascades over the Nyanga Escarpment into the Honde Valley. Ruben Marinda, ZIRRCON staff interview, 3 January 1994. In correspondence, Pearson Chitare of EHTE suggests that because the Pungwe River flows throughout the year this may be related to the connotations of perseverance in *pupupu* and *kupupudzira*.

[18]Young people often celebrate the harvest with an all-night dance, the *tsabatsaba*, for instance, in central Mashonaland. Some dances, called *ngororombe*, are held at the full moon, and others at the new moon. Pearson Chitare, interview, 20 May 1991. The term *pasichigare* ('below the chair') echoes the custom of young people sitting at the feet of an elder who tells stories of traditional Shona society. The term is used in both popular and scholarly contexts for Shona society prior to its contact with Western culture. See O M Kabweza and others, *Pasichigare: essays on Shona culture in retrospect* (Gweru: Mambo Press, 1979).

Pungwe! Pungwe!
spearheaded by
Thomas Mapfumo (Mukanya (his *nom de guerre*))
Zimbabwe Musicians' Co-operative stages
A National Show
on Saturday, 1st January
at Sanganayi Inn Open Air Garden[19]

Mapfumo's use of the term is complex in combining SSR and *Chimurenga* themes with a rock concert, for many of his songs mention the spirits, and during the war he wrote and circulated songs that were enormously popular at the wartime *mapungwe*, prompting his harassment by the Rhodesian authorities. A new occasion that prompts an all-night dance in some places, such as Eastern Highlands, is the annual celebration of Zimbabwe's independence on 18 April. During the day the national anthem is sung, a local government official makes a speech, and traditional dances are performed. Dancing continues through the night to rock music provided by radio, recordings or a live band. In sum, the word *pungwe* has long tradition and continuing use in connection with all-night social dances.

Pungwe is not a content-specific term in Shona Spirit Religion, for each ritual has its own name, but the word has always been used to characterise religious rituals that continue through the night until dawn. A Roman Catholic Christian in Masvingo, for instance, recalls that while he was growing up *pungwe* was used to refer to nocturnal rites of SSR, when people invoked the ancestors, drank ritual beer and undertook particular tasks related to spirit possession, whether healing, offering ritual animals or initiating spirit mediums.[20] In trying to explain the term's use before the Liberation War, informants illustrated the point by way of a hypothetical dialogue along these lines:

Two people meet each other walking at around sunrise.
A: Oh, where have you been?
B: Well, I was at a dance *or*, I was at the cleansing of my uncle's spirit *or*, We were celebrating the harvest *or*, My sister was initiated as a spirit medium.
A: Ah! When did you finish?

---

[19]*The Herald* (Harare), 1 January 1994.
[20]Clever Zunde, ZIRRCON staff interview, 3 January 1994.

B: Oh, we did a *pungwe* until we were overtaken by dawn! (*Taita pungwe kusvikira tayedzerwa.*)

As the frequency of social dances declined in some areas, the term *pungwe* became more exclusively associated with the rites of SSR. In a shrinking social world, some Zimbabweans before the Liberation War heard the word only in connection with the traditional religious rites:

> When the society was much more traditional, it was a formal thing and we could have *ngororombe* (a traditional dance) here and there, in this village and in that village. Then the society continued to change and these *ngororombe* became fewer, and so this term could not be used as widely as it was ... Then the term was used ... with the ceremonies for ancestral spirits and not so much at choirs and not so much when an old man is teaching his children during the night.[21]

Thus the term *pungwe* is used widely in discussing the all-night rituals of Shona Spirit Religion.

Night vigils in the traditional rites

Throughout Shona religious culture night is the normative and preferred time for community gatherings with the spirits. The possession that diviner-healers experience with individuals who come for divination and healing can and often does occur during the day, but in general, community ritual is nocturnal.[22]

Mystical danger: vigils at the time of death

Death is an event that always and in all places prompts a *pungwe* in Shona communities, whether the people involved are adherents of SSR, are exclusively Christians, or have dual religious affiliation. The spiritual sensitivity of the time after a person dies makes all-night vigils imperative for followers of SSR as they sit beside the body and

---

[21]Solomon Zvanaka, ZIRRCON staff interview, 3 January 1994.

[22]Wizardry, discussed later in this chapter, is exceptional in that it is an individual activity pursued at night.

spend the time in song and discourse.[23] Death is the point of transition between a person's embodied life and one's continuing life as an ancestral spirit, or *mudzimu*. On account of the family's enduring relationship with the *mudzimu* – especially its power to admonish, harm and punish as well as to guard and protect – the survivors' conduct of the transition rituals is a matter of great concern.

Keeping company with the corpse, called *kugarira chitunha*, doubtless serves emotionally as a transition in bidding farewell to a loved one whose company one kept in life. Beyond the psychological function, however, religious views about the body and its spirit prompt people to spend a full two or three nights without sleep until the burial, at which point they are in an extremity of exhaustion. Among the Budga, a Shona people in north-eastern Zimbabwe, for instance,

> ... at this stage the body of the deceased is a source of mystical danger to them. The unity of their kin group has been broken by an as yet unidentified power and until it has been restored by the ritual which unites the deceased with the *vadzimu* of the family, the members are vulnerable to this 'power' and to the possible wrath of the departed spirit as well ... The period beginning immediately after death and running through a few days after burial is one of great mystical danger, not only for the relatives of the deceased, but for the spirit of the deceased itself. During this period his *mudzimu* has become an independent and active entity, but since the proper rituals have not yet been performed to permit it to join the spiritual hierarchy it is 'outside', restless and insecure.[24]

Dangers associated with the corpse prompt people to stay by its side in order to protect it from evil forces and to detect and address adverse signs. In life, the dominant spirit of a person is that of his or

---

[23]The details of burial and the complexity of subsequent rites have so captured the attention of commentators that the relatively undifferentiated time of waiting that precedes burial has received little notice in the literature, eg Bourdillon, *Shona peoples,* 2nd ed, 192. Although death vigils are mandatory for adults, they are not always held for children, who may be buried the same day that they died. Perhaps as a social response to high infant mortality, children, especially infants, are sometimes regarded as not having become full human beings.

[24]Murphree, 35–37.

her grandfather (*sekuru*), and the person's own spirit is latently present as a small, white shadow, called *mvuri* or *bvute,* that awaits death in order to realise its full being as a *mudzimu.* If the spirit of the deceased is displeased after death the white shadow becomes visible, hovering over the body or lingering on a nearby wall or floor.[25] Dominic Mandaza writes:

> If a shadow from the dead body appears while the body is being wrapped, it means the father has refused the cloth of the son because of wrong committed against the dead father. The son has to put things right immediately or face future trouble. Sometimes the shadow may appear when the body is about to be carried out for burial. This means that there is something which has been left undone or that something is wrong. In this case, a *nganga* has to be consulted before the burial can be undertaken. As soon as the required thing is done, the shadow disappears and the body is placed on the bier (*banda*) and taken for burial.[26]

If wizardry was involved in the death, the wizard may try to return at night to take a piece of flesh or otherwise interfere with the corpse, intensifying the need for protection.

Death, therefore, is the event that invariably prompts a *pungwe,* and the worldview of SSR is the determining influence on this practice. A person's death entails spiritual events and possibilities to which the community is directly exposed. The community must see that its part is carried out well and must guard against pernicious spiritual influences, by night as by day. With such an understanding, those who live by SSR keep watch with their dead in *pungwe.*

'We are drinking your beer': vigils for the ancestral spirits

Shona Spirit Religion responds to two central human realities: the

---

[25]Each person is also thought to have a large black shadow that represents his physical being. Daneel, *Major movements*, 97. However, this shadow dissipates with the person's physical remains. For accounts of the movements of the white shadow, see Murphree, 37; Bourdillon, *Shona peoples*, 2nd ed, 192; Gelfand, *Spiritual beliefs*, 34.

[26]Dominic M Mandaza, 'Traditional ceremonies which persist', in *Shona customs: essays by African writers*, eds Clive and Peggy Kileff (Gweru: Mambo, 1970), 56.

experience of powerlessness over the events of life, especially adversity, and the experience of broken relationships. Power to control events and prevent misfortune and power to regulate and restore relationships are, therefore, overwhelming needs. For this power, the Shona turn to the ancestral spirits, because they are believed to have a dominant role in the life of the kinship group. Clear, immediate contact with the *vadzimu* is the great *desideratum,* and SSR offers an impressive array of ritual occasions designed to provide such contact. Nocturnal activity plays an important part in most of these.

The central focus of SSR is on rituals that enact the continuing relationship of the family group with the spirits of the deceased. Recognition that the family would not exist were it not for the existence of the progenitor is expressed in the statement made to the spirit of a grandfather, 'Grandfather, you are my creator' (*Sekuru, ndimi musiki wangu*) and the statement by a grandfather spirit through a possessed medium, 'Without me you are not here.'[27] This primal role entails spiritual power over most aspects of life. The *vadzimu* own the land and control its fertility. They guard the kinship group and seek to ensure proper and harmonious relations within it, including the carrying out of ritual obligations to themselves. Health, prosperity, harmony and good harvests are thought to show the approval of the *vadzimu* for the good behaviour of their descendants. On the other hand, illness, poverty, discord, drought, death and other misfortunes are attributed to the ancestors' anger against their descendants. In the case of the land, the *vadzimu* become angry and cause drought when people spill blood on the land in war, have sexual intercourse on the ground, or fail to give the land a weekly day of rest, or *chisi,* from being tilled. In the area of family relationships, adultery, theft, incest and the failure to observe ritual obligations to the *vadzimu* prompt the spirits' anger.[28]

The important ritual of bringing home and settling the spirit of the deceased is held at night. Variously called *kugadzira mudzimu* ('to pre-

---

[27]Gelfand, *Spiritual beliefs*, 73, 85.

[28]Helpful reviews of the role of the *vadzimu* and their ambivalent relations with living persons are found in Bourdillon, *Shona peoples*, 2nd ed, 217–239; and in Hubert Bucher, *Spirits and power: an analysis of Shona cosmology* (Cape Town: Oxford University Press, 1980), 56–83. Gelfand provides a wealth of detail in *Spiritual beliefs, passim.*

pare the spirit'), *kurova guva* ('to beat the grave'), *kutora mudzimu* ('to take the spirit'), or *kuchenura munhu* ('to purify the person'), this ceremony occurs up to a year after a death and has a common pattern:

> A large number of relatives and friends of the deceased gather to sing and dance in honour of the spirit through most of one night; there follows in the morning a procession to the grave or some other spot outside the homestead where various rituals are performed including generous libations of millet beer and the spirit is requested to come home; this is followed by further music and feasting in the homestead to welcome the spirit home.[29]

The inheritance rite has a celebratory tone that continues through the night until morning:

> The guests begin to gather on the evening before the ritual is to be performed. Some of the millet beer is consecrated to the spirit and the spirit is informed of the forthcoming ceremony in a formal address by the senior *muzukuru* (sister's son) of the family. Others present may also make a formal address to the spirit and pay their respects with token gifts. Late into the night, funerary songs are sung in mourning for the deceased and in honour of his spirit and men and women dance in his honour. Then young boys and girls take over with a gay dance lasting into the following morning to welcome the spirit and make it happy.[30]

The annual honouring of a spirit elder follows a similar pattern, with the addition that two nights may be included and the people disperse during the intervening day. In all these rites the community gathers at night, people celebrate by dancing and singing, and the ceremony continues until dawn, when important ritual actions are undertaken. They do not include spirit possession, for they are focused on fulfilling an obligation to the spirit rather than on receiving the spirit's initiative.

Fulfilling family obligation includes frequent addresses to the spirits during the nocturnal ceremonies. In preparing for the purification ceremony for his deceased wife, the bereaved husband puts the grain for the ritual beer on the potshelf in the home and sings to his spirit elder:

---

[29]Bourdillon, *Shona peoples* 3rd ed, 209. In Manicaland the beer is brewed with *rapoko,* another grain.

[30]Ibid, 210–211. For a description of *kuchenura* in Manicaland, see Gelfand, *Spiritual beliefs,* 102.

'Now, grandfather, we are going to brew beer for purification for my wife, who died a month ago.' At the ceremony itself:

> The woman's eldest relative stands up, takes a cup and fills it with beer from one of the biggest pots on the floor. He drinks saying, 'We are drinking your beer. See us. We are gathered in your room.'[31]

In a ceremony focused on the sacrifice of a bull or goat, the son-in-law in the family addresses the ancestral spirit when he sets aside the grain and then again when he offers the ritual beer on the potshelf:

> This is the *muderedzo* (libation) to wash down your bull, which I gave you before the beer. Tell your relatives with whom you are living and invite them to come and join the ceremony. We want to be kept by you and we want you to protect the villages day and night.[32]

He makes a similar address as he offers the liver of the slain bull or goat during the succeeding *pungwe* and as he pours beer on the ground for the ancestor: 'This is your beer from your grandson. Inform your relatives. Free our children from all sickness and other dangers.' In a nocturnal ceremony conducted for healing, an ill man's eldest brother addresses their deceased father's spirit, saying, 'Here is your beer, father. The beer is brewed by your son, whom you have made sick.' At the ceremony's close he says, 'This is your last pot of beer. We have enjoyed the ceremony today. Be so good as to release our sick brother from his illness. He is very sick.'[33]

Documentary evidence of the prominence of all-night ritual in SSR goes back to the 1890s. In one of the few early descriptions of Shona ritual, Anglican missionary Frank Edwards wrote to his brother about how his church-building project west of Harare was delayed by a five-day rainmaking ritual that included a sacrifice at the grave of a deceased chief. As more people came, the celebration became a long-running *pungwe*:

---

[31]Gelfand, *Spiritual beliefs*, 102. The potshelf, called *rukuva*, is usually a masonry shelf built out from the bench encircling the interior of the round Shona kitchen structure. On it rests the family's cooking pots and, usually, a set of shelves for plates and cups. Simple and unadorned, it becomes a ritual centre at nocturnal ceremonies.

[32]Ibid, 109.

[33]Ibid, 109–110, 79–80.

The third day many people came from surrounding Villages as to a feast bringing cooked food – Dancing & Drinking *Doro* (ritual beer) then commenced and has been going on almost without intermission Day & Night for 3 days ... Last night I went to see a Mutzimo (*mudzimu*, ancestral spirit) festival or Sacrifice to the Dead ... My Native Catechist said to me yday afternoon, There is going to be a sacrifice tonight. I said I wd go & see the ceremony – presently a crowd of men & women came along from the Kraal on their way to the grave, which is placed high up in the Rocks about 3/4 mile away so I followed them. arrived (sic) at the place I found several people had already stationed themselves there perched like so many huge crows on the several surrounding boulders, one woman was shaking a small gourd with a Rattle inside shouting and moaning for the dead (I understood to be her son) in front of the grave was set a huge pot of Native Beer & two pots containing water – The chief came up and poured some of the Beer into a small open pot, then taking a fowl from a Boy who was holding it cut its head off with a Knife and mixed the Blood in the pot with the Beer. Then with a bunch of leaves he sprinkled the outside of the grave with the mixture ...[34]

In short, all-night ceremony has long been a prominent feature of the ritual complex in Shona Spirit Religion.

'They want to be roused': vigils for spirit possession

Spirit possession is the centrepiece of SSR, and most possession rituals occur at night. In possession, people meet the supernatural directly, and the living community receives guidance and correction from the living dead. Nocturnal possession, believed to be at the spirit's initiative, occurs in a variety of settings: individual meetings between a diviner-healer and a suppliant, family feasts where the spirit elders speak through their mediums, large gatherings at the *kraals* of chiefs to pray for rain, and audiences that official messengers from chiefs have with the mediums of Mwari at Matonjeni.

Various ritual actions precede possession at communal *mapungwe*. The family may slaughter a bull, cow, or goat previously dedicated to

---

[34]Frank Edwards, Fort Salisbury, to J Edwards, ALS, 19 September 1892, Zimbabwe National Archives, Harare.

the spirit, and the community participates in a meal during which the senior family member verbally offers the animal to the spirit. Ritual beer, *doro*, that women of the family have brewed over the previous four days is drunk in large quantities. Finally, several family members begin a fast-paced and loud drumming (*kuridza ngoma*) that continues with little interruption throughout the night. Each type of spirit is associated with a particular drumbeat, and people believe that drumming powerfully influences the spirit to come and disposes the medium to receive the spirit.

The medium invites the spirit to come by sniffing deeply several pinches of tobacco snuff (*fodya* or *bute*), and in nocturnal community gatherings everyone present may take snuff as an indication of general receptivity to possession. The medium's possession usually begins with shakes and jerks of the body, and the medium moans, hums or mutters for a time. Entering a trance, the medium assumes a tense, rigid position and speaks in a voice similar to that of the deceased. Formal greetings may be exchanged between the medium and the group, the medium usually has counsel for the community, and the dances of particular spirits may consume much of the night.[35] Possession ends with more shaking and moaning, often accompanied by sneezes and other noisy expulsions of breath that suggest the spirit's departure. The most common verb for possession, *kusvikirwa*, 'to be arrived at,' emphasises the initiative of the spirit in entering a person. Among other terms, the verb *kukumbirwa*, 'to be requested, asked for,' highlights the spirit's choice of a particular person as a devotee and spokesperson. The verb *kubudirwa*, 'to be come out of,' stresses the coming forth of the spirit through a person.[36]

What revelations emerge from spirit possession, whether at night or

---

[35]A *pungwe* convened by Mai Muzanenhamo at Zindi in the Honde Valley included a dozen different dances, each with its own rhythm and costume. Most songs consisted of a single line sung repeatedly, while in some there was elaboration through stanzas. Frequent references to violence and war reflected the history of the Honde Valley: skirmishes among indigenous groups, killings among migrant workers, the Liberation War, and the more recent violence of the Mozambican conflict. *Pungwe*, festival of Shona Spirit Religion, 24–25 May 1991, Zindi Township.

[36]The verb *kukirwa* is also used, but the meaning and derivation of the term are unclear. Some of the terminological variety was gleaned from the *nganga*. Samson Matsanzike, interview, 1 January 1994.

otherwise? Mediums' utterances in a variety of settings highlight people's experience of the spirits as a source of wisdom and guidance. In a *mhondoro* possession described by David Lan:

> The *mhondoro* speaks. His voice is low and rough but his speech is clear. He explains why he has called the people to his village. A discussion starts. Problems are raised by the elders and by younger men as well. Herds of elephant have gathered in the bush outside the villages. The crops will be destroyed as soon as they grow ripe. What is to be done? Some men object to the siting of a new village. They fear the fields will encroach on their own. In three villages children have sickened and died for no good reason. They address the *mhondoro* face to face and soon the awe his appearance had called up wears off. The discussion is respectful but vigorous and free. The medium listens but says nothing until everyone has had his say. Then he gives his advice and his instructions. When everybody's problems have been raised he asks who is to take the offering to the senior *mhondoro* who controls the rain.[37]

At a *mhondoro* possession for drought, the female medium of a *mhondoro* said to the family involved:

> Drink what I am giving you. This is my beer prepared for me by my people. I have heard what you had to say. I want you to keep special days. Keep the day of rest *(chisi)*. When you walk in the woods, walk well, don't talk nonsense, otherwise I shall frighten you. Don't listen to those who say, 'Look at that small hill.' This is mockery because it is where most of the spirits live. Don't carry the pot to the river or wash a mat in it. This is strictly forbidden, otherwise you will meet a crocodile or hippopotamus ... Stay well, plough well, but keep the ritual day of rest *(chisi)*. These days are mine. I strongly urge you to keep them.[38]

In a possession that responds to family crisis, the spirit's communication is personally specific. In the case of a sick woman, a possessed family medium called the invalid and spoke for the spirit elder:

> I am the one who made you sick. You are not brewing beer for

---

[37]David Lan, *Guns and rain: guerrillas and spirit mediums in Zimbabwe* (Harare: Zimbabwe Publishing House, 1985), 47.
[38]Gelfand, *Spiritual beliefs*, 59.

me. Don't you know that I asked for beer several times and made your children ill? Do you recall the time I made your boy sick but you did not heed? I am the one who brought illness to your son – you did not hear me. I caused your sickness. I can take you as a medium now or I can make you die. I can destroy your eldest son whom you love or your husband so that you can feel painful remorse.

Initiation of a family member as a spirit medium always takes place at an all-night ritual, a *pungwe.* When a family member experiences a persistent illness that does not respond to either herbal remedies or Western medicine, the family consults a *nganga,* and the answer may be that the spirit of a recently deceased relative wishes to possess that individual as the spirit's medium, through whom the spirit will regularly communicate with the community.[39] Alternatively, this message may be received through dreams. The initiation occurs in an all-night ritual that comes to a climax in possession very late at night or just before dawn:

> The ceremony usually starts late in the night before the initiation ritual when the senior medium, the initiand and often other hosts in the cult become possessed to the accompaniment of appropriate music ... The mediums spend much of the night in consultation, discussion and instruction. Early in the morning the senior medium initiates the new medium with a hair-cutting ritual.[40]

The convening of night-long rituals depends partly on the type of spirit being invoked. Samson Matsanzike, a *nganga* in Chipinge, puts it this way:

> There are the spirits of rain – they want to be roused at night. The spirits of the ancestors want to be roused at night also. The spirits of the Ndebele and the spirits of people in the bush who were killed by the Nguni people long ago want to be roused during the afternoon.

Matsanzike does most of his healing individually with people during the day, and his own ancestral spirit can possess him at any time. However,

---

[39]See Gelfand, *Spiritual beliefs,* 39; Bourdillon, *Shona peoples,* 3rd ed, 238.
[40]Bourdillon, *Shona peoples,* 2nd ed, 229. For other accounts of nocturnal initiation, see Gelfand, *Spiritual beliefs,* 28–30, 63–66.

when he encounters an especially stubborn illness, he organises a night gathering of the family or community, saying, 'The child is being sought by the ancestral spirit of healing.' Nocturnal rituals, including initiations, he calls feasts (*mabiko*) or sacrifices (*mapira*), generic terms people use throughout Manicaland. Chiefs are responsible for convening the night rituals to ask for rain and to celebrate the harvest, and these ceremonies are called collectively *makoto*.[41]

All-night rituals culminating in spirit possession shortly before dawn are prominent with clan and territorial spirits:

> Vital to the ritual is the prior brewing of beer in the prescribed way. On the morning of the ceremony some of this beer is placed in the *rushanga*, a hut sacred to the *mhondoro*, which is built outside the village where the medium resides. In the evening the ritual begins in the hut of the medium, when he is also given some of the beer to drink. Music and dancing follow throughout the night and in the early morning the medium is possessed with the spirit of the *mhondoro*. He then drinks water placed in a wooden bowl to which an ember has been added, to 'cool off' his spirit. He is then approached by his assistant with the various requests that the people may have. At daybreak he leads a procession of attendant followers to the *rushanga*, where further prayers are made. A return is then made to the village, where the ceremony is brought to a close.[42]

The time immediately before dawn is especially potent in a *pungwe* of SSR. This period, roughly between 3 am and 5 am, is termed *mambakwedza*, 'beginning to dawn'.[43] During the initiation of a new medium, other mediums may become possessed early in the rite and may encourage the chosen family member for much of the night, but often the initiate is not possessed until *mambakwedza*. As an informant in the Honde Valley puts it, 'The most important spirits come out just before dawn.'[44] That is when the most powerful manifestations of

---

[41]Matsanzike, interview, 1 January 1994.

[42]Murphree, 46–47. See also Michael Gelfand, *Shona religion: with special reference to the Makorekore* (Cape Town: Juta, 1962), 31, 47.

[43]Defining the term as 'very, very early morning', Hannan cites its derivation as the combination of *mavamba*, 'you have begun', and *kuedza*, 'to dawn' (sv).

[44]Pearson Chitare, interview, 4 January 1994.

possession occur and when the most important messages from the spirits are heard. The pre-dawn period is also when the most frenzied dancing occurs, involving the largest number of people in a gathering.[45] The greatest excitement at a certain Honde Valley *pungwe* began at about 2:45 am, when the mediums began a dance dedicated to Chaminuka, the greatest ancestral medium of the Shona people. The *pungwe* in SSR, therefore, is not simply a night-long period of undifferentiated time and activity. Instead, ritual action builds through the night toward the pre-dawn climax of *mambakwedza,* a time of spiritual sensitivity and power.

The factors that make night so central in the religious experience of Shona people are not easy to determine, for informants generally assert the importance of night without advancing specific reasons for it. People generally agree that spirits are more accessible at night, and religious specialists have ideas about the habits and preferences of certain spirits. Some explain that the inherent dangers of night draw the spirits to protect their descendants:

> ... the ancestors, as guardians of their families, are near the homesteads of their kith and kin. During the daytime they will occasionally reveal their presence in the tree leaves rustling in the wind, but they normally dwell in the 'wards (ie places) without water' (*matunhu asina mvura*) until the sun sets and they draw nearer home to protect their relatives. That is why spirit-possession or the ritual communication with the ancestors mostly takes place late in the afternoon, at night or early in the morning.[46]

Spirits are more accessible at night because that is when they wander. The spirits' accessibility to human yearning for spiritual experience is one side of the encounter. The other side is human accessibility to spirits yearning for hosts in whom they can 'come out'. Many informants simply take it for granted that the spirits' preferred time of manifestation is night. A related theme in Shona discussions is the fact that, once they have put aside the desire and need for sleep, people have

---

[45]The unanimous stress of informants on the importance of *mambakwedza* is borne out by indications in the research of Lan, 50–51, and Gelfand, *Witch doctor: traditional medicine man of Rhodesia* (London: Harvill Press, 1964), 59; *Spiritual beliefs*, 28–30.
[46]Daneel, *Major movements*, 98.

plenty of time at night for religious experience. Possession rites take considerable time. Night is a time when the spirits' accessibility to people is matched by people's accessibility to the spirits.

The fact that audiences with mediums of Mwari at the shrine at Matonjeni occur exclusively at night confirms the centrality of night in Shona religious experience. Marthinus Daneel's monograph on the Mwari cult was written on the basis of the only audience known to have been granted to a researcher. His photograph of the entrance to the shrine bears the explanation: 'Cave entrance at Wirirani shrine – Matonjeni. Photographed from a distance with tele-lens, since approach of shrine during day-time was prohibited.'[47] He writes:

> Several days of deliberation passed in the priest's colony before I was allowed to accompany the priests to the cult cave ... and on a bleak moonlit night Simon Chokoto led us up the slopes of Mt SaShe in single file. Fifty yards from the cave we took off our shoes and then approached the place where High Priestess Kombo and Simon's wife were already seated, facing the east. We followed suit and sat down with our backs to the cave ... I was warned beforehand that turning round to face the cave while Mwari is speaking is strictly prohibited. Way back in Gutu some of the tribal elders had told me that I ran grave risks of being blinded even without trying to observe Mwari's actions at the cave.[48]

Night as the time of spiritual encounter can be traced, therefore, into the precincts of the most sacred shrine of the greatest spiritual reality of SSR, Mwari – God. Access to the deity is prohibited during the day and is perilous even at night.

Night here plays a complex role. Mwari is a spirit being of great mystery, whose privacy must be guarded during the day, a time when too much is visible. Night both conceals and reveals the deity. People can approach Mwari at night because night hides the deity's fullness. From partial concealment, Mwari communicates deity in the ways that Mwari chooses, through the sound of the voice shrouded in the mystery of

---

[47]Daneel, *Matopo Hills*, Plate 2. In describing her 1992 visit to Matonjeni, Marcelle Manley notes, 'No one is allowed near the shrine by daylight, I was told: you are not *supposed* to see the holy of holies.' 'The pilgrimage to Matonjeni', in *Annual Report: June 1992–July 1993* of ZIRRCON: 4.
[48]Daneel, *Matopo Hills*, 77, 93.

darkness. The concealing function of darkness also serves to protect people who come to consult the deity, for they would be maimed or destroyed if they were to see more of Mwari than the deity chooses. Darkness that conceals in mystery and reveals in intensity is a theme of the Mwari cult that appears throughout Shona Spirit Religion in people's nocturnal encounters with the spirits.

The nocturnal evil of wizardry

Wizardry, *uroyi* in Shona, is an important aspect of the worldview in which the all-night rituals of Shona Spirit Religion take place. Wizards (*varoyi*) are people who use evil spiritual powers to harm others. The literature distinguishes witches and sorcerers among wizards, with significant differences in gender, type of activity, source of power and social implications. Witchcraft is associated mainly with women who operate through psychic phenomena to harm others in the community by inflicting illness or death. The spirits through whom witches work are generally alien, wandering spirits with a generalised desire to harm communities of the living. Sorcerers are usually men who use physical objects and concoctions (rather than spirits) to harm others through motives of jealousy or greed and so enhance their own social or economic position.[49]

A common form of sorcery in the Honde Valley is the practice of casting pernicious spells, called *chitsinga* or *makona,* against people with the use of potions or other charms (*mishonga*) concocted from a variety of materials. One type of *chitsinga* is a thorn or needle that the sorcerer impregnates with poisons and places in the path of the intended victim.[50] A small packet of materials thought to be potent, called a *gona,* may be placed at the victim's home (in the thatch or near the

---

[49]Daneel, *Major movements,* 156–160; Bourdillon, *Shona peoples,* 2nd ed, 165–175; Leny Lagerwerf, *Witchcraft, sorcery and spirit possession: pastoral responses in Africa* (Gweru: Mambo Press, 1992), 5. Shona makes no linguistic distinction between sorcerers and witches, for the term *muroyi* is used for both types. Distinctions in English assist discussion so long as the Shona linguistic situation is kept in mind. Analysis must confine the negative connotations in English to those functionaries whom the Shona *themselves* see as evil.

[50]Wilma Muzvidzwa, interview, 4 January 1994.

doorpost), from where it casts a harmful spell by virtue of its psychic power. Sorcerers are thought to do much of their work during the day as well as at night.

The strongest source of evil in SSR is witchcraft. Appalling acts are attributed to witches and their work is thought to occur almost exclusively at night. Witches or their psychic 'shadows' are thought to travel at night, riding naked on that unsavoury nocturnal beast, the hyena. People believe they enter homes in order to plant poison or to commit incest or adultery, sometimes changing themselves into snakes or crocodiles. Indulging their predilection for human flesh, especially that of children, they rob graves and feast on corpses. Court cases where cannibalism has been confessed by accused witches indicate that these Shona beliefs are not necessarily imaginary.[51] A member of an independent church described the source of the illness she had before her conversion as follows:

> It was caused by an avenging spirit *(ngozi)* that had been put into me and by the wizardry *(uroyi)* that had been put into me so that I practised wizardry, eating the flesh of people, so that I killed people and ate the flesh of the dead *(vanhu vachifa ndichidya)*.[52]

This account stresses that the nocturnal malevolence of witches is prompted by the malice of the spirits who empower them. Avenging spirits are thought to wander chiefly at night, when the witches are available to them, so that together they can work the evil they desire. How witches manage to carry out their bizarre activities is worked out in a matter-of-fact way in the popular imagination, as evident in an essay written by a secondary school student:

> A *muroyi* travels at night visiting those places and people she wants to harm. Before she departs from her home, she bewitches her husband so that he falls into a deep sleep and cannot wake up until she returns. In order to bewitch a person, the *muroyi* must know the victim's family *(dzinza)* and his clan name *(mutupo)*, otherwise her witchcraft is harmless. To travel the

---

[51]Gordon Chavunduka, *Traditional healers and the Shona patient* (Gweru: Mambo Press, 1978), 14–18; Daneel, *Major movements*, 161–164; Gelfand, *Spiritual beliefs*, 192; Lan, 35–36; Bourdillon, *Shona peoples*, 2nd ed, 166–168.

[52]Violet Mushunje, interview, 22 April 1991.

muroyi usually rides on the back of a hyena. When she reaches her destination she bewitches the house and the surroundings so that the victim falls into a coma. Then she recites a number of praises connected with his family and clan names. In so doing, she begs his ancestral spirits to allow her to do what she wants with this person ... She sends her ghosts (*zvidhoma*) into the victim's house to kill him. In some cases she calls the victim's name and the sleeping person wakes up hypnotised. In this state he does as she commands and unlocks the door. Such a bewitched person rarely dies while the witch is present and operating on him because his matrilineal *vadzimu* ... prevent this. When the witch has departed, the victim wakes up yelping, shivering, powerless and half mad.[53]

The association of witchcraft with night is so strong that a contemporary Shona novel that focuses on witchcraft is titled simply *Zvousiku,* 'Things of night'.[54]

The practice of wizardry in these forms and, equally important, the supposition, diagnosis or accusation of wizardry, function to analyse, explain and make explicit the social tensions within a community. Bourdillon writes:

Witchcraft is the paradigm of all evil and anti-social behaviour ... Witchcraft can refer to any threat, involving an element of furtiveness, to personal security by the violation of the human person or of human life, or by the violation of any deeply held value. A witch or sorcerer (*muroyi*) is a person in any way responsible for such a violation ... Open accusations of witchcraft are almost always preceded by tension and conflict within the community.[55]

Explaining how the witch 'personifies the evil and disruptive forces in society,' Daneel quotes J R Crawford:

Cannibalism is the most detested of all crimes, therefore she (the witch) is a cannibal; family ties are the most sacred of all ties, therefore she destroys members of her own family; medicine and

---

[53]Ignatius M Zvarevashe, 'Witches and witchcraft', in Kileff, *Shona customs,* 48.

[54]Jonathan J Mukandi, *Zvousiku* (Gweru: Mambo Press, 1983).

[55]Bourdillon, *Shona peoples,* 3rd ed, 183–184.

61

magic are the forces with which one can control the environment in the interest of one's society, therefore they become perverted in the hands of the witch; animals such as snakes are dangerous because they can kill; owls are feared because they fly when all other birds sleep, therefore the witch has these creatures as her familiars. She is associated with all that is feared and that is detestable.[56]

The extreme threat associated with the nocturnal activities of *varoyi* results in a religious and social sanction against individuals travelling or moving about the village alone at night. The medium of the *mhondoro* at Nyamaropa declares, 'People should not travel after dark, when they should all be in their villages.'[57] Activity on an individual's part during the night is often regarded as a sure sign that the person is a witch.[58]

On account of the intense danger associated with witchcraft, people cloak their suspicions about a particular person in almost as much secrecy as the witch uses in her activities. Witchcraft is regarded as a dangerous charge on account of both the enmity it causes and the possibility that, if the accused is actually a witch, she will kill or otherwise harm her accusers with more witchcraft. Suspicions of witchcraft may lurk even beneath overtures that seem friendly and complimentary:

> In many cases, after the witch has been named by a *nganga*, the relatives go to that witch and implore her to cure the sick person. They don't tell her that she is the *muroyi*, but they flatter her saying, 'A certain person thinks you are able to help. If you can cure

---

[56]Daneel, *Major movements*, 158–159.

[57]Gelfand, *Spiritual beliefs*, 60.

[58]Bourdillon, *Shona peoples*, 2nd ed, 177. In view of this prohibition, one may ask how people manage to participate in *mapungwe*. One answer lies in the distinctions between individual and group activity, and between intentional travel and apparently inexplicable activity at night. A family group walking to a *pungwe* is above suspicion, as are most individuals who are travelling to a known destination for a credible reason. An individual sauntering about the village at night, however, or even doing chores in the vicinity of someone else's homestead may be suspected of performing wizardry. Another answer is that Christians holding *mapungwe* in deserted places at night have sometimes been suspected of wizardry on that very account. For this last point, see Daneel, *Major movements*, 434–435.

him we will give some money or a goat.' Then the *muroyi* may reverse her spell and the sick person recovers.[59]

The prominence of fears and suspicions about witches and about the harmful spirits who work with them gives night a sinister connotation of spiritual threat for the individual and the community.

SSR tends to link women with the threat of evil and with night. Female spirits threaten their descendants with illness and death more often than male spirits do. Similarly, witches are regarded as more evil and a greater threat to society, because witchcraft brings fatal illness and death, whereas sorcery may simply advance the economic or political fortunes of the male sorcerer. The greater power and more intense malice attributed to witches is inherent in the fact that their power comes from spirits, who are independent sources of volition, rather than from physical objects and concoctions. The greater threat that women represent is consistent with the fact that in a patrilineage they are the strangers brought from outside into the patriarchal line. Misfortune in that line is more likely to be attributed to the malevolence of a female witch than to a male sorcerer, for the latter is thought less likely to deal his own family a crippling blow. As a social construct, witchcraft merges the conflicts endemic between men and women in patriarchal society with the Shona spirit world, positing women as powerful at the same time that it associates their power with spirits dangerous to the social order. It is important for our study that the greater threat associated with women also appears predominantly as a nocturnal phenomenon. The woman who lives on the margin of the patrilineal family carries out her destructive work in a marginal time – in secret, at night, when malevolent spirits are abroad and when most people are asleep.

Night's meaning in Shona ritual

Night is a supremely important time in SSR. The period between dusk and dawn is when people encounter spiritual reality with greater immediacy, power, fear and celebration than at any other time. The drama of the entire range of spirit beings that the religion offers centres in nocturnal possibilities and events. At night the spirits are acces-

---

[59]Zvarevashe, 48.

sible to the human family and the human family is accessible to the spirits. With this access comes knowledge and power as spirits communicate and share their potency with the human community.

The spiritual power of night is profoundly dualistic, for it includes the spirit beings that SSR holds up for honour and reverence and the spiritual influences that SSR regards with horror and disgust. Night is the time when descendants fulfil their obligations to the ancestral spirits, receive their presence in the experience of possession and hear the pronouncements of territorial spirits and the very words of Mwari. Night is also when avenging spirits seize their victims, ghosts appear, and witches travel on their appalling errands.

The power of night gathers members of the human community to celebrate their human and supernatural kinship, and to stand in solidarity against the evil powers that seek to harm and divide them at night. Corporate ritual at night strengthens community bonds, offers ecstatic experience, initiates religious leaders and protects the community from harm. Nocturnal wizardry brings personal catastrophe and threatens the community by spreading suspicion.

Night as the time of spiritual power is the religio-cultural foundation on which Shona people developed *mapungwe* in SSR. With this foundation, the guerrillas of the Liberation War and the Christians of the Shona churches both brought the *pungwe* to the centre of their efforts to build communities of political and spiritual solidarity. On this foundation, the churches have developed an abiding dynamic of Christian mission.

CHAPTER 4

Mass mobilisation: night rallies in Zimbabwe's Liberation War

The vigil movement in Shona Christian churches owes much to the night-time rallies held by guerrillas during Zimbabwe's War of Liberation in the 1970s. Churches had held night vigils since the early days of Christianity in Zimbabwe, but the power of the wartime rallies brought *pungwe* practice to the centre of popular consciousness and catalysed Christians to develop it as a major form of renewal and mission.

In their rallies, the guerrillas built on the nocturnal rites of Shona Spirit Religion and incorporated the cult of the spirits whom they were invoking to assist in the struggle. The interreligious tension they felt with Christianity prompted them to promote the spirits with missionary zeal, giving Shona Spirit Religion a missional thrust for the first time in its history. In organisation and format, the guerrillas built on their experience of vigils in the churches, but in content they articulated a radical rejection of Christianity and its links to Rhodesian domination. In an especially vivid instance of this dynamic, choruses extolling the war effort were often set to the tunes of hymns guerrillas had learned in the churches.

Night was the theatre for these complex interactions of religion, culture, politics and military initiative. Like the vigils of SSR and the churches, the guerrillas' rallies were a form of ritual action, and this proved to be an ideal vehicle for the synthesis of divergent themes in thought and practice. The rallies' overall success in mobilising the masses is a major factor in the growth of the *pungwe* as a movement in the churches, for the missional thrust of the churches' vigils is essentially a mobilisation of Christians to advance the gospel in their communities and throughout the country.

This chapter introduces the guerrillas' *pungwe* practice and traces the roots of their gatherings both in SSR and in the practices of the churches. The first section highlights the central role of *mapungwe* in the liberation forces' strategy of peasant mobilisation, and the second details how guerrillas organised and conducted their night meetings. Subsequent sections discuss the role of violence in wartime *mapungwe* and the development of the word *pungwe* as a technical term in the struggle. The chapter then details how the complex religious overtones of wartime *mapungwe* offered the churches a ready vehicle for passionate and liberative spirituality in the post-war period.

The *pungwe* as a political and military strategy

When I ask Shona people about the *pungwe* phenomenon in their churches, they often open their response with the words, 'Well, during the war ...' They then recount how the guerrillas, usually called 'the comrades' or *vakomana* ('the boys'), used to summon people from the villages out into the bush for night-long sessions of political talks and the singing of liberation songs. Such meetings were called *mapungwe.* The cover of darkness helped to conceal both the presence of the guerrillas and the gatherings themselves from the security forces of the Rhodesia Front (RF) government. The meetings were illegal, for dusk-to-dawn curfews were imposed throughout the rural areas of the country.

The night-time gatherings were the only context in which the freedom fighters could regularly meet with large groups of people for 'consciousness raising' or 'politicisation of the masses', the processes by which rural people were persuaded not only to acquiesce in the Liberation War, or *Chimurenga,* but to support and participate in the struggle.[1] This was especially crucial in Manicaland, the border area across which most guerrillas of the Zimbabwe African National

---

[1] *Chimurenga* is the popular name for the Liberation War. The verb *kurenga* denotes causing to act with harmful force, and the noun *murenga* includes warlike spirit and rebellion among its meanings. Hannan, sv. *Chimurenga* is an extended form of *murenga* that developed in the Rhodesian struggle. Unlike the neutral term *hondo,* which refers to any war, *Chimurenga* connotes the struggle to throw off oppression. In the sweep of history, the 1896–97 rebellion has come to be seen as the First *Chimurenga* and the 1966–1980 war as the Second *Chimurenga.*

Liberation Army (ZANLA) entered from Mozambique. For ZANLA and for the Zimbabwe African National Union (ZANU), the political party of which it was the military wing, Mozambique and Tanzania functioned as external bases of logistical support for prosecuting the war in Rhodesia. Zimbabwean recruits were smuggled out of Rhodesia and assembled in camps where they received ideological education and military training. They were then mobilised into small teams that re-entered Rhodesia to engage the RF forces.

Mozambique emerged as a training ground for guerrillas after ZANU formed an alliance in 1970 with the Front for the Liberation of Mozambique (FRELIMO), which was waging a guerrilla struggle against the colonial forces of Portugal.[2] Mozambicans won independence in 1975, after which ZANLA could mobilise there freely with the official sponsorship of then-president Samora Machel, who had led FRELIMO to military and political victory. It was through FRELIMO that the nationalist parties and their military wings realised that only a sustained and well-organised guerrilla war could wrest majority rule from the determined and powerful RF forces:

> In the Sixties there had been a tendency among liberation movements and particularly the Zimbabwean movements, to believe that all that was necessary to end white minority domination was to train some guerrillas and send them home with guns: this would not only scare the whites but would ignite a wave of civil disobedience by blacks. It was a belief psychologically founded on the relative ease other African countries had in achieving independence in the early Sixties.[3]

The Battle of Chinoyi in 1966 had been a psychological lift, but the military defeat it represented gradually convinced nationalist leaders that a different strategy was imperative:

---

[2]ZANU marks the Battle of Chinoyi on 28 April 1966, in which seven guerrillas were killed, as the official beginning of the Liberation War. In 1967 forces of the Zimbabwe People's Revolutionary Army (ZIPRA) and the African National Congress (of South Africa) engaged the Rhodesian army in a major battle in the Hwange National Park in south-western Rhodesia. A lull in the war extended from 1968 until an attack on Altena Farm in December 1972 opened the war's decisive phase.

[3]David Martin & Phyllis Johnson, *The struggle for Zimbabwe: the Chimurenga War* (Harare: Zimbabwe Publishing House, 1981), 11.

It was realised that the people had to be mobilised if we were to conduct a successful struggle. (Josiah) Tongogara (chair of ZANLA's high command) in particular had learned in China that it was vital to mobilise the people and it was that lesson which shaped future strategy. He brought the new strategy which said if you want to win a revolution it is not only a revolution of the gun but a revolution of mobilising the masses.[4]

ZANU and ZANLA aligned themselves with China and its history of peasant struggle:

In his analysis of *The three stages of protracted war*, the late Mao Tse-Tung identifies the first stage as being the 'strategic defensive phase' involving political mobilisation of the population prior to the commencement of guerrilla warfare, which is limited to small scale operations and in which conventional positional warfare must be avoided. In the second phase, having secured a base in the rural areas by mobilising the people and retaining the tactical initiative, the guerrillas can take on the enemy on a large scale. Finally, in the third phase, having secured liberated zones, positional warfare and attacks on urban centres become possible.[5]

Many ZANLA fighters received specialised training in China, Yugoslavia and Tanzania, but more were trained for peasant mobilisation and military action by the FRELIMO forces close at hand in Mozambique. One of the first four ZANLA guerrillas sent to the Mozambican province of Tete in 1970 said later:

We had to learn by observation how the masses lived. We had to learn from FRELIMO how to keep prisoners. We had to learn how they taught the masses co-operative work like agriculture and also how to establish cordial relations with the masses. We wanted to see how they taught them about war and how they prepared their minds for war.[6]

As a political and military strategy, the guerrilla *pungwe* itself appears

---

[4]Ibid, 11.

[5]Ibid, 27. The Zimbabwe African People's Union (ZAPU) and its military wing, the Zimbabwe People's Revolutionary Army (ZIPRA) were, by contrast, aligned with the Soviet Union.

[6]Ibid, 26.

to have emerged through the instincts and circumstances of anonymous fighters on the ground. It was not prompted by the ZANLA high command and its emergence has not been identified with any particular freedom fighter or guerrilla group. Guerrillas had been trained in the Maoist stress on peasant mobilisation, but they did not learn about *mapungwe* in Mozambique and Tanzania. All-night vigils were not a generic revolutionary strategy imported from other contexts.[7] The *pungwe* was the Shona way in which the guerrillas applied and implemented the mass mobilisation theory they had learned was so important. It emerged when guerrillas moving back into Zimbabwe engaged the traditions of SSR and drew on their experience in churches to devise a relatively safe way to meet with the people and a powerful way to mobilise them. Once sprouted from the grassroots, it proliferated almost immediately throughout the war effort. About 80 per cent of guerrillas' time was spent in mobilising the masses,[8] and much of this was spent in almost nightly *mapungwe.*

The freedom fighters' movements had a general pattern:

> The guerrilla groups crossed European farming areas and game parks as rapidly as possible and made for the relative safety of the densely populated Tribal Trust Lands. They moved from kraal to kraal or along a network of base camps until they reached their area of deployment ... The guerrillas normally operated in sections of 10 men comprising the commander, political commissar, security officer, medical officer, logistics officer and three to five cadres.[9]

Manicaland's location along the Mozambique border and the Honde's valley geography made these areas especially prominent in guerrilla operations, for a secure base needed to be established here for operations to be launched further west. Both along the way and in their

---

[7]'We were never taught about *mapungwe* while we were in Tanzania,' says Chamutenga Munetsi, a former guerrilla in the Honde Valley. Interview, 24 May 1991. Other former guerrillas confirm that the *pungwe* was neither taught in the training camps, nor does it appear to have been practised much there.

[8]Paul Moorcraft & Peter McLaughlin, *Chimurenga! The war in Rhodesia, 1965–1980* (Marshalltown, South Africa: Sygma Books and Collins Vaal, 1982), 127.

[9]Ibid, 125.

deployment areas, fighters focused much of their attention on organising *mapungwe* with the local population. Far from being peripheral to the main business of the war, *mapungwe* were the principal method for implementing a major revolutionary strategy of the twentieth century.[10]

Patterns of a guerrilla *pungwe*

The Honde Valley's role as a conduit for guerrilla entry from Mozambique made its control a high priority for both ZANLA and the Rhodesia Front. The guerrilla presence was intense, conflict was frequent, and night meetings were important in ZANLA's efforts to secure the loyalty of Honde residents.

Organising a *pungwe* was the first objective for guerrillas when they entered an area, and when they appeared they expected immediate support from the local population:

> If they came in the vicinity, they would have a place where they would go and stay ... If it was during the day, you would send people who would go and give them some food where they were. Their scouts – they could be girls, they could be boys – they were the ones who would give them food.[11]

Some residents recall night rallies being held several times a week close to the border:

> Because we were so close to the border, there were many groups (of guerrillas) operating around us at one time. There might be as many as five – one down by the villages, another behind us here,

---

[10]Rhodesian forces sometimes attacked *mapungwe,* especially when given information about specific gatherings, but government soldiers often feared moving at night because local support gave the guerrillas an advantage in making ambushes. The RF failure to respond more actively to the *pungwe* movement was a major blunder. Its defensive posture inclined it to respond to events that were clearly military and miss the populist movement that was well under way. 'This was the key element of ZANU strategy that their opponents never really understood: that (until the war entered a new and more conventional stage at the beginning of 1978) ZANLA was not on the offensive but was engaged in defending the process of mass mobilisation.' Martin & Johnson, 88.

[11]David Mubaira, church members interview, 13 April 1991.

another at the top of the mountain and so on. This was one of the main routes for guerrillas to come in with men and material for transporting into the interior.[12]

A former freedom fighter describes operations from the guerrilla viewpoint:

> When we would arrive (in a particular locale), we would set up what we called a Day Base, where we would stay during the daytime. We would stay where there was a good deal of cover, with many trees. Where we would have the *pungwe* would be an open place and there we would explain how the *Chimurenga* was going on, how the war was progressing. That was called the Night Base. We would come out of the hidden places to the Night Base. We would find where there were some houses but an open space and that's where people would come to meet. Then we would instruct them about how the war was going.[13]

He describes the pattern of a typical *pungwe* as follows:

> Many times we would be eating at 6 or 7 o'clock. Food would come with people from their homes, but at other times it was dangerous because some people had a system of wanting to bewitch or poison us. So then we would want to be cooked for there. We had a soldier we called *seglanza,* so this person would do the work of tasting the food to check if it had poison. He would stay for an hour before the food was eaten by others. Then from 8 o'clock we would begin singing. If we had said we would have a *pungwe,* we would then do the *pungwe*. At dawn (*kana kwoda kuti hwe*) people would be dismissed and they would go to their houses.
>
> Q: You would continue until what time?
>
> A: Up to about 4 am.

---

[12]Shepstone Muzvidzwa, interview, 3 January 1994.

[13]Thomas Marira, church members interview, 13 April 1991. The RF mounted a well-organised campaign to stimulate pro-government enthusiasm through a variety of media. Kenneth Dzutsumwa Manungo, 'The role peasants played in the Zimbabwe War of Liberation, with special emphasis on Chiweshe District' (PhD diss, Ohio University, 1991), 158–162. The banning of nationalist publications made the dissemination of war news through *mapungwe* crucial to the guerrilla cause.

Q: Would you sing songs?

A: A great many of them, while we were telling people how the war was going, where we would be, where the enemy would be, how we would be fighting the enemy – all that.[14]

A former guerrilla's account of operations in the Dande area of the Zambezi River valley provides more political detail:

When we came to a village, the first thing we would do is hold a rally. The Commander and the Political Commissar would go to the place where the rally was to be held. The rest of us would go to all the houses and make sure that everyone came. Some people would want to come, others would not but there was no choice about it. You had to come. We wanted everyone there because if anyone wasn't they could go off quietly and betray us. First we would explain who we were. We were ZANLA. We were not ZANU … We explained the structures of the ZANU party. We then explained the structure of the army and told the masses about the army high command and described their duties. Next we explained national grievances, then colonialism, then neo-colonialism and capitalism. We explained that ours would be a socialist government and what that would mean to the masses. The pattern of the meeting would be: talk for half an hour, then teaching the masses songs for an hour, then talking for another half hour and so on, so that people did not get bored … At the end of the meeting we would say to the older people: 'Mothers and Fathers, go home now and sleep in peace. But children you must stay here.' The younger people would stay and we would then say: 'What is our support here? Are people in favour of us, are people speaking against us and who is doing so?' Then they would tell us, for example, that some people were saying that they didn't have enough food to eat themselves without giving some to us. And many other complaints came out as well.[15]

War-related fiction in Zimbabwe often features the guerrilla *mapungwe*, evokes the tone of the gatherings and reconstitutes the content of speeches. A representative sample appears in Garikai Mutasa's 1985 novel, *The contact*:

---

[14]Marira.
[15]Lan, 127–129.

It was the *Pungwe* night and there was singing and political education. Bazooka (a guerrilla) came into the clearing which was surrounded by about fifty people; men, women, boys and girls. The small piece of land was wholly covered with thick trees in the virgin forest which paralleled the Musabezi River. Only three guerrillas were seen by the peasants at one time as the others took it in turn to guard the meeting. They knew that it was necessary for the people to hold them in esteem and to trust them completely.

'Forward with the *Chimurenga!*
Forward with the War!
Forward with the Central Committee (of ZANU-PF)!
Forward with the High Command (of ZANLA)!

'Forward with the ZANLA Forces!
Forward with the Masses of Zimbabwe!
Forward with Chama chaMapinduza! (the Tanzanian ruling party that was supporting ZANLA)
Down with the sellouts!
Down with destroyers!
Down with Smith and Janet! (Prime Minister Ian Smith and his wife, Janet Smith)[16]

After each slogan had been shouted out by Bazooka the people responded in unison with a loud *'Pamberi'* (Forward) or *'Pasi'* (Down) to endorse what was being said. The politicisation continued, 'Parents ... do we understand each other ... ?[17] We are fighting a war like this NOT for racial superiority ... we are not fighting the war so that whites will become second class citizens ... we are not fighting against the colour white, parents ... we are fighting against what that colour represents ... against capitalism and colonialism. We are fighting against the capitalist stooges and their lackeys.'

He paused a moment and breathed deeply, 'VIVA ZANU!'

'VIVA!' The people roared back.

---

[16]Although the novel is written in English, the slogans appear in Shona, and I have provided an English translation.
[17]These ellipses appear in Mutasa's text. It is unclear whether they represent pauses, dramatic effect, or omissions of material from interview accounts on which he may have based his narrative.

'We are fighting the war, parents and comrades, (Bazooka continued) so that we can have land to till. How many of you parents
were removed from their land and placed in this desert? How
many of you children do not have land? How many of you wouldn't
want to repossess what was once owned by your parents? How
can someone from Europe own land in our forefathers' country?
How can they dig gold and carry it overseas?

'They got what they got through the gun ... our own country
through the gun. They killed Kagubi and Nehanda (spirit mediums
executed by the BSAC authorities during the 1896 *Chimurenga*) ...
Now we want to right the wrongs. This is a war to end war. To end
the aggression, to end the *'makandiwas'* (agricultural contour
ridges mandated by the Land Husbandry Act and other government regulations) and *'muteros'* (taxes). Our spirits will never be
free until every inch of Zimbabwe is liberated.'

The chanting of slogans, the speeches and the discussion continued until daybreak. The people ambled back sleepily to their
homes full of the new things which they had learnt. To discuss
such things in Rhodesia was taboo and now issues upon which
they had long pondered were put concisely to them. Trying to gain
a knowledge of the authentic history of Zimbabwe, their country,
was to invite the devil into your quarters.[18]

Singing was central to the propagandising and mobilising function of
the guerrillas' night rallies. As the chorus of one song said, 'You must
communicate your stand clearly to the masses, / They must know the
party line.'[19] Singing provided continuity between the guerrilla *pungwe* and people's general cultural experience, for Shona people sing
when they gather, regardless of the nature of the occasion. As all could
participate simultaneously, singing strengthened cohesion and gave
pungwe groups a sense of shared identity. Singing stimulated joy and
celebration when people had reason to fear both discovery by the
enemy and summary executions of sellouts. Often quite ideological in
content, the songs imprinted the substance of the guerrillas' historical
and ideological lectures on the minds of uneducated and illiterate

---

[18]Garikai Mutasa, *The contact* (Gweru: Mambo Press, 1985), 37–38.
[19]Alec J C Pongweni, *Songs that won the Liberation War* (Harare: College
Press, 1982), 9–10.

people. Proclaimed one song,

> Forward with the year of the people's power!
> Forward!
> Down with exploiters!
> Down with them! ...

> What did the exploiters bring to Zimbabwe?
> They had nothing but empty stomachs
> Sagging because of no food in Britain.

> They won't leave our country to us
> Because they claim, 'We have businesses',
> Saying they have investments,
> Saying they have farms.
> These are the inheritance of the blacks,
> You masses of Zimbabwe ...[20]

Many of the young were well into primary and secondary school, but many parents and grandparents experienced the guerrillas' historical and economic concepts as intellectually challenging. The songs distilled the teaching to short, mnemonic lines set to appealing tunes, many of them melodies from church hymns, and made people more receptive to the lectures. Singing also kept people awake and alert, so that the group could disperse quickly if a lookout spotted an army patrol.

In the Honde Valley guerrillas held night rallies on the plantations freely early in the war years and tried to disrupt operations by persuading workers to leave the tea estates. In August 1975 they emphasised their point by marching 22 workers from Aberfoyle Tea Plantation and shooting them to death at Eastern Highlands. The execution was so widely perceived as unjust that by the next day two of those responsible for the shooting were dead, presumably at the hands of either their colleagues or outraged locals. Such events at *mapungwe* did prompt many workers to leave. In December 1976 Eastern Highlands responded by moving many of its workers to a camp near Penhalonga, from where they were trucked to EHTE daily by armed convoy. When, in late 1977, the company moved workers back but enclosed its villages with

---

[20]Ibid, 12. I have altered the translation to reflect more closely the Shona original.

security fences the frequency of *mapungwe* decreased greatly:

> There was nowhere they (the guerrillas) could come in to take us to the *pungwe*. Guards would be guarding in here. The *pungwe* that we would see, that is when we would go away from here and go to places like Bocha and Marange and Zimunya (south of Mutare). If you would go there, that's where you would have a *pungwe* with the boys. But before the security wire was put up people would be able to go out of here and we would go and meet with the boys ... There were six of them. They asked us, 'Where do you stay?' We said, 'At the tea.' They said, 'Leave and go to your villages. Stop working.'[21]

Among many people, the mobilisation rallies achieved their objectives. Written responses to the question, 'What experiences did you have of *mapungwe* of the *Chimurenga*?' in the Essay Project on Christianity and Tradition included answers such as the following:

> My experiences in *mapungwe eChimurenga* (were that they) were there to give people morale. Even if people knew of the war, they had high morale at *mapungwe*. The *pungwe* played a big role, because they helped the people to forget about possible attack from enemy soldiers.

> *Chimurenga pungwe* experiences were to drive people to be brave and to inject them with the spirit of war so that they could fight till the enemy surrendered.

> The *pungwe* of the *Chimurenga* was meant to strengthen the war by ensuring that people continued to work together.

> *Mapungwe eChimurenga* were helpful, because they gave us a vivid understanding of what was happening and what was going to happen.[22]

The guerrilla *mapungwe* were hampered by the government's establishment of 'protected villages' (PVs), beginning in 1973, where about

---

[21] David Mubaira, church members interview, 13 April 1991. Major facilities at EHTE still exhibit high barbed-wire fences as a legacy of the war.

[22] Elias Chibvuma, Rodrick Dhliwayo, Mai Mabvaka, Joseph Nymuchengwe; Essay Project on Christianity and Tradition, questionnaire circulated by author, 1991.

two thousand people typically were settled on about 100 acres surrounded by barbed wire.[23] The RF justified the PVs on the grounds of protecting local inhabitants from guerrilla violence, but the initiative had obvious objectives of insulating local people from guerrilla influence and depriving the fighters of logistical support. The policy was implemented in the Honde in 1975 as Rhodesian military units destroyed villages throughout the valley and sequestered the inhabitants in ten large keeps.[24] Residents' movements were closely monitored:

> Life was very hard in the keeps. We were searched when we went out and when we came back. When we went out to work in our fields, we had to leave our identity cards with the guards so that they could check to make sure that we returned at night. We were not allowed to carry any food outside, because they thought that if we carried food outside we might give it to our friends the freedom fighters.[25]

Rhodesian consistency in maintaining the keeps varied with local military fortunes:

> … new PVs were constantly being erected, while at the same time the guerrillas were destroying the 'keeps' by cutting the fences and burning down the temporary shelters in order 'to liberate' the

---

[23]The people called them 'keeps', while nationalist leaders called them 'concentration camps'. Models for the policy were the New Villages established by the British in Malaya and the Strategic Hamlets established by the Americans in Vietnam. 'Families were usually allotted fifteen square yards for shelter, latrine, and accommodation for chickens and goats. Huts were laid out in grid fashion and in straight rows for unobstructed observation.' Lewis H Gann and Thomas H Henrikson, *The struggle for Zimbabwe: battle in the bush* (New York: Praeger, 1981), 74.

[24]By mid-1974 the security forces had moved 100 000 people into keeps in the north-east. By mid-1976 there were 581 000 people living in 203 protected villages nationwide: 159 in north-east Mashonaland, 31 in Manicaland, and two in Masvingo Province. Diana Auret, *Reaching for justice: The Catholic Commission for Justice and Peace looks back at the past twenty years, 1972–1992* (Gweru: Mambo Press, 1992), 65, 67. Ten of the 31 Manicaland keeps were in the Honde, indicating the valley's strategic importance.

[25]Kingston Marohwa, interview, 20 January 1994. Many Honde people lived in PVs for over three years, but life in the keeps is not a frequent topic of conversation. I attribute this reticence to the painfulness of people's memories.

people. By the beginning of 1977 seventy such attacks had occurred.[26]

Thus, although night rallies became less frequent, they could not be eradicated and they continued to be a feature of wartime life in the Honde through to the end of the war.

The dominance of young people, some of them even teenagers, in the liberation movement and in the guerrilla *mapungwe* prefigured the prominent role of youth in the post-war night vigils of the churches and the vigils' role in recruiting members. The young fighters established networks of younger scouts – male *vanamujiba* and female *zvimbwido* – who helped them mobilise the local population, especially for *mapungwe*.[27] The scouts spread word of the guerrillas' arrival, announced the *pungwe*, provided food for the fighters and gathered intelligence. There were an estimated 50 000 *vanamujiba* and *zvimbwido* throughout Zimbabwe at the height of the war.[28] So many scouts and other teenagers became guerrillas that by late 1975 1 000 recruits were crossing into Mozambique every week.[29] The

---

[26]Auret, 67. Divided loyalties often prompted the African district assistants charged with maintaining security in the villages to be lax in enforcing regulations, a practice that further facilitated guerrilla access. Gann and Henriksen, 76.

[27]People associate these words exclusively with the Liberation War, and neither of them is attested in Hannan's *Dictionary*. Participants in the liberation struggle developed their own vocabulary to designate unique roles. In his memoir, Peter Godwin defines *vanamujiba* as 'local kids used by the guerrillas as their eyes and ears to keep them informed about the movement of the security forces'. *Mukiwa: a white boy in Africa* (New York: Atlantic Monthly Press, 1996), 250.

[28]Lan, 125.

[29]Martin & Johnson, 205. In correspondence, Irene Mahamba recalls a *Chimurenga* song that summarises the point: 'Mother and Father, you stay: I have gone to the Liberation War/You will see my blood under the flag of Zimbabwe.' For routes taken, see Henry Moyana, *The victory of Chief Rekayi Tangwena* (Harare: Longman Zimbabwe, 1987), 39. 'By the time of Zimbabwe's independence, there were eight refugee camps in Mozambique, not including military camps, with a total population of up to 150 000 people, of whom 20 000 were attending school.' Janice McLaughlin, "We did it for love': Refugees and religion in the camps in Mozambique and Zambia during Zimbabwe's Liberation Struggle', in *Church and state in Zimbabwe*, eds Carl Hallencreutz & Ambrose Moyo (Gweru: Mambo Press, 1988), 128, 130.

night rallies were a major source of recruits; as one informant put it: 'Recruitment was done during the *pungwe* ... All new recruits were taken at dawn.'[30]

Often these enlistees had voluntarily devoted their lives to the liberation cause, but sometimes the guerrillas left young people little choice about participating. Leadership by young people was revolutionary in Shona society, where the young are expected to defer to their elders. The war turned this chain of command upside down. Now elders were challenged to accept the leadership and obey the orders of young people. The transition was not easy, and some older people suffered when they hesitated.

Violence and the guerrillas' *mapungwe*

Violence at their *mapungwe* was part of the guerrillas' missional strategy, for they used violence not only to coerce compliance with their wishes but also to persuade people to support the liberation cause. When guerrillas suspected individuals of collaborating with the Rhodesia Front forces they held summary trials, and findings of guilt resulted in threats, beatings or executions, depending on the severity of the offence, the certainty of guilt and the guerrillas' own circumstantial needs to demonstrate power.[31]

Violence at wartime *mapungwe* is controversial in the post-war period. Partisans of the struggle do not deny that violent incidents took place, but they minimise their frequency and suggest that they were instigated by the exceptional, undisciplined guerrilla. Accounts by Manicaland residents, however, suggest that violence was common. 'The *mapungwe* of *Chimurenga* were very menacing,' wrote one person in this study's Essay Project on Christianity and Tradition, explaining that among the five rallies he attended two people were killed at one rally and seven at another. Other responses include the following:

---

[30]Pearson Chitare, Essay Project on Christianity and Tradition.

[31]Trials of suspected collaborators were so common at *mapungwe* that in Masvingo Province the term *pungwe* came to mean simply a trial held by guerrillas, whether by day or by night. Marthinus Daneel, *Guerrilla snuff: spirituality of a bush war* ((Masvingo: Typescript, 1991)), 262–266. Use of the term *pungwe* for daytime meetings is not attested in other parts of the country.

Their (the guerrillas') aim of having these *pungwes* was to gather with the people and share ideas, methods and routes of attacking the whites. Their preaching was under the title of death, so they preached death. When they had got all they wanted from the people they then proceeded with war. So at the *Chimurenga pungwes* the people shared evil spirit, the spirit of killing, demolishing, demoralising, etc, the creatures of the Lord. People were taking one another as enemies. Those who were found to be enemies were beaten up, hung, shot and some arrested.

Mapungwe eChimurenga were horrible, because that was the time when many innocent people were killed for no apparent reason.

I did not attend one, but oral tradition states they were places where discipline could take place and even a death sentence could be passed out. These *pungwes* were bitter places, because no one had freedom of speech.

After commending the rallies' for helping to achieve liberation, one respondent wrote:

Though *mapungwe eChimurenga* had their advantages, they were also a horrible experience. At times, other people would be ill-treated after having been falsely condemned as traitors. It was a rare case having the whole *pungwe* without witnessing acts of terrorism or bullying by the guerrillas. At times, innocent people would be butchered and false charges laid against them. At some meetings the guerrillas were a threatening sight especially to adolescents since they would forcefully take some with them to join the war.[32]

What ordinary people report is confirmed by post-war writers of historical fiction. Alexander Kanengoni's short story 'Things we'd rather not talk about' focuses on a young man forced by a guerrilla band to kill his father with a pickaxe at a *pungwe* while the villagers stand by, resolutely singing 'an ominous song that told of the grim fate that befell sellouts and enemy collaborators.' A youth leader relates the father's offence: 'Your father's store is used by the soldiers to send out telephone messages to various camps across the district', but the

[32]Togarasei Kahlari, Noah Madenya, Peter Matinenga, Maxwell Muparutsa, Leon Semu; Essay Project on Christianity and Tradition.

story suggests that the accusation is trumped up by the rival businessman next door.[33] Kanengoni tells the story from the perspective of the young man being tormented years later by psychotic hallucinations of that night, thus emphasising the enduring power that the wartime *mapungwe* continue to exercise in the consciousness of Zimbabweans who lived through the struggle. The story illustrates the perennial reality that war is not only a military and political fact but also a psychological event that has massive repercussions in the group consciousness of a people. Kanengoni himself was not an ambivalent bystander in the war but a guerrilla who fought for seven years and whose ideological credentials won him a post as head of television services with the Zimbabwe Broadcasting Corporation. Thus a former guerrilla acknowledges the moral ambiguity of tactics that guerrillas used to enforce loyalty among the people. In the story, the band's commander is depicted as a cruel maniac, but his deputy tries to moderate at least the means of execution and, at the denouement, walks 'wiping the tears in his eyes with the smoking barrel of his gun, away into the outlying bush'.[34]

Violence was inherent in the guerrillas' commitment to politicise and mobilise the masses for the struggle. By appearing openly before the peasants, the guerrillas put themselves at risk: all would now know them, and a few would know where their 'day base' was located. This risk entailed, from their point of view, a reciprocal obligation of absolute secrecy and loyalty to themselves on the part of the locals. Betrayal could cost the guerrillas their lives and impede the war effort in that area. Therefore, the fighters believed that sellouts had to be dealt with immediately and harshly.[35] One summary of guerrilla violence puts the case as follows:

> Rhodesian propaganda often spoke of an indiscriminate reign of terror inflicted on the African population by the guerrillas. There was a deliberate reign of terror, but only against those who sym-

---

[33]Alexander Kanengoni, *Effortless tears* (Harare: Baobab, 1993), 59, 60, 58.

[34]Ibid, 63. Violence at *mapungwe* also appears in Mutasa's novel *The contact*, 51–52, 100–101. Included are two incidents in which guerrillas hand captives over to peasants with the confidence that the local people will kill them at a *pungwe* scheduled by the guerrillas.

[35]The Shona word corresponding to 'sellout' is *mutengesi,* which usually refers to a storekeeper or anyone who sells a commodity.

pathised with or aided the Rhodesian cause. 'Collaborators' or 'sellouts' were brutally murdered, or mutilated and often whole households and kraals were destroyed. But the targets were normally carefully selected and the local population could usually see the point of the executions or mutilations.[36]

Less sanguine about guerrilla policy, Norma Kriger's extensive research in the Mutoko area corroborates the general climate of fear to which Honde residents testify in their relationship with the wartime guerrillas:

> Peasants inform us of how much they suffered, not only from the abuses of government forces but also from guerrilla coercion. Even though they worked very hard and sacrificed their meagre resources to meet the guerrillas' logistical needs, they were often beaten and threatened by the guerrillas … It is impossible to know how many 'sell-outs' were killed, but official figures show that the guerrillas killed more African civilians than regime force members.[37]

The consequences for popular support were serious: 'Oral data from active participants about their behaviour in the civilian support organisations challenge the entrenched view of popular support for the guerrillas. At best,' Kriger concludes, 'peasants were reluctant supporters.'[38]

Guerrillas sometimes used *mapungwe* to bring force to bear on social issues not directly related to the war. Liberation of women is a notable example. Irene Mahamba recounts how guerrillas explained their intervention in a family to ensure that a daughter would not be married to a man she hated:

> Right now in our liberation army we have got women who fight side by side with us, women who have suffered with us, faced the hardships of attacks by Smith's bombers with us … The present war of Liberation in Zimbabwe has proved that women are as tough as the men. However, it should be understood that women

---

[36]Moorcraft & McLaughlin, 130.

[37]Norma Kriger, *Zimbabwe's guerrilla war: peasant voices* (Cambridge and New York: Cambridge University Press, 1992), 7, 156–157.

[38]Ibid, 169, the conclusion a chapter on guerrilla-civilian relations (116–169).

have always been equal to men. Men have taken unfair advantage of them and mistreated them ... It is no longer possible to force a woman to marry a man she does not want ... We can no longer say a woman should earn less money for the same job ...[39]

Mahamba describes a *pungwe* where guerrillas condemned prostitution as a form of collaborating with the Rhodesians' disintegrating effect on Shona society and urged the villagers to identify not only the local prostitute but the men who patronised her. The prostitute was humiliated simply by being identified, but the men were forced to lie on the ground and submit to severe beatings by their wives.[40] In such cases the *pungwe* became a forum for extending into society the active egalitarian role of women that the guerrillas themselves experienced in prosecuting the war.

Severe violence from the Rhodesian forces was an ongoing experience for rural Zimbabweans. RF soldiers routinely searched kraals and interrogated suspects, and they were brutal in punishing those they believed were cooperating with the guerrillas. Legislation made harbouring or failing to report 'terrorists' crimes punishable by life imprisonment or death.[41] The military judged that *pungwe* attendance constituted such violation of the law, so participants were considered fair game in any attack on a *pungwe*. Individuals suspected of attending a *pungwe* were often beaten and tortured for information about guerrilla movements. While rural people felt caught between the competing violence of the RF and the guerrillas, violence from the security forces

---

[39]Irene Ropa Rinopfuka Mahamba, *A woman in struggle*, 2nd ed (Gweru: Mambo, 1986), 24–25.

[40]Ibid, 36–43. In correspondence, Mahamba explains, *'Pungwe* sessions were not only arenas for educating the masses, they were also the revolutionary *dare* (traditional court) in which problems that plagued society were dealt with ... the struggle was not just a military matter but an overhaul of society.' In Dande, 'The prostitutes were killed because the comrades said: You are holding us back from winning our country. The comrades were saying: the country is ours, we blacks. People who were putting Ambi (skin-lightening cream) on their faces were killed.' Lan, 129.

[41]Martin and Johnson, 102–103. For accounts of Rhodesian enforcement tactics, see Terence Ranger, 'Holy men and rural communities in Zimbabwe, 1970–1980', in *The church and war*, vol 20, *Studies in church history*, ed W J Scheils (Oxford: Basil Blackwell, for the Ecclesiastical History Society, 1983), 447, 453–456; McLaughlin, 131; Auret, *passim*. For a vivid statement of the balance of terror, see Godwin, 272.

was a grim fact of life that they simply expected. People recall their interaction with the guerrillas, by contrast, as a relationship of high drama in which great themes mingled: the power of a righteous cause, the mobilisation of the masses, the violent means used to enforce loyalty and the complexity of motives and personal relationships. Guerrilla violence was brutal and scarring, but it stirred souls and raised profound ethical issues that people are still seeking to resolve.

Pungwe as a *Chimurenga* word

The all-night mobilisation rallies were such powerful experiences for many Zimbabweans that they associate the word *pungwe* primarily with the guerrillas' wartime practice. Although the word *pungwe* has long referred generically to any gathering in which people stay up all night, all informants recall the term emerging into special prominence during the Liberation War. Some even credit the guerrillas with coining the term:

> We say the word *pungwe* was brought by the comrades. They were the ones who came with the *pungwe*. We used to have meetings where we were overtaken there by dawn (*misangano yekuedzerwa tiriyo*). Now they (the comrades) came, saying, 'Come, today there is a *pungwe*.'[42]

The term *pungwe* became a technical term of the liberation struggle. In its use with social dances and the rites of SSR, the term describes the nocturnal aspect of various gatherings and ceremonies that have their own names. An inquirer might ask, 'You did a *pungwe* last night, but what sort of gathering was it?' In wartime use, however, the term *pungwe* became the specific and self-explanatory name for an all-night meeting convened and led by guerrillas for the purpose of political education and practical mobilisation. If someone said, 'I'm tired today, because last night I went to a *pungwe*', the listener would understand immediately the precise nature of the gathering. This association continues today when people discuss the past, although the churches' post-war use of the term for its own practice sometimes calls now for additional specification, such as *pungwe reChimurenga* (*pungwe* of the Liberation War) or *pungwe revakomana* (*pungwe* of the

---

[42]Mai Kachali, interview, 25 August 1987, Tsonzo.

guerrillas). Fiction writers often assume their readers will understand the wartime reference and so do not provide any explanation. In a novel about women in the war, Irene Mahamba writes:

> The other thing that *mbuya* (grandmother) talked of that interested me was the freedom fighters who were operating in the Bikita area at the time. I had heard many stories about them and worshipped them as heroes. When I showed interest in them *mbuya* said they actually had *'pungwe'* sessions almost every night with the secondary school boys and I could see them as soon as I was fully recovered. I was very delighted and my imagination ran wild.[43]

A story by G Shuro begins:

> It was the year 1976 in the month of April that we were at a *pungwe*. Many people were there. All had been called to come to be with the guerrillas. The *vanachimbwido* cooked *sadza* and the comrades ate. When the people gathered around the fire that had been kindled, one of the comrades said, 'When I say, "Forward with the war!" you say, "Forward!"'[44]

In secondary literature on Shona life and culture, the word *pungwe* never appears, even when authors discuss rituals that are nocturnal, but it does appear in works on the Liberation War, confirming its particular association with the struggle.[45] *Pungwe* became a *Chimurenga* word that was almost as distinctive as the words *mujiba* and *chimbwido*.

A possible nuance of the term relates both to the Liberation War and to the Pungwe River. In one of the most notorious Rhodesian raids on ZANLA in Mozambique, Selous Scouts killed over a thousand people in August 1976 at a large camp located near the confluence of the

---

[43]Mahamba, 14.

[44]G Shuro, *'Chisingaperi Chinoshura'* (Eternal bad luck). In *Hondo YeChimurenga: Nyaya dzeHondo dzakaunganidzwa neLiterature Bureau* (The Liberation War: stories of the war, collected by the Literature Bureau) (Gweru: Mambo, 1984), 196. (English translation mine.)

[45]J Frederikse, *None but ourselves: masses vs mass media in the making of Zimbabwe* (Harare: Zimbabwe Publishing House, 1982), 367; Lan, 127; Manungo, 157–179; Godwin, 258. *Morari* was the term for a night rally in the Dande and Mutoko areas.

Nyadzonya River and the Pungwe River.[46] The raid provoked international attention, including that of the United Nations High Commission for Refugees, which had been assisting refugees at the camp. The association of this major incident with the Pungwe River may have strengthened the guerrillas' resolve to use the term *pungwe* for their nocturnal mobilisation meetings. The term also acquired the connotation of memorialising the many *Chimurenga* supporters killed so close to the Pungwe River.

Guerrillas were able to transform the *pungwe* into a powerful political tool, because they built on the practice's deep foundations in Shona social and religious life to give their meetings a populist appeal. The strength with which the term took hold may be compared to the power of the liberation songs, many of which cannot be traced to particular authors and which appear, as a common Shona expression would have it, to have 'come up from the ground' (*kubva pasi*). Use of a term shared by the general population accorded well with the guerrillas' overall effort to take the liberation struggle beyond their own ranks and mobilise the population, so that the struggle became not the preoccupation of an ideological elite but the shared struggle of black Zimbabweans as a national community.

Religion and the guerrilla *pungwe*

Conversion of mind and heart, popular mobilisation, social transformation – these were the objectives and achievements of the guerrillas' rallies that had a signal impact on *pungwe* practice becoming a movement in the churches after independence in 1980. This impact was virtually assured by the strong, albeit complex, religious dimension of the guerrilla *pungwe*. Guerrillas organised night meetings in order to achieve the political objective of grassroots consensus favouring the Liberation War and the military objective of logistical support for fighting units. For both the fighters and their rural audiences, however, these objectives had religious themes that included the heritage of Shona Spirit Religion and the traditions of Christian churches. The guerrillas' appeal to SSR to legitimise the war contributed to a

---

[46]Ron Reid Daly, as told to Peter Stiff, *Selous Scouts: top secret war* (Cape Town: Galago, 1983), 321–406.

revival of ancestral veneration and also subjected it to serious scrutiny that continues today. The fighters' disparagement of Christianity alongside their use of church traditions sharpened popular reflection about Christianity's relation to colonialism even as it set in motion the widespread vigil movement of today.

The integration of religion with mobilisation in the guerrilla *pungwe* is well articulated by a Honde Valley Anglican who lived through the war:

> The *mapungwe* of *Chimurenga* expressed the view that the whole Zimbabwean nation was drawn to the one and only cause – fight for the liberation of the country. Yet the aspects of the *Chimurenga* itself and the associated *Chimurenga mapungwe* were culturally, traditionally and spiritually symbolic, hence religious orientated. I experienced pain, grief and sorrow – it was the bleakest period of my life. Hence the whole nation sang religious orientated songs. These *mapungwe* of *Chimurenga* played a very important part during the liberation struggle insomuch that I have termed them *the gene (factors) of unity to a genuine cause.*[47]

'Forward with the spirits!': guerrillas on mission

Invoking the ancestral spirit guardians of the land and promoting their veneration was normative practice in the *mapungwe* of the freedom fighters. Their missionary zeal had important consequences for Shona Spirit Religion. SSR became a mission religion, probably for the first time in its history. It became a topic of serious reflection among the people, for it was promoted as a religion alongside other religions, not simply as a cultural custom. Through the ancestors' stewardship of the land, SSR became linked integrally with nationalism and liberation. These consequences, in turn, boosted SSR's competitive position with Christianity, which was identified as the religion of the oppressors.

The *pungwe* was the chief context in which guerrillas promoted SSR. Commented one person in the Honde Valley: 'People were taught to respect the *vadzimu* which were said to be rendering great help spiritually.' Fighters often opened their *mapungwe* by greeting the spirits with the customary reverent clapping. Opening acclamations extolled

---

[47]Shadreck Mapudzi, Essay Project on Christianity and Tradition.

the spirits and the great mediums such as Chaminuka, Nehanda and Kaguvi, who had empowered the First *Chimurenga* of the 1890s and who might now turn the earlier defeat into a decisive recovery of the land. Said one informant of the fighters, 'They used to drink (ritual) beer, take snuff, beat drums and sing the songs of the *mashavi*.'[48] In echoing the patterns of night vigils in spirit religion, the guerrillas joined their rallies to the deep and perennial stream of Shona spirituality and so claimed religious legitimacy for their struggle.

The prominence of the land issue in *pungwe* rhetoric mirrored the centrality of land in the rationale of the *Chimurenga*. One valley resident reconstructed a typical piece of guerrilla teaching as follows:

> A guerrilla would instruct people in political education: 'Forward with ZANU, with unity, with resistance and with courage! Down with oppressors and sellouts! Our country belongs to us and to our ancestors. We're not going anywhere, but it was seized by the whites. They used the Bible and then the gun. Now we are oppressed by the white … So all this came with the missionaries. They came deceiving the people with the Bible.'[49]

The appeal to SSR as the religion of liberation was based not on a desire for *any* alternative to the religion brought by whites but on the spirits' historic association with the land. Indeed, the Shona worldview made it inevitable that the war would take on a religious tone, that the guardian spirits would focus religious authority and the night rallies would promote Shona Spirit Religion.

Significant alliances with spirit mediums lay behind the guerrillas' promotion of spirits at *mapungwe*. Fighters sought and received the support of territorial spirits through their mediums, who also offered tactical assistance. The guerrillas responded by taking initiative in the traditional practice of eliminating wizards. Initial efforts by ZANLA guerrillas in the 1960s to forge solidarity with peasants failed until they followed local people's advice and consulted spirit mediums. When the ZANLA High Command endorsed this practice, albeit reluctantly, popular support grew quickly and recruits came forward in large numbers.[50] While in some cases the approval of the territorial *mho-*

---

[48]T Makunike, Essay Project on Christianity and Tradition.
[49]David Mubaira, interview, 20 May 1991, EHTE.
[50]Ranger, *Peasant consciousness*, 202–216.

ndoro was extracted by threat, common concern for the land and shared reverence for the ancestors often made this a genuinely religious exchange. The mediums placed the guerrillas under the traditional discipline of holy warriors: no sex while on active duty, no killing of wild animals, no eating of certain vegetables and certain parts of cooked meat and so on.[51] Mediums taught guerrillas how to interpret signs displayed by wild animals:

> The spirit mediums gave us many good ideas. The *chipungu* (eagle) was a very important sign ... If you saw two eagles fighting in the sky that meant that the bomber planes were coming. In March 1979 we saw two eagles fighting near Gonono. We made off. The planes came and bombed but no one was hurt.[52]

In some instances mediums guided the operations of guerrillas in the field with tactical counsel derived from revelation received in possession. Premonitory dreams attributed to the spirits could provide counsel, and some guerrillas were mediums themselves who guided their comrades out of difficult situations through possession.[53] Supporting the mediums' advocacy in the struggle was the sanction of Mwari, the High God, who in the mid-1950s had declared a second *Chimurenga* through the messengers sent from the southern districts to hear God's word at Matonjeni:

> You will see, it is going to be a war of the spirit mediums. Through the *masvikiro* Mwari will make the second *Chimurenga* a people's war. Then we will regain our lost lands. Already Mwari is saying at the *dombo* (rock) that if his black sons and daughters heed his call to arms and if they obey the directives of the ancestral war council, victory over the oppressor will be theirs. Mwari says: 'Forward with the struggle! Blood will flow. There will be deliverance from oppression. The land is ours!'[54]

---

[51] The substantial role of spirit mediums is detailed by Lan, especially 136–175. See also Ranger, 'The death of Chaminuka: spirit mediums, nationalism and the guerrilla war in Zimbabwe', *African Affairs* (June 1982), 349–69; *Peasant consciousness*, 202–216.

[52] Lan 157–158; see also Daneel, *Guerrilla snuff*, 15, 105.

[53] Daneel, *Guerrilla snuff*, 88–89, 115–129, 133–164.

[54] Ibid, 73.

Many guerrillas felt that, through the *vadzimu,* Mwari intervened to protect them from ambushes and even from bullets in battle.

Having championed the spirits, the guerrillas then entered SSR's most vigorous struggle with evil, the identification and elimination of wizards:

> When the *vakomana* had a *pungwe* they would speak against the rural councils, against the dip tanks and the Agritex (Rhodesian Agricultural Extension) officers. They would ask, 'Do you know any wizards (*varoyi*)? Bring any diviner-healer (*nganga*) you know. And also bring collaborators.'[55]

Punishing or eliminating wizards varied with particular fighters and circumstances. For the guerrillas, it sometimes represented a crude *quid pro quo*: the fighters would punish people the peasants hated and feared if the peasants would identify people the guerrillas hated and feared.[56] People's accusations of wizardry could express local rivalries rather than occult malevolence or collaboration with the Rhodesians. However, sometimes the guerrillas' witch-hunting expressed a genuine conviction that the spirituality of liberation entailed an effort to free people from the oppression of others in league with evil spirits. This campaign went forward at *mapungwe,* meetings held at night, when the evil spirits and their human agents were believed to be abroad on the suffering land.

'Down with Jesus!': guerrillas and Christianity

The other side of the mission coin in the guerrillas' promotion of Shona Spirit Religion was the attempted suppression of Christianity. In Manicaland people recall that generally guerrillas denounced Christianity and the churches at *mapungwe.* The following is a typical exchange on the topic:

Q: Now at these *mapungwe* did the boys talk about the church?

A: Yes, they talked a lot about the church.

Q: And what did they say about the church?

A: They used to teach people to say, 'Down with Jesus! Down with

---

[55]Michael Mbona, interview, 20 May 1994. See also Lan, 167–168.
[56]A possible case in point appears in Daneel, *Guerrilla snuff,* 107.

the teaching of Jesus! Down with going to church! Forward with the ancestral spirits! (*Vaidzidzisa vanhu kuti, Pasi naJesu! Pasi neudzidzisi hwaJesu! Pasi nekuenda kuchechi! Pamberi nemidzimu!*)

Q: So why were they saying, 'Down with the church!'?

A: It was caused by this idea that Christianity was brought by the whites, so the whole idea was white, (so) down with the church. Just because religion was brought by the white people, so down with religion, down with the church and down with Christ.[57]

Anti-Christian rhetoric was backed up with forceful strictures against congregational life as guerrillas forbade Christians to meet and sometimes punished leaders for holding services. While urban churches continued to meet, many rural churches throughout the country suspended services for long periods, especially between 1976 and 1980. As one lay leader at Eastern Highlands put it:

It was difficult to worship during the time of the war. People were coming to church, but just a few at a time. But those who were members of churches outside (the tea estates) were not worshipping; that was not possible.[58]

Guerrilla pressure inhibited personal religious devotion as well. Many church members buried their Bibles, prayerbooks, Mothers' Union uniforms and Fishermen materials so that they would not be found by searching guerrillas.[59]

For freedom fighters with an agenda to recover the land and control the country, it was a natural *political* move to condemn the religion of those they regarded as usurpers of the land and political power. Christianity was the religion of the white settlers who had seized the land and ruled the country. Although there was no officially established church in Rhodesia, the Anglican cathedral's location next door to Parliament House on the former Cecil (Rhodes) Square (now Africa Unity Square) in Harare symbolised a mutual interest between

---

[57]Elisha Gunda, church leaders interview, August 1987. Accounts of guerrilla hostility to churches in other areas appear in Michael Bourdillon and Paul Gundani, 'Rural Christians and the Zimbabwe liberation war: a case study', in Hallencreutz & Moyo, 152; and Lan, 150.

[58]David Mubaira, church members interview, 13 April 1991.

[59]This phenomenon is documented for central Zimbabwe, as well. Bourdillon and Gundani, 157.

Christianity and the colonial establishment. Denouncing Christianity was also a natural *religious* move for people whose traditional religion highlights spirits who are strongly identified with the land and its tenure. With such a link between religion and land, it was difficult to disengage Christianity from its settler adherents, and it was natural to condemn a religion that co-existed with land usurpation.[60]

The mission-founded churches' variable and complex stances toward the liberation struggle in public debate did little to modify guerrillas' negative impressions of them. Representing the Protestant churches, the Christian Council of Rhodesia initially criticised the RF government and then took an intermediate position between the moderate African National Council of Abel Muzorewa and the radical approaches of ZANU and ZAPU. Late in the struggle it moved from conditional support to open criticism of the Internal Settlement of Zimbabwe-Rhodesia and finally appealed for national unity and an end to the war. The Roman Catholic Church initially opposed the RF's Unilateral Declaration of Independence (UDI) of 1965 but then accommodated itself to Rhodesian concessions. Its own Commission for Justice and Peace later became the major internal monitor of wartime conditions, and the commission's findings prompted the church to criticise government policy frequently.[61] Anglican leaders generally took their cue from the white bishop in Salisbury, who gave lukewarm support to the liberation cause in general and backed up Rhodesian claims in many

---

[60]The link between land and biblical mandates for justice made the Anglican St Faith's Farm experiment of the 1950s very significant for black Zimbabweans and, conversely, threatening for the Rhodesian authorities, who eventually suppressed it. Weller and Linden, 75–76; Patricia Chater, *Grassroots: the story of St Faith's Farm in Southern Rhodesia* (London: Hodder & Stoughton, 1962). The veneration accorded to Anglican missionary Arthur Shearly Cripps responds to the fact that he opposed colonial land tenure policies not on secular political grounds but on the grounds of Christian principle. See Douglas Steere, *God's irregular: Arthur Shearly Cripps: a Rhodesian epic* (London: SPCK, 1973).

[61]Carl F Hallencreutz, 'A council in crossfire: ZCC 1964–1980', in Hallencreutz and Moyo, 99–101. The efforts of the Commission for Justice and Peace are documented comprehensively by Auret; see also Martin and Johnson, 103–104. Bishop Donal Lamont of Mutare was especially outspoken in his opposition; after being sentenced to a year in prison for not reporting the presence of guerrillas, he was deprived of his citizenship and deported.

particulars.[62] In the United Methodist case, Bishop Abel Muzorewa, one of the early nationalists, and his Africa National Council differed increasingly with ZANU(PF) as the war progressed, with the result that the church as a whole was suspected of collaborating with the enemy. Muzorewa became the enemy when he won the 1979 elections and was made prime minister under the internal settlement that instituted Zimbabwe-Rhodesia. Although the changing positions of churches influenced political debate in Rhodesia, they do not appear to have affected the guerrillas significantly.

The attitudes and actions of local church leaders, whether white or black, were what most shaped guerrilla responses to the mission-founded churches in their operational areas. The folk Christianity that Roman Catholic missionaries developed in the Makoni district and the personal risk they undertook in forging solidarity with local people catalysed trusting relationships with freedom fighters, although even there the differing heritage of particular mission stations made for significant differences in guerrilla policy.[63] Black Anglican leaders at Bonda and a white Anglican priest at Penhalonga cooperated substantially with the guerrillas and so preserved their missions from harm to personnel or property, while the reputed intransigence of a white priest at Daramombe resulted in the nearly total destruction of that major Anglican mission. The fanatical commitment of Arthur Lewis to the Rhodesian cause affected the Honde Valley on account of Lewis's long tenure as priest-in-charge at St Peter's Mission at Mandea. By the time of the war, Lewis was long gone from Mandea, but resentment against his stance may have motivated the gutting of the Mandea rectory.[64]

---

[62]Michael Lapsley commends Bp Kenneth Skelton of Matabeleland for opposing the Rhodesian government and criticises the mixed signals offered by Bp Paul Burrough of Mashonaland and Dean John Da Costa of the Cathedral of St Mary and All Saints in Harare. *Neutrality or co-option? Anglican Church and state from 1964 until the independence of Zimbabwe* (Gweru: Mambo, 1986), *passim*. See also Kenneth Skelton, *Bishop in Smith's Rhodesia* (Gweru: Mambo, 1985).

[63]Ranger, 'Holy Men', *passim*.

[64]Lewis is reported to have said in church that the hearts of the nationalist leaders were 'as black as a crow', whereupon most of the men of the church walked out and did not return. Such legacies reduced Anglican church attendance during the war. It may also have fuelled guerrilla charges against the Rev Mashingaidze, Lewis's successor, that he was a sellout. When summoned for execution at a *pungwe*, Mashingaidze, whose name means 'you

Guerrilla attitudes toward African Initiated Churches depended entirely on local cooperation, for the AICs' oral culture did not produce written pronouncements intended for the public. In a historical novel based on incidents in Masvingo Province, Daneel cites *Ndaza* Zionist prophet Musariri Dhliwayo:

> For months he had been hearing rumours about comrades harassing church leaders in the Bikita district. At Norumedzo an uncooperative Zionist leader had his church burnt down. Bibles and garments were burnt. *VaPostori* who openly criticised the guerrilla slogan, 'Down with Jesus', had their beards shaven off and were forced to drink ancestral beer in public. It was even whispered that defiant believers had been martyred for their faith.[65]

When guerrillas approached Dhliwayo for logistical support at his Zion in Patmos centre in Gutu South District, they mocked his Christian convictions and threatened his church. As mutual trust developed, however, the guerrillas sought out the prophet's ministrations and depended on his spiritual discernment in their military manoeuvres:

> So there was no rest for the man of God. He prayed for the safety of the fighters. He prophesied about enemy movements and how these had to be countered. He warned the guerrillas of ambushes. He sprinkled their AKs with holy water, declaring their campaign a holy war against oppression. He preached that Mwari was on the side of the oppressed, that his whore son was the true liberator of all humankind. At night he sometimes prayed with comrade Nyika for a speedy end to the suffering of war. Patmos became a kind of operational base from where the war of liberation was masterminded, guided, inspired by the powerful *Mweya Mutsvene* (Holy Spirit) of Zion.[66]

Thus, many guerrillas first approached the churches with hostility, but the support of leaders in both MFCs and AICs sometimes transformed adversaries into allies for liberation. Bourdillon and Gundani suggest that the degree of local Christian strength influenced guerrilla approaches:

---

have thwarted', overcame the charge by publicly challenging the local people to specify any grounds that might justify it. When no one came forward, the guerrillas released him. Shepstone Muzvidzwa, interview, 5 May 1991.
[65]Daneel, *Guerrilla snuff*, 167.
[66]Ibid, 170; see also 106–109.

... where Christianity was relatively uninfluential ... the guerrillas found no need to pay much attention to it. Where communities had become largely Christian ... the guerrillas were obliged to respect Christianity. The word *obliged* is important: guerrillas often treated peasants with scant respect, but they needed food from the local population ... On the other hand, we suggest that where there was no dominant religion and Christians comprised a significant section of the population, their position was difficult in the extreme. The guerrillas had to stress unity. Where there were divisions in a community between Christians and non-Christians, Christianity was easily associated with the Whites and the other side in the war.[67]

Strategic as well as ideological concerns contributed to guerrillas' distrust of church life. Churches drew gatherings where contrary opinions could gather momentum:

It's because among the people and in worshipping there were enemies who would take what we would discuss with the boys and go and give that to the enemy. So that's why the boys were not permitting the churches (to continue).[68]

Fighters sought to disrupt all the normal processes of society, except smallholder economic production, to enable people to direct all their energy to the armed struggle. Meetings of other groups, whether religious or secular, offered the appearance of normalcy, distracted attention from the pre-eminent goal and provided alternative forms of solidarity where anti-war sentiment could take hold. Shutting down churches disrupted normal life and demonstrated the fighters' power to their opponents. One former freedom fighter declared that the guerrillas' policy saved lives:

The reason we were discouraging churches is not that we did not want people to worship, no, but we were preventing situations where people could die in large numbers if fighting broke out where they were gathered. We wanted to minimise people gathering in one place. But worshipping? – Yes. We (the freedom fighters) also worshipped while we were at war, but what we did not want

---

[67]Bourdillon and Gundani, 149–150.
[68]Bernard Matseketsa, church members interview, 13 April 1991.

was for people to gather in large numbers in one place, because many people used to die (that way). We were trying to ensure that people would not be bombed in large numbers by airplanes, because the airplanes had a system such that when they saw where there were many people they would say, 'This is a base', and then bomb.[69]

Sometimes guerrillas forced villagers to destroy church buildings and their associated schools in order to prevent the Rhodesian army from using them as barracks.[70] Despite the tactical purpose, such events confirmed the impression Christians received at *mapungwe* that the freedom fighters were hostile to Christianity.

Co-existing with the prevailing disparagement of Christianity was a secondary but important theme of quiet Christian affirmation. Many guerrillas retained their Christian commitment intact, and since explicit Christian profession was politically dangerous they simply refrained from religious comment. The guerrillas' use of church hymn tunes as settings for *Chimurenga* songs communicated two contradictory messages. On the one hand, it demonstrated the fighters' power to claim any cultural artifact and use it to advance the war. On the other hand, the tunes constantly reminded *pungwe* audiences of their own roots in the churches. Similarly, the very form of the guerrillas' *mapungwe* owed much to the longstanding tradition of night meetings in the churches. The alternation of singing and political lecturing that constituted the bulk of a guerrilla *pungwe* resembled not so much the *pungwe* of SSR as it did the night-long alternation of singing and preaching in the *pungwe* of the churches. Even as the guerrillas promoted the spirits, the form of their *pungwe* implicitly declared their dependence on church practice as well as on the rites of SSR.

The mission paradigm of the wartime rallies

Religious mission consists of the spiritual vision and practical means by which people promote their faith and work and invite the adherence

---

[69]Thomas Marira, church members interview, 13 April 1991.

[70]In the Bonda Church District, the quartering of Rhodesian troops at St George's Church and School at Dziwa prompted guerrillas to demand that the villagers of Chirarwe, several miles to the east, raze St Gabriel's Church and its associated school.

96

and participation of others. The all-night rallies of the guerrillas became a major wartime movement in Shona society. Alongside its political and military dimensions, the equally prominent religious dimension took on a strongly missional tone in explicit competition with Christianity. Politics was integrally related to religion in the guerrilla *pungwe* and contributed to the freedom fighters' missionary fervour in promoting the spirits.

A major claim of this study is that Christians experienced the guerrilla *pungwe* as a potent paradigm for religious mission, notwithstanding the fighters' denunciations of Jesus and the churches. Experienced but not generally articulated, this paradigm had several principal features. The guerrilla *pungwe* offered a spiritual vision that brought spiritual life to bear on pressing problems of the people that were experienced both individually and in the body politic as a whole. Mwari and the spirit elders were anguished about the alienation of their people's land. Second, the engagement of the spirit world with the nation's oppression promised to make a difference. In prosecuting a war, the guerrillas were activists in the extreme and their night rallies expressed this activism. Third, the wartime *pungwe* rejuvenated the *pungwe* of the spirits by drawing it into the orbit of the war effort, using its spiritual power and focusing the traditional activism of the spirits on the task of national liberation. To the traditional rites' emphases of spiritual encounter and community cohesion, the fighters added the theme of liberative empowerment. The guerrilla *pungwe* thus achieved a remarkable ritual transformation of religio-cultural resources. Fourth, in this transformed ritual, the guerrilla *pungwe* demonstrated the power of discursive talk and celebratory song to persuade people intellectually and energise them emotionally to commit themselves to a religious vision with a practical goal. This conversion of heart and mind was the essence of the missional thrust of the night rallies. A fruit of such conversion was often the volunteering of young people to join the liberation movement, so that the *pungwe* became a major source of recruitment.

The results of guerrilla mission on behalf of SSR were mixed, but they included substantial success. Church life was disrupted, buildings were destroyed, and at *mapungwe* some church leaders and people accused of wizardry lost their lives. For a substantial proportion of the freedom fighters, the alienation from Christianity they expressed during *mapungwe* became a permanent conviction, and in the 1980s many young veterans stayed aloof from the churches. The role of spirits and mediums in the war renewed many Shona people's confidence that the link between the land and the ancestors had the power to guard them from harm and to liberate them from oppression. No longer an anachronistic relic of a bygone era, SSR played a crucial role in a modern guerrilla war against a colonialist settler regime, and this success stimulated a continuing renaissance of SSR in the post-war period.[71]

Guerrilla violence against rural civilians was, of course, the underside of the wartime *pungwe*'s mission thrust, and for many Zimbabweans the coercive aspect of *pungwe* persuasion was a fatal flaw that limited the fighters' mission success. The coercive history of Rhodesian colonialism helped secure a hearing for the guerrillas, but when their mobilisation rallies turned brutal, many hearers offered their outward cooperation but remained unpersuaded inwardly. Most rural Christians complied with guerrilla demands about external religious observance, but retained their basic religious orientation. Suspension of services did exact a toll on Christian affiliation, for some people who gave up observance during the war never returned to it, or they began to focus on the rites of SSR. Many others, however, buried their Bibles and religious emblems rather than burn them, as guerrillas had demanded. They joined in the slogans lauding the guardian spirits, but they held their own counsel. Meanwhile, they experienced the *pungwe* as an event of compelling power, and this was the vehicle to which they turned for mobilising the churches for spiritual renewal and social liberation after the war.

---

[71]Signs of this renewal include the increasing strength of national associations of diviner-healers, greater interest in publications on SSR, and prominent debate in public forums such as radio and the press about the role of SSR in Zimbabwean life.

CHAPTER 5

Communities in renewal:
night vigils in mission-founded churches

'Big fish are caught in the dark!' This is how a Roman Catholic cate-chist sums up the evangelistic power of the *pungwe* in Christian churches. His church authorities have prohibited all-night vigils and he is frustrated at how mission is held back now in his congregations in the Honde Valley. Without the *pungwe,* he can't fish in the dark, so he isn't catching the big fish or as many fish.[1]

A young Methodist garage mechanic testifies to how his life changed when he was caught in the dark and how he soon began to fish him-self:

> In the past, I was just a person living a hard life. I had no idea about Christianity, but as I attended night prayers, I started to feel I was a man. As I attended for a long time, all that I did started to change – from being an evildoer to being a good man. I started to have control in my life ... I stayed for a year still calling for for-giveness from God. Then I was baptised ... I then started to spread the good news to others and now I know the Spirit is with me.[2]

He is now a passionate preacher and song-leader in *mapungwe* among mission-founded churches at Eastern Highlands Tea Estates.

The unifying effect of the Christian *pungwe* among the churches is highlighted by an Anglican school teacher:

> The *pungwe* plays a very important role in my spiritual life as it uni-fies people from many denominations. Under the banner of God

---

[1]Francis Sanyanga, church leaders interview, St Columba's, 18 January 1994.
[2]Noah Mushunje, Essay Project on Christianity and Tradition.

we are one – in other words, God knows no denomination. I believe therefore that by meeting people of different faiths one becomes spiritually 'richer'. The love of Jesus is conspicuous and his universality is emphasised.[3]

He participates in night vigils both in his home village and at the tea plantation where he teaches during the week.

Conversion, evangelism, church unity – these are among the missional fruits that have issued from the *pungwe* movement among mission-founded churches in the period since Zimbabwe's political independence in 1980. Charismatic renewal, conflict with demons and the liberation of women are other fruits bearing directly on the churches' mission in Zimbabwe. The movement has grown explosively in major denominations such as the Anglican, Methodist and Presbyterian, while church advancement is impeded in churches that hold themselves aloof from the movement, such as the Roman Catholic and the Apostolic Faith Mission. Night vigils among the MFCs share a general ecumenical pattern that largely effaces denominational distinctives, while very distinctive *pungwe* practices appear among the African Initiated Churches.

The church *pungwe* draws on the nocturnal rites of Shona Spirit Religion in its view of night as a time of spiritual encounter and community celebration, but the traditional ceremonies are refocused on meeting the triune God, rather than ancestral spirits, and on building up the church as a new community that transcends the boundaries of family and clan. From the wartime rallies of the guerrillas the church *pungwe* appropriates an emphasis on liberative empowerment that includes activist teaching and engagement with the issues of Shona society. Through striking interactions of gospel and culture, the movement has contributed to the rooting of Christianity in Zimbabwe as an authentically African phenomenon.

The contemporary vigil movement has historical antecedents in early missionary approaches to the relationship between gospel and culture, in the rise of night vigils in the churches and in Manicaland's mass movement toward Christianity early in the twentieth century.

---

[3]Daniel Patrick Kavhuru, Essay Project on Christianity and Tradition.

This chapter's review of the background is followed by a *pungwe* narrative that details the course of a particularly typical vigil that drew a number of churches together. The variety of night vigils in the churches is discussed alongside the missional implications of some churches' opposition to the movement.

Gospel and culture in the churches' vigil history

Early missionary approaches to gospel and culture

The theological, cultural and missiological themes of George W H Knight-Bruce's work as founding bishop of the Anglican Diocese of Mashonaland typify the approach that Western missionaries and their sending churches took toward African religions and cultures. As one of the first missionaries in Rhodesia, the bishop's organisational achievement was considerable. In less than three years, 1891–94, Knight-Bruce established among the Shona and Ndebele peoples a network of growing Anglican mission stations with African leadership, a number of European congregations in such centres as Salisbury and Fort Victoria, and a diocesan pattern of itinerant oversight that continued after his premature return to England and early death.

The bishop's approach to African religion and culture, however, was characteristic of his time in that he believed that Shona religion was rudimentary and Shona culture degraded. Responding to the question, 'What is the religion of the Mashona?' he wrote:

> It is very hard to say that they have any. I have talked to them about God and His sending them their crops and food and they will agree and say He lives in heaven; and then they will tell you soon afterwards that they had a god once, but the Matabele drove him away.[4]

In passing through villages in his successful effort to secure locations for Anglican mission stations, the bishop did learn some features of Shona religious life:

> Their ideas on religion were few and vague. One tribe lived in some awe of an old man on a mountain; another said their chief

---

[4]George Wyndham Hamilton Knight-Bruce, *Memories of Mashonaland* (London and New York: Edward Arnold, 1895), 43.

knew about heaven and what happened after death, resting satisfied with this delegated faith; another village had a subterranean cavern, apparently treated as sacred, for they would not allow the Bishop, as a white man, to go down to it ... Here, too, the men spoke more fully about their religion, saying that God lived in the sky, though once he had lived with them, before the Matabele drove him away; that God had made them and taught them to sow; and that they learnt all this from their chief.[5]

Beyond this, Knight-Bruce's writings indicate no awareness of such central Shona religious realities as the prominence of ancestral spirits in daily life, the role of Mwari as God, the experience of spirit possession and the nocturnal rituals of SSR. His ability to discern religious conviction and activity appears to have been strongly shaped by the evidences of religion his own culture had led him to expect: a readily recognisable group of religious leaders, distinctive buildings for ritual, and public gatherings for worship during the day. Further, Knight-Bruce did not build upon the fact that in using the Shona name Mwari when he talked with Shona people about God he was himself affirming, however unwittingly, Shona religious understanding.[6]

With regard to Shona culture, Knight-Bruce's attitude is aptly summarised in this reflection from his published journals:

> No one who has not had dealings with the really heathen native can credit what a degradation of humanity they are. To live somewhat intimately among them is the best refutation of the belief that heathen natives are better than Christian and is the strongest argument of raising them.[7]

The bishop's views on Shona religion and culture illustrate European intellectual and mission thought during the time that most mission

---

[5]Knight-Bruce, *Journals of the Mashonaland Mission, 1888 to 1892* (London: Society for the Propagation of the Gospel in Foreign Parts, 1892), 6–7.

[6]Similar attitudes are evident in Francis R T Balfour, Fort Salisbury, to Canon Tucker, (SPG, London), LS, 15 September 1891, Zimbabwe National Archives, Harare.

[7]Knight-Bruce, *Journals*, 9. For his views on Shona abilities in morals and politics see *Memories*, 143–44.

churches were founded in Rhodesia.[8] Europeans in Rhodesia were ill equipped to envision the interaction of Christian gospel and Shona culture that the Christian *pungwe* now represents.

As an African missioner working within a mission-founded church, Bernard Mizeki illustrates a contrasting approach that could affirm as well as confront African religion. A Mozambican who converted to Christianity in South Africa, Mizeki entered Rhodesia with Knight-Bruce in 1891 as a catechist. While ministering at Mangwende near Marondera, he was martyred during the First *Chimurenga,* the Shona rebellion of 1896. As a cross-cultural missionary for whom Shona culture was new, Mizeki found within SSR much on which to build:

> In a letter to Archdeacon J H Upcher, Bernard said that the people in his area knew 'a great deal more about God than any other heathen'. He realised, when he examined the religion of the Nhowe people, that acceptable foundations already existed on which he could base his teaching of the Christian religion. They believed in Mwari, the Creator, the One God, but He was remote and far removed, unconcerned with individuals or their problems. They did not pray to Him but to their ancestors, or to their *mhondoro,* or tribal spirits ... Bernard's task was to transfer the fatherly, benevolent, protective attributes of past ancestors to Mwari Himself and reveal Him as the living, personal Father of all men, while at the same time he sought to preserve the reverence and awe traditionally accorded to Mwari for His might and majesty, His omniscience, omnipotence, infinity and 'otherness'.[9]

Exploiting a point of contact with local religion, Mizeki persuaded Chief Mangwende to proclaim every Sunday a *chisi,* the day of rest given to the land in deference to the ancestral spirit guardians. Yet Mizeki did not hesitate to articulate what he regarded as the discontinuity between spirit veneration and Christianity. A German woman, Paula Dorothea von Blomberg, recounted Mizeki's testimony to Africans in Cape Town on the subject of fear of spirits:

---

[8]Titus Leonard Presler, 'Missionary Anglicanism meets an African religion: a retrospect on the centenary of Bishop Knight-Bruce's entry into Zimbabwe', *Missionalia* 17, 3 (November 1989),171–174.

[9]Jean Farrant, *Mashonaland martyr: Bernard Mizeki and the pioneer church* (London, UK, and Salisbury, Rhodesia: Oxford University Press, 1966), 143–144.

He stepped forward and I can still hear the burning eloquence, which no one would have expected from this quiet young man. Without any hesitation, he started talking about the Father and Maker of all spirits, Who could at will send them all out or call them all back to Him. Without His permission, he said, they were powerless to harm us. He said that at one time, like his listeners, he had been afraid of all these spirits and had honoured them and made sacrifices to them, but now he had given his soul and life to the One Holy and Loving Spirit, Whom we call God. Because of this he had lost all anxiety and no one could ever again disturb his peace and happiness.[10]

Thus two perennial missiological approaches to the encounter of gospel and culture appeared very early in the life of one MFC in Zimbabwe. Knight-Bruce illustrates how a European leader's religious and cultural judgments could set a trajectory of mutual hostility between church and local religious culture. Mizeki illustrates how an African leader close to the people could set a trajectory of theological and liturgical interaction between church and local religious culture. There were many intermediate positions adopted by Europeans and Africans, but these two major approaches set the tone for later debate and development within Shona Christianity, including the *pungwe* movement.

'A mass movement' toward Christianity

The first decade of the twentieth century featured what missionaries called a 'mass movement' toward Christianity, especially in Manicaland.[11] It built the foundation of the churches' intensive presence in the province and was a precursor of the post-1980 mass movement that features the *pungwe* so prominently.

African initiative in mission was centre-stage in the mass movement as congregations proliferated through local vision and enterprise:

---

[10]Ibid, 51.

[11]George E P Broderick, *History of the Diocese of Southern Rhodesia (formerly the Diocese of Mashonaland)*, (1953), TMs, Zimbabwe National Archives, Harare: 269; S J Christelow, 'The Bonda years, part 1' *The Link* (January 1969), 4. The movement is dated to 1901 by John Weller and Jane Linden, *Mainstream Christianity to 1980 in Malawi, Zambia and Zimbabwe* (Gweru: Mambo, 1984), 86.

(The Rev E H) Etheridge (principal and chaplain at St Augustine's Mission, Penhalonga) wrote in July 1907 that at Tsonzo, 19 miles away, he opened a pole and *dagga* (mud) church where work had been started by pupils from St Augustine's in their holidays. The teacher was Fabian Chitungu who with Charles Hill had built the church and some huts ... Going westwards from there he visited a place called Bonda where other pupils living at Ruwendi's *kraal* had made an opening, this he already foresaw as a good place for a new centre. Summing up his trip he said, 'It seems to me as though a really big movement towards Christianity among the natives of this district is not at all improbable in the near future.'[12]

'Here is Church History in the making, being made so rapidly that we hold our breath,' exclaimed George Broderick, Bonda's priest-in-charge between 1911 and 1916, to supporters in Britain. 'It is the work of the people themselves – what will it grow into?' Etheridge added:

Here in Manyikaland it is no longer a question of the conversion of individuals ... it is the question of the conversion of a district, practically of the people of the Manyika. The movement is obviously of God: we can do and have done, extraordinarily little. Every tour brings home to me the little we can do. And yet the thing is being done. What we are working for is being accomplished, not by us, but by the Power of God.[13]

Christian adherents were multiplying rapidly, and it was clear to the missionaries that indigenous, not foreign, agency was the key factor:

... truly the work of the priest was not so much evangelisation, which was being done by the people themselves, but he was continually overwhelmed with shepherding the crowds brought in by those who had glimpsed a little of the Light and always he was faced with the travelling to be done, mostly on foot, in that roadless and mountainous country. Already in 1913 a station had been opened at Buwu (in the Honde Valley) on the Portuguese border which alone had 300 people in school.[14]

---

[12]Broderick, 269–270.
[13]Ibid, 273.
[14]Ibid 334. Christelow wrote, 'The spread of the Gospel was brought about as much by the African converts themselves as by any forward movement from the central station.' 'The Bonda years, part 5', *The Link* (May 1969), 4.

The Manicaland mass movement is a striking instance of Africa's embrace of the Christian gospel, for conversions far outstripped foreign missionary efforts within only a few years of the gospel's first proclamation in Zimbabwe.

The early mass movement invites comparison with Manicaland's religious renewal after independence. Each period followed a decade of war, but the contrasts are equally salient. The First *Chimurenga* ended in defeat for the Shona. Prominent spirit mediums were executed for aiding rebellion, and the establishment of a Rhodesian socio-political order in the late 1890s encouraged affiliation with the new and apparently victorious religion:

> ... the war of rebellion had been presented to the Shona as a war of religion by their own leaders who had promised supernatural immunity against bullets and the support of Mwari with all the tribal Spirits or *Mondoros*. Not only had the living Shona been defeated but with them their dead chiefs and their God.[15]

The Second *Chimurenga,* on the other hand, brought victory over the Rhodesians and secured black majority rule. In the flush of their success, the freedom fighters' promotion of SSR and condemnation of the links between colonialism and Christianity seemed to presage a decline for the churches. Spirit religion did gain, but the greater Christian revival challenges the common assumption, shared by the guerrillas, that Christian growth in Africa depended on the dominance of European colonial powers. In fact, Rhodesia colonialism inhibited the genuine Christianity that took hold from 1901 onwards, and political independence released the full creative initiative of Zimbabwean Christians to relate the depth of their faith to the depth of their culture. A new mass movement was the result.

Night vigils in the history of the churches

Night vigils became prominent in the early decades of the churches' presence, both expressing and accelerating the mass movement toward Christianity. It prompted controversies similar to those that occur today as many Shona Christians met at night and others in the churches opposed the practice. Cultural fears, denominational rival-

---

[15]Weller & Linden, 55.

ries and Shona Spirit Religion's ties to the night all played a part in the developing discussion.

Shona Christians sometimes met at night in the early decades. Missionary accounts do not mention all-night vigils, but Shona oral testimony indicates that mission centres held *mapungwe* on major festivals and that outlying congregations held them more frequently.[16] Missionaries were uncomfortable with night vigils on account of the similarity they perceived between them and the nocturnal rites of SSR. George Broderick's account of night life at Bonda between 1911 and 1916, when he was priest-in-charge, highlights an execution his wife witnessed within a religious ritual:

> They saw before them within the circle of huts a great fire burning and a large group of people kneeling in dead silence: the drums were beating their terrifying rhythm and later out of some huts came a group of figures grotesquely disguised who circled the kneeling folk dancing and singing for a time, then suddenly one of these kneeling people was stabbed with an *assegai* (spear), the fire was extinguished and silence fell.

Horrified, the missionaries felt called to combat spiritual forces at work at night:

> ... there were other mysterious happenings at various times, attributed to witchcraft and who shall say that 'explanation' is untrue for we could, many times, feel the power of the Evil surrounding us and were sometimes called in to help fight the evil things. For a time the whole district was in a state of terror at certain phases of the moon, for a local headman was reputed to be a 'Mondoro' (sic) and to have the power of turning himself into a lion; on such occasions the countryside was paralysed after sundown, but strange to say the people revolted against the terror and the 'Mondoro' fled for safety to our house one night, after which his power was broken. But it was often nerve-wracking for those who lived in the mission house.[17]

---

[16]Also, service record books indicate multi-day festivals which probably included some night services. At Bonda, for instance, Canon Christelow included such references in service registers during the century's second decade. Service Register, St David's Mission, Bonda, 1915–1918, St David's Church archives, Bonda.

[17]Broderick, 339–340.

Revivalist American Methodism was a powerful catalyst for the spread of night vigils among MFCs, beginning from the church's flagship Old Mutare Mission in 1898. Language training at Old Mutare included residential time with families in local villages, not a priority for Anglican missionaries. With such grounding in the people's life and language, missionary leaders at Old Mutare were prepared to nurture local initiative in strengthening the spiritual life of Shona Methodists:

> In Manicaland the American methodist (*sic*) Pentecost came in 1918. It began at a revival meeting at Old Umtali (now Old Mutare) mission in March, when African teachers and preachers were seized with the Spirit and rushed out on to the mountain-side to pray. They then spread out to carry the Pentecostal message to all the stations. It reached Makoni in July 1918 – the Holy Spirit came down on Gwidza mountain and the people 'made confessions of Adultery, theft, bewitching'. Soon there occurred a spectacular healing.[18]

Climbing mountains to pray is so integrally associated with *mapungwe* in Shona Christian spirituality that it is certain that all-night vigils were part of this revival. The 1918 revival strengthened an already strong Methodist practice of long camp meetings that featured *mapungwe* prominently. Four large gatherings, called *magungano,* were held each year in the area north of Mutare, with thousands camping for two weeks at Nyatande in Manica Communal Area.

It was routine for many camp-meeting nights to be *mapungwe,* sleepless with preaching, singing and praying. 'For very many of the African teachers and preachers and converts,' says Terence Ranger, 'the camp meetings were occasions also for exorcism of evil spirits, for the healing of confessed witches and so on.'[19] Exorcism helped make nightlong vigils especially prominent at the encampments. A Methodist pas-

---

[18]Terence O Ranger, 'Medical science and Pentecost: the dilemma of Anglicanism in Africa', in *The Church and Healing: Papers Read at the Twentieth Summer Meeting and the Twenty-first Winter Meeting of the Ecclesiastical History Society,* ed W J Sheils (Oxford: Basil Blackwell, for the Ecclesiastical History Society, 1982), 352–353. On the Anglican side, missionary Edgar Lloyd at Rusape in 1921 wrote of how the spirituality of local church and school represented 'an indigenous effort of raw natives to come to the light of the knowledge in Christ.' Broderick, 394–395.

[19]Ranger, 'Pentecost', 353.

tor who grew up at Murewa in northern Mashonaland in the 1950s recalls how spirit possession and exorcism at the annual 'Ten Days Meetings' brought night into the foreground:

> Some of those spirits would come out at 9 (pm), others at 10 (pm), but others would not come out until just before dawn (mamba-kwedza). And the spirits would not come out with just two minutes of praying or three minutes of praying, but the Vabvuwi had to work the whole night to get some of those demons out. That's why they said, 'It's not enough for us to meet during the day at these meetings, but we must meet right through the night.' Because of that, mapungwe became common at the Ten Days Meetings and not only that – people began to organise more weekend meetings and they began to organise them so that on Friday people retired at 10, but for Saturday the program was planned so that they would meet right through the night to Sunday morning.[20]

The evangelistic power of the Methodist gatherings attracted non-Christians, but initially the Methodists discouraged attendance by MFC members who tolerated beer and tobacco.[21] The movement's vitality was irresistible to others, however, and Methodist leaders could not obstruct their desire to attend. Anglicans in the Bonda area remember their parents going to the Methodist revivals at Nyatande in the 1930s:

> Yes, they used to go and spend the whole night singing with the Marombe (a group similar to the Vabvuwi) ... So when those fathers and mothers returned, they would tell and show others what they had seen and heard at the gathering. That is how awareness (of mapungwe) began to enter our church and people saw that it was good.[22]

Anglicans attended in large numbers, but they were not allowed to

---

[20]Samuel Mukata, interview, 12 January 1994.

[21]Mai Kachali, interview, 25 August 1987.

[22]Elisha Gunda, church leaders interview, August 1987. The importance of the 1918 Methodist revival to other churches is confirmed in a 1948 letter from the Rev Langton S Machike, an Anglican, to a Fr Smith in which he resists pressure to adopt pentecostal measures (such as public confession and burning witchcraft paraphernalia) that he says the Methodists have been practising since 1918. Machike, St Mary's Mission, Salisbury, to Smith, St Faith's Mission, Rusape, ALS, 11 February 1948, Zimbabwe National Archives, Harare.

preach, a limitation that prompted them to organise their own night meetings. Typically, the practice first took hold in outlying congregations and then moved to the mission centres, depending on the receptivity of clergy. At Bonda, occasional night meetings, called *magungano*, commenced in the late 1940s under the leadership of the Rev Matimba. As today, a simple meal was served, but without tea, which was scarce then. Few Christians had their own Bibles, so preachers focused on one verse that was read out. MU members testified about how they had become Christians, how their lives had been transformed and how they had overcome the marital obstacles they faced in becoming members.

Anglican leaders, black as well as white, often had misgivings about the practice:

> When these gatherings took place Baba Masara used to think that people wanted to form another church. That was his idea. His main theme was, 'If you do it you'll do crazy things' (*kuita zvoubenzi*) ... Nevertheless, people used to meet, not very often, but from time to time.[23]

The priest feared that night vigils would evoke ecstatic spiritual manifestations that he found difficult to distinguish from craziness, which, in the Shona worldview, is often attributed to demonic powers. Maintaining adequate clerical control over pentecostal-inclined church members was a clear concern at mid-century:

> When the first group of Anglican African clergy and formally trained teachers emerged in the 1930s and 1940s they had a vested interest in emphasising their control over the formal liturgy and the set lessons as against the improvisations of the older and untrained teacher-catechists. They had also imbibed much of the individualism then inherent in Anglican theology. They took up similarly cool positions, rebuking the teacher-catechists for excessive emotionalism and criticising both catholic and methodist popular religion.[24]

In the Honde Valley clergy from Penhalonga and Bonda discouraged *mapungwe* in the 1920s and 1930s, but in 1952 people at Zindi

---

[23]Elisha Gunda, church leaders interview, St Gabriel's, August 1987.
[24]Ranger, 'Pentecost', 358.

began meeting for *pungwe* in their homes. The Honde history traced by an Anglican church warden illustrates the ecclesial, moral and inter-religious tensions that the *pungwe* provoked:

> When we started doing *pungwe* we copied from the Methodists. We accepted the custom from the Methodist *Vabvuwi* when we saw that it helped us to strengthen our Christianity. Many Anglicans were against the Methodist practice, because Methodists opposed people who went to beer halls and danced *mashavi.* Anglicans wanted to go to beerhalls and play traditional drums, saying that was what protects one's spirit from dying. Anyway, we invited the Methodists, and we developed the desire to have *mapungwe.* We grew with the practice until 1957, when Bishop Cecil (Alderson) and the diocese (of Mashonaland) stopped it, say-ing, 'What you have been doing is different from the church.' They forbade people from doing *pungwe.* When we were forbidden, we used to do *pungwe* in our homes, not at the churches. Bishop Cecil then said, 'Let them do it. If it is of Christ, it will proceed. If it is of Satan, it will come to an end.' So we went ahead with *pu-ngwe.* Bishop Cecil allowed us all to do *pungwe* in the churches and not (only) in the villages. That is how the *pungwe* began in the Anglican Church ... 1957 was when we started doing it, with the Methodists teaching us that African tradition (*Chivanhu*) and Christianity do not go hand in hand.[25]

Methodists combined the American camp meeting with the Shona all-night religious meetings, and the *pungwe* became the primary vehicle for an evangelistic group that confronted SSR. When some Anglicans became interested, others were scornful on account of the strict behaviour codes of the Methodists with whom the *pungwe* was asso-ciated. Anglican *leaders,* on the other hand, believed that the move-ment was too *close* to SSR and feared that it would encourage unde-sirable pentecostal manifestations. When the go-ahead was given, the movement took off among Anglicans and it grew as a *confrontation* with SSR and as a movement with pentecostal overtones.

Mubatanidzwa: an ecumenical vigil

Highlights of a particular *pungwe* held at Eastern Highlands Tea

---

[25]SaMubure, interview, 18 May 1991.

Billboard in Mutare advertises a rock concert as a *pungwe*

Anglican women cook *sadza* for an ecumenical *pungwe* at Eastern Highlands

Enduring through the night: in the early-morning hours, some participants are overcome with slumber during the preaching at an ecumenical *pungwe* at Eastern Highlands ...

... but they spring to life when someone begins a song!

Estates illustrate the main features of night vigils in the mission-founded churches and stress their mission vision. This *pungwe* was an explicitly ecumenical gathering, designed to welcome all churches to a common sharing of song, word and prayer. The term for this is *mubatanidzwa*, which means 'a holding together' or 'a uniting'.

The ecumenical vigil in the community hall at Village No 3 was convened by the local Anglican congregation and participated in a growing tradition of *mibatanidzwa* that grew directly out of the exigencies of war and the guerrillas' *pungwe* practice. *Mibatanidzwa* among Mothers' Union chapters took hold north of Mutare in the mid-1970s when Methodists from Nyakatsapa experienced daytime ecumenical services in Harare and began holding them in their own area. Joint services among the churches were often a necessity in the 'protected villages' when the movements of clergy were restricted and people felt the guerrillas' pressure to reduce the number of church services. The interchurch appreciation that flourished in these adverse circumstances prompted MU leaders and a few clergy to revive the *mubatanidzwa* after the war, but the guerrillas' *mapungwe* and the desire to spend more time together soon transmuted a midday meeting into a *pungwe*:

> When the boys would come, they would choose a day, saying, 'Today we are doing a *pungwe*. No one is to lie down and sleep.' So now we took that up and said, 'That's the custom that has stuck in people's heads. Let's use that and call it *pungwe*. [26]

By the mid-1980s *mibatanidzwa* that were *mapungwe* had become a movement in themselves among Mothers' Union chapters of MFCs from Old Mutare to Bonda. Gatherings were organised monthly by an interdenominational MU committee led by Methodists, Anglicans and Salvation Army leaders, with members from many more churches attending. Frequently over a thousand women participated, so that the meetings had to be held outside even the largest church buildings.

'Watch and pray': meals and songs at a *pungwe*

Eating together is customary at a church *pungwe*, and the meal is part of the *pungwe* itself, providing a physical experience of common nour-

---

[26]Mai Kachali, interview, 25 August 1987.

ishment before a night of spiritual nourishment. By mid-afternoon on the *mubatanidzwa* Saturday, about twenty women from the Maronda Mashanu (Five Wounds) Anglican congregation at EHTE were cooking *sadza* in large oildrums over fires behind the hall and preparing vegetable and meat relishes. By dusk, several hundred people had gathered in and around the hall and supper was served by the women, many of whom had now changed into their MU uniforms. In addition to sustenance, the meal offered people an opportunity to socialise and talk about work, family and politics.

Such a meal is universal in *pungwe* practice except when a *pungwe* is organised without advance planning or when the event focuses on visiting someone at home. The opening meal is consistent with the meals that invariably open the nocturnal rites of SSR. It also echoes the meals that guerrillas generally had at the start of their *mapungwe* during the Liberation War. While the church *pungwe* supper is not explicitly cultic, as meals for the *vadzimu* are, the cultic aspect does appear in the general practice of offering the Lord's Supper or Eucharist at the end of the *pungwe* in the morning, if a clergyperson is present.[27] The *mubatanidzwa* at Village No 3 ended this way as the district Anglican priest celebrated Eucharist, after which the group gathered outside for the customary breakfast of tea and bread.

The group singing so central at a *pungwe* generates enthusiasm, strengthens group cohesion, keeps people awake and reinforces declarations that preachers make in their sermons. At the EHTE *mubatanidzwa* the youth began singing after eating, and others joined them until the hall was packed with 300–400 people singing in full voice the first of at least 35 hymns and songs sung during the *pungwe.* Several opening songs highlighted *pungwe* themes and illustrated the close relationship between singing and *pungwe* practice.

The first song was a spirited, rhythmic chorus sung primarily by the thirty or forty young people. The term 'chorus' is used routinely by Shona Christians in referring to songs that have arisen recently in the life of the churches, that are simple in structure and easy to learn and

---

[27]Morning Eucharist at the end of an ordinary *pungwe* is practised only among the MFCs, for eucharistic worship tends to be much more infrequent among the AICs.

that usually alternate between a refrain and a verse.[28] Choruses are very popular with young people, and this one ran as follows:

Refrain: *Elia waenda, waenda nengoro yemoto.*
Verse: *Kana uchida kunamata, kutanga wadhingura Satani.*

Refrain: Elijah has gone, has gone in a chariot of fire.
Verse: If you want to pray, you must first dethrone Satan.[29]

The implied message of this very condensed lyric appears to be as follows. The validation of Elijah's life and message as a prophet of God was sealed in the dramatic way in which God took him up to heaven in a whirlwind and in a fiery chariot (2 Kings 2:1–12a). The fiery chariot recalls the other fiery event in Elijah's ministry, the calling down of fire on the sacrifice offered to Yahweh on Mount Carmel during Elijah's great contest with the prophets of Baal (1 Kings 18:20–46). Elijah's victory was due to the faithfulness he showed in his public prayer on the mount (1 Kings 18:36–37), through which Baal's prophets were routed and, so the interpretation would run, Satan was dethroned. The application of the story to Christians is that those who wish to pray seriously must be prepared to confront and dethrone the evil power of Satan.

The song had important implications for the *pungwe.* First, the night's work was summarised as the work of prayer, an interpretation later echoed by the evening's chairperson in his opening remarks. Second, the song highlighted confrontation with evil powers as a crucial feature of this work of prayer. The gathered Christians were reminded that they faced spiritual conflict; prayer and, indeed, the entire *pungwe* would be crucial for victory. Third, the night's work was placed in the history of God's people by reference to a great prophet who by prayer dethroned God's competitors. Elijah's example reminded the *pungwe* community that it lived, as the prophet did, on the border between God's realm and the realm of the world. As the prophet was willing to

---

[28]The church 'chorus' was American in origin, designating early nineteenth-century camp meeting choruses and late nineteenth-century gospel choruses. The term became current in Britain as a result of the American revivalists' visits in the second half of the century. John R H Moorman, *A history of the church in England* (London: Adam & Charles Black 1953), 366.

[29]*Pungwe, mubatanidzwa*, 12–13 April 1991, Eastern Highlands Tea Estates. Material from this event is not further footnoted.

stand alone in witness and confrontation, so also the community must be willing to stand in witness and confrontation. Fourth, the song's stress on fire emphasised that the community's *pungwe* witness was a spiritual test. The fiery chariot is an image of glory, but it also recalls the destructive and purifying function of fire in Elijah's great test. As the prophet subjected himself to a test by fire, so also the community must be willing to be tested. Participants often interpret *pungwe* sleeplessness as just such a test, and the test motif becomes more explicit in a major African Initiated Church, the Apostles of Johane Marange, whose night vigils are literal ordeals by fire. The glorious reward for those who remain steadfast in the test is the fiery chariot of salvation.

The second song was less exuberant in tempo and rhythm and more reflective in content:

> *Pamuchinjiko pakarwadza moyo wangu*
> *Parufu rwaJesu.*
> *Zvakaitwa naJudah zvakarwadza moyo wangu*
> *Parufu rwaJesu.*

> On the cross my heart was broken
> When Jesus died (literally, At the death of Jesus).
> What Judas did wounded my heart
> When Jesus died.

The song's stress on the death of Jesus highlights the christocentric focus that is universal in Christian *mapungwe.* The chorus dwells on the emotional and spiritual effect that Jesus' death has on the believer, not on a theology of the atonement. It assumes that the death of Jesus is theologically central and that all know who was accountable for that death. The song is thus purely devotional, intent on emotional engagement with the central events of God's work with humanity.

The virtual theme hymn of night vigils in the mission-founded churches was led by the women and, indeed, Hymn 130 in the Anglican Shona hymnal was sung four times during the course of this vigil:

Mukristu usanete,	Christian, do not tire
Inzwa Ngerosi yako,	Hear your angel's word,
Uri m'kati memhandu;	You are in the midst of enemies;
'Namata urinde.'	'Watch and pray.'

Hondo dzese dzedima,	The armies of the darkness,
Dzisingamboonekwi,	That are invisible,
Dzinoda kukubata;	Want to seize you;
'Namata urinde.'	'Watch and pray.'
Tora mapfumo ako	Take up your spears,
Abate misi yese,	Hold them on all days,
Satan anorindira;	Satan is watching for them;
'Namata urinde.'	'Watch and pray.'
Inzwa vakakurira	Hear those who overcame,
Vari kukuringisa,	They are conquering,
Ivo vese vachiti,	All of them saying,
'Namata urinde.'	'Watch and pray.'
Inzwa zvikuru Tenzi,	Especially hear the Lord,
Unomudisisisa,	Whom you love infinitely,
Chengeta izwi rake;	Keep his words;
'Namata urinde.'	'Watch and pray.'
Rinda panguva dzese	Watch at all times,
Ndicho chiro chikuru,	That is the great thing,
Kumbira rubatsiro;	Ask for help;
'Namata urinde.'	'Watch and pray.'[30]

The Shona text, so rich in resonances of Shona spirituality and *pungwe* practice, translates an English original by Charlotte Elliott (1789–1871). The Shona version emphasises central *pungwe* themes of darkness, spiritual conflict and the imperative of watching through the night. People hear the opening imperative, 'Do not tire', not only as an injunction to be faithful, but also as a directive to resist the natural inclination to sleep at night and to persevere in the spiritual struggle which the hymn highlights and which is centre-stage in the *pungwe* itself.[31]

---

[30]*Ndwiyo dzomuchechi.* (Hymns for Church Use), rev ed (London: SPCK, 1966), *ad loc.* Used with permission. English translation is mine. The original appears as No 308 In *Hymns ancient and modern: revised* (Np: Hymns Ancient and Modern, Ltd, 1981), 414. The multisyllabic character of Shona necessitates considerable condensation of thought when an English text is translated into Shona with the intention of setting the Shona text to a reasonably short musical line.

[31]Another song sung at *mapungwe* is more explicit in its charge to remain wakeful: 'Do not sleep / There is still work to do / Come, let us proclaim the gospel / To our villages.'

The second stanza portrays spiritual struggle in stark terms. 'Principalities and powers', in the English original echoes Ephesians 6:10–18, and the entire hymn can be taken as a meditation on 'the whole armour of God'. When 'principalities and powers' is rendered into *Hondo dsese dzedima*, 'All the armies of darkness', the liberation struggle is recalled through *hondo*, the main Shona word for the war. Spiritually hostile forces are termed forces of darkness, *dima*, a description that does not appear in the English original but echoes the elaboration in Ephesians 6:12: 'For our struggle is ... against the cosmic powers of this present darkness ...' Darkness emphasises the nocturnal setting of the hymn being sung at a *pungwe*, and night is understood as a time of spiritual hostility, a perception that arises directly out of the beliefs of SSR.

In the third stanza, the English 'armour' for the various weapons in Ephesians is specified in the Shona as *mapfumo ako*, 'your spears'. Spears were the primary weapons of warfare in pre-colonial southern Africa, and they also appear in the ritual paraphernalia of spirit mediums as they invoke the spirit elders. 'Spears' thus recalls the historical experience of Shona people using *mapfumo* in warfare. Its application to spiritual affairs both reflects the Ephesians passage and recalls SSR's use of ritual spears. The resonances of this single line anticipate the interplay of confrontation and dialogue in *pungwe* sermons, where the 'armies of darkness' so often cited as the enemy are the concepts and representatives of SSR. The *mapfumo* of the gospel go to war against the *mapfumo* of avenging spirits.

The repeated chorus, '*Namata urinde*', translates the words of Jesus to his sleeping disciples in the Garden of Gethsemane in Mark 14:38, '*Watch and pray*, that you may not enter into temptation.' Here is a graphic and obvious link between the hymn's message of the hymn and the *pungwe* setting. Jesus undertakes a vigil of prayer as he contemplates his imminent suffering. His Gethsemane comment to Judas at Luke 22:54, 'This is your hour and the power of darkness', is another nocturnal echo corroborating the general *pungwe* theme of night as a confrontation with evil. In *pungwe* sermons preachers often cite Jesus' vigil in Gethsemane as an example of perseverance that Christians should emulate.

In sum, Hymn 130 emphasises Shona images of weaponry and darkness, and it highlights the nocturnal and conflictive themes that are especially strong in *mapungwe*. The hymn's provenance alerts us to how the simple translation of a Victorian English hymn can become a vehicle for indigenous spirituality and the particular themes of all-night vigils. Its biblical overtones connect the gathered Christians with Jesus at Gethsemane and suggest that they themselves are at a similarly crucial point of decision, when they are challenged to follow Jesus' example and watch through the night in prayer.

The *pungwe* was then opened by the designated chairperson, Silas Mhlaudzi, a field assistant at Eastern Highlands. Two clergy (Methodist and Anglican) were present, but obligations in other congregations meant that one left early and the other arrived late. The multiple responsibilities of any rural MFC pastor have for decades made strong lay leadership crucial and continue to preserve the lay-led quality of the *pungwe.* Following Shona custom, the chairperson addressed the people in their principal familial roles — 'Excuse me, excuse me, fathers, mothers and aunts' – and he invited them to a night of prayer: 'Let us begin our prayer. We give these times to the Father' (*Totangisa hedu munamato wedu*). He then invited all to stand and sing a classic Anglican evening hymn, 'Sun of my soul, thou Saviour dear', *Zuva rangu Muponisi* in the Shona, which invokes the presence and protection of God in a time of darkness.

The complex relationship between particular songs and the *pungwe* is evident in a particular song sung between two sermons during the *mubatanidzwa.* When asked to sing a chorus, the youth responded with a simple line repeated six times: 'O be brave: / We are on the cross / Until we find rest' (*Shingirira: / Tiri pamuchinjiko / Dzamara taona zororo*). Participants in the *pungwe* faced a long night through which to stay alert and sleepless before they could rest, and the *pungwe* itself identified them with Jesus' suffering. Watching all night was a way of obeying Jesus' injunction, 'If any want to become my followers, let them deny themselves and take up their cross and follow me' (Mark 8:34). This analysis does not assume that the youth chose this song consciously for these reasons, nor does it claim that the song is exclusively a vigil chorus. Rather, the *pungwe* focuses attention on certain themes, and through a process of association during the night people employ liturgical and theological resources that amplify themes that are naturally evoked.

120

'O Jesus, move us': prayer in a *pungwe*

In the MFCs, singing and preaching are the principal *pungwe* activities, and explicit spoken prayer is secondary in time and attention. Prayer opens and closes the *pungwe,* and it may be included at other times as well. To open the *mubatanidzwa,* the Rev David Manyau, who at that time was priest-in-charge of the Anglicans' Mandea Church District, led the group in the Lord's Prayer, which stressed the group's interdenominational unity in Christ. The priest then moved into an extemporaneous prayer that struck many distinctive notes of *mapungwe*:

> We give thanks to you, our Father in heaven, this evening. We thank you because you have gathered us together in this place. We thank you because you have managed to lead us from our villages. We thank you for this time you are giving us, such an important time in our life.
>
> We thank you, good God, for the care you give us all the days of our life. We thank you for your son Jesus Christ, who came here on earth. We thank (you) for his death which set us free. We are thankful for his resurrection which gave us confidence and hope. We thank you for his going up to heaven. We thank you for the salvation which you brought to earth so that we could be at peace with others. We thank you for the relationship (*ukama*) which you brought between us and you, so that we can become your children. We are thankful, good God, for the Holy Spirit you poured (*wamakadurura*) on earth to lead us in our thoughts and to move us close to you (*nokutiswededza padyo nemi*).

This last phrase moved Manyau to break out into a slow, deeply meditative chorus:

> Jesus, you are redeemer.
> You came down to earth.
> Move us (*Tiswededze isu*)
> Close to your Father (*Padyo naBaba venyu*).
> Lord, you have a good heart
> Close to your Father.
> May we find rest
> Close to your Father.
> O Jesus, Redeemer,

> You were sent down here,
> O Jesus, move us
> Close to your Father.

He resumed:

> We ask this evening that you move us closer to you (*kuti mutiswededze padyo nemi*). We ask, our Father in heaven, through the Holy Spirit, that when your people speak you yourself will breathe into them (*muchafemera*). We ask for the opening of our ears outside and inside, so that your word may abide inside our hearts and move us close to you, because near you, good God, there is no sin which stays.

> So, our Father in heaven, we ask to be cared for by you and that the whole family (*mhuri yose*) gathered here be cared for by you, asking that when tomorrow dawns (*kwoedza*) we be awakened by you and that we rise (*nokumuka*) from the dead, as our Lord Jesus Christ rose (*akamuka*) from the dead, being the first from among all those who were asleep. So we also ask that you wake us from the life of sin and bring us to the life of righteousness through this time you have given us and through Jesus Christ our Lord. Amen.

Closeness to God through the Holy Spirit is the prayer's central theme. It recurs so often in the vigils of all communities that we may regard it as the most universal *pungwe* theme. As Manyau makes a major pentecostal reference to the Spirit being 'poured out', he summarises the Spirit's work as bringing people closer to God, the focus of the song. Through the Spirit, God breathes into people, an image that recalls both God breathing into the first human creature at Genesis 2:7 and the risen Jesus breathing on his disciples as he sends them out on mission with the words, 'Receive the Holy Spirit' (John 20:21–22). Manyau cites hearing the word as another way of approaching God, a way that the *pungwe* highlights through multiple sermons. The new relationship God has brought in Christ constitutes Christians as a family, or *mhuri*. The family's watching through the night and rising in the morning to a life of righteousness is analogous with Jesus rising from the dead after the night of death. Sleep is Manyau's image for death here, an obvious allusion to the apostle Paul's discussion of resurrection: 'Christ has been raised from the dead, the first fruits of those who have fallen asleep' (1 Cor 15:20, RSV).

122

Manyau's prayer is an archetype of *pungwe* spirituality. The contrasts between night and dawn, and between sleeping and waking, correlate with the contrast between sin and righteousness, between death and life. As the Christian community resists sleep and watches through the night until dawn, they resist sin and death during a death-dealing time. In their watching they open themselves to the Holy Spirit to bring them closer to God. Dawn and the Christians' rising to a new day in righteousness become a resurrection experience. Manyau frames the *pungwe* in the most comprehensive and powerful themes of biblical revelation: creation and re-creation, distance and closeness, sin and righteousness, death and resurrection in Christ. By staying awake and watching through the night until dawn Christians experience these themes as vivid and powerful.

With the news that the brother of one participant had suffered a stroke recently, the chairperson called for song and prayer, demonstrating how even a large *pungwe* can focus on the need of one person. Manyau's healing prayer focused on the power of God's word and on God breathing the Holy Spirit into people:

> We come to you again at this time, when you are breathing (*muri kutifemera*) into us your Holy Spirit. We are thinking of our relative (*hama*) whom you know and see at this time, because you are God who is everywhere. In times of bodily illness, we know that when you came to earth, many called their relatives (*hama*) and friends who were sick so that you could help us. Although you might be far away, if you only said the word everything would be possible. Therefore we ask for your word which created all things at the beginning – the word that said, 'Let there be water;' the word that said, 'Let there be the sun;' the word that said, 'Let there be trees;' the word that breathed into (*rakafemera*) a human being so that it became a living creature. That is the same word that was created and lived and was made flesh among us. That is the word we are asking for, our heavenly Father, for our relative (*hama*) who is ill. We put him before you that you might just speak, so that his spirit and body might be restored again, if it is your will.

Around midnight a man and a women offered prayers on behalf of the whole group, and a similar pattern was followed in the morning. The latter prayers echoed not only the earlier theme of closeness to God but also the fruit the *pungwe* should bear in evangelism:

You are quite amazing. You seek those who are suffering and you invite them nearer. Now this morning we thank you, Lord, that you have knocked on the door of their hearts, so that when they go to their homes they will know and remember that you died for us on the cross. In that way, Lord, you will stay with us forever ... We spent the whole night doing your work. Our Father in heaven, we ask that as we go out of this village of Maronda Mashanu our hearts will carry the little that we have heard so that we preach to those who stayed at home.

'We are seeing the kingdom!': ecumenical vision

Celebrating their ecumenical calling, communities gathering for a *mubatanidzwa* recognise all the church groups present by name, and this sets the stage for the interchurch cooperation that continues through the night. On this occasion, the church introductions also highlighted the separation between MFCs and AICs.

As the chairperson called out the name of each congregation, its members stood and the chairperson invited the assembly to welcome them, 'Let us greet them!' (*Ngativachingamidze hedu!*). As they rose, assembly members raised hands high in a single loud clap to welcome them. Often this custom is amplified verbally as those who stand say, 'We are here!' (*Tiri pano!*) and the assembly cries out, 'You have come!' (*Mauya!*). About 15 congregations were welcomed, including nine Anglican and several Methodist groups and single congregations from the Church of Central Africa- Presbyterian (CCAP), Faith Apostolic Mission, Unity of African Apostolic Faith Church (Mugodhi) and Roman Catholic Church. The number of people from the host congregation, about 100, well exceeded its normal Sunday morning attendance of 60, demonstrating the effectiveness of vigils in mobilising attendance. The chair called out in quick succession the names of churches from which he expected that no members would be present: '*VeZviratidzo ... veJekenishen ... veZioni ... veZAOGA ... ve*Full Gospel *... vePentecosti ...*' All the churches present were MFCs, with the exception of the Mugodhi, and all the absent churches were AICs, with the exception of the Full Gospel congregation, which associates closely with the Zionists.

The gap between the two church types was dramatised by the ripple of laughter that greeted the chair's call for *Vapostori*, members of the

African Apostolic Church of Johane Marange. The amusement issued from the incongruity that struck people as they imagined the AICs participating in this conventional gathering, where people sat on benches in a meeting that was coordinated by a chairperson from behind a table at the front. The prospect that brilliantly costumed Zionists whirling in their dances, or Jekenishen members with their enormous drums under the moonlight, or especially the *Vapostori* walking on fire, might join this gathering struck people as a laughable clash of styles. More seriously, participants knew that AICs were absent because they question the legitimacy of the MFCs and, conversely, participants knew their own reservations about some beliefs and practices of the AICs. The night's first preacher, for instance, disparaged the Marange Apostles' practice of handling fire. He went on to distinguish this *pungwe* from those of AICs when he bemoaned parents' failure to nurture their children in the ways of their own churches:

> That's why you see our children, when they see these other small churches, you will hear them saying, 'I was baptised at night, because at our church we are baptised at night. I do not like your church, because it does not pray (properly)' – (this happens) because you do not pray with them.

The roll-call emphasised two signal facts about churches in the Honde Valley. The large number of people and churches present indicated widespread enthusiasm for the MFCs' common tradition and spirituality, shared language of faith and similar norms of practice. The roll-call highlighted also the deep divide between MFCs and AICs in liturgical style, approaches to spiritual life and, in some cases, ethical norms such as polygyny. An important asymmetry in the picture is that in the Honde Valley and throughout Zimbabwe the AICs' awareness of themselves as a church type distinguished from the mission-founded type is qualified by strong differences among themselves that inhibit their meeting together.[32]

---

[32]There is a major exception in south central Zimbabwe where, beginning in 1972, the *Fambidzano* movement convened a large number of AICs to cooperate in development and theological education. More recently, the Association of African Earth-keeping Churches (AAEC) has drawn AICs of Masvingo Province to plant millions of trees in the 1990s. The catalyst for both *Fambidzano* and AAEC has been Marthinus Daneel, whose 1960s research into AICs prompted him to concretise the AICs' expressed desire to cooperate in theological education and community development.

The group's satisfaction with the ecumenical spirit of sermons at the *mubatanidzwa* was expressed by a woman preacher who summarised her impressions at about 4 am:

> Truly God is good. We heard the Bible saying that there is no church so designated (by the statement), 'This is the only church.' Moreover, all churches speak of Jesus. I have not seen one church speaking about things that are not of Jesus. If we are seen to be failing to follow Christianity, we will be seen as despising churches.

David Manyau expressed a wider ecumenical interest during the morning Eucharist as he noted how Rahab the woman of Jericho (Joshua 2:1–21) and Cornelius the centurion (Acts 10) were people who feared God even though they were outside God's covenant with Israel. He concluded that if God can save even such strangers to Israel's faith, Christians attending the *pungwe* should not be complacent in thinking that mere self-identification as Christians, without transformation of life, would save them.

With the ecumenical stage set, the young people led a chorus that is extremely popular at night vigils in the Honde Valley MFCs:

> Refrain: We are seeing the kingdom of heaven.
> (*Tiri kuona umambo hwokudenga.*)

> We will pray and love him until we have gone (to heaven).
> (*Tichanamata nokumuda dzamara taenda.*)

> Jerusalem is the Father's country.
> (*Jerusarema inyika yaBaba.*)

It is difficult to convey the joy, conviction and group solidarity with which communities sing this chorus, the people rising to their feet and swaying to the rhythm. Enthusiasm raises the overall tonal pitch substantially higher across the many repetitions, people break into numer-

Marthinus Daneel, *Fambidzano: ecumenical movement of Zimbabwean independent churches* (Gweru: Mambo Press, 1989). The Zimbabwe Institute for Religious Research and Ecological Conservation (ZIRRCON), founded by Daneel in Masvingo, promotes cooperation among AICs. It plays a similar role with yet another organisation catalysed by Daneel, the Association of Zimbabwe Traditional Ecologists (AZTREC), which draws SSR leaders into environmental projects.

ous part lines, and all who have brought *hosho* immediately produce them. The community proclaims the kingdom of God with both eschatological expectancy and confident joy in the kingdom's presence in their midst. Later in the gathering, a woman preacher expressed as much when she said:

> We are not at a dressing competition, nor have we come to eat, but this is all about a journey, to prepare while there is time. We are being sung to well, prayed for well, preached to well, all the while being reminded that we are on a journey. Blessed are they who have eaten these words ... Now my heart will sing my song which says, 'I am seeing the kingdom of heaven.' That is the kingdom that we are now seeing.

'Fire from heaven!': *pungwe* preaching

Occupying the bulk of *pungwe* ritual time in the MFCs, preaching is a major source of evangelism, teaching, interreligious polemic and social reflection in the mission-founded churches. Over half the members of a typical MFC congregation have preached or testified at one gathering or another, and a substantial proportion of these feel comfortable preaching at length and do so with great skill and effectiveness. This intensive engagement with preaching stems mainly from the extensive opportunity provided by the 6–8 hours of preaching time at a typical pungwe, where 20–30 people might speak publicly, whether in sermons or shorter, personal testimonies. Preaching, therefore, is a shared task that nurtures an ongoing community conversation within a *pungwe,* between a *pungwe* and Sunday morning worship and from *pungwe* to *pungwe.* This communal approach accounts also for the enormous capacity of a Shona congregation to listen to sermons at a *pungwe*!

At the *mubatanidzwa,* the chairperson explained the standard pattern:

> May I have your attention. We are now to start the preaching. At this time we are going to hear Baba (Milcent) Chigwande read our Bible (passage) to us. When he has finished, our preacher will be Baba Kahlari (the Methodist pastor), who is the one who will begin preaching to us. We shall have two preachers, with Baba Kahlari starting and Baba Manyau (the Anglican priest) will close. But we will have many, many preachers after Baba Manyau.

After the pre-arranged preachers have spoken, the leaders generally open the floor to anyone who wishes to preach, although the chair may ensure that most groups, congregations or denominations are represented, depending on the nature and scope of the *pungwe*. Shorter testimonies by less confident speakers tend to predominate later in the *pungwe*.[33] The sequence of events on this occasion was as follows:

> Opening preacher: the Rev Kahlari (Methodist), 9 pm
> Other preachers, representing various denominations and congregations
> Prayers by members, 11:30 pm
> More preaching by leaders of churches
> Closing preacher: the Rev Manyau (Anglican), 1:30 am
> Speech of appreciation for the preachers, 2:30 am
> Dramatic play by MU members, 2:45 am
> Homiletic testimonies by wide range of participants, 3 am
> Break, 5:15 am
> Eucharist, 5:30 am
> Prayers for healing, 6:30 am
> Breakfast and dispersal, 7 am

The scripture passage for the night was Luke 24:13–35, the story of two disciples and Jesus on the road to Emmaus, itself an evening story conducive to the *pungwe* setting. About thirty people preached or testified, and all the homiletic offerings were opened, and some were interspersed, with hymns and songs.

Detailed analysis of the opening sermon by Methodist pastor the Rev Togarasei Kahlari offers a glimpse into *pungwe* preaching and highlights how distinctive themes emerge. Kahlari acknowledged the gravity of being the first to speak and asked the congregation to strengthen him by singing Anglican Hymn 158, a meditation on Jesus' words

---

[33]In correspondence, Dana Robert notes a parallel in the organisation of early nineteenth-century ecumenical camp meetings in the USA: 'In camp meetings there was a distinction between preachers and exhorters. Preachers were billed in advance and gave the set sermons. Exhorters, who could be blacks or women, followed.' The Shona distinction is not between the speakers, who collectively are called *vaparadzi* or *vashumairi*, preachers, but between the types of speech: *mharidzo,* sermon, versus *umboo,* testimony or witness.

in John 14:6, 'I am the way, the truth and the life; no one comes to the Father, but by me.' The pastor followed this with an extemporaneous prayer stressing that it was God who was gathering the people together and that they had gathered to feed on God's word. In the first of a number of proverbial expressions he compared resistance to the word with those who say, 'We don't eat the relish (with the *sadza*) because it gives me indigestion' (*Uyu muriwo hatidyi nekuti unondisvota*).

Kahlari's narrative meditation on the Emmaus encounter focused on three elements that he turned into exhortations: grave clothes in the tomb, despondency on the road and the witness to having seen Jesus. The grave clothes Peter and John saw in Jesus' tomb became an image of the grave clothes of sin and sloth that serious Christians must take off. 'What would you say about me if you were to see me entering a river to bathe with my clothes on?' he asked the congregation. 'Crazy! (*Kupenga!*)', all responded with gusto. He elaborated the point:

> Yes, I would be crazy, seriously disturbed. There are some Christians who come to church the whole of their lives, but with their bad habits and deeds that they don't want to take off. They bathe with them. They're insane. So when you plan the things of the church you will see them pulling to the side. They are not bathed in the blood. They bathe in their bad deeds. Do you think they will be bathing? No, they are just joking.

The despondency of the two disciples on the road to Emmaus was a thematic basis for the preacher's regret and sadness at the state in which he believed some non-Christians or would-be Christians were living:

> I feel sorry that you come to look for Jesus, yet you don't want to see him. He is here where you are (*Aripo panewe ipapo*). He is very near you (*Ari pedyo-pedyo newe*). He is standing where you are, but you don't want to see him and you just want to find fault. Now if you just mock him, you will not see him. The men of Emmaus were filled with anguish, anguish that our Jesus has been killed. That is why they saw Jesus. If we need Jesus, we feel emotionally upset. Even if a child is ill, be ambitious to say, 'Is it true, Jesus, that you want to take away this child? I am with you, Jesus.' You will see that child rise up, because you have ambition (*shungu*) with Jesus.

Here Kahlari addressed himself principally to the 40 or 50 people in the hall without a professed or active Christian faith. His assurance that Jesus was very near (*pedyo*) echoed the chorus in the Anglican priest's opening prayer. His allusion to the illness of a child highlighted one of the principal situations in which Shona people feel drawn to consult spirit mediums, and he implicitly challenged people to see such occasions as crucibles for their faith in Jesus. 'The true Christian,' he stressed several times, 'is revealed in the time of suffering.' Kahlari depicted the alternative as a stark spiritual contrast:

> Now you go to church year after year, going there early in the morning, but you have not yet seen Jesus. That's why you see Satan posing in Jesus' place, because if you do not see Jesus, Satan lands on your mouth. So there won't be any Christianity then, it will have gone.

'Fathers, mothers, boys and girls, let us see Jesus!' was the injunction Kahlari drew from the two disciples' encounter with the risen Christ at Emmaus. The pressing task was evangelism. If one naturally shouts a warning when one sees a snake, he argued, why not freely proclaim the gospel when one has seen Jesus? Correlating the sleeplessness of the *pungwe* with the gospel story, he went on: 'These boys of Emmaus, when they saw Jesus they did not sleep in that house. They wanted to go and announce the news to others that they had seen Jesus.' Here the Emmaus story is set forth as a *pungwe* story: evening was at hand, the despondent disciples were looking for Jesus and they shared a meal; when Jesus appeared to them, they resisted sleep and, instead, rushed back to Jerusalem to announce the good news to the others. That joyful reunion was the Jerusalem *pungwe*. Kahlari calls the two Emmaus disciples *vakomana*, 'boys', the standard name for the wartime guerrillas. The pair's defiance of official persecution in traveling and meeting at night may have suggested this terminology. Thus the Emmaus story anticipated the liberating rallies of the war as well as the community-building vigils of the church.

From the Emmaus meditation Kahlari moved seamlessly and passionately into a personal testimony that wove together the themes of night, prayer, fire and seeing Jesus:

> Let me tell you a little piece of my story. When I was 15 years old, that is when I saw the Lord. I and my younger brothers were in

the mountains in the evening. We were praying, we were praying. Fire fell from heaven – this is true. Fire fell from heaven and splashed in front of us – *pu*! I then said, 'Amen! Amen!' Then we were in the fire, we were in the fire. Not that fire which is kindled by those of us who then step on it (the fire ordeals of the Marange Apostles). No, absolutely not! It was fire from heaven, fire from heaven. Alleluia! (Congregation responded, 'Alleluia!') It was fire from heaven, fire from heaven. After praying in the fire, praying in the fire, we went away, leaving it burning there and ran to the village and said, 'Mother, Mother, we have seen Jesus, Jesus! (*Taona Jesu, Jesu!*) We saw Jesus' fire!' When one sees Jesus, one cannot sleep indoors, for the joy. The boys of Emmaus, when they saw Jesus they ran to Peter, telling him, 'Jesus has risen! We have just talked with him!'

For Kahlari, his youthful vision at least 40 years earlier authenticated his spiritual experience and identity. It is striking that it happened in a *pungwe* setting – a group were praying together at night in a remote place, probably with the intention of staying out all night – and it is consistent with the prominent theme of 'going to the wilderness', *kuenda kumasowe*, in Shona Christian spirituality.[34] The nature of the 'fire from heaven' was unclear, but Kahlari insisted that it was real rather than visionary.[35] It recalled Elijah's fiery chariot in the chorus that opened the *pungwe*. The phrase 'Jesus' fire!' (*Moto waJesu!*) recalled the fiery tongues of fire in Acts 2 and its christocentric expression resonated with a later remark about the coming of the Holy Spirit: 'Jesus' disciples had been filled with Jesus.' *Pungwe* theology emphasises the Holy Spirit, but it remains enduringly christocentric.

---

[34]The theme is especially prominent among individuals and groups in AICs such as the Marange Apostles and the Pentecostal Apostolics, as outlined in chapter 6.

[35]Lightning strikes that ignite fires and kill people are so common in Zimbabwe that the nation is said to have the highest mortality rate from lightning of any country in the world. However, there is no reason to believe that Kahlari would have suppressed the fact of lightning, if that were indeed true. Kahlari's successor at Gatsi, the Rev Samuel Mukata notes that Methodists in Mandea had a similar experience. One member of the Methodist group is said to have actually handled the 'fire from heaven' and not been burned, a claim that may signal an effort to equal the feats of the Marange Apostles.

Evangelistic outreach to friends and neighbours would be the fruit of seeing Jesus at the *pungwe,* according to Kahlari:

> I would like you all to see Jesus. If you see Jesus this evening, tomorrow when the light dawns each and everyone will look for your friend and tell him or her, 'I saw Jesus.' Anyone who sees Jesus does not hide the fact. No, you rot (if you hide it).

The exhortation in Ephesians 6:18, 'Pray at all times in the Spirit, with all prayers and supplications', was interpreted as an injunction to resist sleep and persevere in prayer during the *pungwe.* The preacher's passionate peroration focused on the gathering's potential for moral transformation:

> This is our time to pray to God and seek God ... When we want to see Jesus, let us meet with Jesus. When you have been preached to here, tomorrow you will have seen Jesus. Go and tell your friend, 'I have seen Jesus – I will not steal. I have seen Jesus – I do not want to be stingy. I have seen Jesus – I do not want to commit adultery. I have seen Jesus – I do not want to do anything of that sort' – because you will have seen Jesus. In the name of the Father and of the Son and of the Holy Spirit (*Mudzimu Unoyera*), Amen.

Perhaps it was the *pungwe* setting's resemblance to the night vigils of SSR that influenced the pastor's unusual use of the ancestral spirit term *Mudzimu* for the Holy Spirit.[36] Contrasting with his uncompromising christocentrism, the designation illustrates how the *pungwe* itself catalyses theological interaction between Christian gospel and indigenous religious culture.

The sermon was a classic example of the missional power of a *pungwe* sermon in the MFCs. *Pungwe* themes of night, conflict and revelation were woven into biblical exposition, moral injunctions and community critique, all of it delivered with personal testimony, common proverbs and grand passion. The overall tone was revivalist: the preacher sought the conversion of non-Christians, the renewal of

---

[36]People use *unoyera* and *mutsvene* interchangeably as adjectives meaning 'holy' with reference to the Spirit. The former has the nuance of deserving reverence, and the latter has the nuance of rightness and acceptability (Hannan, sv).

believers and an evangelistic outpouring from all attending.

'Donkeys in the night': liberation for women

The liberation of women to exercise leadership in church and society emerged as the dominant theme of sermons at this *pungwe*. Following Kahlari in the preaching order, an elderly male CCAP leader introduced this theme when he requested a reading of Luke 24:8, which the expansive Shona version renders as: 'Then these women remembered his very words.'[37] Preceding the designated reading for the evening, the pericope in which this verse appears focuses on how a group of women saw angels at Jesus' tomb and reported to the eleven disciples of Jesus' inner circle. The preacher reflected:

> Jesus showed himself to women, but now I see only men standing up (to preach). It was supposed to be women who would initiate the word (*vatange shoko*), because it was they who first saw him. Then we men would come next, because it (the word) had not yet reached us. But, while today we are all shown at the same time, I see it is we men who begin, but the women are the ones who were the first to see Jesus. They ran to the grave. We followed later. The word began with the women. They were supposed to open the meeting.

The CCAP congregation at Eastern Highlands does not stress women's leadership any more than other MFC congregations,[38] but in the *pungwe* context the leader made women the centrepiece of his homily, applied the biblical story directly to the life of the churches, and confronted that very meeting's pattern of male leadership. 'We have come to see the Holy Spirit!' the preacher declared in another expression of how the Spirit is a central *desideratum* of the *pungwe* experience. He contrasted the spiritual conversation of the two disciples on the Emmaus road to the earthly and petty conversations participants may have had on their way to the *pungwe* and exhorted them, by way of a chorus, to go to Jesus:

---

[37] *Bhaibheri, ad loc.*

[38] Lay pastors in the MFCs – Anglican catechists, Methodist lay preachers, Presbyterian deacons – are generally men. United Methodist ordination of women as clergy has prompted more local leadership by women, and some Anglican catechists are women.

Ngatiende kuna Jesu, timutende.	Let us go to Jesus, let us thank him.
Pano pasi pakashata.	Here on earth things are bad.
Mwoyo wangu unosuva.	My heart grieves.
Unokuona Jesu Ishe.	You will see Jesus the Lord.

Riveting attention on the role of women was the next speaker, Mai Nyabereka of the United Methodist congregation that meets at the plantation. As owner, with her husband, of a general store in Zindi Township, she moved among the upper economic and social levels of Honde society. Her sermon was notable for its interpretation of the *pungwe* as a journey, her reflection on the effect of my *pungwe* project for the self-image of the churches, her appeal for solidarity in a spiritual war and, especially, her electrifying peroration on the liberation of women in gospel perspective.

Mai Nyabereka spoke quietly and slowly about the *pungwe* as a journey, as though she were searching for the words to characterise the power of the occasion for her: 'It is about a journey ... We are on a journey (*rwendo*).' For the many valley participants, simply getting to the event had indeed been a journey of several hours by foot and by bus. Mai Nyabereka depicted the *pungwe* as a stage in the journey of spiritual growth. She then connected this theme with my project of visiting the churches and investigating the *pungwe* phenomenon:

> That's the kingdom we are now seeing together with our dear friend from over the ocean. Doesn't it seem astonishing to us? There is no other skin (colour) in here but only he who gave himself saying, 'Let me go and see my friends'. He left his parents, he left his relatives, he left his friends, his wife has been left behind, for loving us. That's why there is a verse that says, 'You are people's friends if you do what I say.' We feel credible (*Tiri kunzwa kutendeseka*). We feel happy.

She went on to reflect on the *pungwe* itself:

> If we love and are loved by Jesus, we will fight one war (*Tikada-nana naJesu, tinorwa hondo imwechete*), we will be one family (*mhuri imwe*), we will walk together, we will sing together, we will eat together. So when the Lord was breaking bread, the disciples said, 'Were not our hearts so kindled?' If we had not yet seen Jesus, we would not yet have received salvation. If we experience

134

salvation as pleasing when we are being preached to, if we find salvation pleasing when it is being sung, if we hear good sermons and everything pleases us, we will see everything washed. We will be one army (*hondo*), we will be like one another (*tinonga tafana-na*), we will be the same people. That is why there is another verse that says it is better than gold, it is sweet like drops of honey. (Speaker broke out into singing, 'We are seeing the kingdom of heaven' and congregation followed.)

Mai Nyabereka saw the kingdom of God instantiated in the foreigner's *pungwe* project, because it was enacting racial reconciliation and fulfilling Jesus' desire for mutual love and obedience to his words. In saying 'We feel credible', Mai Nyabereka was declaring that after decades of Shona congregations feeling that their ways of experiencing the gospel were beneath the notice of white Christians and church leaders in the urban centres, the project was recognising and validating the spirituality of Shona churches. From the theme of racial reconciliation, Mai Nyabereka moved naturally to interpret the *pungwe* as a kind of war, a *hondo*. The war she was mobilising, now in loud and impassioned tones, was a spiritual war, but the image recalled the Liberation War still fresh in the memories of many. After the hostility and victory of that war, another step in reconciliation was now being taken in the churches. The context was the *pungwe*, which itself recalled the night rallies where guerrillas built solidarity for winning the liberation struggle. In predicting that mutual love would bring all to fight together, walk together, eat together and be one family and 'one army' (*hondo*), Mai Nyabereka applied the wartime building of solidarity to the life of the churches. The resurrection experience of seeing Jesus would similarly bring diverse races and church groups together, a unity that would manifest the kingdom of heaven.

Fervent with these themes of eschatological urgency and liberation longing, Mai Nyabereka then turned to the liberation imperative close at hand, the liberation of women:

My heart is happy with the word spoken by that father who said women should have been the ones to begin. I have seen that we are that donkey spoken of by the Lord: 'Go and untie it (*munorisunungure*).' It had been tied up outside the village. Stand up, women's group (*Simukai, chita chevakadzi*)! Let us give thanks for this time we were given, the time in which we were

135

blessed. We were not objects (*Taiva tisiri zviroba*). We were not human beings (*Taiva tisiri vanhuba*). But there are many (of us) in here. Some were even sold. To be married to a man – to be sold (*Kuroorwa pamurume, kutengeswa*)! But with the coming of Jesus, we were set free (*takasunungurwa*). That's why he said, 'Be righteous because your Father in heaven is righteous.'

We were made righteous by Jesus, mothers. If it were not for Jesus, we would not be here ... but Jesus came into our houses ... Stand up, mothers of the guild (*Simukai, vanamai vechita*), let's sing: (all sing:) 'The time that we have others lack. / Isn't it a mercy? / It's the mercy, the mercy, the mercy of the Father.'

We are thankful for the mercy of the Father, which makes us stay in houses. It is the Lord's grace. Isn't it mercy, dear ones, to bear children of the same kin? (Otherwise) we would have been saying, 'This one with this man, this one with that man.' ... I am thankful for experiencing the setting free of the donkeys (*kanguva kekusunungurwa kwemadhongi*) that were in darkness and that are now moving by night, being freed from being sold. But on account of the coming of Jesus all people can do as they please – have a man, get married and produce a good race.

In suddenness and power, this exhortation fell like a lightning strike, a discursive version of the Methodist pastor's 'fire from heaven'. She seized the opening provided by the previous speaker and compared the state of women under the old dispensation to the donkey tied up outside a village near Bethany (Mark 11:4). She moved instantly from Jesus' words, 'Untie it', to her appeal for the women to stand up and be free. The phrase 'to be married to a man – to be sold!' asserted that the custom of a bridegroom paying a bride-price (*lobola* or *roora*) for being a bride reduces a woman to the status of a possessed commodity.

Jesus' coming assures women that they are righteous as persons in themselves rather than derivatively from their husbands, according to the preacher. The freedom Jesus gives women recapitulates the freeing of the donkey and the relevant verb, *kusunungura,* is commonly used for human freedom in both the political rhetoric of the Liberation War and in Christian theological discourse. Mai Nyabereka's non-biblical image of the freed donkeys moving by night drew simultaneously from the wartime *mapungwe*, when people defied the national curfew, and from this *pungwe*, where women were moving at night as Jesus liberated them from social oppression. The preacher announced an eschatological vision, not accomplished facts, as she rejoiced in what had been accomplished and declared what its fulfilment would entail. The donkeys were moving, but still by night; day had not yet dawned. Remedial rather than revolutionary, Mai Nyabereka did not envision an entirely new social structure but argued that women must be free to make choices within marriage and child-bearing. Still donkeys, women continue to live subordinate to men in a patriarchal society. Yet, as women bore the resurrection news unmediated by men, so women can still bear the presence of Christ without men, just as the humble donkey bore Jesus on his entry into Jerusalem.

The 'donkey sermon' established a theme for the night, and it profoundly affected a number of women. In concluding her testimony late in the *pungwe*, Mai Mubure of St James' Anglican Church at Nyamhingura said, 'Now this morning I heard another woman give an example of a donkey that was set free. In coming here to Maronda Mashanu I also have been set free. Thank you, people of God!' One woman used the tragic story of her infant Nyarai to encourage young women, including teenage members of the St Veronica's Guild, to lay aside their fear of exposure and to preach:

> I used to go to church with others, but I could not stand up and talk in front of others, although I heard good songs and sermons. Whenever I thought of preaching, my husband would come and give me the baby and I failed to preach. So my husband and my child prevented me from doing God's work, because Nyarai would cry and then I would begin to comfort her.

Eventually the child was killed by her first husband, she said,[39] but she transformed the story into a startling exhortation:

> There are some girls who are still carrying that baby Nyarai ... When they want to stand up they feel shy about looking at people, because their husband would have given them the child to quiet since the child may be crying. If only Jesus could enter their

---

[39]She did not explain the circumstances or clarify whether, for instance, she meant physical murder or death by the occult means of wizardry.

hearts so much that the child would appear to be killed and they would be given a good child. When I say a very good child I mean that the girls will not be shy about standing in front of people and preaching the word of God.

The exhortation prompted a number of young women to make short testimonies and lead songs.

The challenge of men's oppression of women was taken up by David Manyau as the main theme of his hour-long sermon:

I would like to take hold of that theme of the woman, because I see that it is a major issue in the life of us blacks. I see that we have not yet understood what a woman is in our life. I do not know how long it will take for us to understand, but since we have men and young men here, I thought we could have enough time so that if we still do not understand that gospel about the life of a woman our life will always be troubled!

Biblical and theological themes that Manyau emphasised were the creation of woman as well as man in God's image, the time Jesus spent in the homes of people and the resurrection appearances to women. On these bases he discussed a broad range of issues in women's oppression: men's treatment of women as property rather than as persons in the negotiation of bride-price; their tendency to commend women verbally but behave unjustly toward them; the socialisation of men to be violent toward women; the ease with which some men divorce their wives; the injustice of polygyny; and the imperious behaviour of mothers-in-law toward their daughters-in-law. Other speakers, both male and female, denounced the role of men in infecting their wives with Aids through frequenting prostitutes at Zindi's Pungwe Hotel, often called *Rambanai,* which means 'divorce'.

The emergence of women's liberation as the night's principal theme demonstrated how the *pungwe* becomes a forum for the church to address social issues and include them in its mission. The preaching initiative of two individuals catalysed people to explore complexities of the issue and build on one another's insights. The *pungwe* offered ample time for in-depth discussion and for the inspirational singing so crucial for group mobilisation among the Shona.

'Satan is there': conflict and community in the *pungwe*

Themes of social and spiritual conflict arise frequently in *pungwe* sermons. We have just seen how conflict between men and women was prominent in sermons at the *mubatanidzwa*. Stimulated by Pastor Kahlari's reference to youth being baptised in 'churches of the night', a number of preachers discussed conflict between parents and children. A drama presented by the MU at 2:45 am focused on conflict between a mother and daughter about the daughter's sexual promiscuity and absence from church. When she was stabbed by a disgruntled boyfriend, the daughter changed her mind and experienced a religious conversion. The daughter's story functioned as a warning to young women, but the play's depiction of the mother's vanity also highlighted the danger of parental hypocrisy. Typical of Shona drama, the play focused on family conflicts and violence vividly and powerfully, yet elicited plenty of laughter even as it communicated a strong ethical message. In the *pungwe* the play offered yet another mode of communication and group life. Presented between the cycles of preaching and testimony, it restored dozing attendees to wakefulness and unified all as spectators of entertainment.

Conflict with the spiritual forces of SSR and with Satan were prominent themes, as they are at most *mapungwe* in the MFCs. A young Methodist man declared that the sacrificial system of SSR was no longer necessary on account of God's work in Christ:

> If you place your heart in God and say, 'God, you died for me, so now I will not kill any more goats; today, take care of my heart, because you are a live goat that died and conquered death', God will look after your heart.

An Anglican youth, Joseph Tangwena, encouraged people to discard any charms tied to parts of their bodies. Mai Ruona, an Anglican MU leader and church council member, challenged women to renounce their traditional role of brewing beer for *mashavi*. SaMasamvu from St Peter's, Mandea, declared that the *vadzimu* are deceptions of Satan and exhorted people to develop self-reliance in interpreting the gospel:

> Now there came teachers, priests and evangelists to teach us to know God's word within us. The country refused to listen. The country began making surprising things, for Satan has conjuring

tricks. The ancestral spirits that we are using today are the works of the devil. We are reverencing Satan's creature. Now, fathers, if you start climbing onto a bicycle, do you ride on your own or are there some who hold it for us so that we ride until we know how to ride on our own? Now, beloved, the time for the bicycle being held is over. The gospel needs to live inside each and every person. Let each one live with Jesus in one's heart.

Conflict with Satan was important for many speakers. A teenaged girl, Agnes Mabvunyaroya, attributed to Satan her reluctance to speak during the testimony time:

I am here and I thank the Lord Jehovah who made me come to this time, Amen! During all this talk about striving to preach, I have been repressing myself in the corner there, because Satan had seized me. When that was being said, I wrapped myself in my blanket. Now I have seen that God is not happy with what I am doing. That is why I have stood up to thank my Lord Jehovah who saved me, Amen!

One *mubvuwi* illustrated the eager malevolence of Satan with a parable from the rural countryside of the Honde Valley:

The eagle goes and builds its nest high up and below it there is a pool. There are crocodiles and fish in the pool. Now an eagle laid her eggs and they hatched. But she said to her chicks, 'My children, listen to each other. If you are not united, there is a pool below. Fish are there. If you fall, you will be eaten. You will leave this place when you are able to fly so that you can perch outside.' The eagle chicks became united. Now to us, the Bible is saying something. Satan is waiting for us. As we go out of here, Satan may be waiting for us. Satan is waiting to eat us, to take us into evil. The eagle warned her chicks. We are warned by the Bible. Throw away the evil, throw away the works of darkness. Do not be envious. Work hard. Love each other.

David Manyau encouraged women to see their struggle as liberation from the deceptive and oppressive power of Satan, which, in turn, drew him into a critique of SSR:

Be careful: people will come wearing sheep's skin, but they are destructive wolves. So that is Satan. There are some things that we think are good, but they are destroying us internally. The one (spirit) who we think is grandfather – we are being destroyed by him. The one who we think is grandmother – we are being destroyed by her. People who we think are ancestors – we may be destroyed by that. Some people are absent from work for five or six days, dancing to the drums at their home. They lie to their boss, saying, 'My wife is very ill', but would be at a beer ceremony dancing ... Let's understand the gospel. If the Holy Spirit descends on us and if we read the Bible, we will be freed forever.

As the social and spiritual conflicts besetting Christians become clear in a *pungwe,* the community draws together in solidarity against the forces it perceives arrayed against it and its members draw strength from one another for perseverance and witness. The *mubatanidzwa* illustrated the various ways in which this occurs: singing, praying, play-acting, preaching, Eucharist and healing. A frequent critic of the churches who usually stands aloof from church events stood up and declared, 'I thank you, beloved, for empowering me. You have empowered me and I shall go praising you wherever I go.' He pointed out that the gathered community would become a body of mutual accountability as a result of the *pungwe*:

I have come to be encouraged by you. You are seeing me, because I have presented myself before you so that you would see me. Tomorrow I might meet you. You are now my police, because I have put myself before you. I am also your police, because you also have stood up here and we have met in here.

There was broad agreement that a major purpose of the *pungwe* was to strengthen the faithful for evangelism. Simply summoning the courage to testify at the *pungwe* was for some a first step in embracing the evangelistic task. The woman who offered the final extemporaneous prayer during the closing Eucharist summarised the group's evangelistic resolve:

We have spent the whole night doing your work, our Father in heaven. We ask that as we leave this village of Maronda Mashanu we will carry the little that we have heard so that we will also preach to those who stayed home.

The closing Eucharist enacted the spiritual and social solidarity in formal liturgy, after which almost every person present went forward to receive the laying on of hands with prayers for healing from the clergy,

141

a process that took more than half an hour. In a final act of communal solidarity, all shared enthusiastically in the breakfast of tea and bread outside the hall. Thus the *pungwe* ended as it began, with a meal.

Varieties of *pungwe* in mission-founded churches

Various events and occasions prompt *mapungwe* in MFCs: death vigils, remembrance rites, gatherings of gender- and age-based groups, church festivals, sacramental transitions, ministry initiatives and pastoral care. In these gatherings the basic pattern of the *pungwe* is what we have seen in the *mubatanidzwa*: a meal, welcoming remarks, a scripture reading, prayers, an alternation of sermons and songs throughout the night, testimonies, a closing service and breakfast. The church *pungwe* is remarkably versatile in its occasions and its interactions with Shona religious culture.

Vigils of death and remembrance

Paralleling the practice of SSR, the death of a family member prompts Christians in both MFCs and AICs to hold a *pungwe* with the body and with the family each night until burial. Spending the nights in the same *rondavel* as the body, mourners encourage one another with Christian songs, sermons based on scripture and prayers. As exhaustion sets in over several days, the number awake at any nocturnal hour dwindles to ten or five as people take turns sleeping, but they consider it important that at least a small group be awake at all times.

Interpretations of this vigil vary with MFC members' views about spirit elders, and the issue's prominence indicates ambivalence and dual religious affiliation on the part of many. For the minority of Christians who eschew any involvement with *vadzimu*, the all-night vigil invokes God and expresses mutual care and solidarity, although some in this category also wish to protect the corpse and the family from wizards. Some Christians are sceptics who suspend belief about the ancestors and wizards but perform SSR's rites in order to protect themselves from what might be true and from later accusations of wizardry. Many sincere Christians believe it is important to facilitate the necessary transitions of the departed spirit and to protect the family from

142

wizardry. Opinion becomes more divided on the controversial question whether to call a *nganga* to determine the spiritual cause of death. Many who reverence the spirits balk at engaging a *nganga,* both because they know that someone will be blamed for the death and because they believe that the explicitly cultic character of the diviner's activities conflicts with Christianity. For others, the reason someone died is a personal, social and spiritual question that demands an answer that only a *nganga* can divine. This diversity does not mean that MFC members are simply switching to a second religious affiliation. Christian songs, prayers and sermons are offered with confidence that the trinitarian God can vanquish the hostile spiritual forces that may appear at night.

A related type of Christian *pungwe* is the *runyaradzo,* the 'consolation' service that MFCs and AICs are increasingly offering to bereaved families. Held after a customary lapse of time after death – between a month and a year – these observances are designed specifically to replace the rites of SSR that would otherwise be held. An instance took place at the homestead of Sylvester Gorogodo, a *mubvuwi* and the senior catechist of St George's Anglican Church at Sadziwa near Bonda. Gorogodo's son Maxwell had died suddenly one year earlier in his apartment near Harare leaving his wife and several small children. According to SSR, the circumstances called for divination, but the father refused entirely. At the one-year anniversary of Maxwell's death, when SSR's purification ritual would normally be held, Gorogodo held a *runyaradzo* to which he invited all his relatives, the SaDziwa congregation and other villagers and members of Bonda's other congregations. His invitation was put simply: 'Let us do *pungwe* for Maxwell' (*Ngatiite pungwe ngeMaxwell*), and he made it clear that he intended a purely Christian event.

Drawing several hundred people to an outside worship area, the event had a major theological impact in the local area. Following the normal *pungwe* sequence, preaching focused on such questions as: What happens to the spirit of a dead person? Is it right to offer prayers to the *vadzimu*? What is the relation between Christ and the ancestral spirits? Not surprisingly, speakers were critical of the traditional rites, but they also celebrated a resolution to the perennially difficult issue of how to honour the dead without reverencing their spirits. At dawn after the Eucharist, Beavan Tsinakwadi, Gorogodo's assistant cate-

143

chist, declared exultantly, 'Ah, now, the people know it can be done!'[40]

The *runyaradzo* offers both continuity and discontinuity with the purification rite of SSR. The community responds to the longing of Shona spirituality to remember and care for the departed and to do so at night. Yet preachers stress that the parents and church leaders are commemorating the departed, not appeasing the spirit. They commend the departed to the company of Christ, rather than restore him to the homestead or initiate him into *vadzimu.* Gatherings include not only relatives but also the wider community of church members, related spiritually to one another in Christ. Prayers are addressed to the trinitarian God and not to the spirits of the departed. Finally, Eucharist replaces ritual beer and *vadzimu* communion with the communion with Christ and, depending on particular theologies, the saints. With these emphases, the *runyaradzo* both builds on the traditional rite and transforms it.[41]

Mapungwe of gender and age groups

The strong identity and relative autonomy of age- and gender-based groups within the MFCs prompt them to hold numerous night vigils on their own.[42] In addition to the *mibatanidzwa* held by the Mothers' Union, the women's organisations of the various churches organise vigils within their denominational life for general revival or to enroll new members. Less numerous, the Fishermen *(Vabvuwi)* organise

---

[40]*Pungwe, runyaradzo* for Maxwell Gorogodo, 31 May–1 June 1986, Dziwa.

[41]AICs share these emphases but, like some MFC Christians, they sometimes ascribe more power to the spirit of the departed than was ascribed at the Gorogodo *runyaradzo.* Overall, however, Daneel remarks, 'The substitution of the *kugadzira* ritual (another term for the purification rite) with its Christian parallel, the *runyaradzo* ceremony, provides us with a unique example of how the IC (independent church) leaders try to eliminate an old practice without neglecting the traditionally conceived need which it had served ... the former inducts the spirit into the ancestral hierarchy by bringing it home, while the latter effects a passage into heaven. Thus the Zionist *runyaradzo* is not merely a superficial adaptation to the old system'. *Old and new in Southern Shona Independent Churches,* vol 2, *Church growth: causative factors and recruitment techniques* (The Hague and Paris: Mouton, 1974), 117–118, 131.

[42]See appendix 6 for the history of the Mothers' Union and the Fishermen.

fewer gatherings and they nearly always include chapters from a wide area. Very enthusiastic about night meetings, young people organise frequent *mapungwe* in their congregations and districts.

A weekend *gungano* of United Methodist Fishermen held at Nyangombe, west of Nyanga on the plateau, was billed as the 'MUMC (Men of the United Methodist Church) South Convention Revival'. Held outside under baobab trees at a long-standing Methodist campground, it drew over a thousand people, including six or seven hundred *Vabvuwi* from all over Manicaland, church officials from Harare, women and young people from *Vabvuwi* families and members of other MFCs. The unusual mimeographed schedule specified that Friday night people were to retire at 10 pm – many stayed up and held a *pungwe* anyway – but the night between Saturday and Sunday was designed explicitly as a *pungwe*:

9:30 pm – 10:00 pm	Singing by MUMC Makoni/Mutasa
10:00 pm – 11:00 pm	Sermon by the Rev FK Mukwindidza
11:00 pm – 11:30 pm	Singing by MUMC Mutare South
11:30 pm – 12:30 pm (*sic*)	Tea refreshments
12:30 am – 1:30 am	Sermon – the Rev Mazarura
1:30 am:– 5:00 am	*Pungwe/Umbowo* (Testimonies) – MUMC
5:00 am – 6:00 am	Rising Devotions – MU Mutare South
6:00 am – 8:00 am	Breakfast
8:00 am – 10:00 am	Main Service – Head Office[43]

As one Methodist pastor said afterwards, 'We don't feel satisfied unless we have a *pungwe* on the last night.'[44]

Evangelism, conversion, relations between men and women and spiritual conflict were prominent themes in preaching. The revival's thematic verse was James 1:22a, 'Be doers of the word', which the evening's lead-off speaker related to Jesus' commissioning of his disciples in Matthew 29:19 and to Andrew's witness to Simon Peter in John 1:40–42. Witness was enacted in stories of conversion,

---

[43]S E Chikonzo, 'MUMC South Convention Revival' (Schedule), (10–12 May 1991), mimeographed. Although the document uses the English name for the organisation, participants referred to themselves and to the organisation simply as *Vabvuwi*.

[44]Lloyd Nyarota, interview, 12 May 1991.

Preacher at United Methodist *pungwe* at Eastern Highlands

United Methodist pastor Togarasei Kahlari (left) supervises the burning of a
spirit medium's *gona*, or basket of ritual objects, at a Methodist men's
gungano pungwe at Nyangombe

146

especially in the early-morning testimony time, when speakers recounted the struggles they experienced with their families and with the spirit world when they became Christians. Clergy exhortations for more equitable relations between men and women were amplified by women speakers who sought the community's prayer and moral support in the abuse they were suffering from their husbands. Stories of family rejection, children's deaths and wife-beating elicited tears and groans of sympathy from the hearers. These conflicts echoed the general conflict preachers emphasised with Satan, spirits and the practices of SSR. 'You know, this evening we have come face to face with the fact that we have a great war with Satan,' one preacher said. Using the special cloths of the ancestral spirits, he said, was like using crutches to walk, and he prayed to God that the group would be able to discard them.

Perceived conflict between Christ and the *vadzimu* became overt in a number of incidents. An elderly MU member brought to a small group of clergy and lay leaders her late husband's *gona*, the basket of materials he used in his work as a *nganga*. They proceeded to burn it while they prayed and sang hymns around the flames. Just before dawn, at *mambakwedza,* a young woman leaped up from the gathering, ran to the nearby Nyangombe River and threw herself into the water, from which several quick pursuers rescued her. As Pastor Togarasei Kahlari and others gathered around her on the riverbank, she appeared to be in a trance, but when she recovered she said that an *njuzu* had called out to her in a vision, filling her with an overwhelming urge to meet the spirit in the water. Sessions of intense prayer and exorcism ensued. Throughout the night Pastor Kahlari and others were sought out by *pungwe* participants for prayer and exorcism in connection with physical ailments and reported harassment by spirits.[45] In general, night evokes conflicts that are implicit in Shona life and spirituality, and the *pungwe* offers a setting where the community can discuss them openly and deal with them directly.

---

[45]Pastor Kahlari is a 'locally ordained' pastor rather than a seminary-trained minister of the UMC. Occupying a lower place in the denominational hierarchy, he therefore did not receive one of the high-profile preaching opportunities that went to his more educated colleagues. It was clear, however, that many attendees believed he had special authority in the spiritual matters that were most important to them. This dynamic illustrates yet again the populist nature of the *pungwe* phenomenon.

Youth *mapungwe* tend to be especially open to pentecostal phenomena such as speaking in tongues, ecstatic prophecy and exorcism. At an Anglican youth *pungwe* in the Honde Valley a young preacher led the group of two hundred youth and adults in a long season of spontaneous and confessional prayer that evoked glossalalia and weeping in a number of participants.[46] When some Anglicans who were disturbed by this worship style convened a night meeting to discuss it, debate was heated between older Anglicans arguing for orderly worship and younger members pressing for spontaneity and openness to the Holy Spirit.[47] *Mapungwe* in all the MFCs highlight pneumatological features of Christianity and blur denominational distinctives and hierarchical lines of authority.

The pentecostal tendency of youth gatherings and the possibility of sexual activity among the youth at night have prompted some church authorities to discourage youth *mapungwe*. In a 1989 circular to youth in the Anglican Diocese of Harare, the then Bishop Peter Hatendi wrote:

> MEETING TIME: Ideally the congregation should pray and worship and learn together. When need for an exclusive youth service arises the best time is during day light. Satan is the ruler of darkness. This is why 'Pungwes' have resulted in unwanted pregnancies and false teaching. There is need for girls and boys to meet separately for lessons on husbandhood/wifehood and fatherhood/motherhood.[48]

Young people in that diocese chafed against this restriction, which has since been relaxed somewhat. 'It's our culture,' declared Alice Chimbidzo, a youth group member in an Anglican congregation north of Harare. With a delighted smile, she explained, 'We like to get together to sing and to dance and to preach and to pray. We like to do it until the morning comes.'[49] Dismissing the concern about sexual activity, a Honde Anglican lay leader annually takes his youth group back to his home area in Mashonaland specifically to hold a *pungwe*

---

[46]*Pungwe*, youth rally, 15–16 January 1994.
[47]Night service, *Rutandadzo*, 20–21 January 1994, EHTE.
[48]Peter Hatendi, (untitled circular to youth), 7 December 1989, mimeographed.
[49]Alice Chimbidzo, interview, 30 December 1993.

and so encourage the young people there. The effects have been dramatic:

> Each time we take the youth there the church grows in size, because many other people come in. So for several years that church has been growing. At first the priest opposed it, saying, 'No night meetings!' But now he enjoys it and encourages it. In fact, this year he took some youth from that place to his own home area to hold a *pungwe*.[50]

Thus the vigil movement and, in particular, youth *mapungwe* help revitalise congregations and promote numerical growth. The youth's role parallels their part in the *mapungwe* of the *Chimurenga,* where a liberation movement led by young people challenged the older generation to shift their ideological stance and to become involved personally in a community struggle. Movements of Christian youth from one area of the country to another to mobilise youth groups recapitulates the wartime movements of guerrilla groups for mass mobilisation. Where the *pungwe reChimurenga* mobilised people for a liberation struggle against colonialism, the *pungwe remayouth* mobilises people for spiritual engagement with Christ and liberation from powers they consider evil in their lives.

Congregational *mapungwe* for festivals and pastoral care

MFC congregations regularly hold *mapungwe* to celebrate festivals and transitions in the lives of their members. Indications in the gospels that the resurrection of Jesus occurred before dawn, during the spiritually powerful time Shona people call *mambakwedza,* make a *pungwe* especially appropriate at Easter, and some congregations also observe Christmas with a *pungwe.* At Bonda, from 1984 to 1986, I synthesised the Great Vigil of Easter with a *pungwe* to produce a dramatic night: the new fire was lit after dark; all nine lessons were read and catechists preached on them in sequence through the night; during a midnight break the youth presented a passion play and new lay leaders were commissioned; testimonies followed the preaching; baptisms occurred shortly before dawn; and the first Eucharist of Easter was celebrated at first light. When combined with a district-wide choir

---

[50]Shepstone Muzvidzwa, interview, 3 January 1994.

festival Saturday morning, this Easter observance became a major event in the area and the celebration attracted a large following. Methodist and Anglican congregations often celebrate their patronal festivals with *mapungwe*. The annual festival of Bernard Mizeki prompts *mapungwe* both at the martyr's shrine near Marondera – which drew 15 000 pilgrims for the Mizeki centenary in 1996 – and in individual Anglican congregations.[51] Other common occasions include initiatives in stewardship, evangelism and family life; the visits of ordained pastors, superintendents and bishops; and liturgical observance of life transitions, such as confirmation and marriage.[52]

Pastoral care is the purpose of some *mapungwe*. Christians often hold all-night vigils at the homes of members homebound by illness or old age. Such outings are usually led by lay members of the congregation and participants can number from 10 to 60. The *pungwe* becomes a vehicle for the church to extend itself corporately to those in need and to offer an alternative response to illness, which is a major preoccupation of SSR. On one such visit a Baptist preacher encouraged the sick woman to put her entire trust in Jesus and to reject the counsel of those encouraging her to offer a cow or a goat to her *vadzimu*. A person feeling vulnerable may request a visit:

> If I have an evil dream at my home, I will summon my congregation, 'Come, put your prayers on my house. The *pungwe* is very useful in many such cases.'[53]

All-night pastoral visits from the churches challenge the tendency of some MFC members to seek out mediums when misfortune strikes, for the churches offer their presence at precisely the time of greatest anxiety and vulnerability.

---

[51]See Titus Presler, 'Mizeki pilgrims "see God with new eyes"'. *Episcopal Times* 19, no 5 (September 1996):20–21; 'From Boston to Zimbabwe: young pilgrims find the "heart of God"', *Episcopal Life* 7, no 8 (September 1996), 1, 3; 'An immersion in Africans' living experience of Christ in community', *Cowley* 20, no 4 (Spring 1995), 8–12.

[52]Church members commonly hold night meetings in their homes that end at 1 am or 2 am and are not, therefore, *mapungwe*. Called a *rutandadzo,* such a gathering includes prayer, song and mutual encouragement. The small, informal nature of the meeting prompts free discussion among the participants on topics similar to those that preachers treat at large *mapungwe*: SSR, ethical issues, social movements, evangelism and the like.

[53]Gilbert Masiyakurima, Essay Project on Christianity and Tradition.

The *pungwe* is also a ready vehicle for ventures in economic develop-ment. World Vision International, the California-based evangelical Christian development organisation, has an office at Chisuko in the Honde, where a local director coordinates projects in carpentry, dress-making, welding, milling, building, sanitation and water supply. The organisation sponsors two *mapungwe* each year to encourage churches to mobilise for these development initiatives, A 1991 a *mubatanidzwa* drew over 1 500 people from ten MFCs and AICs. The format of these gatherings is similar to others already discussed, and the full range of pneumatological expressions appear in the pre-dawn hours of *mambakwedza*.[54]

Church opposition to the vigil movement

In the midst of the widespread and growing *pungwe* movement, there is also substantial opposition to night vigils in the MFCs. St Columba's, the major Roman Catholic mission in the Honde Valley, illustrates the post-war growth of the movement, the reasons for opposition and the efforts of a church hierarchy to ban *mapungwe.* Like their Protestant and Anglican counterparts, Roman Catholics have always kept all-night vigils in the homes of bereaved families, but before the Liberation War, official, congregational vigils generally occurred only at Christmas and Easter.[55] Church attendance declined as a result of the Liberation War:

> The guerrillas were saying, 'There is no God and we do not want to hear you talking about God – we will shoot you.' Those people who were not strong in their faith, they started to get away from the church.

As catechist at St Columba's, Francis Sanyanga used the *pungwe* to renew interest in the church after the war:

> You see, it was a means of just motivating those who were no longer coming to church or to their stations ... *Pungwes* were not just held at a central place but at any place. And now those peo-ple were also invited to accompany us or to join us. By joining us,

[54]A F Chimuti, interview, 10 April 1991.
[55]Phillip Kembo, church leaders interview, St Columba's, 18 January 1994.

in fact, they found they were now interested. They thought it's necessary now to start going with others. It encouraged them to come back to church even with those people they were having *pungwes* with ... That's how we started these *pungwes,* because we were just trying to fish people who were defecting.

Competition with the Anglican, Methodist and Mugodhi Churches energised the catechist's *pungwe* promotion:

Our youth were now just going to attend these *pungwes.* And we were surprised: 'What's going on?' They would say, 'There is this big meeting.' The youth were no longer interested in their churches but in other churches, because they were spending much time doing *pungwes.* So why not start our own *pungwes?*

The logistical advantage was that Sanyanga could take the church to the people where they were, instead of attempting to persuade them to come out to services:

The *pungwe* seemed to draw people to the church ... Let's say people from Muparutsa up there, it's very far away from church. Let's say there are so many people in this area who are no longer coming to church. We then do *pungwe* there and do the readings and not just ordinary readings but choose a special reading ... We found it better to do in the evening, not the youth only, but me and the adults. The adults said, 'We will be busy working in our fields, the youth will be at school and some working.' So evening time was the time they said it's better to start our prayer, from 6:30 until the following morning.

Sanyanga discouraged ecstatic manifestations as devil-inspired, but he realised that night was a time of spiritual power for his congregations. He summarised the evangelistic power of the *pungwe* in the Shona proverb, 'Big fish are caught when it is dark' (*Hove huru dzinodyira kwadoka*).

After a *pungwe* heyday in St Columba's District between 1984 and 1989 under Irish missionary Tony Cahill, a new Shona priest took a different view:

When Father Sakarombe came down to the Honde Valley, he said, 'I do not want these *pungwes* because in Mutare they are no longer doing these systems, because the youth are getting the

152

chance to do what they want during *pungwe* time.' So he said, 'No, I am no longer much interested in people going for *pungwes.*[56]

The bishops of Mutare Diocese 'totally discouraged' the practice, citing concern about illicit sexual activity among the youth.[57] In response to the people's entreaties, yet another Irish priest granted *pungwe* permission on a limited basis. Ironically, the Roman Church's opposition to nocturnal ritual has undercut its own efforts to promote an official, 'christianised' version of SSR's purification ritual for the dead, in which participants bless ritual beer and address the ancestral spirits. By drawing these elements into the orbit of trinitarian prayer and the communion of the saints the rite seeks both to affirm the traditional impulse and to replace the traditional ceremony.[58] The fact that the Roman ritual is held during the day, however, has largely neutralised the effort. Such is the power of night that many families agree to the church's rite and then also hold the traditional ceremony at the traditional time, at night.

Theological questions are raised in some quarters. The general prohibition by the former Anglican bishop of Harare issued not only from concern about pregnancies but from the association of night with SSR:

> Another form of hypocrisy which is widespread in our diocese is syncretism – the mixing of Traditional and Christian religions. When shall we stop hopping from Traditional religion at night to the Christian religion during the day-time? The climax comes at national holiday weekends. There is a rush back by bus, car or on bicycle to traditional or ancestral homes to placate our angry gods (*midzimu*). During the same period rivers of the blood of innocent bulls, goats and sheep flow to no avail because Christ is our perfect sacrifice. At our baptism we were converted from worshipping idols to worshipping the true God through Jesus

---

[56]Francis Sanyanga, church leaders interview, St Columba's, 18 January 1994. The preceding four quotations are also from Sanyanga.

[57]Tafirenyika Nyagope, church leaders interview, St Columba's, 18 January 1994. The Apostolic Faith Mission is another MFC that discourages *mapungwe*. Costa Matunia, interview, 24 April 1991.

[58]*Shona ritual: kuchenura munhu, kana kuti kurova guva, kana kugadzira mufi* (Purifying the person, or beating the grave, or preparing the dead) (Gweru: Mambo Press, 1982).

Christ. By returning to the blood of bulls or goats we are eating our own vomit, while others rush to holiday resorts for self-indulgence in the pleasures of this world.[59]

In the bishop's view, SSR's ceremonies stigmatise night as a gathering time. Even the United Methodists, whose camp meeting tradition catalysed *mapungwe* in other MFCs, are experiencing such tensions. 'Some leaders are questioning why meetings that exorcise demons and so on have to be held at night,' reports one minister at Old Mutare Mission, 'Why not bring it out into the daylight?' In a historical counterpoint to the pentecostal outpouring at that mission in 1918, pentecostal manifestations at some *mapungwe* in 1990 caused such a commotion among secondary school students there that district officials became cautious about holding more such meetings at Old Mutare.[60] In general, however, UMC leaders' reservations about the *pungwe* have had little effect on congregations.

The nature of opposition to the *pungwe* movement in the MFCs highlights major features of the movement. Concern about the control of youth echoes the leadership role that young people took in the nocturnal rallies of the Liberation War. Concern about pentecostal expressions at *mapungwe* confirms that night is a time of particular spiritual sensitivity in Shona spirituality. The fact that it is church hierarchies, not ordinary members, who oppose the *pungwe* emphasises the movement's populist, grassroots quality, in which real power is shared by many, sometimes at the expense of established hierarchy. Finally, the fact that it is difficult to prohibit or suppress the *pungwe* demonstrates the movement's power. In the *pungwe* Christians are taking charge of their own ecclesial life as they develop new theologies, build communities of solidarity and reach out in mission to the world.

---

[59]Peter Hatendi, 'The bishop's charge – 1986', TD, mimeographed, 4.
[60]Shirley DeWolfe, interview, 2 May 1991; Togarasei Kahlari, interview, 30 April 1991.

CHAPTER 6

Communities on fire:
night vigils in African Initiated Churches

African Initiated Churches are proliferating in number and growing in size in Zimbabwe and throughout black Africa. Thousands of Honde people are being drawn into their life as the major churches consolidate their ministry and new churches enter the valley. AIC growth testifies to African initiative in mission, and among the Shona the movement of all-night vigils is a major vehicle of that initiative.

'The *pungwe* helps especially in places where there are no believers,' said a Full Gospel Church leader whose evangelistic congregation is growing rapidly at Eastern Highlands Tea Estates:

> The *pungwe* of Christianity restores the person who has been involved in sin. One is attracted to come and hear and receive forgiveness. When folks inclined to fight at night hear the singing of God's songs, they come away and leave their quarrels.[1]

A member of the indigenous Zimbabwe Assembly of God, Africa, recalled how he attended a *pungwe* the week of his conversion:

> At midnight there was the Holy Spirit session and I was filled by the Holy Spirit. Since then, I love and admire to be in a *pungwe*. I always feel my soul filled in a *pungwe* because that is where a lot of time is spent preaching the word and rejoicing in the swimming pool of the Holy Spirit. Yes, that is a blessing. Time and again, whenever I think of a *pungwe* I see it as the best blessing God ever gave to man.[2]

---

[1] Isaiah Shawati, Essay Project on Christianity and Tradition.
[2] Aneck Taulo, Essay Project on Christianity and Tradition.

Conflict with spiritual forces of evil is what stands out for pungwe participants in the Pentecostal Apostolic Church of God. One writes, 'We drive out the spirits of demons, avenging spirits and spirits of wizardry', and another says, 'We take out unclean spirits that live on the mountains and in the trees.'[3]

Mission has particular expressions among various AIC groups. The Marange Apostles seek to prepare people for the world's fiery end, while *Ndaza* Zionists enact God's present reign in feverish drumming and dancing. Pentecostal Apostolics liberate women from oppressing male spirits, and Mugodhi members combine strong teaching with regular healing and exorcism. All of these groups promote evangelism as a perennial imperative, encouraging their members to share the gospel with others and invite them into the church fellowship. The gospel proclamation and invitation implicit in Christian mission are thus inherent in the life of AICs, and their activism has produced dramatic church growth. AICs are not attempting to replicate the schools and hospitals that historically have been prominent in the outreach of MFCs, but their work in spiritual healing and disciplined lifestyle has a significant social impact. In addition, AICs in the Masvingo area are cooperating in a substantial project in ecological renewal.[4]

'Churches of the Spirit' (*chechi dzoMweya*) is the popular name for the AICs that are drawing attention and members. Amid the substantial disagreements AICs have on many points of belief and practice, emphasis on the presence and power of the Holy Spirit is a passion they share in common. Tea pluckers, peasant farmers, clerks and shopkeepers alike agree that they joined AICs on account of the prominence such churches give to the Holy Spirit and to the ministry of healing.[5] The night vigils that are so central for AICs feature many

---

[3]Thomas Makunike and J D Mvumih, Essay Project on Christianity and Tradition.

[4]See chapter 5, note 32.

[5]In contrast, Ethiopian-type AICs, where worship and organisation follow MFC patterns, are not growing and are now a relatively minor presence. Ethiopian-type AICs in the Honde valley include the First Ethiopian Church, known as Topia; the African Congregational Church, called *Chibarirwe*; and *Zivezano*. The categories, 'Spirit-type' and 'Ethiopian-type', are Daneel's revision of Bengt Sundkler's earlier distinction between Zionist and Ethiopian churches. Race was a factor for both types in their secessions from MFCs. Daneel, *Major movements*, 285–287, 350–351.

of the elements found in MFC vigils, but each church has practices that distinguish it not only from MFCs but from other AICs. In this chapter, the AIC contribution to the *pungwe* as a mission initiative is illuminated by the practice of three particular churches: the Marange Apostles, the Pentecostal Apostolics and the Mugodhi Church.

Trial by fire: the African Apostolic Church of Johane Marange

Open-air Sabbath services of congregations in white robes; bald and bearded men walking with ceremonial shepherds' staffs; wailing songs in the night at great encampments; men and women walking on fire and picking up burning logs with their hands – these scenes manifest a powerful community. The movement founded by Johane Marange is remarkable for its rapid growth, the distinctive ways it has combined Christian gospel with Shona religious culture, the dogmatic conviction of its members and the persistence of the subculture it has created. Fire-handling, the great distinctive of its all-night vigils, undergirds the church's theology as a community literally preparing for the end of the world.

Gospel and culture in the life of the Marange Apostles

Understanding the Apostles must begin with the late Johane Marange, the founder whose example, precept and presence are powerfully felt by members of his church. Born Muchabaya Momberume in 1912 in Marange, south-west of Mutare, he experienced visions from the age of six. He completed Standard 2 (the present Grade 4) at the American Methodist Mission school, where he studied catechism and received baptism before leaving to work as a labourer in Mutare.

> On the evening of the 17th July, 1932, Johane was on his way home, having visited his in-laws. Near Mt Nyengwe he suddenly noticed a strong light falling on him. He heard a voice saying, 'You are John the Baptist, an Apostle. Now go and do My work! Go to every country and preach and convert people! Tell them not to commit adultery, not to steal and not to become angry! Baptise people and keep the Sabbath Day.' Johane described this experience as

157

being awesome, his soul 'becoming very small' while the light was on him.[6]

Mission vision and task are central in this vision, which signalled not Johane's conversion but a missionary vocation that included evangelism, international proclamation and moral reformation. For *pungwe* practice it is striking that Johane's crucial vision came in the evening, *manheru,* which designates any time near sunset to about midnight. The vision's strong light suggests darkness rather than dusk. Some of Johane's visions occurred in the afternoon, but another revelation of his authority, where his bundle of grass grew bigger than his brothers', also came in the night. The Apostles' evening services and night vigils are thus grounded in the pivotal experiences of the founder.

Worship and mighty works carried out through the power of the Holy Spirit were central in Marange's call by God:

> You will have power to cure the sick by laying hands on them and by consecrating water for them to drink; you will be able to drive away any kind of *shavi* through the laying-on of hands. Take the long staff, wherever you go, for healing purposes! Through your hands fertility will be conveyed to the barren and when you step in fire you will not be burnt ... When you want to lay hands on a new convert so that he can perform miracles, so be it. If you want him to have the Holy Spirit, so be it. If you want him to heal others, he will do so. If you want him to prophesy or preach it will be so.[7]

The Holy Spirit's presence could not countenance other spirits, so in full-scale confrontation with SSR Marange exorcised the spirits as demons rather than inviting them into the family as ancestors. This stance continues to define the approach not only of the Marange Apostles but also of the various other *Chipostori* ('Apostolic') AICs related to it. In the spirits' absence appeared a rich repertoire of pneumatic experience and works such as healing, miracles, prophecy and fire-walking.

---

[6]Daneel, *Major movements,* 319. For AACJM history, see also 315–339, and Benetta Jules-Rosette, *African Apostles: ritual and conversion in the Church of John Maranke* (Ithaca and London: Cornell University Press, 1975).
[7]Daneel, *Major movements,* 320.

In other areas Johane reaffirmed impulses of Shona religious culture. Continuing the family focus of Shona society, Johane's pivotal vision was immediately confirmed, shared and elaborated among the members of his family as they experienced glossalalia and falling down, the phenomenon called 'being slain in the Spirit' in Western pentecostal traditions. Johane appointed family members to authoritative positions in the new church, thus replicating the familial basis of Shona Spirit Religion, but with a radical Christian conviction. The church was one of a number of AICs that emerged in Rhodesia after World War I from roots in holiness churches that Americans established in Johannesburg in the 1890s and that subsequently became pentecostal.[8]

The prominence of visions in Johane Marange's spiritual experiences contributes to the Apostles' expectation that night brings special revelations from God. He had visions of being with Jesus in heaven, of preaching in many countries and gathering a large following, of protecting believers from fire and of his pre-eminence as a religious leader.[9] Johane's elevation of visions and dreams to a privileged place in divine communication in the Christian context accorded well both with SSR, where immediate supernatural communication is the principal religious experience, and with the prominence of dreams and visions in the Bible. Apostolic spirituality's consonance both with Shona culture and with biblical precedent accounts for the extraordinary confidence Apostles have in their way of life.

The Apostles' exclusive dependence on prayer for healing contributes to the frequency and intensity of their *mapungwe*. Many members say they joined the church after Apostolic prayers enabled them to bear children or to recover from major illnesses that neither MFCs nor Western-style hospitals could cure. After every liturgy healers lay hands on the sick for healing and exorcism, and they bless water that people take away and drink at their homes to continue the healing process. Apostolic insistence that true faith requires them to avoid clinics and hospitals provokes controversy in Zimbabwe, and deaths that could have been avoided if medical care had been sought prompt

---

[8]For details, see Sundkler, *Bantu prophets*, 48; Daneel, *Major movements*, 285–286.

[9]Daneel, *Major movements*, 316–318. Johane recorded his revelations in *Humboo hutsva hwavaPostori* ('The new revelation of the Apostles') a document that the Apostles consider an authoritative addition to the Bible.

criticism from government officials and the press.[10] Some scorn what they call the hypocrisy of *Vapostori* men who keep their wives and children away from clinics but do go when they themselves are ill. *Chipostori* healing both emulates and confronts the healing institutions of the *nganga* and the MFC, each of which offers divine revelation and physical healing. Just as Johane asserted that the spiritual dimension of his 'new revelation' superseded that of both the missionary and the *nganga,* so the practical ramifications of the revelation also had to supersede both, according to the logic of the movement. Condemning the *nganga*'s medicines was a foregone conclusion, for everything connected with the *nganga* was seen as evil. Mission medical institutions were seen not so much as evil as irrelevant. In practice, Apostles view consulting them as a spiritual lapse, a sign of weak faith, and anyone who goes to such institutions is required to confess the lapse as a sin. The Apostles' night vigils enact a similar dynamic of both emulating and confronting the traditional religious matrix.

The Holy Spirit's reported delineation of church ministries has issued in an elaborate hierarchy that is very evident in the church's *mapungwe.* There are four orders of ministry, each with strong biblical precedent: *Vabapatidzi* (baptisers), who are the first order; followed by *Vavhangeri* (evangelists), who preach and teach; *Varapi* (healers) and *Vaprofiti* (prophets). Each order has three grades, the highest of which is *Rabhauma* (a word of uncertain provenance), and each congregation constitutes its council from the ranks of this highest grade. This hierarchy reflects the norms of *pasichigare* Shona society, where avenues of communication, initiative and authority are clearly circumscribed by age, gender, kinship location and spiritual role in the ritual complex.[11] In the midst of colonialism's increasing impact on Shona society, the prophet instituted an independent source of authority and group identity, but his new structures reassured many by replicating the strong boundaries of *pasichigare* society. Apostles encourage polygyny (*barika*) on the grounds that Hebrew custom in the Old Testament supports this traditional Shona practice. Arguing that

---

[10]See, for instance, 'Rural round-up', column, *The Herald*, 1 April 1991; editorial, 7 April 1991.

[11]AIC hierarchies often replicate kinship authority structures. Marthinus L Daneel, *Old and new in southern Shona independent churches*, vol 3, *Leadership and fission dynamics* (Gweru: Mambo Press, 1988), 10–47.

women's subordination to men is consonant with Shona custom and with scripture, Apostles allow women to hold only the offices of healer and prophet, and promotion to *Rabhauma* and the church's ruling councils is closed to them.[12] Johane's own ministry, however, did not evolve into the chiefly type of leadership common in many AICs, for the founder continued to focus on itinerant preaching and healing while family members administered the church.[13]

Marange Apostles are such a conspicuous subculture that many Zimbabweans consider them the archetypal AIC, although several Zionist churches antedate it by more than a decade. Polygyny is a major factor, for it is difficult to leave the *Vapostori* and join a MFC once one has made the social arrangements connected with polygyny. Entrusting health exclusively to the believing community's prayers strengthens the church's solidarity and contributes to the large number of *mapungwe*. Apostles' frequent camp meetings and their stress on Saturday worship point away from conventional employment's expectation of a Monday-to-Saturday work week, so many families are agrarian or self-employed in business with strong and lucrative mutual ties. *Vapostori* men shave their heads and grow long beards, so they are visually identifiable. Saturday Sabbath observance and strict avoidance of alcohol and pork further set the Apostles apart.

Mission vision, local and international, has drawn many into the Marange fold, where *mapungwe* play a strong role in outreach. Johane himself travelled south to the Transvaal and north to the central Congo, and today the church has substantial membership in Malawi, Zambia, Congo, Mozambique, Botswana, Ghana and Uganda. *Vapostori* were tireless in village evangelism, offering a joyful and persuasive witness that could not be reduced to personal or corporate aggrandisement. With 910 000 affiliated members in 1995, the AACJM is the largest AIC in Zimbabwe and the second-largest single church body, after the Roman Catholics' 940 700 affiliated members, in 1995.[14] The Apostles' enthusiasm for evangelism suggests that part of the impetus for independency was simply a desire for a more clear-cut

---

[12]See Benetta Jules-Rosette, 'Women as ceremonial leaders in an African church: the Apostles of John Maranke', in *The new religions of Africa*, ed Benetta Jules-Rosette (Norwood, NJ: Ablex Publishing Co, 1979), 127.
[13]Daneel, *Quest for belonging* (Gweru: Mambo, 1987), 142.
[14]See appendix 2, table 3.

commitment to evangelism. For persons who sensed the mission thrust of the gospel, Johane's movement may have appeared to offer more opportunity than could be found in the MFCs.

Training for the fiery end: night vigils of the Apostles

Apostles of Johane Marange hold night vigils during encampments of several days that they call *magungano*, 'gatherings',[15] thus differing from the single-night pattern of most other churches. In the Honde Valley each congregation holds a *gungano* at least once a month at established campgrounds they call *misasa,* the name of the booths they erect on site.[16] Households bring food, cooking utensils and bedding for camping in the booths, some of which are large enough to accommodate fifty people.

The encampments' bush location highlights the wilderness motif of night vigils in *Chipostori. Vapostori* have no church buildings, so the Saturday daytime services are always held outside. An evangelist of the church offers a representative explanation:

> The Apostles do not build a house for the church, because God says, 'I do not fit in a building.' God is everywhere. God says, 'What type of building would you build for me? The earth is where my legs and my hips are, heaven is where my body is, so what type of a building would you build for me in which I could fit or live?' That is what the Bible says. But erect tents in which to worship as did Moses. We can be twenty thousand at a *gungano,* so what size of a building could we build that could accommodate all of us? Moreover, Jesus prayed in the mountains *(kumakomo)* in the bush *(kusango).*[17]

The desert motif in Hebrew history and Jesus' ministry grounds the Apostles' wilderness spirituality in biblical revelation. Campgrounds are

---

[15]This term echoes Marange's upbringing in Methodism, where camp meetings were called *magungano,* the term Methodists use today.

[16]Hannan (sv) defines *musasa* (the singular form) as follows: 'Shelter. Temporary camp. Roofless enclosure (eg for wedding feast).' The word appears in Exodus 33:7 with reference to the camp of the Israelites at Mt Sinai *(Bhaibheri rine apokirifa: ad loc).* Johane Marange saw people staying in *misasa* in one of his visions.

[17]The reference is to the annual Paseka services at the church's headquarters in Macheke, and the crowd estimate is accurate.

shifted occasionally, partly to accommodate health concerns and partly to reproduce the experience of moving through the wilderness. The *gungano* is a mid-point between ordinary life at home and truly going out into the wilderness, which they term *kuenda kugomo*, 'to go to the mountain', or *kuenda kumasowe*, 'to go to the wilderness'. The latter are one- or two-day ventures in prayer, either individually or in groups, that continue through the night as participants fast without food or water, whereas at a *gungano* the Apostles have shelters, sleeping mats and plenty of food. *Gungano* deprivation consists of members camping by gender and ministry groups, rather than as families, with the discipline of frequent worship, night vigils, Bible study and discussion. Thus the encampments of the *Vapostori* enact a pilgrimage through wilderness in the great drama of God's people that includes the Sinai trek, the retreats of Jesus and the visions of Johane Marange.

'God bless Africa!': night life at a *gungano*

Night vigils are important at a *gungano*, especially for the young people and it is during these *mapungwe* that *Vapostori* walk on and handle fire as a sign of the presence and power of the Holy Spirit. Arriving after dark among the many campfires and the pole-and-grass booths of the Chikomba congregation near Eastern Highlands, I was asked by the first Apostle I met to remove my shoes, for I was now on the holy ground of their *temberi* (temple), and he directed me to a group of about fifteen *vavhangeri*, evangelists dressed in white ritual garments and gathered around a campfire. Presently some prophets appeared in the clearing in the centre of the encampment and arranged themselves beyond the central fire in pairs, with the two in each pair facing each other with enough space for one person to fit between them. These were the 'gates' through which the faithful must pass, confessing their sins and having unconfessed sins discerned by the prophets.[18] Women also wore white, flowing garments, so that the entire assembly was dressed in white. Two long queues formed in the darkness before the gates and people passed through them quickly as they confessed their

---

[18]Confession gates are common in AICs, where the term has been carried over into Shona as *magetsi*. The Zion Apostolic Church has elaborate physical gates in the form of arches that members construct out of bent saplings and decorate with coloured fabrics similar to their own spectacular liturgical garments.

sins and sometimes received direction from the prophets.

Those who had passed through the gates gathered at the great fire, the women on the west side, the men on the east, singing as they convened:

O, we have gathered at Jerusalem – Alleluia, Father!
Ondeya, ondeya, ondeya – The glory of heaven, Father!
You have gathered at Jerusalem – We thank the Father!
Are you happy there at Jerusalem? – Alleluia, the Lord rose!
O, we have gathered at Jerusalem – St John (Marange) was blessed!
O, you have gathered at Jerusalem – The Lord died and rose again![19]

Apostles sit on the ground in a remarkably uniform manner, the women with their legs to one side, the men with knees drawn up and their long staffs resting on one shoulder. Male song directors lead from a standing position, sometimes directing with slow swings of their staffs. Apostolic music, quite unique in tone to this church, avoids drums or rattles on account of their source in SSR, but the young men's percussive hand-to-mouth hooting supplies a strong rhythmic base. The high status of Johane Marange was evident in the plaintive chant that followed:

He came, the king of heaven. Hosanna!
John is the king of heaven. Hosanna!
   (*Johane ndiye mambo wekudenga.*)
We thank him, the king of heaven. Hosanna!
   (*Tinomutenda mambo wekudenga.*)
Remember the king of heaven. Hosanna!
He shall come, the king of heaven. Hosanna!
You loved us, the king of heaven. Hosanna!
Here is the kingdom of angels. Hosanna!
The king of kings of heaven. Hosanna![20]

---

[19] *Pungwe*, Chikomba congregation of AACJM, 12–13 April 1991, Mutemangao. This reference serves for all songs, prayers, and sermons in this section that are not otherwise referenced. *Ondeya* is simply a rhythmic utterance.

[20] The song raises the important question of *Chipostori* christology, which cannot be detailed in this study. AACJM christology is orthodox, but there is a tendency towards Johane Marange being absorbed into the godhead by theological apotheosis. On one hand, I have heard Johane described as 'the sent one' for black people, as Melchizedek, and as 'king of kings'. On the other hand, Apostles constantly invoke Jesus' example, test spirits according to whether they profess Jesus, and in prayer invoke the trinitarian God.

When the three hundred women, men and children had finished confession and gathered, all turned and knelt toward the east with arms raised in the *orans* position, palms facing forward. A young man stood and led the missional and invocational song that Johane received from the Spirit and mandated to open all services:

> Everywhere we see people who do not know Christ,
> They are lost, that is why they sin,
> Our mighty God, send the Holy Spirit to those who do not have it ...
> God bless Africa and hear our prayers, God bless it!
> Come Holy Spirit, come Holy Spirit, come Holy Spirit!
> Bless us, your servants.[21]

After the Lord's Prayer and a song about following Johane Marange, two men stood up, a reader and a preacher, to begin a season of preaching, alternating with singing, on Mark 16:15–17, where the risen Jesus commissions his disciples and speaks of the signs they will be able to perform.[22]

The second preacher's sermon highlighted classic Apostolic themes of mission, spiritual gifts and eschatology, and it is reproduced here in full:

> Peace be to us! (People: Amen!) Peace to those who believe! (Amen!) We have the words at Mark 16, verse 15:
>
> (Reader: 'And he said to them, "Go into all the world and proclaim the good news to the whole creation."') These are the words that were said by Jesus Christ to those people who were there during

---

[21]The latter part of this song became Zimbabwe's first national anthem and has had similar status in South Africa. Known by its first line, *Ishe komborera Afrika*, it was forbidden during the Rhodesian period. The song is said to have been a Methodist hymn, so the Apostles' use may derive from Johane's upbringing. The Apostles are not known for political activism today, but Daneel notes in correspondence that their sermons were nationalistic in the 1960s. Their use of the hymn symbolises the impulse for religious independence that was integral to the political struggle, and it constitutes an enduring witness to the central place of African initiative.

[22]Although Mk 16:9–20 is of ancient provenance, textual and stylistic evidence indicate that it was not part of the original gospel of Mark. Modern English Bibles take pains to inform the reader of such anomalies in the text, but no Shona Bible yet provides marginal notes, so preachers have nothing to alert them to nuances of authenticity and interpretation.

that time, so that they could follow the words of Jesus Christ. It was said, 'Go into the world and preach to all creatures. Anyone who believes what you preach will be saved.' Peace be to us! (People: Amen!)

(Reader reads vs 16: '"The one who believes and is baptised will be saved; but the one who does not believe will be condemned."') Peace be to us! (Amen!) That refers to when you ministers go and travel over all lands, when you arrive and when you preach these words. A person who does not believe in these words will be judged. Peace be to us! (Amen!) So the problem we have in being in the bush like this is to spread the words so that all people, when the world comes to an end, will have heard that God's words are there. Peace be to us! (Amen!) There should not be anyone who would say, 'I did not hear them', because each person knows that the world will come to an end. During Noah's time it happened like that: people refused to build the ark, but when the flood came each and everyone had to cry. This world in which we are today, we know that it will be destroyed by fire (*richaparadzwa nemoto*). And it is true that it will come to an end. Peace be to us! (Amen!) No matter how many riches we gather, no matter how much we accumulate, no matter what families we have, this world will be destroyed by fire. Peace be to us! (Amen!)

(Reader reads vs 17: '"And these signs will accompany those who believe: by using my name they will cast out demons; they will speak in new tongues."') So right now, these signs were given to us who believed. We cast out evil spirits. We do not have alien spirits. We are told of everything that will happen in the next five years by the Holy Spirit (*Mudzimu Unoyera*). Peace be to us! (Amen!) We are being led by the Holy Spirit. John (Marange) was sent and was told, 'Go and teach them to make people repent and whoever believes and is baptised will be saved.' Peace to us Apostles! (Amen!) So this is the problem we have: we children of Africa were told, 'You shall enter the Gehenna of fire.' We shall enter the Gehenna of fire if there are some who will not have believed and understood. Those of Noah's time entered the catastrophe of water. Peace be to us! (Amen!) Those of Moses' time were bitten by cobras, some were swallowed by the earth on account of not heeding Moses. So we have this messenger. We are

166

expecting fire in our destruction. There is no other war or misfortune that we will meet, but we will be destroyed by fire. Peace be to us! (Amen!) The king be honoured forever! (Amen!)[23]

The frequent exclamations of peace assure church members of God's favour and their status as a saved community. Since *Vapostori* consider themselves the only community that God will save at the world's end, the exclamation 'Peace be to us!' is exclusive in its frame of reference.[24] Conversely, the missionary obligation to proclaim the gospel is an absolute imperative, for the entire non-*Chipostori* world must be saved. With clear calls from both Jesus and Johane Marange, the AACJM has mission concern for other countries and peoples which is laid on all Apostles but especially on the baptisers and evangelists, who ordinarily preach. Genuine conversion to Christ entails entering the AACJM, for God accepts no other Christian profession. The Holy Spirit has equipped the Apostles for mission with power to vanquish the evil spirits of SSR and authenticate the AACJM as God's chosen community.[25] Mission is urgent, because the world is about to end in fire, when God will judge unbelief. God's destructive fire is intended for the unbelievers, but if Apostles are slack in evangelism they could

---

[23]In contrast to the MFCs, AACJM sermons are very brief. Day and night services are similar in form, with three sermons at night, six at the daytime sabbath service.

[24]Exclusive claims were explicit in the charge Johane said he was given in heaven: 'If you go and do the Lord's work on earth, whoever does not follow what you say and do it will not come into this temple. All who do not follow my word that I say to you will not enter here in heaven ... Whoever runs away from you has denied salvation and will not be saved. Whoever forms his own congregation is lost, even if he goes and makes people repent and baptises them. If they (followers of a dissident leader) come to you, baptise them, because he is lost in his deeds.' *Umboo hutsva hwavaPostori*. Although aware of my Anglican ordination, evangelists at one *gungano* urged me to receive baptism at their hands, thus becoming 'born again', and to become a missionary of the AACJM in North America.

[25]Mk 16:18, where Jesus promises protection from snakes and poison, was omitted from the scripture reading, probably to deflect attention from practices the Apostles do not seem to follow. However, a non-Apostolic eyewitness recounted to me how prophets called forth two poisonous snakes, a hyena, and two owls – all associated with wizardry – from the river one year at the annual *Paseka* at Macheke and cast them into the fire. Both snake-handling and poison-drinking are practised by some pentecostal groups in the United States.

be consumed, for God might interpret the existence of any unbelievers as a sign that the Apostles have been unfaithful. Apostles have reason to be confident that they will be saved from the catastrophe, but they must avoid complacency.

With such exhortations about spiritual gifts and fire it was not surprising that during the praise song that followed, 'Angels of heaven worship', the young song leader entered into an ecstatic state in which his shoulders and head jerked rapidly and he ran about; he was seized by the Holy Spirit, participants said. The man then walked on the fire with bare feet, stomping hard on the coals and ran about on the ground before entering the fire again. Various people began crying out, reportedly also seized by the Spirit, and there was general excitement. When these manifestations subsided, an evangelist rose to preach on John 3:3, where Jesus speaks of the necessity of being born again, but the scripture reading was abruptly halted by a woman prophet who said she discerned unconfessed sin in the preacher. As all knelt toward the east again, general simultaneous prayer followed, in which a few miscellaneous snatches could be caught:

> Good God, we thank you this evening ...
> We beg for the power of the Holy Spirit this evening ...
> It is you who looks after us day and night, O King ...

A slow, meditative song took over:

> To the Father in heaven, Amen ...
> Jehovah, look after all the people, Alleluia,
> Who believe in you, Lord God.
> Lord God, you are theirs.
> Hosanna! We shall enter into there.
> Jesus Christ, Alleluia, is in heaven.

The service then closed with a final grace and blessing.

Many people stayed on for the ministry of healing with the laying on of hands, which sometimes brought on seizures in the Spirit. Some people then retired to their sleeping booths, while others went to their ministry booths to spend the night in ministry or conversation. Evangelists were available for the confession of sins, prophets for prophecy and so on. Those who slept did so to dream dreams from God. As one evangelist put it,

Some will go sleep and dream dreams of heaven. They will have dreams that will say that such is bad and such is good ... Tomorrow they will tell their dreams. Anyone can dream, so tomorrow when they tell their dreams, others may interpret what they mean.

Joel's prophecy of dreams through the Spirit was cited as scriptural warrant, as were the visions of Johane Marange. Dreaming thus becomes a counterpoint to the motif of sleeplessness in the church's *pungwe,* another opportunity for divine fellowship and communication. For the sleepers as well as for the watchers, night brings God close.

The one group for whom a sleepless *pungwe* is an absolute obligation as well as a desire are the singers, called *maharklos.* At the Mutemangao *gungano* a group of about sixty young people – from teenagers to a few people in their early 30s – gathered by the fire for singing that continued through the rest of the night:

> We have gathered (*taungana*) there at Jerusalem – Alleluia, Lord!
> *Onde, onde, onde!* Hosanna of heaven!
> We thank Johane – Hosanna! Alleluia!
> Look at Jerusalem there!
> We thank Aberu[26] – Hosanna!
> We will follow Johane – Alleluia, Johane!
> Johane was sent – Alleluia, he was sent!
> Alleluia, Father! – Will we see Anrod?[27]
> We will go with Johane – We will go to the Father.
> Apostles, let us go! – O, we go with him, Alleluia!

The song leader jumped continuously up and down in the narrow corridor formed between men and women, spearing the air with his staff. The men hooted continuously, while the women carried the tune and the entire group rocked and swayed. By exhaling noisily and simultaneously jerking a hand toward their faces, some cantors produced a remarkable percussive roaring. Even higher agitation in the Spirit that

---

[26]Aberu was Johane Marange's senior son.

[27]Anrod was Johane Marange's full blood brother who, in concert with Johane's senior son Aberu, took control of the AACJM in the inheritance struggle that followed Johane's death in 1963. Daneel, *Major movements,* 333–339.

Evangelists of the Marange Apostles gather under their *musasa* at a *gungano* at Murara in the Honde Valley. Ernest Mutasa is in the foreground; research assistant Leon Semu (with unshaved head) is seated on the right

Marange Apostle walks on fire at a *gungano* at Murara. As in most Shona churches, women and men sit and stand in separate groups

In fever-pitch excitement in the pre-dawn period of *mambakwedza,* one of the *maharklos* at a Marange Apostolic *gungano* at Mutemangao in the Honde Valley grasps a burning log in his hands ...

... then presses in on his shaved head. He later put it in his mouth

broke out about 2 am issued in a number of *maharklos* walking on the large fire stoked with tree trunks. In apostolic practice, individuals walk on the fire with bare feet, neither lingering nor rushing, but passing over in a leisurely fashion from which one would expect serious burns. On this occasion, some went further. One ecstatic standing in the fire picked up two burning coals and held them in his hands as he danced in the corridor of the singing group. Another put a burning stick two inches thick into his mouth and danced. Another pressed a burning log down onto his bald head. Not only was no one burned, but firewalkers' garments were not singed. While the *maharklos* sang in the *temberi,* other ministry groups preached, taught and healed around fires on the outskirts, and firewalking occurred there as well. At dawn, those who were still awake or recently roused gathered for a short prayer service.[28]

'God walks at night!': interpretations of night worship

The missional power of the Apostles' night vigils is supported by an especially robust theology of night and of the fires they kindle and walk on at night. Apostles' interpret night meetings on the basis of biblical precedent in the life of Jesus and their experience of evil spirits.

Jesus is central in the Apostles' spirituality of night worship:

> The idea of praying during the night came from Jesus Christ. Jesus Christ went with his disciples at night. For instance, when he went to Gethsemane, he went at night and told his disciples to pray. There we see that he prayed during the night, so we also can pray during the night. We follow the custom of Jesus.[29]

Some incidents in Jesus' life are projected into night-time:

> When Jesus was born, he went to the temple in Jerusalem where the high priests and the scribes were. They discussed questions together with him at night and honoured their God. Night is a good time for honouring God and moreover it shows love. At twelve years old Jesus was asking questions with the chief priests at

---

[28]The absence of firewalking in Harvey Cox's vignette of an AACJM vigil suggests an unusual gathering or limited field observation. *Fire from heaven: the rise of Pentecostal spirituality and the reshaping of religion in the twenty-first century* (Reading, Mass: Addison-Wesley, 1994), 243–245.

[29]SaMajaro, evangelists interview, 19–20 April 1991.

night. He was talking about the greatness of God, and he spoke with love. Likewise, we have not received a plan that we should meet in the afternoon only, but that we should honour our God at all times, night and day. This shows love.[30]

On the basis of Luke 6:12–16, the establishment of the Marange Apostles themselves is regarded as occurring in Jesus' nocturnal prayers:

Now that is where the *foundation* of us Apostles is, in the footsteps of Jesus Christ. (This is the foundation) that he asked from God and for which he spent the whole night praying. That is the *foundation* we have that we are the true apostles, that we be seen to be following the true footsteps of Jesus Christ. We are the apostles. Jesus went on until dawn, through the whole night (*Jesu akayedzerwa usiku hwese*), that he might search for the word 'apostles'. When he called the disciples, the word 'apostles' (*vapostori*) was not there. That is what we ask for in worshipping, that we worship as true apostles, who know that we are following the true steps of Jesus Christ.[31]

Influenced by SSR's belief that evil spirits circulate at night, Apostles cultivate receptivity to God's power at night. They project Jesus' historical exorcising activity into the night and see God as travelling at night, ready to do battle with evil:

Many times Jesus used to work at night; that is when the alien spirits used to come out. They did not usually come out during the day, but they usually came out at night. Moreover, it is easier to do something at night because you will not tire or want to rest as you do in the afternoon. God makes everything easier at night. That is when the power of God is there. That is when God walks, because the demons also come out at night. The real power of God is at night. Alien spirits also travel at night, which means that the power of Satan is also there at night. The power of God and the power of Satan are equal.[32]

---

[30]SaNyeredzo, evangelists interview, 12–13 April 1991.
[31]Ernest Mutasa, evangelists interview, 19–20 April 1991. SaGogodi (ibid) extended the argument to the startling conclusion, 'Jesus was an Apostle' (*Jesu aiva Mupostori*).
[32]Sa Chimbuwa, evangelists interview, 12–13 April 1991.

Here all the latent themes of the religious *pungwe* become explicit. Night is the time of supernatural encounter in SSR, and Christians are called to continuous struggle against the spirits of SSR. God is abroad at night to help God's people do battle with those spiritual powers. Prayer at night is therefore especially powerful, and night is an especially good time to fight the spirits that must be cast out.

On the side of praise rather than battle, the *maharklos* are thought to enact in their all-night singing the eternal praises of God's angels in heaven: 'Most of the time at night is spent in singing. In heaven there are angels that sing "Hosanna" time and again. In the worshipping that we do, singing for God is great worship.'[33] One leader specifically charged the *maharklos,* 'Sing until it dawns outside', and he declared that anyone who disturbed their singing would have to appear before the prophets for discipline. The *maharklos* unite the Apostles on earth with the praises of the apostolic company of heaven.[34]

'God is fire!': interpretations of fire-walking

Night and fire are linked by the fact that Apostles kindle ritual fires only at night, so fire-walking occurs only at night. Fire itself functions as an icon of God's presence that recapitulates one of the pre-eminent appearances of God in Hebrew scripture, the burning bush seen by Moses:

> We have an observation about whenever the Holy Spirit is sent, as from the time of Moses. When Moses spoke with God he saw a bush burning. God's word comes through fire (*Shoko raMwari rinoburikidze mumoto*). God is fire, if we are explaining it (*Mwari moto kana tichidudzira*), because Moses saw a burning bush. The word said, 'Moses, take off your shoes, for the place on which you are standing is holy.' There was no person, but fire was burning. So that is where our *foundation* is, that if we are worshipping God we are obligated to have a fire. Because it was said, 'Take off your

---

[33]Philip Moda, evangelists interview, 12–13 April 1991.

[34]The name *maharklos* is said to have been given by the Holy Spirit, and it has no evident roots in Shona or the biblical languages. A speculation: as a boy at the Methodist mission, Marange probably sang in English the Christmas carol, '*Hark,* the herald angels sing!'; possibly, he associated the word 'hark' with angelic singers and so named the church's singers.

shoes', we take off our shoes, as you see. If we look at the scripture, when shoes were to be taken off a bush was burning.[35]

'God is fire!' – the connection between fire and the divine cannot be stated more strongly. Since the Apostles kindle ritual fires only at night, night becomes a sacred time of privileged experience and special revelation. Apostles see many biblical precedents linking fire with particular aspects of God's presence: God's righteousness when Moses received the law at fiery Mt Sinai (Exodus 19:16–18); the visionary gift in a prophet's vision of fires (Ezekiel 1:4–14); the Holy Spirit's anointing of apostles in tongues of fire at Pentecost (Acts 2:1–11); and John the Baptist's prophecy that the Coming One would baptise with the Holy Spirit and with fire (Luke 4:16–17). Johane Marange's visionary identification with the Baptist links the God-fire-Jesus-Spirit complex of scripture with the mission of the church's founder. Moreover, Marange himself set the example. The day after his pivotal vision, he 'surprised a party of beer drinkers at Mazodza's village. In an effort to convince them of his calling he stepped into a fire and did not get burnt.'[36] Ability to handle fire was the competitive mode of legitimation between Johane and one of his lieutenants, Ruka Mataruka, in the schism that occurred between them in the 1940s, and Marange won by demonstrating that even his Bible and liturgical garments could withstand being burned in a fire.[37]

Biblical images appear to have been the decisive influence in Marange's theology and practice of fire, for there is no known antecedent in the founder's experience, and, indeed, its uniqueness may have been attractive.[38] Fire-handling was also another way to con-

---

[35]Ernest Mutasa, evangelists interview, 19–20 April 1991.

[36]Daneel, *Major movements*, 322.

[37]Ibid, 332. St Luca's Apostolic Ejuwel Jekenishen Church, the church founded by Ruka Mataruka in 1932, does not promote walking on or handling fire, but does use fiery logs in chasing away demons. Explained a prophet, 'The burning log is strengthened by the Holy Spirit, so that when an evil spirit sees it, the spirit flees for fear of being burned'. *Pungwe*, SLAEJC, EHTE congregation, 30 April-1 May 1991, Buwu.

[38]The practice had not appeared in other AICs in Rhodesia, such as the Zion Christian Church. It is not known whether Johane had any exposure to fire-walking among AICs in the Lower Congo from 1920 to 1930. Jules-Rosette, *African Apostles*, 84. For a non-Christian parallel today among the Kung people of Botswana, see Richard Katz, *Boiling energy: community healing among the Kalahari Kung* (Cambridge, Mass, and London: Harvard University Press, 1982), 120, 122.

front SSR, where fires generally are not lit during the nocturnal rites because the spirits are reputed to dislike smoke and the image of fire in dreams at night is an omen of injury, death, or some other misfortune. Thus, in embracing fire Apostles manifest a superior power that enables them to conquer destructive spiritual forces as conceptualised by SSR. That power, of course, is the Holy Spirit, whose presence in the individual and in the group is verified by firewalking:

> The power of the Holy Spirit (enables people) to step on or hold fire without being burned. So these signs were sent in Johane Marange so that he would come and show the power of the Holy Spirit on the earth.[39]

Apostles believe that Christian history is culminating today in an 'age of the Spirit':

> We have three stages. If we say, 'In the name of the Father', that's the ancient time of the Old Testament in the time of Abraham; 'and of the Son', that's the time of Jesus, when he was here on earth; and now we are in the last stage, 'and of the Holy Spirit'. That's the period we are in now. That's why you see our church is mostly led by the Holy Spirit.[40]

Members of other Shona churches often doubt reports of fire-walking, but even those who credit the reports wonder whether it is by the power of some other spirits, not the Holy Spirit, that the Apostles handle fire.[41] *Vapostori* acknowledge that evil spirits can imitate the Holy Spirit's signs, just as Pharaoh's seers matched Moses' signs, but they insist that profession of Jesus is the crucial criterion:

> The one who has God's Spirit steps on the fire and speaks in tongues and in the end says, 'Jesus Christ' – that is when we know that it is the Spirit of Jesus. That which is not of Jesus will not say, 'Jesus Christ'. Some just say, 'D-r-r-r-r' and cry, shedding tears – then we know it is the spirit of a demon.[42]

---

[39]SaManhare, evangelists interview, 12–13 April 1991.

[40]Philip Moda, evangelists interview, 12–13 April 1991.

[41]For instance, a Zion Apostolic Church member asserted that the Marange Apostles' fire-walking contravenes Deut 18:9–10, which proscribes anyone 'who makes a son or daughter pass through fire'; he charged that fire-walking is a type of wizardry arising from Chivanhu. Sheadman Mupinda, interview, 17 April 1991.

[42]SaNyeredzo, evangelists interview, 12–13 April 1991.

Fire as the instrument of God's judgment is what brings the Apostles' nocturnal fire-handling into sharpest focus. They cite many biblical references: John's panorama of the earth's destruction, a final judgment and fire for the wicked (Revelation 20:11–14);[43] Jesus' numerous predictions of judgment by fire;[44] the fiery judgment of Sodom and Gomorra (Genesis 19:24–28); and the fire that consumed complaining Hebrews in the wilderness (Numbers 11:1–3). Specific testing by fire is warranted by the fiery refining and testing in Zechariah 13:9 and exemplified by Daniel's companions walking in the fiery furnace (Daniel 3:19–30). Paul expects church leaders' work to be tested by fire (1 Corinthians 3:12–15). It is clear that, however literalist the Apostles' hermeneutic of fire may appear, they have not magnified a peripheral biblical image but have built on a theme that plays a major role in many parts of Jewish and Christian scripture.

With fiery judgment imminent, preparation is crucial. Those who will be tried by fire must first practice with fire:

> One who has entered into this fire, he will not burn, even at the end of the world. When we light a fire we are doing a practice so that when the fire comes, (we will be able to answer the question,) 'Can we (withstand it)?' This world will burn. Now those who are not righteous will burn like husks.[45]

While prophets and *maharklos* make a habit of handling and walking on fire, virtually every baptised Apostle is expected to walk on fire at least once in a lifetime as a test of purity and fitness for judgment. Apostles believe that when they walk on fire without being burned God is confirming their righteousness and, therefore, their acceptability at the time of judgment:

> Those stepping on the fire will not get burned. If you are righteous, at the end of the world we will enter fire, but you will not be burned. If you have a sin you will not walk on the fire, because you will be burned by it and your garment will be burned.[46]

---

[43]Other passages cited for their emphasis on fiery judgment include Mal 4:1 and Rev 20:7–10; 21:8. One preacher assumed that Patmos, the island on which the writer of Revelation was exiled, was an 'island of fire'.

[44]Mt 5:22; 7:19; 13:40–50; 18:9; 25:41; Mk 9:43–49; Lk 12:49; 17:28–30; Jn 15:6.

[45]SaMuura, evangelists interview, 12–13 April 1991.

[46]Ibid.

Trial by fire brings symbolically, even sacramentally, the eschatological judgment into the present. The Apostles anticipate it, enact it and undergo it in a way that appears severe by ordinary standards but that the Apostles regard as modest when compared with the coming great conflagration.

A need and desire to clarify one's moral standing in relationship is a universal human impulse that people express in their relationships with supernatural beings. Among the Shona people, and perhaps among other African peoples as well, this impulse is especially strong and explicit. We have seen how SSR encourages belief that personal moral agency not only shapes personal relationships but also causes events such as illness and misfortune through spiritual influence. Clarifying relationships is an intrinsic function of religious ritual, and SSR's entire system of ritual divination is directed to discerning, articulating and clarifying spiritual influences and to resolving the relational conflicts that they provoke. The Marange Apostles explicitly reject that system in favour of obedience to the triune God as expressed in biblical norms. Fire-walking at *mapungwe* tests purity and verifies obedience through an extreme means, even for the Shona context. Some Shona people choose it to express their need for moral clarification when their religious scruples proscribe divination. When the ancestor and the diviner have no role, moral status is communicated directly by the Holy Spirit through a public ordeal that demonstrates conclusively where one stands with God. Handling fire thus contextualises a Shona religious and cultural sensibility in Shona Christianity.

The Apostles' theology that brings together the themes of God, spiritual warfare, night, the Holy Spirit, righteousness, fire and the end time is coherent and well reasoned within their literalist interpretation of scripture. A step-by-step summary follows. Righteousness is the call that God issues to God's people. Those who would follow Jesus must be righteous, and righteousness will be the criterion of acceptance by God in Christ for eternity. At the final judgment, God will use the simple test of fire, which will function as the discerning word of God, for fire has always revealed God. If one wishes to live with God eternally, one will need to withstand that fire, for the sinful will be consumed by fire in the judgment, but the righteous will survive. That judgment is very near, and God's people must prepare for it. The faithful prepare by gathering at night. Night is a time of testing, for the powers arrayed against God and against God's people are especially active at night. Night is also the time when God's presence is especially near and powerful. At night, God's people kindle the holy fire of God's presence, and God pours out the Holy Spirit on them, just as God has always done through fire. Handling and walking on fire helps God's people prepare for the end, for these practices test whether they are truly righteous and whether they have received the Holy Spirit. If they are not burned, God is reassuring them as righteous bearers of the Holy Spirit. If they are burned, they know they must amend their lives while there is still time before the end.

The Marange Apostles' theology and practice of fire at night vigils appears bizarre not only to Western Christians but to many Shona Christians as well. It is, however, a salient feature of their life, and I testify personally to its magnetism. I suggest that the practice is a principal feature in the missional power by which this church has become the largest AIC in Zimbabwe and the country's second largest single ecclesial body.

A church for women: the Pentecostal Apostolic Church of God

The Pentecostal Apostolic Church of God (PACG) is a new AIC with several distinctives: it was founded by a woman, it continues to be led by women prophets, and its mission focuses on liberating women afflicted by the spirits of murdered men who come back to claim a woman from the family of the murderer. The church's ministries of prophecy, exorcism and healing climax in the group's *mapungwe,* especially when church members go out to meet God in the wilderness.

'You have gathered': from prophet to church

In contrast to the maturity of the Marange movement, the Pentecostal Apostolic Church of God is in an earlier stage of growth and development, during which the founding prophet continues to be the energising source of its identity and activity. The PACG exemplifies the rapid growth of a new African-initiated mission movement and the centrality of the *pungwe* in its formative period.

Mbuya Maunganidze, the founding prophet, was born as Beulah in

Mbuya Maunganidze (centre), founder of the Pentecostal Apostolic Church of God. Her chief assistant, Violet Mushunje, kneels on the left

PACG members sent out to pray in small groups are visited by Prophet Evelyn Mhlambo during a wilderness *pungwe*

about 1935 to Isaac and Lucia Mashita, poor agricultural labourers at Odzi, west of Mutare. The family held membership in the Apostolic Faith Mission (AFM), a pentecostal group from South Africa that began work in Rhodesia in 1918. Very early in her life Beulah had a dramatic spiritual experience that propelled her into ministry:

> I myself began doing God's work when I was seven years of age. When I was born there was the Faith Apostolic Church. My father used to live on a farm at Odzi. That year (of my call) I was not yet going to school. I then started going to school, and that is when we saw (AFM) Apostles baptising people at the Jordan (in the Odzi River). We went there to look; we were many. Now while I was staring like that, I was just seized (*ndakangobatwa*) by the power of the Spirit. I don't know how it happened. I was lifted up (*ndakasumudzwa*), then plunged in the water where they were baptising. The elder who was baptising was called Joel. This Joel then baptised me when I was seven years old. I then began to be seized with the great power of the Holy Spirit. Continuing in the Faith Apostolic, I then ministered in it until I was married and had my own house, doing only God's work.[47]

The young Beulah attended school up to Standard 6 (Grade 8) and for a short period she taught kindergarten. As her ministry became more focused in prophecy – understood as the discernment of spirits, sin, the future and the causes of illness – conflict arose with the Faith Apostolic Mission:

> Then I began prophesying (*kuprofita*) and seeing hidden things and healing the sick and catching those with evil spirits doing things like wizardry. In the ministry I used to do we failed to agree with the Faith Apostolic about the fact that they did not want me to be doing what I used to do, removing evil spirits. They said, 'Stop casting out evil spirits.' That is when I began living here, healing people. I said I did not want (to found) a church, I only

---

[47]Mbuya Maunganidze, interview, 22 April 1991. Beulah's conversion occurred in a period of ferment in Shona Christianity that included the Zionist initiatives of the 1920s and the movements begun in the early 1930s by Johane Marange, Ruka Mataruka (founder of the Jekenishen Church), and Elijah Mugodhi (founder of the Unity of African Apostolic Faith Church). This study's discussion of the PACG is the first account of the church by an outsider.

wanted to heal ... There were white leaders; I have just forgotten their names; I did not talk with them. I only talked with the blacks. They are the ones with whom I disagreed, the ones who were saying, 'Stop.' I said, 'All right. I was given a gift by God when I was still small. It is impossible that I stop, but I will live praying for people at my house.' I then stayed here, praying for people.[48]

In 1956 she married David Machare Johns of Odzi, who was descended from Scottish as well as Shona forebears and who had been adopted by a Roman Catholic from India. Johns worked as a transport overseer with the roads department, and in 1957 the couple moved to the Florida section of Mutare. The growth of Beulah's ministry prompted calls for a church to organise around her:

A great many people repented and were healed. Some who had no children were given children. The blind saw. So these people then said, 'We would like to establish our own church.' That is when this Church of Pentecostal Apostolic began. We then established our many *branches*.[49]

The new church emerged around 1960 and Beulah adopted the name Mbuya Maunganidze, meaning 'Grandmother, you have gathered together.'[50] As she and her husband brought up their three children, the comfortable home they bought in 1959 also functioned as Mbuya's healing centre and soon the church's headquarters.

Mission to distant places was an early focus of Mbuya's ministry, with the result that there are at least twenty-five PACG congregations in Zimbabwe today, including all of the country's major cities, with additional congregations in Zambia, Mozambique and South Africa. The 15 000 members estimated by church leaders represent a considerable achievement, as would a figure half as high. Healing is central in Mbuya Maunganidze's view of her mission outreach:

I do not stay here much. Many times I travel outside the country;

---

[48]Ibid. The issue of prophecy prompted many breakaways from the AFM. Costa Matunia, interview, 24 April 1991.

[49]Mbuya Maunganidze, interview, 22 April 1991.

[50]Some church members understand the name in terms of her leading a group of people she has gathered, while others believe it refers to her collecting and burning materials used in wizardry. Another name members use is Mutumwa, which means 'sent one; messenger'.

I go and I come back. Just now I wanted to go to England; that is where my child is, the *number-two girl*; she was married there. But it happened that I went to Johannesburg, in South Africa; I itinerate there, doing prayers ... I go there to pray and come back to sleep at the hotel. I will be having some people (with me); at times we will be twelve. I have helpers with whom I work. I work alone on some complicated diseases and on making the blind see. If God's power comes, those who have BP (blood pressure) or asthma (will be healed). We work on all such diseases without using injections.[51]

Financial support comes from members' regular contributions and from special thanksgiving gifts made by persons who have been healed.

Responding to the sharp increase in orphans resulting from the Aids epidemic and the Mozambican civil war, the PACG has an orphanage mission that is being institutionalised on the model of MFC institutions. The present 40 orphans are housed at the healing centre and another property, but church leaders have established the Beulah Johns Organisation, which is charged with constructing an orphanage for two hundred children. The 1993 proposal for the US$400 000 project persuaded the Mutare City Council to sell 3,75 acres of municipal land to the church.[52] Also on the MFC model, the church has built a large cathedral in Mutare.

The church's story in the Honde Valley illustrates how its mission of healing and women's liberation attracts new members and promotes rapid growth. Until the late 1980s Ezekiel and Evelyn Mhlambo were leaders of the African Methodist Episcopal Church (AMEC) congregation at Hamudikuwanda, a small hamlet near their home at Pimai.[53] The Mhlambos moved to the PACG when Mbuya Maunganidze healed their son Abel's abdominal illness after neither the AMEC congregation nor conventional western medicine could heal him. In 1990 they established the Pentecostal Apostolics' Pungwe Branch, named for the river,

---

[51]Mbuya Maunganidze, interview, 22 April 1991.

[52]I S Munyame, acting town clerk, City of Mutare, to Organising Secretary, Pentecostal Apostolic Church of God, 4 August 1993, TLS, photocopy.

[53]The AMEC has roots in the American church of the same name (which entered Zimbabwe in 1900), but in South Africa and Zimbabwe it became an AIC of the Ethiopian type.

with ten members meeting in a thatched shelter about fifty metres away from the AMEC. By 1991 the PACG congregation had grown to about 200, some coming from other churches and many from non-Christian backgrounds, while the AMEC next door languished. The dynamic leadership of Evelyn Mhlambo, whom Mbuya chose to be chief prophet and healer for the Honde, and the church's focus on avenging spirits attract so many young women that by 1994 the Pungwe Branch had grown to 400 members, with 380 women and 20 men. It had also started two additional congregations for a total Honde membership of 700. Frequent evangelistic *mapungwe* spur much of the growth, assisted by regular visits by Mbuya Maunganidze from Mutare.

Festival and wilderness vigils in the PACG

Mission activism marks Pentecostal Apostolic life strongly, and night vigils are inherent in virtually every initiative of the church, from exorcism to building construction, from general revival to planting new congregations. The PACG uses *mapungwe* to combat spirit adversaries, purify the community, build solidarity, celebrate church festivals and conduct evangelistic outreach.

Evangelism is highlighted when Mbuya Maunganidze travels among her congregations, where she invariably holds *mapungwe* to gather the people, cast out evil spirits and attract new members. The church's uncommonly explicit invitation to the public is distilled in a large cloth banner lettered in English (for urban dwellers) and hung at the *pungwe* site:

The Pentecostal Miracle Gospel Crusade: Welcomes You!
To the great miracles of God during these precious end-times of
God's appointed hour of salvation.
The blind see! The deaf hear! The crippled will walk again!

The banner attracted considerable attention in the Honde Valley for Mbuya's Easter (*Paseka*) visit to the Pungwe Branch. A *pungwe* was held on Friday, the first night of the revival, and this was followed by a large outdoor communion service on Saturday afternoon that continued into a *pungwe* on Saturday night. The founder's visit for the annual *Paseka* included the year's only offering of the Lord's Supper, so many of the 400 people attending were church members, identifiable by various age- and gender-based vestments, but there were at least 50 visitors.

184

In the pre-dawn period of *mambakwedza* at a wilderness *pungwe,* prophet
Evelyn Mhlambo wrestles with an afflicted woman in the process of
exorcising a *chikwambo* spirit from her

Worshippers sing at an outside Mugodhi Church *pungwe* at the Chitambo
kraal at the southern end of the Honde Valley

The mass laying-on of hands Mbuya conducted outdoors Saturday afternoon was characteristic of the church's pentecostal ministry of exorcism and healing:

> The laying-on of hands by Mbuya Maunganidze was offered as she worked her way down a line of people. Sometimes she would pace up and down before starting in, and she began to work up a sweat in the warm, humid air. She carried a staff in her left hand, and she would place her right hand firmly on the head or forehead of a person, sometimes with some words – inaudible in the uproar – sometimes not. Clearly the expected effect of this procedure was that people would fall back, for a rank of people stood behind the line ready to catch people as they fell. Practically everyone did fall down backwards. Some lay still with their eyes closed after they were laid on the ground by attendants, in which case they would lie for a minute or so before coming to, as it were, and getting up, sometimes with the help of an attendant. Others would manifest signs of ecstasy or spirit possession: their bodies shaking, their heads shaking violently from side to side, limbs shaking; sounds included a simple glottal perseveration, shouts, glossalalia and the like. If this seemed especially violent or if it persisted for an extended period of time, the person would be taken into the care of one of the leaders. With the constant singing at a high volume, most of the vast crowd joining in, with the considerable activity at the front, with people surging forward and others being dragged off, and with Mbuya Maunganidze in constant concentrated motion, the scene was not far off pandemonium. Yet at the same time it was quite orderly in that everyone knew what was expected and what course things would take. The third class of response to the laying-on of hands, equally important, was persons who clearly had not felt very affected by the anointing, who either did not fall down at all or who awkwardly threw themselves into the waiting arms behind them and who then cooperatively sat or lay on the ground for awhile before getting up and departing the immediate scene.[54]

[54]From author's research journal. Unlike the Marange Apostles, the PACG does not require its members to rely on spiritual healing alone. Medical care in clinics and hospitals is tolerated, although some frown on it. Ezekiel Mhlambo, church leaders interview, PACG, 30 March 1991.

Such public settings facilitate the evangelistic outreach Mbuya says she intends: 'When I see visitors, my heart honours God. Relatives (in Christ), this is the message that we want our worship and our welcoming of visitors to convey – that God is truly there.'[55]

Daytime services, however, are preludes to the serious nocturnal work of a *pungwe*:

> After the communion we went to what is called *General Treatment* this afternoon. Everyone has been *treated,* but in the evening we will have *special cases* of those who are very ill, those with demons – all those will be given *special attention.*[56]

During the *pungwe* that followed, Mbuya and her assistants worked intensively with people they believed were afflicted by demons and, in particular, *zvikwambo,* the avenging spirits of murder victims. Exorcism occurs by day as well as by night, but the spirits' habits focus the ministry at night:

> Evil spirits are more *active* during the night time *than during the day.* That is when you will see a person who is asleep appear to be choked by the neck – those are some *actions* of evil spirits. So, observing the way evil spirits come out during the day and at night, we find that at night they are *easier* (to detect) than in the afternoon ... Evil spirits mostly visit people during the night, often when someone is asleep. So that is the time when we fight against them, casting out the evil spirits.[57]

Theologically, the major preacher of the night, SaMukasi of the church's central committee in Mutare, confronted SSR by way of the difference between what he termed the 'good resurrection' (*kumuka kwakanaka*) available in Christ and the 'bad resurrection' (*kumuka kwakaipa*) of the ancestral spirits. He contrasted the Christians' faithfulness in attending the *pungwe* with the involvement of others in SSR:

---

[55]Easter communion service, Pungwe Branch of PACG, 30 March 1991, Hamudikuwanda.

[56]Ezekiel Mhlambo, church leaders interview, PACG, 30 March 1991. Italicised words reproduce English words the speaker interspersed in his Shona.

[57]SaMukasi and SaNemutenzi, church leaders interview, PACG, 30 March 1991.

In God's will you have been chosen by God to come and gather at the Pungwe (Branch) and spend the whole night worshipping and praying, spending the whole (Easter long-weekend) holiday, giving ourselves to God, giving our spirits to God, because we know that we are living in him. At this time, some people are fighting with (ritual) axes, someone is on the way from the diviner-healer's to hear why his younger brother's child died unexpectedly, but we have come to remember his (Christ's) resurrection and to wait for his resurrection ... I have said that I want us to learn together about good resurrection and bad resurrection. The good resurrection is that we are expecting our Lord Jesus to rise.[58]

To demonstrate 'bad resurrection', Mukasi detailed the story of a family near his village who invoked the spirit of a dead relative but fled in terror when the *mudzimu* actually appeared. Christ's resurrection, he said, has prepared for them a place of peace in heaven, from where they will never need to wander and trouble their descendants.

Energising the *pungwe* phenomenon in all Christian churches is people's expectation that they will meet God most immediately and powerfully beyond the ordinary and routine, on the edges of human experience, where people have pressed themselves to an extremity. Going to an actual wilderness place emphasises this dimension by adding fasting, travel and isolation to the theme of sleeplessness. Two interrelated expressions are used: *Kuenda kumasowe* means 'to go to the wilderness', on the model of the people of Israel, John the Baptist and Jesus;[59] while *kuenda kugomo* means 'to go to the mountain', with biblical antecedents in Moses, Elijah and Jesus. In Manicaland's rural and mountainous terrain Christians can bring wilderness and mountain together in their pilgrimage.

---

[58]*Pungwe*, PACG, 30–31 March 1991, Hamudikuwanda.

[59]The provenance of the word *masowe* is unclear, but it is a technical term of AICs. Shona versions of the Bible use the word *renje* for wilderness. Hannan defines *masowe* as 'Uninhabited part of country to which people (eg *vapostori*) retire for a penitential fast' and speculates that the term was derived from Massah, the wilderness place where the Hebrews asked for water and thereby 'tested the Lord' (Ex 17:7). Hannan, sv. The word was popularised by Johane Masowe, a messianic figure who around 1932 retired to the Marimba Mountains for a few days and returned to present himself as Johane Masowe, John the Baptist from the Wilderness. Sundkler, *Bantu prophets*, 324.

Going to the wilderness is central to Pentecostal Apostolic practice, with most of its night vigils involving treks to mountainous and deserted places. The PACG, along with some other AICs, thus differs from MFCs, which hold *mapungwe* in their regular meeting places, whether church or classroom, and from the Marange Apostles, who hold vigils at their *misasa*. Mbuya Maunganidze strongly encourages the practice, taking the lead in organising extended wilderness stays of up to two weeks.[60] When the Hamudikuwanda congregation wished to construct a church building, Mbuya directed the group to hold midweek *mapungwe* on five different mountains over five weeks in order to facilitate discernment, purify intentions and test resolve. The final *pungwe* on Dombomupunga Mountain, reached in darkness after a climb of almost two hours, was a classic example of PACG *pungwe* practice with serial confession, individual desert time, prayer litanies and exorcism of *zvikwambo*. The meeting place, which church members call 'Paradise', is an unusually stony and desolate spot, well beyond any human habitation and overlooking the darkness of Mozambique to the east, where a full-scale civil war was raging at the time.

Confessional scrutiny and purity is intensified in the PACG by multiplying the 'gates' by six: each member must confess to five prophets in succession and then, finally, to the chief prophet before entering the meeting place. While the 100 women, men and children crowded to pass through fifteen prophets, most of them women, a women's choir sang about the task at hand:

> Come, let us confess to the Father,
> and let us be righteous.
> Confess and go to Paradise.

---

[60]During the 1991–92 drought congregations in Masvingo Province held many all-night vigils on mountains: 'From several holy mountains supplications for rain went up. In towns and in rural areas IC (independent church) members could be seen regularly on their pilgrimages to these mountains ... At least once a week each congregation ascends the holy mountain. Many hold all-night vigils.' Solomon Zvanaka, 'Mountain vigil', in *Annual report: June 1992–July 1993*, of the Zimbabwean Institute of Religious Research and Ecological Conservation (ZIRRCON). Hezekiel Mafu documents several movements that ally or fuse SSR and Christianity in responding to the crisis. 'The 1991–92 Zimbabwean drought and some religious reactions', *Journal of Religion in Africa* 25 (3) (August 1995), 288–308.

189

We have waited to go to the Father.
Mothers, come,
Confess and be righteous.
Come, we are going to Jerusalem.
Jesus is coming,
He is coming with power.
Let us confess and be saved.[61]

Improvised stanzas highlighted various sins to confess: murder, wizardry, gossip, adultery, theft and so on. Participating in the exercise myself, I was quite edified by it, for it required me to delve more deeply into my life than I might in a single confession, and the prophets' assurances of forgiveness were correspondingly deeply cleansing. As in other AICs, prophets sometimes detect unconfessed sin:

> Last month when we came up here one woman did not confess all her sins. She got so sick she almost died, but then we prayed for her ... She revealed that she practices witchcraft. She was denounced in the presence of everyone, and I said, 'You are now suffering because you have not said this and this and that.' Thus, anyone who has come here has come prepared that he or she has not got anything that would make him or her suffer such consequences. However, that woman has continued coming to church.[62]

When, after over an hour, all had confessed and gathered around a large fire, Mai Mhlambo introduced the night's work – 'to talk with God, to be healed and to be given various gifts' – and the *pungwe* was under way with songs, sermons and prayers.

As the PACG intensifies the confessional pattern of AICs, it also intensifies the wilderness experience by sending individual participants out to pray alone during the *pungwe*. Several times during the night Mai Mhlambo walked among the group during a hymn and touched individuals as a signal that they should move out to the flat, open area and pray alone, and when they were dispersed she would move among them with prayer and counsel. This unique practice individualises the

<hr/>

[61]*Pungwe*, wilderness mountain vigil, PACG, 8–9 May 1991, Dombomupunga. Subsequent quotations from this event are not further referenced.
[62]Ezekiel Mhlambo, interview, 8 May 1991.

wilderness experience, pushing each adult to encounter God alone and providing individual pastoral care in the all-night communal experience. Equally unusual, Mai Mhlambo at one point dispersed people in groups of five to go and pray. With such ritual flexibility, the wilderness night becomes a setting where people engage their spirituality in a variety of modes: individually, in small groups and in the assembled congregation.

Long litanies of prayer to invoke God's power in the church's mission outreach distinguish the PACG's *masowe* from the night vigils of other churches. With the group standing or kneeling eastward, the leader bids the group pray for a certain concern, and at the leader's concluding 'Alleluia!' everyone bursts loudly into individual prayer, which the leader brings to a close with another Alleluia!' that signals the start of another bidding. Focusing group prayer while affirming individual intercession, three or four litanies can be called in a single night, each of them up to 45 minutes long, with such biddings as the followings:

> Let us pray for our preachers. We want learned preachers. Let us pray to God for guidance. Let us all fast regularly, for this is a blessed mountain. Alleluia!

> Let us pray for our fellow Christians who have backslid, so that they will hear God's calling and return. Let us pray to God that more people will become Pentecost Christians, so that by Christmas our number will have doubled. Alleluia!

> Let us ask for power from God so that the world will come to know God through healed people. Alleluia!

> Let us pray for those who pull in the opposite direction from others, so that God will punish them. Let us pray for the Holy Spirit. We must pray for our own needs also, for God to help us. Pray for gifts to touch where it pains you and God will heal and help. Let us pray for the gifts of healing, preaching and singing. Alleluia!

Another litany at Dombomupunga had five biddings: family life in homes, faithful prayer in families, protection of children from harmful influences, the need for a permanent church building and strength to resist sleep during the *pungwe*, 'that we not be like Peter, who could not watch'. Two seasons of prayer ended with ecstatic dancing around the fire.

The *pungwe* came to a climax in a full-scale confrontation with *zvikwambo* between 3:30 and 4:30 am, precisely the pre-dawn time, *mambakwedza,* when many people expect spirits to come forth with special intensity. Preachers had been alluding to evil spirits abroad, and now Mai Mhlambo opened the exorcisms with a thematic song:

> Sicknesses will end
>> In the name of the Father.
> Demons will come out
>> In the name of the Father.

For the exorcisms, ten or fifteen participants gathered expectantly in a line, while others stood to the side, singing strenuously. The prophet moved down a line of about 15 women, attending to each member while others stood aside singing. Shouting as she worked, Mai Mhlambo commanded the evil spirits to come out and go elsewhere as she called on God's power and asked Jesus and the Holy Spirit to free supplicants from disease and harassment. She rubbed and shook supplicants' heads and sometimes slung their bodies roughly from side to side. Reactions included falling down in a trance, speaking in tongues, running off into the bush shouting with hands aloft, and remaining unaffected in any visible way. The general frenzy was interpreted as the coming out of evil spirits, including *zvikwambo* both new and returning, who were more than matched by the manifestations of the Holy Spirit. When the group settled down again, the *pungwe* ended with another litany of prayer and another dispersal to individual prayer. At dawn, all stood and sang 'God bless Africa', but substituting 'Pentecost' for 'Africa'. Members then recounted dreams for interpretation and retrieved jugs of water that Mai Mhlambo had blessed for healing.[63] As the sun rose, people walked back down the mountain to the work that awaited them in their homes and fields.

Exorcism for women's liberation

Founder Mai Maunganidze is the source of her church's mission of exorcising from women at night vigils the spirits called *zvikwambo,* which return from murdered men to claim a woman from the murderer's family. She explains it simply:

---

[63]The Jekenishen Church stresses holy dreams by specifying about two *pungwe* hours specifically for sleeping, after which members' dreams are discussed and interpreted.

Let's say your father kills a person. The spirit of that person rises to say, 'I was killed for no crime' and goes and rests on this child and says, 'I was killed in your home. Your father killed me.' That's how unclean spirits come. Children are bothered by the spirit of that person saying, 'You are my wife. You are not to be married. You are not to be taken by any other man.' Now we cast out that spirit and the woman then goes right out and gets married. That is an avenging spirit *(ngozi)* ... She will be oppressed by this avenging spirit. We then cast out this avenging spirit, saying, 'You! Go to the one who killed you. This child knows nothing.' That avenging spirit then agrees.[64]

This ministry has enormous appeal: nationally, 75 per cent of the church's members are women; at the Pungwe Branch 95 per cent are women; and Mai Mhlambo estimates that half of the women in the branch have been delivered of *zvikwambo*. In combating a phenomenon that impedes the normal fulfilment of women's marriage and child-bearing expectations, the PACG initiates a major confrontation with both the spirit world of SSR and the institutions of patriarchy which shape that world.

In instituting a traditional Shona marriage, the 'bride-price' (*lobola* or *roora*) that the bridegroom pays to the bride's family is not so much for the bride as her *child-bearing capacity*, for patrilineal continuity is pre-eminent.[65] The long time over which instalments are arranged – many years may be stipulated – anticipates that if no children, insufficient children or insufficient male children are born, portions of the

---

[64]Mbuya Maunganidze, interview, 22 April 1991. In general Shona usage, *chikwambo* is the 'faculty, conferred by *shave* (spirits), of recovering property, and of punishing those who refuse to restore property'. Hannan, sv. The plural is *zvikwambo*. David Maxwell notes in Katerere, north of Nyanga, a wave of women-possessing spirits who must be appeased by 'the gift of a young girl to the family of the murdered victim'. 'Witches, prophets and avenging spirits: the second Christian movement in north-east Zimbabwe', *Journal of Religion in Africa* 25 (3) (August 1995), 325.

[65]Traditionally, the bride-price was paid in the form of essential articles such as hoes, but cattle became an almost universal medium in this century. Today cattle continue to be prominent in *lobola*, but sums of cash are usually included as well. See Joan May, *Zimbabwean women in customary and colonial law* (Gweru: Mambo Press; Edinburgh: Holmes McDougall, 1983), 48.

bride-price can be suspended, delayed, or withheld permanently. If a husband divorces his wife or takes an additional wife, for whatever reason, he normally retains the children in traditional society, which assumes they were born to continue his family.

Under customary law, a woman had no legal standing on her own but was always represented by her father, husband, or other male relative.[66] The Legal Age of Majority Act (LAMA), which became law in December 1982, overturned customary law by specifying that all persons attain legal majority at age eighteen:

> When someone attains majority age, it means that person no longer has a guardian. In other words, it means he or she can sue and be sued in his or her own right, can own property, sell it or give it away without interference from anyone as long as that property is his/hers to give and a major can enter into any contract without the need of a guardian. By virtue of this Act, it follows that any two people wishing to enter into a contract of marriage can do so with or without the consent of the woman's father or other male relative. Therefore, nobody can legally stop them from marrying simply because *roora* has not been paid. Another implication is that women can also become guardians of their children, irrespective of whether these children were born in or out of wedlock.[67]

Still, uneducated people are unaware of the Act or are confused by the ambiguous relationship between civil and customary law. Many people have resisted the Act because they believe it undermines male authority, a man's accountability to his wife's family, incentives for marital fidelity and the general stability of the Shona family. Customary norms often prevail because they enact the interlocking authorities of culture and religion.

It is the spirit world's interaction with Shona kinship patterns which makes patrilineal continuity so crucial in traditional marriage and which, in turn, evokes the *chikwambo* phenomenon. In SSR the spirits

---

[66]Joyce Kazembe, 'The woman issue', in *Zimbabwe: the political economy of transition, 1980–1986*, (Dakar: Codesria, 1986), 385.

[67]Ibid, 391. For detailed analysis of changes in marital customs and attitudes, see Dominique Meekers, 'The noble custom of *roora*: the marriage practices of the Shona in Zimbabwe', *Ethnology* 32 (1) (Winter 1993), 35–54.

authoritative for the family are the husband's spirits: his father, grandfather and so on. The spirits of the husband's mother and grandmother are also important, but only as members of the husband's lineage; they do not represent their own natal families. A woman joining the family through marriage does not relate formally with the spirits of her own birth family, for that is her brothers' responsibility. Instead, she adopts her husband's family spirits, brewing their ritual beer, cooking their *pungwe* meals and bringing up her children to honour them. Sons are crucial, because only sons can make offerings and formally represent the family in ceremonies invoking the family spirits.[68]

With such a weight of social and spiritual sanction, the phenomenon of *chikwambo* is not only natural but inevitable. Belief in *ngozi,* spirits who return to avenge death, provides the conceptual structure and spiritual ontology for the social and spiritual construction of the *chikwambo.* When a childless man has been killed without just cause, it is a spiritual catastrophe, because his *mudzimu* has been deprived of any male descendant to invoke, honour and receive him in possession. Hence the man's spirit returns and through possession claims a daughter from the family of the murderer. As in an ordinary marriage, the spirit claims not so much the woman herself as her capacity to bear children for the deceased and so provide him with descendants. When the woman is possessed, she communicates the spirit's claim by speaking in the murdered man's voice and can attack with male strength any man who enters into marriage arrangements for her. Typically, a family responds to this spiritual onslaught by renouncing any hope of marrying the woman off and, instead, assigns her a permanent plot on their communal land. Through a steady boyfriend, a succession of lovers, or prostitution she may then bear children and so provide descendants for the *chikwambo.*

Violence in the Honde Valley has made it fertile ground for the phenomenon. Immigrant workers were often murdered by residents in the early days of the tea estates, and deaths from lowveld tropical dis-

---

[68]'Perhaps the most potent single reason for having children is that through them the parents and grandparents are remembered in the next world. A marriage must provide sons to pray to the *vadzimu* and daughters to provide the sons and daughters for the next generation'. Michael Gelfand, *The genuine Shona: survival values of an African culture* (Gweru: Mambo Press, 1973), 175.

eases are often attributed to occult murder by wizards. The *Chimurenga* resulted in many deaths, and these were followed by others as the Mozambican civil war of the 1980s spilled over into the valley. Thus, there have been many old scores to be settled in the social, economic and political history of the valley.

For the woman involved, being claimed by a *chikwambo* is a catastrophe both practical and spiritual, intensifying all in Shona religious culture that places women in a secondary position. Marital romance with the man of her choice is impossible, and any current marriage is threatened by dissolution. A threat of violence often hangs over her sexual encounters, for the *chikwambo* is ambivalent about the woman's sexual activity. The spirit wants children, but if a sexual liaison prompts talk of marriage, the *chikwambo* may beat up or even kill the suitor while possessing the woman. In marriage a woman's childbearing capacity is bought, but at least with a partner whom she has chosen, whereas the *chikwambo* represents a man she does not know and her partner is an unseen spirit. In marriage a woman becomes part of her husband's family, but in time she becomes a matriarchal figure in her own right. A woman claimed by a *chikwambo*, however, is denied social standing and is confined to the orbit of her family of origin. In marriage a woman does eventually become an honoured figure in the spirit world, albeit in that of her husband's family. A host to a *chikwambo*, however, loses any status in the spirit world, because she is never incorporated physically into a man's family.

In liberating women from the power of the *zvikwambo*, Mbuya Maunganidze and the PACG both accept and revise the spiritual ontology of Shona Spirit Religion. They affirm that spirits of dead men do return and claim women and thereby accept SSR's socio-spiritual construction, rather than dismissing it. Within that worldview, however, they also confront SSR in fundamental ways. Most basically, they challenge the assumption that what a spirit states must be accepted and what a spirit demands must be given. SSR counsels people to accept spirits' demands as justified by familial and moral obligation and warns that refusal to comply will bring misfortune. Mbuya Maunganidze views the claims of spirits as a kind of harassment:

> Now if that child (a young woman) says, 'I no longer want ancestral spirits' and does not know what happened with the elders, we also cast out that ancestral spirit and it goes out. We say, 'Get out,

ancestral spirit! This person will no longer perform veneration.' She brings the cloths here that she bought (for divination) and we burn them ... The ancestral spirit is there, but we do not want it to be venerated, because if you venerate it, it bothers you.[69]

With a theological framework that relates the spirit world of SSR to Christianity, the church addresses the *chikwambo* phenomenon at its all-night vigils. The prophets deny that a *chikwambo* has a moral claim and demand that the *chikwambo* go and trouble the murderer. This approach liberates women in several interconnected ways. In addressing the woman's situation rather than the relational obligations between families, it asserts an individualistic perspective that challenges society's assumption that women exist to provide patrilineal continuity. In simply rejecting the claim of the *chikwambo*, the polemic asserts the woman's freedom from being subjugated to the wishes of a man, whether alive in the flesh or as a spirit elder. The polemic also asserts that a woman has a right to bear children in the circumstances she chooses rather than in restitution to a man she does not know. The PACG's confrontation with *zvikwambo* represents not a rejection of marriage but an effort to remedy particular disabilities Shona marriage may impose on women. The church's emphasis on prayer for conceiving children is a similar effort to remove the stigma of barrenness. Its efforts to bring reconciliation between women and the men who have divorced them has a similar thrust.

In confronting *zvikwambo* during its all-night vigils, the church engages the avenging spirits in the time they claim as their own and so highlights for believers the contrast between spiritual oppression and liberation in Christ. Night is when spiritual evil manifests itself and also when God's Holy Spirit is especially near. Night is when the community can gather in solidarity with its afflicted members. Night is when those oppressed by *zvikwambo* can be liberated, with far-reaching implications for their spiritual, social and even economic lives. The *pungwe* catalyses this transformation for individuals, for their families and for their communities. The *pungwe* becomes the theatre in which the Pentecostal Apostolics fulfil the mission to which they feel called.

---

[69]Mbuya Maunganidze, interview, 22 April 1991.

Pastoral outreach: the Unity of the African Apostolic Faith Church

The church that may hold more night vigils than any other is the Unity of the African Apostolic Faith Church (UAAFC), a long-established but vital and growing AIC. Its *mapungwe* combine strengths of both the MFCs and the AICs, making the church attractive to an exceptionally wide spectrum of people. Much of the church's pastoral outreach occurs in *mapungwe,* and a strong emphasis on evangelism has led to growth throughout the country. The church's synthesis of diverse elements in its life leads to considerable negotiations for power in liturgical and leadership life.

Syntheses of mission and African models

In 1931 Elijah Mugodhi, a young man living near Wedza in western Manicaland, called a group of people together and announced that the Holy Spirit had come to him at Maguni Hill in Gangaunze and had audibly spoken the words of Exodus 20:3, 'Thou shall have no other God before me.'[70] Like Mbuya Maunganidze, Mugodhi was a member of the Apostolic Faith Mission and left that church on account of its rejection of prophecy, and the church he founded is popularly known by his name, simply the Mugodhi Church.

The touchstone of single-minded devotion to God in the Spirit's communication with Mugodhi was followed by a number of other injunctions that highlight the church's emphases:

1 Thou shalt not smoke.
2 Thou shalt not drink alcohol.
3 Thou shalt not commit adultery.
4 Thou shalt not be treated (by conventional Western medicine) except when seriously injured. Mark 16:15.
5 Thou shalt not worship ancestral spirits.
6 Thou shalt not be married to non-Christians. Deuteronomy 7:3.

---

[70]This is the way this verse is reproduced in a booklet published by the church, *The formation of the Unity of African Apostolic Faith Church,* from which much of the historical material in this section is taken. I am indebted to Lovemore Mupinda, who copied the booklet by hand and provided much supplementary information. This study's discussion of the UAAFC is the first account of the church by an outsider.

198

He/she who marries a non-Christian shall be charged. Deuteronomy 22:14.

7 The church has prophets who prophesy members of the church. He/she who shall invite or come to us to be prophesied we shall do so. If we visualise any unwanted on possessions (sic) ie witchcraft, *mushonga, nyoka,* etc, we shall burn.

8 Our church permits us to marry. Genesis 29:20, 1 Samuel 3:2.

9 Our church has judges who try cases between or among its members. Deuteronomy 1:13.

10 No member of the church is allowed to immediately report his/her case to court of law before notifying church members.

11 Any member of our church who breaks any law of the church is liable to undergo a charge given by judges of the church.

12 Our church permits us to eat some of the beasts as per the Holy Bible. Deuteronomy 14:3.[71]

Church discipline and conformity with Old Testament norms are clear concerns in these rules, which also provide for enforcement. Strictures against drinking and smoking are common among AICs and among the MFCs' women's and men's groups. Provision for internal adjudication of disputes reflects 1 Corinthians 6:1–8 and stresses the community's separation from the world. The church is similarly unequivocal in opposing the rites of SSR, and prophecy is strikingly promoted as the Christian alternative to divination. The UAAFC conforms to the general pattern of *Chipostori* in discouraging Western medical treatment, but it makes a concession for cases of serious injury.

The mission of the church is remarkably holistic as set forth in its 1952 constitution:

1 To evangelise to all nations the word of God.

2 To establish believers into the whole truth of the Bible – Old and New Testaments.

3 To assist widows, orphans and all in need. James 1:27, Galatians 6:10.[72]

---

[71] *The formation of the Unity of African Apostolic Faith Church,* Ms copy by Lovemore Mupinda, May 1991, 1–2. Most of this document is written in English.

[72] *Formation,* 3.

Evangelism and international mission are the church's first priority in a threefold vision that also stresses teaching and outreach to those in need. The UAAFC consequently spread throughout Zimbabwe, although it is strongest in Wedza, where its leaders plan to construct a new headquarters. Central church funds have supported missionaries sent to establish congregations in Zambia, Malawi and South Africa. In the Honde Valley, Mugodhi has ten congregations that are part of a district north of Mutare that includes 53 congregations, which compares well with the 75 or so that the Roman, Anglican and Methodist Churches each have in the same area.

The UAAFC promotes a high level of activity among its members and, correspondingly, a large number of *mapungwe.* In addition to Sunday services, local congregations are required, like MFCs, to offer women's meetings, prayer meetings, Sunday School and Bible studies. Like other AICs, the Mugodhi Church holds an annual *Paseka* in April, which church literature associates with the Passover theme of Deuteronomy 9:14 and Numbers 26:27, although it is pre-eminently the annual celebration of the Lord's Supper. Two other festivals have a strong Old Testament tone: the Festival of Weeks (*Mutambo Wemavhiki*) is held in April or May on the model of Deuteronomy 16:9–12, and the Festival of Booths (*Mutambo WeMatumba*) is held in October on the model of Deuteronomy 16:13–17. A Ten-Days Prayer Meeting is held in August or September, and the Annual Conference convenes at Wedza in July. Although the church is not dogmatic on the point, church buildings are not customary in the UAAFC, and congregations generally meet outside in communal areas or on church members' land.

The church's organisational life exhibits an unusual combination of MFC and AIC elements that create the context for the negotiations of power that are so prominent in the church's night vigils. Contrary to the pattern of some AICs, Bishop Mugodhi's four successors since his death in 1970 have not been relatives but simply other qualified leaders. 'Presbytery' is the term used for governing bodies throughout the church, including local congregations, districts, national headquarters and the church at large, which is overseen by a general presbytery that meets at the annual conference at Wedza. In the episcopal transition of 1982 the hierarchy was supplemented by twelve 'disciples' to assist the bishop, and in the transition of 1985 the terminology was altered to provide for twelve 'elders', with seven 'disciples' appointed to serve widows and orphans.

Church members are called *vanamati*, 'pray-ers', an unusual term among Shona churches, which generally call their adherents members (*nhengo*), Christians, or believers (*vatendi*). Men wear white lab-style jackets in worship and women are expected to wear white head coverings. For congregations, the church's constitution provides pastors, elders, evangelists, deacons and deaconesses, but in practice this MFC-derived list undergoes subtraction and addition toward the AIC pattern of charismatic offices. The congregation at Samanga, for instance, has a pastor (*mufundisi*), an assistant pastor, evangelists (*vavhangeri*), preachers (*vaparidzi*), secretaries (*vanyori*), healers (*varapi*) and prophets (*vaprofiti*). As among the Marange Apostles, only the offices of healer and prophet are open to women. Unlike the Apostles but following the MFCs, the Mugodhi has a women's organisation equivalent to the Mothers' Union and called *Sangano raVanaMaria*, the Fellowship of Mary, which assigns roles to women on the basis of the offices their husbands hold in the congregation.

Anyone who speaks in tongues shares the gift of prophecy, but the office of prophet gathers around particular persons both locally and nationally; the bishop has a senior prophet and there is a head prophet to oversee all local prophets. Prophets and seers (*vanoratidzwa*, 'those to whom it is revealed') must have their spirits purified before they undertake their work and they may not receive payment. Similarly, the church's midwives should not be paid with cattle or goats but can receive simple gifts of soap and head coverings. These provisions represent an effort to distinguish the ministry of prophets and healers from the income-generating divination and healing of the *nganga*. In marriage arrangements the UAAFC engages and regulates Shona custom: polygyny, accepted but not encouraged, is practiced by only a minority of men, and the church protects the rights and standing of first wives.

A steady diet of *pungwe*

All-night vigils are remarkably frequent in the Mugodhi Church. During a single week, leaders of the Mugodhi congregation at Zindi, just outside Eastern Highlands, encouraged members to participate in three *mapungwe*, on Tuesday, Thursday and Saturday nights. The two weekday gatherings were held 'on the mountain of Paradise', a remote wilderness spot high on the escarpment above EHTE. The first *pungwe* was convened to respond to a prophecy that an unspecified woman of the church would die in the near future, and the Thursday *pungwe* was called to pray for the congregation's pastor. The Saturday *pungwe* was a general revival held in concert with a number of other Mugodhi congregations. The wilderness and mountain motifs have a prominence similar to that found among the Pentecostal Apostolics. Confrontation with evil is so integral to the wilderness experience that when the challenge of evil arises in Mugodhi community life, going to the wilderness to engage the battle is the natural response. A distinctive feature of the Mugodhi mountain vigils is that the group moves up the mountain in stages, periodically stopping for confessions, prayers, songs and prophecies along the way and arriving at 'Paradise' toward midnight.

Pastoral care is the most frequent purpose of a *pungwe* as people visit the sick, celebrate an important family event, or comfort a family with a *runyaradzo* gathering on a death anniversary.[73] While driving about the valley one night in search of *mapungwe* in various churches, I heard the sound of singing coming from a *rondavel* some distance off the road and saw people gathered in the doorway in the moonlight. Mugodhi members were visiting an ill and housebound member of their congregation. Twenty people were crowded into the invalid's small dwelling and by candlelight they were doing all that a *pungwe* calls for: reading and preaching on scripture, singing songs and praying for healing. On another occasion five men made seven house calls in a single night, concluding their itineration at 3 am. Gathering around the needs and celebrations of individuals and families stresses the grassroots role of the *pungwe* in strengthening community life.

General congregational *mapungwe* in Mugodhi are characterised by a

---

[73]The Ndaza Zionists (ZAC) celebrate the birth of a couple's first child with a *pungwe* that they call a *dhiri*. Worship takes the familiar Zionist form of a great deal of dancing interspersed with prayers and sermons, but midway through the *pungwe* the congregation greets the young couple, offers special prayers, and offers them gifts of cash and household articles. A high birth rate and the high proportion of young people of marriageable age, both locally and nationally, results in the Zionists holding many *mapungwe edhiri*.

202

A woman preaches at about 3:30 am at the Mugodhi *pungwe* at Chitambo

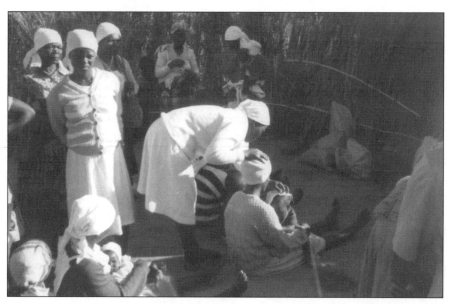

A woman healer prays with worshippers on the morning after the Mugodhi *pungwe* at Chitambo

unique form of confession, regular seasons of prayer, strong emphasis on biblical preaching and a constant negotiation of power between leaders who have authority to speak and other members of the congregations. A large Mugodhi *pungwe* held at the Chitambo *kraal* at 'Honde Green' gathered at David Chitambo's invitation because work kept him from Sunday services; the *pungwe* became both a Chitambo family celebration and a revival for the twelve Mugodhi congregations represented. It drew about 250 people, who included a number of visitors from nearby, gathered in the open area, or *chivanse*, at the centre of the *kraal*.

Public confession followed supper and the opening song, as all 250 people articulated their sins publicly before God. As in other AICs, confession is an indispensable prelude to worship, but in the UAAFC each member's confession is heard by the entire congregation instead of by the prophets alone. The procedure is remarkable in being both public and private in tone. The confessing member speaks quietly, typically with eyes open looking forward into space, addresses God about particular habits or incidents and asks God's help in amending behaviour. Typical sins include scolding, anger, gossip, dishonesty, harshness with co-workers and lust, and people often cite particular incidents and relationships. Confessing aloud ensures public accountability, but the quietness of the proceeding preserves the sense that each person is confessing primarily before God. Others do not comment, nor is any general absolution offered. This form of confession may be unique among Shona AICs.[74] The large number of people at the Chitambo *pungwe* extended the process close to two hours. After the confession, a great fire was kindled in the middle of the *chivanse* and all gathered round in the moonlit and chilly night.

The assembly then faced east and knelt as the *mufundisi* offered a long pastoral prayer. As in the PACG, a summary 'Alleluia!' from the *mufundisi* prompted the entire congregation to pray extemporaneously. A loud clamour followed as most prayed in a combination of speech and ecstatic tongues with hands raised and bodies swaying, a pattern consistent with the church's roots in the AFM. The group expression subsided after several minutes, and the *mufundisi* closed with a summary prayer. There were two other such seasons of prayer

---

[74]The Jekenishen Church has yet another variation, in which members gather in pairs and confess to one another quietly.

during the night, one when the men's time for preaching ended at 2:45 am and the other at sunrise. At the mid-point prayer time a woman led a song on the theme of prayer, and another woman offered a long pastoral prayer to open the women's time of preaching. The common eastward orientation for prayer in AICs is especially effective when the believers are brought through a *pungwe,* as they were on this occasion, to pray once again as the sun actually rises before them.

The song, 'We ask the Father for power' (*Tinokumbira masimba kunaBaba*), made way for one of the secretaries to welcome all and to announce the order in which preachers from the various congregations would speak. He stressed that only designated preachers – understood to be men – were permitted to speak and exhorted them to concentrate on the thematic passage:

> So, preachers, you will follow that order. If a branch (congregation) does not have a preacher, let no ordinary person who is not a preacher stand up. Do not pass yourself off as a preacher, for you are a child of your congregation ... What we ask of you preachers is that you stick to the passage that has been chosen. We are not allowing folk tales *(nyambo).* But let us follow what is said in the passage.[75]

As in the *mapungwe* of the MFCs, sermons occupied most of the night, although songs also took a substantial amount of time, concluding each sermon and introducing another preacher. As in the AICs, however, preachers punctuated their sermons with frequent repetitions of the phrases 'Peace be with you, apostles!' or 'Peace be with you, children of God!' or 'Alleluia, children of God!' to which the people responded, 'Alleluia! Amen!' Also in AIC style, preachers expounded the designated passage (Colossians 3) verse by verse, the scripture being read by an evangelist who stood with each preacher at all times. The reader's visual prominence emphasises the authority of the written word and the preacher's accountability to it.

The season of preaching that occupied the first five hours or so featured men in the various offices of the congregations, beginning with the secretaries, proceeding to the preachers and including the pastor

---

[75]*Pungwe*, Samanga congregation of UAAFC, 28–29 April 1991, Chitambo. Unless otherwise referenced, sermons, songs and prayers quoted in this section occurred at this event and are not separately referenced.

of the hosting Samanga congregation. The verses of Colossians 3 that drew the preachers' particular attention were:

> So if you have been raised with Christ, seek the things that are above, where Christ is, seated at the right hand of God. Set your minds on things that are above, not on things that are on earth (vv 1–2) ... Put to death, therefore, whatever in you is earthly: fornication, impurity, passion, evil desire and greed (which is idolatry) (v 5) ... As God's chosen ones, holy and beloved, clothe yourselves with compassion, kindness, humility, meekness and patience (v 12) ... Above all, clothe yourselves with love, which binds everything together in perfect harmony (v 14).

Host David Chitambo highlighted the mission imperative in his sermon and went on to representative warnings and exhortations to righteous living:

> The word of God says that the world will not end until people have heard. Stop gossiping if you grew up together with Christ. Kill the desires of the flesh that prevent you from entering heaven. Do not wait to be reprimanded by the prophets, because every person knows where he or she sins. If you refuse to listen to the messengers who are sent with God's word, the wrath of God will fall upon you. It is necessary to have a passport of heaven and of faith in order for you to go to heaven. We are not forcing each other, but each person already knows whether he or she is a holy one or a sinner ... You must be righteous and merciful for God's mercy to be upon you. Let God's word take root in our hearts. The word tells us what to do and what to reject, but anyone who rejects the word will be destroyed.

The conflict between good and evil, sin and righteousness, was objectified and transferred into the arena of prophecy as another speaker put the community on notice that 'an animal (spirit) is circulating here that we must intercept'. Exercising the interrupting power of a prophet, the wife of the pastor then specified the evil spirit and warned of its wide power: 'I ask the mothers of children: look after your children and do not neglect them, because there is a hyena here, so (there is the danger) that when you go from this meeting place the children will carry evil spirits.'

Such pronouncements are characteristic of Mugodhi prophecy, which

206

one church leader defined as 'letting the church know what is wrong and what it must do'.[76] The presence of evil was expressed in a classic SSR image of evil, the hyena, which consorts with witches. Conversations indicated that people understood the prophet along these lines:

> An evil force is abroad among us, and one person in this gathering may be the wizard who is the source. The wizard is prowling through a hyena, for I sense that presence here. You may not see a physical hyena, but that spirit is here, and it may enter anyone in this company. Do not be surprised if you do see a real hyena, for the wizard is around somewhere.[77]

The host of the bewitching spirit was never identified, but the warning drew the community together in self-examination and solidarity against evil powers of the night and prepared people for the prophecies and healings that concluded the *pungwe* next morning. With similar impressiveness, a non-Mugodhi traveller from Mt Darwin rose at 12:30 am to tell how he had actually been turned into a snake through wizardry and how he had been healed through the ministrations of six Mugodhi young people, whose care for him he compared to Paul's description of love in 1 Corinthians 13. People heard his story with audible expressions of awe, for some had read about the case in the popular press and were amazed that the man stood before them. The progression by which meeting at night in a *pungwe* heightened awareness of life's spiritual conflicts could not be more clear: a scripture passage was mined for its theology of good and evil, sin and righteousness; the presence of evil was highlighted through the imagery of SSR; and the fact of conflict was exemplified in a person reputed to have been restored from being a snake. Although outsiders might consider the sequence to be a digression from Colossians 3, it presented

---

[76]Lovemore Mupinda, interview, 2 April 1991.

[77]While driving home at about 2:30 am one night from the first part of a *pungwe* in the Honde Valley, I saw a hyena crouching by the road in the darkness. When I mentioned the incident to others it evoked a high level of interest quite beyond zoology. It was as though spiritual antennae immediately went up, and I was questioned closely about the sighting. At what time did I see the hyena? What was it doing? Was it seated, or was it walking? Was it alone, or did it have the company of other animals? How did it react to my presence? The hyena signified occult communication, and people felt obligated to search for clues that might indicate its meaning.

the theme scripture's call for transformation in Christ through vivid images of how people in Shona culture experience the struggle between good and evil, between the earthly and the heavenly.

Negotiation for power through prophecy and song was a constant feature of the *pungwe*, as it is of Mugodhi services in general. In the church's elaborate structure, the secretary had reminded all to respect official preaching positions at the outset. Women do not receive those offices, and so they were excluded from the prize preaching time, for some people were dozing when the women began preaching at 3 am. By prophesying about the hyena, however, a woman was able to seize the stage during the men's time, because anyone can prophesy at any time. The democratic gift of prophecy provides access to spiritual power that balances the liturgical and juridical authority accorded to male officeholders. Moreover, prophecy is usually directed to individuals and it is no respecter of persons. Frequently a young or otherwise marginal person in the congregation calls upon a church leader to stand and hear a prophecy that has come to the young person about the elder. Prophecies may concern illness, impending decisions, struggles with SSR, work conditions, relationships and financial viability. At the Chitambo *pungwe*, preaching itself was subjected to the negotiation of power for, while the women received much less time as a group, the fact that they preached at all was significant, for women do not preach at Sunday morning services. Moreover, the women chose to focus on the role of women in the church, with reference to the strictures found in 1 Timothy 2 and 1 Peter 3. Their interpretations were not revolutionary, but they told humorous stories and celebrated women's roles in ways that implicitly challenged assumptions of male superiority and privilege.

Music is an important tool in the negotiation of power. All Mugodhi songs – none of them written – are variations of one musical line, on which a cantor sings a phrase which the congregation repeats. Virtually every song ends with a strongly rhythmic and exultant refrain of 'Hosanna!' sung many times before the song finally ends with a coda of 'Alleluia! Amen'. Singing for the Mugodhi faithful is a kind of chanting that provides a common thread throughout their liturgies, whether by night or by day. Sermons can be interrupted at any time by songs led by anyone in the congregation. Those who lead songs are expected to do so only at the inspiration of the Holy Spirit, and their role thus becomes a locus of spiritual authority alongside preaching and prophesying.[78] Interrupting a preacher with a song is extremely common in a Mugodhi service and the interrupters are people who are otherwise on the outskirts of power in the church: women, children and those whose personalities marginalise them, male as well as female. While participants generally give song leaders the benefit of any doubt about the Spirit's moving, some cases are transparently competitive situations where song leaders simply want the preacher to sit down on account of the length or the content of his sermon. My field notes of one instance illustrate the point:

> Baba Samanga, first of the *Vavhangeri – Garai muchidanana* (Live loving one another) – Seems to be working on marital issues. Turned back 2 musical interruptions. Accepted third because theme (matches his topic) ... Tough fight with men who began Alleluia – Finally gave in. Finished shortly after that.

Negotiation of power, not sharing of power, is centre-stage, for preaching, singing and prophecy express different kinds of power. The authority to expound scripture locates the preacher closest to what the congregation considers the word of God, but simultaneously he can mobilise a wide range of cognitive, emotional and imaginative resources. The power of a song leader consists in the opportunity to energise and unify the group to produce a single and overwhelming expression of worship. Thought to speak at the direct inspiration of the Holy Spirit, the prophet can suggest particular images and urgencies that guide the group's spiritual movements in reflection, prayer and exorcism. Although the church honours each type of power, the preacher's power tends to be most decisive over time, and preachers possess the power to govern. While the preacher speaks out of the creativity of his thought and imagination, a song leader catalyses an existing community artifact, the song, although she has some freedom for improvisation. In addition, she must insist on seizing the occasion,

---

[78]In the ZAC women and men interrupt preachers in a similar fashion, and men can also initiate a whirling dance which is difficult for any preacher to overpower. In such cases, the drummer becomes the crucial decision-maker: if he supports the singers with a beat, the dance will proceed, but if he drums half-heartedly or remains silent the attempted interruption dies away. Similar but less pronounced interactions appear in the Jekenishen Church.

for preachers often resist interruptions.[79] Prophets, both male and female, have a freedom about content similar to that of the preachers, but their work is limited mostly to designated times. The musician's and the prophet's roles are excluded from the congregation's power centre, where the elders decide the congregation's direction. Similarly, scores of people after the *pungwe* expected the healers, mostly women, to heal them through prayer and the laying-on of hands, and they set out jugs of water to be blessed, for healing ministry is at the heart of the UAAFC. Yet women so central to healing at the *pungwe* are sidelined on Sunday mornings when male officeholders take the lead. They are excluded from the roles of pastor, elder, evangelist and secretary in the presbytery, where basic decisions are made.

The necessity of constantly negotiating power in the Mugodhi Church's life is inherent in the church's mediating position between MFCs and AICs. Polygyny is accepted, but it is regulated. The Old Testament is normative for some social arrangements, but preaching focuses on the New Testament. Confessions are required of all, but they are shared with the entire group. Prophecy is prized, and it can include highly charged statements. However, it is a gift to which all have access, there is no private prophesying, and the prophet is subject to the witness of the community. In these ways the UAAFC incorporates features of Spirit-type AICs, but it moderates and rationalises them. Similar moderation and rationalisation are inevitable in the area of power distribution. Only men hold office, but there are avenues through which non-officeholders exercise power and challenge the leaders. Only men can preach, but prophets can challenge them, and any member, including a child, can interrupt them with a song at any time. Only men can preach on Sunday, but women can preach at a *pungwe.* These avenues do not lead to the same type of power that the male officeholders have, but they do lead to discussion and challenge, and in that continuing negotiation of power the *pungwe* is a central forum.

---

[79]Drawing on her experience of the AACJM in Zaire, Zambia, and Zimbabwe in the early 1970s, Jules-Rosette describes how *Vapostori* women interrupt preachers in that church and says they 'can use their song interjections as a form of preaching'. *African Apostles*, 141. AACJM services in the Honde Valley today feature men much more prominently than women in singing. Moreover, although songs do suggest images and guide thought, Jules-Rosette's terminology of 'sung sermons' exaggerates the parallel in the interest of portraying the Apostles as less patriarchal than they are.

The confluence of two factors makes the UAAFC especially significant for the *pungwe* movement. First, although numerical estimates are difficult to make, the Mugodhi Church may hold more *mapungwe* than any other church. Second, the church resembles both the mission-founded and African Initiated Church types. The spirituality of each church type is attracted by the *pungwe* and finds its fulfilment there. AIC concern with spiritual warfare and pentecostal experience comes to full flower at night when spiritual reality is especially close. MFC concern with a communal and discursive theological process finds its audience in the all-night vigil. Mugodhi spirituality is unusually comprehensive, and, as it embraces both streams of Shona Christianity for mission outreach, the church's life is engulfed with *mapungwe*. The Mugodhi Church's mediating position yields distinctive *pungwe* features: confession that is both public and private, wilderness treks alongside long sermon festivals, and an unusual approach to the uneasy relations between men and women. The *pungwe* is the interactive arena where these elements seek equilibrium.

Mission through *pungwe* in Shona AICs

This overview of the *pungwe* movement as a mission initiative among African Initiated Churches focused attention on three churches that represent a range of Spirit-type churches. The Marange Apostles constitute the largest, most-established and best-known AIC. The Pentecostal Apostolic Church of God is a more recent *Chipostori* church founded and led by women, while the Mugodhi Church occupies a mediating position between AICs and MFCs. All-night vigils are prominent in these churches, as they are in other AICs such as the Zion Apostolic Church and the Jekenishen Church.

The survey demonstrates that the *pungwe* movement is extremely strong among AICs and that it is catalysing mission as each church understands it. Combating spiritual evil, celebrating community and offering liberation are *pungwe* features shared by all the churches. In the AICs, the wilderness mountain focuses these themes by reconstituting the community where spiritual empowerment becomes the sole object of people's attention. Individually, AICs stamp their *mapungwe* with their own distinctives: fire-walking among the Apostles, *chikwambo* exorcism in the PACG, pastoral outreach in the Mugodhi Church,

Ndaza Zionists walk to a *pungwe* at Eastern Highlands, carrying mealie meal, chickens and utensils for cooking the evening meal

Jekenishen Church members worship at a *pungwe* visit to an ill member's *kraal* at Buwu, above the Honde Valley (author in foreground)

212

and constant dancing in the ZAC and Jekenishen Church, with the latter also emphasising dreams. Church leaders have developed theologies of night, fire, spirits and wilderness that represent creative interactions with biblical material and their experience of God in Christ in the power of the Holy Spirit. Their theologies also arise out of creative interactions with SSR, with which they struggle mightily even as they share aspects of its spiritual ontology.

The *pungwe* is the phenomenon that catalyses, energises and integrates these themes. More than at any other time, Christians meeting at night celebrate community, combat evil powers and strengthen their mission initiative. Night is the time for the wilderness journeys up mountains that form the church as a community on pilgrimage. Night is the time that evokes a spirituality of fire and a confrontation with avenging spirits that claim women. The *pungwe* is the setting where people can challenge basic social arrangements between men and women and work toward concrete change that liberates women, however incrementally. It is at the *pungwe* that Christians engage most deeply the theological issues between Christianity and SSR, between Christ and culture. Wilderness nights give birth to the church and forge identity with power and intensity.

Ndaza Zionists confess their sins to prophets at the 'gates' at an Easter *paseka*

Ndaza Zionists celebrate a *dhiri,* a *pungwe* for the young seated couple upon the birth of their first child, at the community hall of Village No 3 at EHTE. Full Gospel Church of God members participate, with leader Isaiah Shawati (centre rear, in white jacket)

214

CHAPTER 7

Taking back the night: appropriation and transformation in the *pungwe* movement

Night is contested ground in Shona religious life, and the Christian vigil movement embodies an initiative to take back the night from the control of Shona Spirit Religion. The movement's power for mission issues from the appropriations and transformations by which Christians both confront the traditional religio-cultural complex and incorporate its central understandings of spiritual and social reality.

We have seen the *pungwe* phenomenon in Shona Spirit Religion, in the early history of Christian churches among Shona people, in Zimbabwe's Liberation War, in the revival of mission-founded churches and in the life of African Initiated Churches. We come now to analyse today's *pungwe* movement as an interaction between Christian gospel and spirit religion in the culture of the Shona people. The interaction features both continuity and discontinuity with Shona culture as expressed in SSR and in the Liberation War.

It is important at the outset to establish historically that the post-war church movement has revived the churches and extended their mission and that the Liberation War was an important impetus for this development. This chapter's second section traces the contours of religious affiliation among Shona people in Zimbabwe and details the debate between advocates of SSR and those of Christianity. It is in this controversy that the interreligious contest over night becomes clear. The third section proposes that two actions, appropriation and transformation, characterise the movement's relationship with Shona religious culture and with Christianity. Spiritual encounter, community-building and liberative empowerment are the three areas of appropriation and transformation that mark the movement and catalyse its mission thrust in contemporary Zimbabwe.

215

Post-war church revival through the *pungwe*

'The naked truth is that now the church has gathered terrific momentum, more than before the war.' So says a United Methodist lay leader in the Honde Valley in discussing the post-war *pungwe* phenomenon in the churches.[1] Christians in most MFCs and in some AICs make similar assessments, and most agree that the *pungwe* has been instrumental in the revival.

The single detailed statistical survey of mission-founded churches since independence states that church membership grew at an annual rate of 10,41 per cent per year, which 'ranks the Zimbabwe church as one of the more rapidly growing churches around the world'. The report continues:

> Some church leaders said this was due to the impact of independence. In the years leading up to independence, people began to leave the church for various reasons. In the years that followed, many who had left began to return to the church ... For a variety of reasons related to post-independence, the Church as a whole grew slightly more rapidly between 1981 and 1986 than between 1986 and 1991. In the early 80s, church leaders worked aggressively to rebuild the damage done by the war to the rural churches. A new surge of growth took place.[2]

This account correctly highlights what statistics and first-hand observation indicate was a mass movement toward the churches after the Liberation War.

The factors that catalysed religious revival stem equally from the *Chimurenga* and from the political independence that was its objective and its achievement. The links between the war and the new nation mingle themes of goal and fulfilment, deprivation and repossession, abiding commitment and new discovery. First, independence brought freedom of religious expression after the severe disabilities imposed on rural Christian communities during the war. Suspended

---

[1]Pearson Chitare, interview, 20 May 1991.

[2]Eight of fifteen denominations for which complete information was available grew 12 per cent annually between 1981 and 1991. Zimbabwe National Evangelism Task Committee, *Target 2000*, handbook for Target 2000 Congress, held 7–10 September 1992, Harare, B16.

services, destroyed churches and condemnations of Christianity during the war threatened the religious identity of many Christians and the churches' role as familiar and reliable community supports. Some church members became disaffected and never returned, but many more found that the religious conflict catalysed a deeper commitment than they had known before. Independence released a religious impulse that had been inhibited for a number of years.

Second, the ideological turbulence of the period raised old questions in new forms. A Mugodhi leader recalls the tenor of the times:

> There has never been so much Christianity in Zimbabwe as in the eighties. Before this time people actually shunned Christianity and the church. When I was at college from '78 to '81, I was a member of FOCUS, the Fellowship of Christian Unions, and there were many strong Christians in that group, but other students actually shunned us.
>
> Q: Was the negative attitude only a result of the war?
>
> A: No, even before the war, the church was mainly for old people, but now you see young people being very active.
>
> Q: What was the source of negativism?
>
> A: People thought that if you were a church member, you had somehow just given up Shona traditions and gone over to the ways of white people.[3]

The missionary heritage of Christianity had always been a mixed phenomenon, sometimes imposing foreign forms and controls even as it offered a gospel that prompted conversion on a massive scale. Was rejecting that gospel and dismantling the church necessary, as many guerrillas suggested? Was the gospel truly liberating, or were Shona Christians simply unwitting accomplices in their own oppression? Could the gospel be separated from how MFCs expressed it? Were AICs anachronistic cultural expressions hiding from the burning political issues of the day? Many missionaries had excoriated SSR, but now many guerrillas were exalting it as the only authentic religion for Shona people. Was SSR truly devoid of helpful religious resources? On the other hand, was SSR sufficient for living through a war and build-

---

[3]Lovemore Mupinda, interview, 1 April 1991.

ing a new nation? The guerrillas' promotion of SSR highlighted the Shona cultural heritage and the potency of the spirit guardians in legitimating a struggle for the land they were believed to own. The guerrillas' advocacy made SSR a missionary religion for the first time and catalysed interreligious debate at grassroots level. For many people, however, independence did not so much validate SSR as free Christianity from foreign associations and enable them to embrace it in a more authentic Shona form:

> When the Liberation War started, people were politicised by the comrades that Christianity was a way Europeans wanted to take land from us, holding the Bible and the gun. But when we took over, I mean with the present government, things changed in churches more than they were before. Things changed more, I think, when people thought deeply that the church was not associated with oppression of any kind ... We soon discovered that the so-called Christianity and the Bible were not associated with these demarcations in pigment ... Africans got deeper into thinking and saw that the bad things about colonialism had nothing to do with Christianity.[4]

Third, independence itself inspired hope for community after the wartime fracturing of community. At independence families were reunited with guerrillas and with scouts who had spent years helping in the Mozambican camps. Families that had fled their villages or were interned in wartime 'keeps' returned to their traditional plots to rebuild their lives. Reconstituting community was high on people's agenda. Churches became a natural and ideal vehicle for such community-building, and community commitment sometimes was strongest where wartime destruction was greatest. At Chirarwe, for instance, where military exigencies resulted in the razing of church and school, the community mobilised after the war to rebuild both institutions, and the small congregation grew to several hundred members. By contrast, a nearby congregation at Bvumba that sustained only light physical damage to its building was slow to make repairs and the membership remained static and relatively inactive.

Fourth, the movement into the churches was a grassroots development in which the major initiative came from ordinary church mem-

---

[4]Pearson Chitare, interview, 20 May 1991.

bers rather than from established church leaders. Leaders did not so much persuade people to return to church as struggle to provide for the large numbers of people seeking a renewed expression of Christian faith and identity on their own. Often, new leaders emerged with vision and commitment to catalyse new communities. In 1985, for instance, I was approached at Bonda by a young man named Augustine Maunga with the appeal, 'Come out and visit our congregation. We would like to join the Bonda Church District.' He held no office in the Anglican Church, but for over two years he had been leading services outdoors for a growing group of people at Nyachibva in the Manica Communal Area. As a wartime *mujiba* during the war, Maunga was wounded and spent two years in a Rhodesian prison. When he returned home to his wife, organising a congregation was one of his major priorities, and after his visit to me I visited the congregation regularly at their meeting place in a meadow high on a ridge.

The factors that promoted post-war growth in the churches – desire to resume church life, theological reflection, community-building and lay leadership – also promoted the explosive growth of the *pungwe* as a movement. Indeed, those factors gave special impetus to the *pungwe* movement, so that it became the principal communal agent of congregational growth and renewal.

The *pungwe* owes its transformation into a mass movement to the transition from war to independence. There is a broad consensus that *mapungwe* are much more common and widespread in the post-war period than they were before the war.[5] A lifelong Methodist missionary resident of Old Mutare Mission recalls that in the 1940s and 1950s all-night meetings were generally limited to the annual camp meetings, and she sees the current resurgence as a post-war movement.[6] When all-night vigils were permitted at Anglican Bonda in the 1950s, they were held only a few times a year, and they later ceased when a dif-

---

[5]People's memories are the major resource for establishing this development. Clergy and academic observers of Shona Christianity have generally regarded *mapungwe* as an adjunct to the real life of the church and thus not worthy of the official notice regular clergy-led liturgies receive. Night vigils usually are not recorded in service registers, nor do they appear in official reports of the churches' life. Thus, there is no written record on which to build a comparison of the pre-war and post-war periods.

[6]Shirley DeWolfe, interview, 2 May 1991.

ferent Shona priest discouraged them.[7] On the independent church side, Lovemore Mupinda of the Mugodhi Church agrees that *mapungwe* are much more frequent in the post-war period and asserts that they are prominent among Christian groups throughout Zimbabwe. 'Churches with *pungwe* are especially attractive and have more growth,' says Mupinda.[8] Although difficult to quantify statistically, the conjunction of the major increase in the number of all-night vigils with rapid church growth after the war indicates a connection between these two developments. The fact that all-night vigils consistently draw many more people than attend Sunday services suggests a causal link whereby *mapungwe* attract large numbers of people, of whom a substantial proportion then affiliate with congregations and generate church growth.

The *pungwe* movement has deep roots in SSR, and it continues a pre-war tradition of night vigils in the churches, but the evidence suggests that the guerrillas' rallies popularised the *pungwe* far beyond its previous currency. The post-war increase in the number of night vigils in the churches and the fact that the very word *pungwe* became general in the churches only after the war indicates a causal link between the guerrillas' rallies and the revival of the churches' vigils. The wartime rallies imprinted the *pungwe* powerfully as an experience of drama, an exploration of meaning and sheer enjoyment. First, the guerrillas' *mapungwe* enacted a drama of communities meeting at night in conditions of danger with great public issues at stake. In church *mapungwe* Christians can maintain such a dramatic dimension in their lives, albeit without the thrill and terror of military conflict. Second, the wartime rallies drew people into explicit reflection about the events that engulfed them. Prosecuting the war by day involved countless details, whether horrifying, thrilling or tedious, and the night rallies were opportunities to explore the meaning of these activities. People moved from action to reflection in the *mapungwe,* and this, in turn, strengthened them for further action. Christian all-night vigils provide a similar opportunity to reflect on experience. Third, the trauma of many mobilisation rallies was tempered by the fact that they could also be enjoyable and thrilling. Asked whether people enjoyed the ral-

---

[7]Church leaders interview, Chirarwe, August 1987.
[8]Lovemore Mupinda, interview, 25 March 1991. The Roman Catholic catechist, Francis Sanyanga, cited in chapter 5, confirms this assessment.

lies, a Honde Valley man responded, 'Chaizvo! Chaizvo!' meaning, 'Very much! Very much!' and others echo this sentiment.[9] Eager enjoyment is also a hallmark of *mapungwe* in the churches.

How do Shona Christians themselves assess the historical link that this study asserts between the guerrillas' rallies and the churches' vigils? The link is easier to see when the general functions of the gatherings are in view, but harder when people focus on the specific content of the two kinds of meetings. A Methodist lay preacher offers an analysis that exemplifies seeing a link at the level of function:

> The boys came and did *mapungwe* with the people, teaching them about the good of self-rule. Now when the war was over, I see that the churches then took the knowledge that if you want to show people the good of something, let us go on until dawn, as in the rallies that the boys used to hold.[10]

The following dialogue with an Anglican catechist, however, illustrates how a church leader can acknowledge the link implicitly but explicitly discount it on account of the difference in the content of the two types of meeting:

Q: Did you say that *mapungwe* are now more popular in the church than they were before the war?

A: They are now more often, because we are doing them every month as a group of churches together.

Q: Okay. So why is it more popular now?

A: Since it is a revival after the war. Since because during the war people were just forced against their wishes. But they knew that it was wrong to say, 'Down with Jesus and the church!' But now because the country is in our hands they are now seeing (the truth).

Q: The *mapungwe* held during the war were compulsory, but it seemed as if people enjoyed those *mapungwe*. Why?

A: You see, people enjoyed those meetings after being mobilised. It was only after being mobilised that people started feeling happy. They developed this habit of liking war things, for example, singing war songs in the daytime.

---

[9]Bernard Matseketsa, interview, 18 April 1991.
[10]David Mubaira, church members interview, 13 March 1991.

Q: So do you think this has got anything to do with the popularity of the *pungwe* in the church after the war?

A: I don't think so ... because this has got nothing to do with the war.[11]

The historical and symbolic linkages this study sets forth for understanding the Christian *pungwe* are not obvious to all Shona Christians, but they are affirmed by many.

The debate between Shona Spirit Religion and Christianity

The role of the *pungwe* movement in the interaction of gospel and culture, of world religion and local religion is shaped by the vigorous debate between the claims of SSR and Christianity that ordinary people carry on in casual conversation, in Sunday liturgies and in all-night vigils. It constitutes the context for exploring how the Christian *pungwe* both embraces and confronts Shona religious culture. Shona people in Zimbabwe fall into three broad categories regarding the relationship between Christianity and SSR: devotees of SSR alone, Christians who avoid any association with SSR, and Christians who participate to some degree in SSR's rituals. These groups define the theological landscape in which interaction between SSR and Christianity takes place. They enact interreligious tension and dialogue pre-eminently through laying claim to night as a central time for religious experience.

'I do not pray': exclusive affiliation with SSR

Shona Spirit Religion is alive and well in Zimbabwe. Its vitality is what makes the *pungwe* in the churches important, for the interaction this study asserts between SSR and Christianity is an interaction between two potent social and cultural realities. As noted earlier, the continuing affiliation that many Christians maintain with SSR demonstrates that SSR has greater influence than adherence statistics would suggest.

---

[11]Richard Masara, church leaders interview, Chirarwe, August 1987. Another church leader asserted the converse, that there is no relationship between wartime rallies and church vigils because there were no Christian prayers at the guerrillas' *mapungwe*. Bernard Matseketsa, interview, 18 April 1991.

Many people live thoroughly in the context of SSR, with little or no contact with Christian churches. The *nganga* Samson Matsanzike in Chipinge exemplifies such a life history in a SSR leader. He was born in 1937, the second son of a *nganga,* and for many years he worked for the parastatal agency Dairiboard in Harare. He became a *nganga* only in 1981, when he began suffering from a mysterious illness that weakened his entire body. His father believed that he was wanted by a spirit, a rite of initiation cured him, and Matsanzike has been a *nganga* full time for the last nineteen years. His family never attended a church, and he was never baptised. With no particularly negative experiences of Christian churches, Matsanzike regards Christianity irenically, but he insists that people should reverence their ancestors:

> Christianity is good, because we (all) heal by the power of Mwari. All people were created by Mwari; that is why we are here. All that people do is given by the power of Mwari, whether one is a prophet, or a driver, or a preacher, or a diviner-healer. If you are inspired to do so, go to church, but all people should reverence their ancestral spirits. As they go to church they must know their nature (*chibarirwe*).[12]

A large number of tea pluckers at Eastern Highlands are non-Christians with no particular church background and no sense of religious continuity between SSR and Christianity. Naison Muzide, for instance, is a young alert plucker in his early 30s for whom even the common verb for praying, *kunamata,* seems alien:

> No, I do not pray (*handinamatiba*). I follow the customs of the religion of the people (*tsika dzeChivanhu*), which have been done since long ago, the customs of the ancestors: the forebears, grandfathers, grandmothers, ancestral spirits.[13]

Many people whose religious experience is confined to SSR have minimal education and, therefore, limited social and economic prospects in a Zimbabwe where education has become crucial to socio-economic advancement. Samson Matsanzike, for instance, has the equivalent of a Grade 4 education, yet as a *nganga* he has considerable social standing, and his fees far exceed what he might earn as a

---

[12]Samson Matsanzike, interview, 1 January 1994.
[13]Naison Muzide, interview, 3 April 1991.

labourer. The influence of education on exclusive belief in SSR is illustrated in the differing attitudes of two of *nganga* Mai Muzanenhamo's daughters at Zindi. The daughter with a primary school education believed in *vadzimu* and was considering a career as a *nganga*, but the daughter who had completed O-Level examinations and who worked as a clerk at EHTE professed not to believe in her mother's rituals.

Tea pluckers are, almost by definition, people with little education, and many of them adhere only to SSR. There they hope to manipulate at least some aspects of their lives in a world where they are generally the manipulated ones, subject to the orders and visions of others. Their strong silent resistance to attending churches may be rooted in the scale of their social and economic world. Life is hard for them. They endure physical labour and minimal pay in order to survive and, if possible, send children to school. Some *vakayi* feel that they do not need to be told of hope by those for whom hope may not be such a challenge, and they are content to remedy what they can through the ancestors who, after all, were people very much like themselves. Nevertheless, all the churches attract many of these same tea pluckers. Among the *Ndaza* Zionists and the Jekenishens, in particular, the poor attain the highest levels of leadership and dress and dance like kings and queens in the coming Kingdom of God.

Relatively few educated people embrace only SSR as their religious profession. MFCs have exercised a pervasive influence on the country's Western-oriented educational institutions, and schools continue to function on the British model, with Christian instruction considered integral, although since independence the Ministry of Education has produced curricular components on SSR as well. Educated people usually have at least a nominal Christian affiliation, and only a few take a specific initiative to embrace SSR exclusively.[14] Among those who reject Christianity entirely, it is more common that they reject all religious faith.

'I don't know about that': exclusive Christian affiliation

At the other end of the theological spectrum are those whose experience of SSR is minimal and whose religious life is defined totally by

---

[14]A well-known instance is University of Zimbabwe sociologist Gordon Chavunduka, who was a member of a mission-founded church but who became a *nganga* in the course of his research into the work of diviner-healers.

their experience in the churches. Raised by Christian families that did not practise SSR, what they know of it they have gathered from casual conversations and general reading. Their basic orientation is similar to that of a foreign visitor – interest, but no inside knowledge of SSR. When asked about an aspect of SSR, one young woman replied, 'Ah, no, I don't know about that. I didn't grow up with all that. I just grew up in the church, and now that I live in town I go to church and just worship Jesus.'[15] Such responses can often be traced back to the first generation of Shona Christians, the great-grandparents of today's young adults, who made exclusive decisions in favour of Christianity that continue virtually intact in their descendants today.

To many exclusive Christians, SSR seems superstitious, capricious and locally idiosyncratic. 'I realised that following or practising the traditional customs is just a matter of wasting time,' says a zealous young clerk affiliated with both the UMC and the Anglican Church. Others denounce SSR:

> In my understanding *vadzimu* means evil spirits ... When a person dies and will not enter or (be) accepted by God because of his or her sins he did on earth, the spirit of that individual is called *vadzimu* whenever it comes from a person of his or her family. So I don't believe in this.

> As far as I am concerned, as a Christian, honouring the spirit elders is just a matter of worshipping Satan. It is a way of pouring (ritual drink) to the devil, Satan. I do not think that people do it knowing that they are worshipping Satan. Many people are perishing because they are lacking knowledge.

> Reverencing the ancestral spirits is evil, because you are praying to gods other than Jesus. I myself do not agree that the ancestral spirits are there.[16]

Biblical arguments are readily adduced by those who see no possibility of rapprochement between SSR and Christianity:

---

[15] Wilma Muzvidzwa, interview, 4 January 1994.
[16] Noah Mushunje, Obvious Hamadziripi, Noah Madenya, Silas Sithole, Essay Project on Christianity and Tradition.

I believe in Jesus' saying which says, 'Let the dead bury their dead', and again, 'There is no communication between the dead and the living.'

In my Christian faith, reverencing the ancestral spirits means breaching the Ten Commandments ... Anyone who does not pass through Jesus Christ is a thief, as far as Christian faith is concerned. One cannot serve two masters. Hence there is no room for worshipping both by an individual. I have no custom(s) I practise in relation to the *vadzimu.* Deuteronomy 5:1–21.

It's 100% evil, according to Leviticus chapter 19 verse 31 and Deuteronomy 18:10–11.[17]

It is hard to estimate the number of people who are exclusively Christian, but it may be between 5 and 15 per cent, much smaller than the approximately 30 per cent devoted exclusively to SSR.

'Drums at the priest's house': dual affiliation

The majority of Shona people occupy a broad middle ground: people who identify themselves as Christians and who may be active in churches and who also participate to some degree in the practices of SSR and share its beliefs. Virtually all churches exhort their members to shun SSR and to commit themselves exclusively to Christ, but the polemic's very prominence confirms that many Shona Christians participate in the rites of SSR as well.[18] 'When shall we stop hopping from traditional religion at night to the Christian religion during the daytime?' asked the former Anglican bishop of Harare,[19] and the first prohibited 'offence' he put on a 1990 list for his clergy concerned SSR:

Publicly and deliberately participating in divination, '*Kurova guvanhaka mudzimu*' practice (purification of the spirit of a deceased

---

[17]Maxwell Muparutsa (refs. Mt 8:22; Lk 16:26), Lovemore Mupinda (refs Ex 20:3–6; Jn 10:1; Mt 6:24), Joseph Nyamuchengwe, Essay Project on Christianity and Tradition.

[18]'It is alleged that 99,9% of native Christian (*sic*) in this country have gone back to traditional religion and that 75% of them still call themselves Christians.' Peter Hatendi, 'The path to God (*Mwari*): Christ or *Midzimu*', TD, mimeographed, 1. Such an allegation is hyperbole, and percentages are difficult to determine.

[19]Peter Hatendi, 'The bishop's charge – 1986', TD, mimeographed, 4.

person), freemasonry, sorcery, occult practices, witchcraft and drunken behaviour. (Deuteronomy 18:10–13).[20]

Occasionally, church members defend participation in both religions:

> My attitude towards reverencing the ancestral spirits is based on the Old Testament – where the Israelites made burnt offering to their forefathers as appeasements against impending evil. I do believe in the practices and offer related things such as beer/slaughtered goats etc to the spirits thereby.[21]

The churches vary in the degree to which they tolerate such participation. MFCs such as the Anglican, Methodist and Presbyterian make pronouncements but generally do not inquire into people's behaviour or enforce sanctions. Spirit-type AICs, by contrast, are alert for infractions and discipline members who participate in SSR. Similarly, when the first mass movement toward the churches attracted people of mixed motivation and spirituality, the Mothers' Union and the Fishermen emerged as reformist groups within the MFCs, with higher standards and stricter rules. Continuing lack of consensus in churches has intensified these groups' rejection of SSR. AICs often regard themselves as more obedient to biblical standards and more faithful in discipleship than the MFCs.

The reproach against Christians comes not only from church leaders but also from practitioners of traditional religion. During a break in a SSR *pungwe* at Zindi Township, medium Mai Muzanenhamo publicly excoriated Christians who condemn *Chivanhu* and then come knocking on her door at night for divination:

> There is a certain priest I helped here, a real priest of the Anglican Church. His child was ill, her face was bruised. He came here with that child. They had taken her to the hospital, but she did not get well. He came with her here. Grandfather (her spirit elder) told them that an ancestral spirit wanted to possess her. The child was a nurse in Mutare. We brewed beer here, we played the drums and the ancestral spirit came. The spirit came and we spent the whole night dancing until the next day. From here we went to their home.

---

[20]Peter Hatendi, 'Ad clerum: of offences', Diocese of Harare, TD, mimeographed, 1990.
[21]Shadreck Mapudzi, Essay Project on Christianity and Tradition.

Drums were played at the priest's house. People wondered how that could be done at a Christian's home. But when the spirit arrived, that child got well and went back to her work. Today she is there in Mutare, she is working, she is a nurse. She is now staying well. That whole work was done by Grandfather. Her parents, even now, believe that it is true that ancestral spirits are there.[22]

The Roman Catholic Church is unique in that, although it discourages participation in SSR, it has designed liturgies specifically to be Christian analogs of SSR rites intended to unite the spirit of the deceased with the other ancestral spirits and welcome the spirit back to the homestead.[23] In an organised theological discussion, a manager at EHTE affirmed the Roman position as a 'localisation' of Christianity and pointed out what he perceived as the similarity between the Ten Commandments and the moral strictures of SSR. A labourer, on the other hand, condemned the Roman ceremonies as contravening the command not to worship anything or anyone except God alone.[24] Some Christians explore SSR out of a desire to reappropriate a Shona culture from which they feel a Western lifestyle has alienated them.

MFC members sometimes accuse AICs of incorporating too much SSR into their approach to healing, spiritual power and leadership. A Methodist leader asserts that some AIC leaders oscillate between being prophets in their churches and diviner-healers in SSR; this indicates, he says, that they are dealing with ancestral spirits in both contexts. How can a prophet's claim to the Holy Spirit be credible, he asks, if, when the same person lapses from his church, he becomes possessed by a *mudzimu* in his role as a *nganga*? Ecstatic manifestations in the church are seen to have a background in ancestral worship:

> Those possessed with Holy Spirit have been previously possessed with either *mudzimu* or *shave.* If one joins the Spirit church without having been possessed of either *mudzimu* or *shave* one won't

---

[22]Mai Muzanenhamo, *pungwe,* festival of SSR, 24–25 May 1991. She herself was a Roman Catholic until the churches' opposition to SSR prompted her to resign her membership.

[23]Eg *Shona ritual: kuchenura munhu, kana kuti, kurova guva, kana kugadzira mufi* (Purifying the person, or beating the grave, or preparing the dead) (Gweru: Mambo Press, 1982).

[24]Church leaders, Forum on Theology, 18 May 1991.

be possessed of the Holy Spirit ... So to me Mweya Mutsvene is either a transformed *mudzimu* ... or something else.[25]

The independents' focus on healing is sometimes criticised as little more than a superficially Christianised version of SSR's instrumental emphasis on religion as the source of personal healing and prosperity. The comparison with SSR is sharpened when the *nganga's* use of various medicines *(mishonga)* is likened to the prophet's use of water, oil, eggs and drawings in the work of healing.[26] To some observers, the similarity is borne out by how some people circulate regularly among diviner-healers and church prophets in search of healing. Even if the leaders are sincere, so the argument goes, their approach does nothing to discourage a purely instrumental quest from superseding genuine spiritual commitment.

Popular critiques of Shona Spirit Religion

At the same time that many Christians practice a dual affiliation that puts the churches on the defensive, many people are also asking serious questions about SSR. If the questions posed to the churches concern the validity of exclusive claims, the questions posed to SSR typically concern the obligations that the rites lay on those who come seeking practical and spiritual assistance.

The ambivalent attitude of ancestral spirits toward their descendants, as expressed in harsh and threatening oracles, often concerns speakers at church *mapungwe.* For instance, at a routine divination session at EHTE, the *nganga* told a young mother that her child's illness was

---

[25]Pearson Chitare, Essay Project on Christianity and Tradition.

[26]Two instances illustrate the point. One PACG prophet asks suppliants to leave jugs of water with their tops off at her healing centre before they go home. If, during the following week, ants and other insects crawl into a jug, the prophet concludes that the suppliant is not following her directions. Owners of the jugs without insects are judged to be faithful. I observed a Jekenishen prophet respond to a suppliant by drawing what appeared to be a star on a piece of paper, roll up the paper, and put it in a bottle of water with directions to take it home and keep it nearby when she prayed. The prophet explained that he drew the picture under the Holy Spirit's direction and implied that having the drawing nearby would ensure the Spirit's continuing ministration to the suppliant.

caused by her husband's failure to brew beer for the grandmother's spirit. The diviner went on to say:

> You still don't want to carry out the rituals for your ancestral spirits (*kugadzira vadzimu*). Let him brew some beer. If he does not carry out the rituals, we will kill her (the child). Now let us go, because he has failed. We told him what the grandmother wants.[27]

The apparent incongruity between a grandparent's love of a child in life but capricious hostility after death is widely questioned, especially in the increasing individualism and isolation of modern Shona society, where the support of the extended family becomes ever more urgent. An Apostolic Faith Mission member put the critique this way:

> The problem with these *vadzimu* is that they are always making trouble for people. They make you sick, they make you die, they make you lose your job. If someone were to say that any of these things happened because of my dead father, I would say, 'My father would never want to do any of those things to me!'[28]

Explaining why he rejected SSR to become a Christian, a Marange Apostle concurred:

> In offering to the ancestral spirits, the ancestral spirits first make one suffer. The person first gets seriously ill. When you consult the *nganga* you hear that grandfather or grandmother is the one who is making him sick. So I found that to be a hard thing, for you pray to grandfather, but he makes you sick.[29]

The fact that ritual practice varies widely among geographical areas complicates the situation in modern mobile society, for what was performed properly by ritual specialists in one area is often deemed improper when a sufferer consults a *nganga* in another area.

Restoring harmony in relationships is a clear concern in SSR divination. When people inquire why their temporal world has been disturbed, they receive an answer based on why the spirit world has been disturbed, and they carry out ritual amends to restore harmony in the relationship between the two worlds. Strong concern for community

---

[27]Divination session, Mai Makwiana, 6 May 1991.
[28]Webster Zizhou, interview, 18 April 1991.
[29]SaDuri, evangelists interview, AACJM, 20 April 1991.

between generations, even across the divide of death, is prominent, and the pattern moderates individual interests in favour of the wider community represented by the spirit elders. The literature on African traditional religions in the latter half of the twentieth century has made much of these qualities.[30]

Evaluation of traditional ritual by many Shona people today is complex. The predominance of ritual infractions over moral infractions in the diagnoses provided by *nganga* is viewed with dismay, especially amid societal problems such as poverty, rape and other violence against women, child abuse, murder and sexual promiscuity that by mid-1998 resulted in the world's highest rate of HIV infection.[31] Diagnoses that attribute misfortune to ritual infractions are sometimes greeted with incredulity and scorn:

> If the *vadzimu* exist why don't they come and put order in a family. For example, when the daughters of a family are heavily indulging into prostitution, or when the sons of a family are involved in thieving, why don't the *vadzimu* come and say, 'Stop thieving, stop prostitution!' But they just come and claim for beer and meat, yet prostitution and theft are at stake.[32]

The sincerity and honesty of diviners is also questioned, for people recognise that a diviner may cite a ritual infraction simply because that is his or her area of expert knowledge, whereas ferreting out important ethical lapses may be more difficult.

---

[30]John Mbiti's analysis is influential and representative: 'In traditional life, the individual does not and cannot exist alone except corporately. He owes his existence to other people, including those of past generations and his contemporaries ... Only in terms of other people does the individual become conscious of his own being, his own duties, his privileges and responsibilities towards himself and towards other people ... Whatever happens to the individual happens to the whole group, and whatever happens to the whole group happens to the individual. The individual can only say: "I am, because we are; and since we are, therefore I am". This is a cardinal point in the understanding of the African view of man.' *African religions and philosophy* (London, Ibadan, and Nairobi: Heinemann, 1969), 108–109.

[31]The United Nations Aids Program reported Zimbabwe's infection rate at 25,8 per cent. Lawrence K Altman, 'Parts of Africa Showing HIV in 1 in 4 adults', *New York Times*, 24 June 1998, A1.

[32]Aneck Taulo, Essay Project on Christianity and Tradition.

A movement for taking back the night

The role of night in both the Anglican bishop's comment and in the spirit diviner's story of a priest coming for divination is striking for our study. For the bishop, nocturnal ritual suggests precisely what he would like Shona Christians to avoid. The central rites of SSR are nocturnal and participation in them leads to syncretism, which the bishop sees as a compromise of Christian truth. His discouragement of night meetings in the churches highlights the role of the *pungwe* in the relationship between Christianity and SSR. The diviner-healer's story confirms the centrality of nocturnal ritual in SSR, and the priest's participation in a night-time divination led him, she believes, to affirm the importance of the ancestral spirits. For her, the day-night contrast is a crux for the integrity of Christians, for she is impatient with being condemned by day but consulted by night.

The place of the *pungwe* in this ritual and theological landscape now comes into focus. The hearts and minds of Zimbabweans are a contested ground between the advocates of Christianity and the advocates of SSR. In that debate, night has also become contested ground. Some Christians claim the day for Christ and believe that night is the time of evil powers. Practitioners of SSR readily acknowledge that their central rites take place at night, but they insist that they deal not in evil (which is the province of wizards) but in the central relationships and obligations of the Shona people. What, then, is happening among the many thousands of Christians who gather for night meetings not in the precincts of mediums and diviners but in their own churches, on mountains, at sacred grounds and in homes? What is happening when they gather at night not to invoke the ancestral spirits but Mwari whom they profess to know as Father and Son and Holy Spirit?

They are taking back the night. Those who take the night back share a confidence in the power of night with those from whom they seize it. In the churches the *pungwe* becomes an arena where visions of the new dispensation are clarified in dialogue with the visions of the old. It is the forum where the claims and counter-claims of all sides are evoked and debated. It is, above all, the crucible in which authentic experiences of the divine are forged.

232

Dimensions of appropriation and transformation

The *pungwe* movement draws deeply from the *pungwe* traditions of SSR and the mobilisation rallies of the Liberation War. Yet it receives nothing without moulding it to achieve objectives conceived within a Christian framework of spirituality, community and mission. The movement's interaction with SSR and the wartime rallies is thus one of appropriation and transformation in the three central dimensions of the *pungwe*: spiritual encounter, community-building and liberative empowerment.

The *pungwe* as spiritual encounter

In SSR and in the Christian churches, the *pungwe* is most fundamentally an occasion for spiritual encounter, a dimension also prominent in the guerrilla *pungwe.*

Night is the time of spiritual encounter in SSR, when the community of the living meets the community of the living dead. The human community believes that spirit beings of every kind are especially active at night and make themselves especially available at night. With this expectation, families and clan groups gather at night to make themselves available to the spirits to whom they owe an obligation. Nocturnal discourse in SSR is not homiletic and people do not primarily talk about the spirits. Instead, people experience the spirits directly in possession. Mediums exhibit the spirits' presence through trance, dance, ecstatic verbalisation, song and instructional declarations. Family elders make ritual offerings to the spirits with customary verbal addresses. Spiritual communion occurs as people talk to the ancestors and hear the ancestors talk to the community.

Spiritual encounter means that night is the time of power in SSR, because ultimate power belongs to the spirit beings who visit people at night. The power of the signs by which spirits signal their desire to come close and speak to the community – illness, misfortune, death – is verified and fulfilled in the power by which spirits possess their mediums. At night people are gathering in an environment of such power. Equally important, night is also the environment of evil power, when avenging spirits express their malevolence through the nocturnal work of sorcerers and witches.

233

Spiritual encounter, with its power, was central in the nighttime rallies of the Liberation War. Calling upon the ancestral and territorial spirits legitimised the wartime *pungwe* by linking it with the spiritual encounters of the *pungwe* in SSR. The power of the spirits was crucial to the fighters' effort to mobilise people to recover power over their own political future. With missionary zeal, the guerrillas brought common religious experience into the arena of public discourse and invited all to enter it and make it their own.

In the dimension of spiritual encounter, the church *pungwe* builds primarily on the *pungwe* of SSR rather than on the wartime *pungwe.* When Shona Christians gather for a *pungwe* they bring with them the longings, expectations and patterns of Shona nocturnal ritual. As it is in SSR, night is a time of heightened spiritual availability for the Christians. At night, the spiritual realm is accessible to them and they are accessible to the spiritual realm. As a United Methodist lay leader says, 'Night is a special time to meet God.'[33] Expectation that night brings especially intense and significant religious experience is the fundamental datum underlying the religious and cultural continuity between the *pungwe* of SSR and the *pungwe* of the churches. Christians even identify the time of *mambakwedza* specifically as a time of particular sensitivity that prompts their interest in *mapungwe.* An ordained UMC minister put it very clearly:

> In our tradition, from 12 (midnight) to 4 (am) is an important time for meeting God. The ancestral spirits are met during that time. The Christian church tradition uses that tradition, only now with Christ as the cause and the source. So when we have testimonies in the early morning people are born again, people repent of their sins and evil spirits are cast out – all around 3 am ... At a *gungano* we don't feel satisfied unless we have *pungwe* on the last night![34]

The Christian *pungwe* expresses the Shona spirituality of encounter, but it simultaneously challenges and transforms the roots of that spirituality in SSR. Christians gather at night to encounter, not the ancestral spirits, but God, Mwari. The apparent contrast also signifies a point of contact, for in SSR it is only at night that people can approach the localised expression of Mwari at the great shrines. In SSR, Mwari's

[33]SaMarange, interview, 11 May 1991.
[34]The Rev Lloyd Nyarota, interview, 12 May 1991.

relative inaccessibility manifests itself in the need to travel to the shrines and work through a hierarchy of intermediaries before hearing Mwari's voice. Using the name Mwari for the God of biblical revelation brings Mwari close, consonant with God's nature as found in Christian revelation. Accessible in all places, Mwari is experienced at Christian *mapungwe* held anywhere. Directly accessible to all people, Mwari's presence is proclaimed and celebrated by all participants at a *pungwe*, not only by religious specialists. Further, Christians enact direct access to Mwari by day as well as by night in personal devotion, family prayers, Sunday and weekday liturgies and various group meetings. No Christian claims that Mwari is accessible only at night. The Marange Apostle's statement, 'Mwari walks at night', signifies that an especially intense and vivid experience of God is available in the context of a *pungwe.*

The church *pungwe* elaborates the nature of Mwari along Christian lines that represent both contrast and continuity with how SSR conceives of Mwari's nature. In focusing on Mwari rather than on local spirits, Christian proclamation highlights monotheism in contrast to SSR's preoccupation with ancestral spirits. At the same time, Christians invoke Mwari as the triune Mwari – Father, Son and Holy Spirit – with Jesus and the Holy Spirit receiving much attention alongside the Father, especially the Spirit in the prophesying and healing work of AICs. The multiple objects of devotion in SSR may equip Shona Christians to embrace biblical revelation's diverse manifestations of God, and their theology has a decidedly trinitarian rather than unitarian cast.

The pneumatological stress of the Christian *pungwe* is a major way in which the *pungwe* of SSR has influenced Christian practice. As SSR offers possession by a spirit as the central religious experience, so Christians at *pungwe* long for the Holy Spirit and profess to be moved by the Holy Spirit. 'Sometimes the Spirit really moves at a *pungwe,'* says an Anglican pastor, 'and you feel that the Holy Spirit is really there.'[35] Most Manicaland Christians consider the Holy Spirit's presence at a *pungwe* to be a criterion of the gathering's success, whereas they may be content with good instruction and faithful prayers at a more subdued Sunday liturgy. Shona people's enduring interest in

---

[35]David Manyau, interview, 16 May 1991.

direct and powerful spiritual experience arises out of SSR and contributes to the pentecostal tendencies of Shona Christianity.[36] The shift from spirits to the Holy Spirit, however, broadens and transforms access to spiritual reality. SSR limits spirit possession to the one person or several people chosen by the particular spirit, who then speaks through the medium. In the Christian *pungwe*, the Holy Spirit is accessible to any member of the congregation, and many members profess to be moved by the Holy Spirit. Reproducing such biblical models of the Holy Spirit's work as are found in 1 Corinthians 12, the manifestations of the Spirit are commensurably more diverse, and church members assess ministries of preaching, praying, singing, prophesying, exorcising and healing as evidence of the Spirit's activity.

Christian scripture plays a key role in broadening accessibility to spiritual encounter. A spirit medium claims to speak the words of a spirit and asserts that the medium must be heeded. Shona Christians' belief that the Bible is God's word means that God's communication is

---

[36]This recognition of pentecostal tendencies is less comprehensive than Harvey Cox's characterisation of AICs (including the AACJM, the ZAC and the ZCC in Zimbabwe): 'These churches constitute the African expression of the worldwide Pentecostal movement', marked by certain patterns of worship and by 'the high-impact spread of the American Pentecostal movement' early in the twentieth century. 'Healers and ecologists: Pentecostalism in Africa', *Christian Century* 111.32 (9 November 1994): 1043. The particular emphasis on the Holy Spirit found in many churches does support analysis of what might be better termed 'communities of the Spirit' on a global basis. Analysis in terms of 'the worldwide Pentecostal movement', however, implies a greater degree of uniformity than exists and diminishes the importance of local and regional distinctives that have grown more prominent since the founding of churches from a common historical source. Several observations are in order. First, the pneumatology of the Shona churches owes at least as much to indigenous sources as it does to the now-distant historical connection with American Pentecostalism. Second, Shona Christian worship exhibits distinct patterns that are as unfamiliar to pentecostal Christians in other parts of the world as they are to Protestants or Roman Catholics. Third, the prominence of the *pungwe* movement, with its pneumatological stress, in MFCs as well as in AICs, defies an easy dichotomy between Spirit-filled AICs and Spirit-deprived MFCs. In sum, as religious communities evolve, paradigms of analysis relevant in one period become less appropriate later as communities respond to different influences and needs. The term 'pentecostal', therefore, is misleading as a primary or comprehensive characterisation of Shona AICs, Shona Christianity, or the *pungwe* movement.

accessible to anyone who reads or hears it, not only to selected individuals who articulate a spirit's words to the community. Being moved by the Holy Spirit, then, means doing the works of the Spirit as set forth in the scriptures and interpreting God's words in scripture so that the community hears and encounters God in the event. Thus, an inclusive vocabulary of inspiration replaces the more exclusive vocabulary of possession; *kufemerwa*, 'to be breathed into', replaces *kusvikirwa*, 'to be entered, possessed'. The contrast between modes of pneumatological experience becomes a full-scale confrontation when, as often happens, exorcism becomes the focus of a *pungwe*.

The celebratory tone of the church *pungwe* draws on the community enthusiasm of the *pungwe* in SSR. The expectancy with which people await the spirits' arrival and the ecstasy that the spirits evoke in an SSR *pungwe* have a direct corollary in the elevated feeling that pervades a church *pungwe*. In both contexts people express their excitement in spontaneous singing and dancing, and the wartime rallies also featured this tone. The content and tunes of songs are quite different in each setting, and the various Christian churches have distinct musical traditions. The 1960s' shift toward drumming in many MFCs expressed a growing belief that African musical instruments could be used in church without importing the ancestral veneration with which they were associated, and a few AICs had always used them. Today, some MFCs and many AICs continue to eschew drums. The diverse percussive instruments and rhythms of the churches, however, are alike in avoiding the drum *rhythms* of SSR's *mashave* dances, which tend to be very strong, fast and complex.

Dancing is a point of nocturnal continuity and contrast. Possession dances in SSR occur mostly at night, and the drumbeat, costume and footwork of each dance often narrate the activity of the spirits involved. So, also, dancing as a full-bodied expression of religious enthusiasm appears much more frequently in most churches' *mapungwe* than during their daytime liturgies, but they avoid the dance patterns and drumbeats of SSR. Methodists and Anglicans often dance at a *pungwe,* and CCAP dances resemble social dances Malawians brought with them to Zimbabwe. Pentecostal Apostolics are happy to dance around their *pungwe* fire in a general way, while the Marange Apostles shun dancing as much as drumming. The Jekenishens and the Zionists, by contrast, spend most of their worship time in dancing, by day as by night, but they too avoid the dance patterns of SSR.

Eucharist at dawn in the vigils of the MFCs expresses ritual continuity with the traditional *pungwe,* for spirit mediums experience their final possession at dawn, when they share special pots of ritual beer. Here again, analog challenges and transforms archetype, for the eucharistic rite focuses on the triune Mwari, not on ancestral spirits. The communion is shared equally throughout the entire community, not derivatively from the medium as the only one who has experienced spiritual reality directly.

Prayer in the church *pungwe* differs markedly from the discourse of possession rituals of the SSR *pungwe.* Brevity characterises people's remarks to the spirits through the mediums whom they possess. Family elders articulate the customary formulas, and people express their particular concerns quickly and deferentially in order to avoid offending the spirits. Similarly, the messages spirits convey through their mediums tend to be brief and peremptory. The high emotion of the community's encounter with a spirit elder finds outlet in the singing and dancing of an SSR *pungwe.* In the Christian *pungwe,* by contrast, people carry the high emotional tone into their prayer. MFC leaders pray passionately and at great length, while others in the congregation murmur assents along the way, and the Spirit-type AICs encourage long periods of simultaneous and spontaneous prayer on the part of all present. In contrast to SSR, the accent is on individual expression rather than articulation of a formulaic address.[37]

In summary, spiritual encounter in the Christian pungwe appropriates key features of the *pungwe* in SSR, but it transforms every feature it receives and moves into direct confrontation on the crucial issue of spirit possession.

---

[37]Incorporation of written liturgies into a *pungwe* occurs gracefully among Anglican congregations, which represent the one 'catholic' tradition that practises the *pungwe.* Shona Anglicans typically begin a *pungwe* with Evensong and end it with Eucharist. Prayerbook worship is deeply embedded in the spirituality of Shona Anglicans, and the move from prayerbook to free worship and back again is a smooth one.

The *pungwe* as community-building

Building community is the second major dimension in which the Christian *pungwe* appropriates and transforms the *pungwe* of SSR and the nocturnal mobilisation rallies of the Liberation War.

The *pungwe* of SSR is the principal setting in which Shona people experience and strengthen community. No gatherings are so frequent, so well attended, so obligatory, or so powerful as the all-night rituals in which people meet to communicate with the spirits of their ancestors. The spirit realm of SSR is an extension of the living kin, and the living kin are an extension of the spirit realm. As the two sides meet each other, full community occurs and group identity is reaffirmed. As the kinship group gathers with its ancestors, it becomes a community in the cultural sense of a group of people who are connected with one another by active networks of mutual communication, shared values and common commitments to accomplish goals. People encounter each other in the ritual roles that enact their familial relations with each other and with the ancestors. As they meet the spirits, they have an opportunity to take counsel about problems facing the community.

Building and mobilising community was a dominant concern of the freedom fighters in the *mapungwe* they organised during the Liberation War. Guerrillas sought to catalyse a new social and national self-awareness in people as they promoted networks of shared commitments and mutual accountability to prosecute the war. By making the *pungwe* their principal instrument in this community-building effort, the guerrillas tapped the celebratory and communal resources of the traditional *pungwe*: people's attraction to all-night gatherings, their joy in being together and their renewed group identity. Guerrillas anchored this strategy by invoking the spirits who are the bedrock of SSR's *pungwe,* thereby asserting continuity with traditional religion. They challenged participants to see that SSR entailed a commitment to liberate the land from colonial oppressors and restore its control to the Shona people and their ancestors.

The liturgical details of the guerrilla *pungwe* not only drew on existing ritual resources but also altered them in the service of promoting the war. The guerrillas incorporated the power of song in the SSR *pungwe* to nurture enthusiasm and commitment. Since the limited and enigmatic content of traditional songs was not useful, a new genre of

239

Chimurenga lyrics developed which, when set to music, demonstrated an eclectic use of cultural and religious sources. Some songs set liberation lyrics to church tunes, some used new tunes developed by local people, and some songs were composed entirely by Shona rock musicians. In giving long and detailed speeches at their rallies, the guerrillas drew not on the SSR *pungwe,* which does not have such a tradition, but on their experience of sermons in the *mapungwe* of the churches.

The guerrillas' community-building *mapungwe* imposed on Shona social structure a new criterion of community membership based on commitment to political liberation and participation in the war effort. The group summoned to a *pungwe* was the local village, but its networks of kinship and friendship were drastically relativised by the criterion of liberation zeal. Leaders were youths rather than elders; prerogatives accrued only to the active and loyal; all were obligated to contribute from their resources; and the marginalised were the sellouts, who might be members of one's own family. Thus, as the guerrillas extended the scope of SSR's concern with the land, they also reconceptualised community as the interdependent cell group marshaling all resources of energy, enthusiasm and vision to the sole task of military victory and political liberation. They sought to implement a new basis of group identity that, nevertheless, would be continuous with the ancestor veneration of SSR.

The community-building function of the *pungwe* in the Christian churches draws on both SSR and the wartime rallies. People's confidence that all-night religious gatherings will strengthen group cohesion and identity issues directly from SSR. Influenced by SSR's implicit assertion that spirituality is not primarily individual but corporate, Christians look to intense group events for primary experiences of their faith. People consider individual commitment important, but they link it to the corporate experience of the *pungwe.* Conversely, SSR influences people to expect that their strongest group experiences will be religious experiences. With such perceptions and expectations, Christians find that their group identity as churches is uniquely strengthened by the *pungwe.*

As the wartime *pungwe* sought to redefine and enlarge the community according to a political objective, so also the Christian *pungwe* redefines the community according to a religious affiliation and enlarges the group beyond the extended family typically present for the rituals of SSR. 'I find that the *pungwe* draws from a much broader spectrum of the society,' says David Manyau, the Anglican priest, 'including young people, people with families, old people. Many more people come to a *pungwe* than come on Sunday morning.'[38] The Christian *pungwe* retains the communal and relational tone of the traditional gathering, but it redefines membership through relationship with the triune God. Community is at once re-directed and broadened: broadened as its membership transcends ordinary kinship and redirected from the ancestor of a particular family to the God of all people as revealed in Jesus Christ. Preachers' use of the terms *mhuri* (family) and *hama* (relatives) in addressing the gathered church indicates that, from a spiritual perspective, a new kinship group comes into being. The triune God is the progenitor, with whom members are related by voluntary association rather than by blood.[39] This is true of Christianity's impact among Shona people in general, but it is especially striking in the *pungwe.* Sunday morning church services generally draw the committed faithful, whereas the *pungwe* also draws the apathetic, the lapsed, the curious and the hostile. In this way it transcends the narrower boundaries of both the SSR rite and the conventional Sunday worship service. It has broader appeal because it both echoes and transforms kinship. The kinship theme is latently present in the very fact of gathering at night, but the traditional kinship is broken open and the community is reconstituted on a broader base and with a more universal focus.

Leadership opportunity in the Christian pungwe likewise appropriates and transforms patterns of the *pungwe* in SSR. Spirit rituals provide for many family members definite roles that reinforce incorporation into the group. The church *pungwe* similarly offers various roles – preaching, leading songs, praying, prophesying, healing, exorcising – but people are chosen for them on the basis of their abilities and calling rather than their place in a kinship system.[40] To the large extent

---

[38]David Manyau, interview, 16 April 1991.

[39]For a full theological development of this theme by a RCC constructive theologian, see Charles Nyamiti, *Christ as our ancestor: christology from an African perspective* (Gweru: Mambo Press,1984); see also Pobee, 94.

[40]As in any religious context, the sociology of the group also influences the assignment of leadership roles in Shona churches. Factors that prompt respect in the wider community – such as education, affluence, professional status and personal connections – play a role, as does position in the kinship system. For role reversals in wartime and in some post-war AICs, see Maxwell, 322–326. It is also important to note that the traditional rites do include some flexibility in role assignments. For the spontaneous and improvised aspects of SSR see Murphree, 59; and Daneel, *Major movements,* 180.

that *pungwe* roles are open to any interested participant, the situation becomes very open indeed, with persons free to preach or lead songs spontaneously as they feel moved by the Spirit. In this way the participatory emphasis of SSR ritual is brought to full fruition.

The Christian *pungwe* encourages participation not only among the self-confident but also by those who ordinarily are at the edges of social interaction:

> Many people who feel too shy to talk about their lives in a regular church service will feel able to talk about their problems at a *pungwe*. You will find that late at night some of these people will stand up and give their testimony.[41]

The general congregational *pungwe* builds community through ensuring that all constituent groups have a chance to be heard:

> Being at a *pungwe* requires patience. Sometimes a youth will stand up and talk about the things that youth are interested in and some of the mothers will just dismiss him. But I tell them, 'No, listen to him, for when you listen to him you are listening to the concerns of your own children. You may actually learn something.' So also, the youth might dismiss what some of the mothers might say. But all must be patient with each other and listen to what each other has to say. People are more free at a *pungwe* to say what they really feel.[42]

Evangelistic outreach and numerical growth are key consequences of the *pungwe* movement's community-building function. The transformation that the Christian *pungwe* has worked on every aspect it receives from the SSR *pungwe* has broadened its appeal and widened its membership: gathering at night, but inviting everyone; meeting for spiritual encounter, but focusing on the universal God; stressing communal tone, but broadening family and community; including many leadership roles, but opening them to everyone. Recognising the natural appeal of these features, the churches have made the *pungwe* a key element in their evangelistic strategy and numerical growth has been a direct result. Thus, the *pungwe* has become a revival movement in the classic sense of a popular movement that features special

---

[41]SaMarange, interview, 11 May 1991.
[42]David Manyau, interview, 16 April 1991.

242

meetings devoted to rekindling the faith of church members and encouraging conversion in non-believers.

All-night vigils were important in Manicaland's mass movement of conversion early in this century. The night-time rallies of the Liberation War brought the *pungwe* to centre-stage again and revealed its potential for activist efforts in affirming identity, strengthening cohesion and broadening participation. By putting a political ideology of liberation at the centre of *pungwe* life, the mobilisation rallies demonstrated conclusively that the *pungwe* was an adaptable practice that did not have to signify ancestor veneration. For churches seeking to rebuild their communities after the devastation of war, the lesson was clear and the instrument was irresistible.

The *pungwe* as liberative empowerment

Liberative empowerment is the third major dimension of the Christian *pungwe* movement that represents an interaction with SSR and with the wartime mobilisation rallies. The movement both incorporates SSR's view of evil into its effort to liberate people from spiritual oppression and radically redefines SSR itself as a locus of demonic power that Christians must overcome. The political dimension of the wartime rallies has enabled the movement to engage social issues and, in particular, promote the liberation of women in Shona society.

Night is the time of spiritual power in SSR, because night is when the spirit beings who hold power are especially available and close. Possession manifests a spirit's power through a medium. In a systematic perspective, all religious ritual seeks to mediate the presence of supernatural reality, and the style and content of rituals in different religious communities vary widely in their relative emphases on instruction, ecstasy, prayer, inspiration, direction and the like. The overwhelming emphasis of ritual in SSR, as in many African religions, is on the power of immediate, ecstatic union with spirit elders and on their direction of the community. As people observe the direct manifestation of power in a medium, they experience in a more diffuse way an aura of power that they express in song and dance. Community empowerment occurs as participants strengthen their group identity and cohesion, renew their networks of relationship, address community issues and decide on courses of action.

The community empowerment that the SSR *pungwe* stimulates often addresses the community's experience of being disempowered by misfortune. The group gathers to hear the spirit's revelation of the personal or corporate violations and errors that have caused an illness, a lightning strike, a poor harvest, a sudden death, or some other misfortune which weakens the community by diminishing its resources of goods and personal resilience. The spirit's analysis may be painful to hear, but its prescription charts the way back to community harmony and wholeness. The nocturnal activities of avenging spirits and wizards constitute the most potent threats to individual and group safety. The *pungwe* enacts group solidarity against whatever threats may be developing under the cover of darkness.

The *pungwe* of the Liberation War concentrated on liberation and empowerment above all else. With the heritage of SSR, the *pungwe* was an environment of power, and the guerrillas' invocation of the spirit elders made the connection with SSR explicit. Earlier patterns of night vigils in the churches also prepared the ground by asserting indigenous initiative over against white superintendence. In a practical sense, the Rhodesian military's relative quiescence at night made night a time of ascendant power for the guerrillas. By eliminating wizards at *mapungwe,* the guerrillas participated in one of SSR's main preoccupations with oppression and liberation.

The guerrillas' principal concern with military and political liberation from white oppression extended the liberation motif of the SSR *pungwe* into the political life of the people under colonialism. The *pungwe* of SSR had always had political ramifications in that it often dealt with community issues, and in the cases of the *mhondoro* and Mwari the issues concerned wide geographical areas and large groups of people. The experience of most people, however, was limited to local *mapungwe,* where the issues were more personal and familial. The broad scope that the guerrillas introduced might have been incomprehensible had it not been that guerrillas invoked the spirit elders, cited the examples of mediums in the First *Chimurenga* and confronted wizards as well as sellouts.

The wartime *mapungwe* empowered people in several respects. First, the rallies empowered the guerrillas themselves. The confluence of strategic alliances formed with spirit mediums, many guerrillas' renewed commitment to SSR and their evident enjoyment of the *mapungwe* indicate that the rallies strengthened the *vakomana* for their military task. Second, rallies mobilised people to realise and exert the power they had to assist the war effort. Frequent executions of collaborators and wizards helped to secure compliance, but such events hampered the empowerment effort by coercing cooperation through fear. Nevertheless, the rallies generated enthusiasm and commitment to the war and thereby empowered local people. Third, the guerrillas sought to empower people for building the new Zimbabwe when independence would be achieved. The guerrillas' language of 'liberated zones' and 'comrades', their frequent predictions about the future independence and their attention to ancillary issues such as prostitution confirm that they believed that their *mapungwe* were shaping the basic units of a new society.

The *pungwe* of the churches draws on the empowerment dynamic of the *pungwe* in SSR as the Christians incorporate the fundamental perception that night is a time of spiritual power because spiritual reality is especially close. As individuals manifest the Spirit's presence and power in prayer, preaching, glossalalia, prophecy, healing and exorcism, the group as a whole is empowered. At the same time that the Christian pungwe receives from SSR's *pungwe* a basic orientation to issues of spiritual power, it launches a frontal assault on SSR by defining SSR as a major source of malevolent power in Shona life. By shifting religious devotion from spirit elders to the triune God, the Christian *pungwe* denies the validity of the obligations SSR asserts that people must fulfil toward their ancestors. The ways in which Christians continue to experience the pressure of these obligations – dreams, the verdicts of mediums, unsought possession – are interpreted as oppression by demons. Theologically, Christian leaders at *mapungwe* assess spirit possession as demon possession and, following Jesus' example, they respond with exorcism, which becomes a major mode of liberation in the church *pungwe.* On this view, the Holy Spirit's conflict with the spirits of SSR expresses God's eternal conflict with Satan and all the forces of evil that rebel against God.

Christians do share common ground with SSR in their opposition to wizards, but their response highlights differences rather than similarities. While SSR locates evil in wizardry, Christian leaders see wizardry and SSR itself as manifestations of Satan's work, differing only in the quality of human collusion. SSR is considered the great deception from which people need liberation through proper teaching and exorcism, but they are not blameworthy unless they resist the gospel and persist in SSR. Wizardry, by contrast, is sheer malevolence. Wizardry is especially feared, but in practice the two form a continuum for Christians, as wizards and diviner-healers alike bring their paraphernalia to be burned and stand together to be exorcised at Christian *mapungwe.*

The political dimension of the wartime rallies influenced the churches' post-war practice by demonstrating that the *pungwe* could become a vehicle for social and political empowerment ranging far beyond the scope of a typical *pungwe* with the spirits:

> By talking to many people, the boys won the people, so that they went over to their side, because during the *pungwe* they taught them (the people) that if we take over the country we would do such-and-so. Now in worship, people spend the whole night talking about how when we do good we will live in blessedness, doing such-and-so and telling one another about the good things that are ahead. Now I see that the churches picked up from the courageous way in which the boys used to talk.[43]

The wartime night rallies alerted some Christians to the political dimensions of the Bible, and the guerrillas' *mapungwe* sometimes dovetailed with churches' night-time gatherings. A United Church of Christ member recalls such a milieu he experienced in the Hilltop section of Mutare during the war:

> During the war people used to come out of church and go to the *mapungwe* of the war. I remember how it was at Hilltop in Mutare, when we came from Harare in 1972. People would go out after a preaching at *midnight* ... The sermon was like the Bible and it was like politics. When you go deeply into the things of the Bible, many times it would be politics.[44]

The guerrillas' liberation message and their anti-church polemic prompted some Christians to formulate a Christian basis for liberation:

> I stayed with the boys. They questioned me, 'Do you worship? Do

---

[43]David Mubaira, church members interview, 13 March 1991.
[44]SaKwadingepi, church members interview, 13 March 1991.

246

you agree (with others) that worshipping will give us the country, or is worship bad?' I said, 'If we fight the war and conquer, it will have come from the children of Israel. They argued with the king of Egypt and on the basis of worshipping they won many wars.'[45]

Thus, the wartime rallies demonstrated the flexibility of the *pungwe* and associated it with creative reflection on issues of power and liberation.

The current emphasis on the liberation of women in the churches' *pungwe* movement applies the wartime *pungwe* experience to one of the principal issues of post-independence Zimbabwean society.[46] The war itself precipitated the issue, for women fought alongside men in many instances and everywhere provided crucial logistical support. Independence raised the question whether Shona society would return to the *status quo ad quem* or wartime changes would be incorporated into societal norms. Important advances were forthcoming from the government, such as the establishment of a Ministry of Community Development and Women's Affairs in 1981, the passage of the Legal Age of Majority Act in 1982 and the enactment of other laws to ensure women's rights to property and children. The *pungwe* movement's initiative for women responds to the need for grassroots transformation. It addresses issues of attitude and social interaction only implied by civil law, and it engages them at the crucial level of religious sanction. The wartime *pungwe* offered a practical vision which the churches appropriated and which enabled them, more than any other local institution, to embody women's solidarity and to give it a religious basis.

Summary

The *pungwe* movement in the churches is not simply the continuation of earlier patterns but is a major post-war development that has been crucial in the renewal and growth of Christian churches in Manicaland. The form and content of the movement is shaped substantially by an ongoing debate between proponents of SSR and those of Christianity about their respective claims. The sensitive and powerful role of night

---

[45]Bernard Matseketsa, church members interview, 13 March 1991.
[46]For a general assessment of the political, legal, cultural, and economic dimensions of women's issues in Zimbabwe during the 1980s, see Kazembe, 377–404.

in Shona religious life means that in this debate night is contested ground, and the *pungwe* movement in the churches represents Christians' attempt to take back the night from the exclusive control of SSR.

The *pungwe* movement's effort to reappropriate night is not simply an adversarial contest with SSR. Instead, the movement interacts with the historical, religious and cultural legacy of night-time activity in a complex pattern of appropriation and transformation that focuses on spiritual encounter, community-building and liberative empowerment. In each of these areas, the church *pungwe* builds on central features of the *pungwe* in SSR and in the Liberation War, but it transforms this heritage by subjecting it to understandings and expectations formed by Christian conversion. At the same time, the heritage of SSR and the *Chimurenga* has shaped the way Christians in the *pungwe* movement understand their faith, live in community and enact their mission in the world.

CHAPTER 8

Catalysed for mission: vigils in the embrace of gospel and culture

Whenever I go for a *pungwe* I experience a great change in my life. I confidently believe that God's greatest chance to deliver messages to his people is during the night at the *pungwes*. One day we held a *pungwe* for the Family of God Church and the whole night was full of amazements. Many Christians were filled with the Holy Spirit and immediately started to speak in tongues. Demons were casted away in the name of Jesus Christ. People who were ill recovered. Myself I started speaking in tongues that night ... This is what is happening in our church. So at the *pungwe* my life is moulded by God. Many Christians attend to the church, hence God has the widest chance to be with his people.[1]

Witness to the mission power of the *pungwe* movement is abundant. All that this study has set forth confirms the assessment of this 23-year-old plantation personnel clerk in the Honde Valley. The always interesting question for Shona people is not, How has something happened? but Why did it happen? When that question is asked about the *pungwe* movement, participants respond simply that it is by the power of God that the movement is advancing mission in the world. Recognising God's action in the movement is, of course, an existentially spiritual matter that each participant and observer decides on the basis of individual experience and discernment.

The question How? continues to be interesting and important. How does the *pungwe* movement exercise such missional power? How has it catalysed such growth and outreach since the Liberation War? How does it carry on from such disparate elements as possession rites and

---

[1]Noah Madenya, Essay Project on Christianity and Tradition.

wartime rallies? Moving beyond Zimbabwe to the global context of religion, what does the *pungwe* movement suggest about the role of primal religions on the world stage? What does it indicate about the rooting of world religions in local cultures? What direction does it offer to world Christianity for mission in the interreligious encounter?

We have explored some central dynamics of the movement's development. The *pungwe* movement in the churches appropriates dimensions of spiritual encounter, community-building and liberative empowerment from Shona Spirit Religion and from the wartime rallies. It then transforms these elements so that the *pungwe* becomes a vehicle of Christian revelation, community life and mobilisation for mission. Understanding the *pungwe* movement as a mission movement invites further inquiry and takes us into this chapter's discussions of the theory of ritual process, the interaction of world religion and local religion and the democratisation of theological initiative. The book concludes with a missiological assessment of the *pungwe* from the perspective of the Christian movement on the threshold of the twenty-first century.

Ritual vitality in wilderness nights

A *pungwe* is a ritual event, and it is as ritual that the *pungwe* catalyses spiritual encounter, community-building and liberative empowerment in Shona Christianity. Night and wilderness are two complementary themes in the ritual process. In the *pungwe* Christians are taking back the night in two senses: they wrest night from the exclusive control of SSR, and they reappropriate night from its exile by Western missionaries. Wilderness experience is a major ritual theme that both explains and extends the movement's nocturnal thrust. Understanding the flexible yet formative role of the *pungwe* in Shona Christianity requires exploration of the power and adaptability of ritual in human social experience.

Ritual meaning involves religion and culture. Clifford Geertz discusses ritual in terms of religion, which he defines as:

> A system of symbols which acts to establish powerful, pervasive and long-lasting moods and motivations in (people) by formulating conceptions of a general order of existence and clothing these

conceptions with such an aura of factuality that the moods and motivations seem uniquely realistic.

A symbol, for Geertz, is a vehicle for a conception; it is the tangible formulation of a notion, an abstraction from experience fixed in perceptible form. Sacred symbols are held to synthesise a people's ethos – the quality of their life and their moral and aesthetic style – and a people's comprehensive view of the world. In the consecrated behaviour and ceremonial form of ritual 'the world as lived and the world as imagined, fused under the agency of a single set of symbolic forms, turn out to be the same world'. Rituals are cultural performances in which the dispositional and conceptual aspects of religious life converge.[2] Ritual experience produces faith as it generates the conviction that religious beliefs are veridical and religious directives sound.

As a ritual form, the *pungwe* synthesises worldview and ethos, for it combines a worldview of spiritual entities with an ethos that expects spiritual encounter, community cohesion and liberative empowerment at night. The separability of the two elements in theory is confirmed by their separability in practice, for the worldview differs substantially in the various settings of the *pungwe,* while the ritual form continues to express a socially constructed ethos. The connection Geertz sees between ethos and worldview in religion prompts him to insist on religion's role as an independent variable in society:

> Religion is sociologically interesting not because, as vulgar positivism would have it, it describes the social order ... but because, like environment, political power, wealth, jural obligation, personal affection and a sense of beauty, it shapes it.[3]

Clearly, the *pungwe* both expresses Shona social order and shapes its continuing development. However, the history of the *pungwe* exposes how Geertz's preoccupation with symbols and meanings and his omission of spiritual reality from his definition of religion results in a failure to differentiate religion from ideology, which also fuses ethos and worldview. In the wartime mobilisation rallies, Marxist hostility to

---

[2]Clifford Geertz, 'Religion as a cultural system', in *The interpretation of cultures* (New York: Basic Books, 1973), 90, 91, 112–113.

[3]Ibid, 119. For a contrasting view, see Mary Douglas, *Natural symbols: explorations in cosmology,* With a new introduction by the author (New York: Pantheon, 1970 and 1982), vii, xiv, 8, 13.

religion fuelled condemnations of Christianity but coexisted alongside appeals to SSR. Developing a new relationship among these religious and ideological options has been a major agenda for the post-war *pungwe* movement. The specifically religious dimension, which concerns relationships between people and supernatural beings, has been a critically important variable in the historical continuum.

The *pungwe* has served a variety of worldviews in its cultural context, and at the same time it has shaped the religious and ideological uses to which it has been put. Ritual thus appears to be both malleable by historical circumstances and influential through the continuum of social experience. This dynamic function of ritual in the setting of culture is difficult to explain in terms of the common Geertzian symbols-and-meanings approach to culture as

> an historically transmitted pattern of meanings embodied in symbols, a system of inherited conceptions expressed in symbolic forms by means of which (people) communicate, perpetuate and develop their knowledge about and attitudes toward life.[4]

The emphasis on historical transmission recognises that culture arises out of a historical continuum and embodies social consensus rather than purely individual perception and understanding. The emphasis on meanings and symbols represents an important recovery of the ideational interest of culture: people do what they do not simply out of habit but because their activities mean something to them.

A dominating emphasis on historical transmission and inheritance in culture theory, however, is not adequate to account for cultural change and for the diversity, vitality and creativity of human cultures. It becomes difficult to explain how the meaning of a ritual can change or how a ritual can continue to shape meaning when its cognitive content has been radically revised. The common terminological bias towards transmitted and inherited material is evident, for instance, in the fact that Shona people using the English term 'culture' often associate it exclusively with *customs they no longer practise,* or with *customs the practice of which prompts experiences of inner conflict.* This is the basis of the complaint, 'Our culture has been destroyed.' In fact, human social life is indelibly cultural and people are just as embedded in culture as ever. The situation is rather that a people's culture

---

[4]Geertz, 'Religion as a cultural system', 89.

has *changed* as a result of their constant and creative interaction with a variety of influences. People are not passive recipients of their cultural heritage but, instead, they interact creatively with it on the basis of individual cognition and experience, which includes personal temperament, individual talents, social interaction and the perceptions shared among subgroups of which people are a part.

The *pungwe* demonstrates that the meaning of a ritual form can change through the historical experience that people bring to it and still maintain continuity with earlier patterns of meaning. The interactive view of ritual advanced by Robert Hefner helps to sharpen analysis of how the *pungwe* both shapes and is shaped by social experience. His definition of ritual is minimal enough to include all types of ritual: 'the physical performance of more or less formalised sequences of communicative behaviour, the form of which is not directly created by the performer'. Most human rituals are 'interaction rituals' concerned with the communication of attitudes and feelings of persons in relationships; in religious rituals, spirit entities are parties to the relationships. The 'reflexive equilibrium' of relationships means that relationships are always being tested; the parties constantly seek information about the quality of relationship; and the relationships are always in flux toward new equilibria of rights, feelings and obligations. Social life consists of a mass of such relationships and human experience is a steady stream of communicative detail in relationship. Ritual lifts a complex of relationship out of this stream, shapes it into an idealised image of the quality of the relationship and places that image on public record.[5]

The question remains, Why is ritual so prominent in religion? Why, in the context of Zimbabwe, is the *pungwe* so persistent in Shona religious life? The answer is that religion posits occult beings as parties to relationships with humans. The combination of their imputed power, their invisibility and the difficulty of verifying their responses engenders an especially intense human need for relational clarification, so that in most societies the most intense ritualism is associated with religion. The *pungwe* of SSR brings the ancestors especially close in the public sphere of the community gathered when it is most receptive, at night. From the disequilibrium of any unwelcome event in a family or

---

[5]Robert Hefner, 'The anthropological study of religion', lectures in Boston University, fall 1989.

clan, the gathering is designed to clarify relationships among the living and with the spirit elders and to reach a new equilibrium. The mobilisation rallies of the Liberation War sought to clarify people's relationships with the spirit elders, with the white settlers and their government, and with the guerrillas and their military programme.

The *pungwe* in the churches seeks to clarify participants' relationships among themselves, with the triune Mwari and with evil spirits. The nocturnal associations of spiritual encounter, community-building and liberative empowerment make night the ideal time to accomplish this. As ritual, the *pungwe* also brings the community to close quarters with oppressive spiritual and social relationships that need the clarification of liberation. Thus, the *pungwe* is the principal setting in which, on one hand, people exorcise evil spirits and, on the other, celebrate the empowering Holy Spirit. It is a major context for engaging with women's liberation. The movement also addresses cultural and historical dimensions of religious disequilibrium. Continuing unresolved and controversial are the relationships between missionary Christianity and Shona culture, between the claims of the gospel and the claims of SSR, and between the churches and the thrust of the Liberation War. The *pungwe* engages those issues and seeks their resolution.

The capacity of the *pungwe,* as a ritual form, to mediate such a variety of relationships in changing historical circumstances confirms Hefner's view that ritual meaning is not a fixed quality stored within invariant ritual symbols; that the internal coherence of a symbolic medium is not a sufficient condition for shared experience; that liturgy does not define an exhaustive belief system but only a core and periphery of meaning; and that religious faith is not generated in ritual performance alone, but is informed by a larger cultural dialogue.[6] The core meanings of the *pungwe* as a ritual form are the dimensions of spiritual encounter, community-building and liberative empowerment that the movement has both appropriated and transformed. These meanings correspond roughly to Geertz's category of ethos, as distinguished from worldview. The worldview has changed substantially in the three principal settings of this study, but the quality of the event persists through the shaping role of ethos. Worldview and ethos

---

[6]Robert Hefner, *Hindu Javanese: Tengger tradition and Islam* (Princeton: Princeton University Press, 1985), 187, 183, 161, 211.

influence each other organically as specifically religious aspects receive characteristic *pungwe* emphases and elements of the *pungwe* ethos are transformed by new elements of worldview.

Analysis of the *pungwe* as ritual sheds light on the mission history of Zimbabwe and on contemporary ecclesial discussions. Western missionaries who condemned night vigils among Shona Christians had too strong a view of the formative role of worldview in ritual and therefore could not credit the *pungwe* with the flexibility and receptivity that it so clearly possesses. As with the issue of drumming, it was easy to believe that if Shona Christians worshipped at night, the *pungwe* would pull them back into SSR. The American Methodists' heritage of liturgical flexibility enabled them early to fuse their own camp meeting tradition with the Shona desire for nocturnal religion without fear of heresy or backsliding. Contemporary efforts to suppress the *pungwe* similarly exaggerate the persistence of worldview in ritual and risk missing a major source of church renewal that is both authentically Shona and authentically Christian. Conversely, those who ignore or marginalise the *pungwe,* on the grounds that Christians can meet God any time, err by minimising this ritual form's unique contribution in building a specifically Shona Christianity.

Night as a wilderness experience is a ritual theme running through all aspects of the *pungwe.* Human beings are diurnal creatures, and in most cultures it is abnormal for people to stay up all night except for occupational necessity or the unusual celebration. The frequency and size of *mapungwe* in their various settings among the Shona are probably unique on a global basis.[7] The power and magnetism of the

---

[7]The typical festival, or *mela,* of mid-India Hindus includes some all-night rituals with ecstatic manifestations. Individually or in small groups, some evangelical Christians in Korea customarily pray for much of the night in mountain hermitages. The nocturnal associations of voodoo traditions in Haiti may stem from Haitian religion's African roots. The East African Revival that swept much of Uganda, Kenya and Tanzania, beginning in the 1930s, featured late-night evangelistic meetings but not the intentional and ritualistic dusk-to-dawn pattern of the *pungwe.* All-night ritual does appear in a number of African contexts. All-night meetings appear in the contemporary *wanamaombi* revival among Tanzanian Roman Catholics, stemming from a Marian apparation to a priest in the 1960s. In his study of Bwiti religion among the Fang people of Gabon, James Fernandez describes all-night rituals, called *engosie,* which trace the spiritual path from birth to death and

pungwe prompts fundamental questions about night: What does night mean? What is it about night that focuses such themes as spiritual encounter, community-building and liberative empowerment? Why is nocturnal ritual so attractive?

In the dimension of worldview or theological apprehension, night focuses the perennial and ubiquitous conflict between good and evil by gathering the community at the threatening time, when malevolent spirits are abroad and wizards do their work. This adversarial quality of night is related to the persistent wilderness theme in Christian *mapungwe*. The *explicit* correlation of the *pungwe* with wilderness journeys in AICs suggests that the wilderness is an *implicit* theme of the general *pungwe* ethos. Among AICs, going out to the wilderness, *kuenda kumasowe*, is a strong *pungwe* theme, and the independents intensify the experience by fasting and walking long distances in the dark to barren, remote places, despite rain and cold. The wilderness practice resembles rites of passage:

> ... all rites of passage or 'transition' are marked by three phases: separation, margin (or limen, signifying 'threshold' in Latin) and aggregation. The first phase of separation comprises symbolic behaviour signifying the detachment of the individual or group either from an earlier fixed point in the social structure, from a set of cultural conditions (a 'state'), or from both. During the intervening 'liminal' period, the characteristics of the ritual subject (the 'passenger') are ambiguous; he passes through a cultural realm that has few or none of the attributes of the past or coming state. In the third phase (reaggregation or reincorporation), the passage is consummated. The ritual subject, individual or corporate, is in

---

which include elaborate ceremonies, multiple songs, long dances, prayer cycles, and brief sermons. Bwiti religion is a thorough amalgamation of ancestral veneration and Christian material, but the deliberate patterning of the *engosie* as a ritual event resembles the *pungwe* in its several settings. *Bwiti: an ethnography of the religious imagination in Africa* (Princeton: Princeton, University Press, 1982), 436–469. The Kung people of the Kalahari Desert conduct all-night healing dances during which they handle fire. Katz, 118–140, 224. Douala traditional healers in Cameroon do their work at night during sessions that include trance, drumming, dancing, singing, and direct healing by the *nganga*. Eric de Rosny, *Healers in the night*, translated by Robert Barr (Maryknoll: Orbis Books, 1985), 1–7 and *passim*. Other instances from Africa could be cited.

a relatively stable state once more and, by virtue of this, has rights and obligations vis-à-vis others of a clearly defined and 'structural' type ...[8]

In SSR and in the Christian churches some *mapungwe* focus on specific rites of passage for certain individuals – the initiation of a medium in SSR, the public recognition of a prophet in an AIC, a Marange Apostle's first walk on fire, or the preparation of confirmands in an MFC – where separation, liminality and reincorporation are obvious. Liminality is equally clear, however, in the ritual process of entire groups as they practice the wilderness *pungwe,* for the event itself enacts a separation from ordinary life, an especially intense experience on the margins of time and geography and then a reconstituting of the community.

The experience of deprivation creates a congruence between night and wilderness. As people deprive themselves of sleep, so in the wilderness journey they are deprived of light, food, comfort and the shelter of familiar village life. The community relocates itself to a setting of adversity and thereby puts itself on trial, testing its power and authenticity in all the dimensions of the *pungwe.* Will people meet spiritual reality and oppose evil spirits once again, or will God's power be absent? Will the community build itself up, or will competing interests and hostilities prevail? Will the group seize liberation from all that enslaves and destroys, or will it succumb to those powers? The wilderness tests the community's mettle. The biblical warrant for wilderness encounter prompts *masowe* Christians to extend a bedrock *pungwe* theme to its logical and spiritual conclusion. What is explicit among AICs is implicit in the MFCs, in the wartime rallies and in the all-night vigils of SSR. An all-night meeting itself constitutes a community dislocation, a self-deprivation and a trial, and members of MFCs often allude to these themes, which were also prominent in the wartime rallies.

The conflictual aspect of wilderness is an underlying theme in the prominence of the *pungwe* in social responses to death. The invari-

---

[8]Victor Turner, 'Liminality and community', in Jeffrey C Alexander and Steven Seidman, eds, *Culture and society: contemporary debates* (Cambridge, UK: Cambridge University Press, 1990), 147.

able communal pattern in the wake of a death is a *pungwe,* and the funeral *pungwe* is the most common in Shona life. Death brings an emotional and spiritual wilderness, and in the wilderness between life and death the community gathers to encounter spiritual reality, rebuild community and experience liberation from death's power. They hold a *pungwe* every night, for night is when the struggle between good and evil on the border with death is most intense. Keeping vigil through the night protects the community from wizards and avenging spirits and thus guards its solidarity. In the Christian context, these themes prompt confrontation between Christianity and SSR. The funeral *pungwe* enacts and projects a variety of clarifications in ongoing relationships that the living have with their deceased relative, the world of the spirit elders, the triune God and the claims of SSR and Christian tradition.

In sum, the *pungwe* is a flexible but formative ritual phenomenon in Shona life. As it carries socially constructed cultural expectations that night is a time of spiritual encounter, community-building and liberative empowerment, this ethos has welcomed diverse religious and ideological worldviews and has both shaped them and been shaped by them. As ritual, the *pungwe* catalyses people's search for new relational equilibria among themselves, with spiritual entities, with political realities and with major religious and ideological options. Wilderness images the ritual significance of night, because by meeting at night the community puts itself on trial, where its spiritual, communal and liberative capacities are tested in its encounter with spiritual reality. The *pungwe* movement is a movement of wilderness nights during which people engage the major spiritual struggles of their lives, gain victory and so make of the wilderness a garden.

Culture and the localisation of world religion

The *pungwe* movement's compelling combination of power and flexibility, of receptivity and normativity, highlights the specifically cultural dimension of the interaction between Christian gospel and SSR that the *pungwe* enacts. In the cultural dynamism of the encounter reside the criteria by which Shona people make decisions about religious appropriation and transformation and thereby put their local stamp on the expression of a world religion.

258

The *pungwe* expressed and catalysed an explosive post-war revival in the churches close on the heels of a full-scale guerrilla war that was supported by *mapungwe* featuring anti-Christian rhetoric and the suppression of congregational life. This study demonstrates that the two developments are related in ways that resist easy explanations such as that the war was epiphenomenal in a longer and deeper cultural stream, or that Christians simply recovered an earlier tradition of their own. How was it, then, that Manicaland Christians traumatised by the guerrillas' *pungwe* practice then embraced the *pungwe* as a principal form of church life? With the frequent night-time shouts of 'Down with Jesus!' still vivid in their memories, how was it that Christians organised *mapungwe* to strengthen their faith and continue to do so? Whence the power that draws people back to the *pungwe* in changed circumstances? Whence the flexibility that enables them to transform what they find there?

In an interactive view of cultural reality, culture is the socially patterned media with which people interact to express and organise themselves. It is the lifeways of a people and it includes the whole range of social experience. The interactive model assumes and expects that every culture is in a state of change because its members continue to think, respond, imagine and create as living members of society. All human activity is culturally conditioned, but it is equally subject to incremental innovation through the creativity of individuals and groups. In this view, the apparent alacrity with which Shona Christians appropriated the *pungwe,* name and all, from the *Chimurenga* becomes easier to understand. The meaning of the *pungwe* is not entirely prefigured – it can be used to express different meanings in different circumstances – but neither is it an empty vessel. The *pungwe* exercises a powerful influence over what it receives. That influence is exercised through the themes that the *pungwe* both appropriates and transforms: spiritual encounter, community-building and liberative empowerment. The Shona sensibility associates this ethos with night for celebration and enactment. If the function of ritual is to fuse ethos and worldview, then the *pungwe* achieves just such a fusion. In the *pungwe,* a worldview of spirituality fuses with Shona cultural concerns for encounter, community and liberation. In this way, the *pungwe* movement's interaction between Christian gospel and SSR is a cultural interaction as well as an interreligious one.

The formative yet flexible role of the *pungwe*, therefore, is due substantially to the fact that culture and religion are variables that operate independently of one another as well as variables that influence and condition one another. Because neither is reducible to the other, an area of interactive freedom opens up that allows for genuine cultural and religious change. The close linkage between culture and religion in the *pungwe* suggests the type of symbiosis that Paul Tillich developed in his view of the relationship between religion and culture:

> Religion as ultimate concern is the meaning-giving substance of culture and culture is the totality of forms in which the basic concern of religion expresses itself. In abbreviation: religion is the substance of culture, culture is the form of religion. Such a consideration definitely prevents the establishment of a dualism of religion and culture. Every religious act, not only in organised religion, but also in the most intimate movement of the soul, is culturally formed.[9]

This formulation illuminates the religio-cultural matrix of meaning, but it threatens to make religion a prisoner of culture at the same time that it voids culture of all meaning except that which religion gives to it. The development of the *pungwe* calls for a view that recognises culture's capacity to convey meanings from its own traditions and acknowledges that interreligious issues may not be reducible to cultural differences. Jeffrey Alexander has remarked:

> Recent developments in cultural studies converge in their emphasis on the autonomy of culture from social structure. The meaning of an ideology or belief system cannot be read from social behaviour; it must be studied as a pattern in and of itself ... We cannot understand culture without reference to subjective meaning and we cannot understand it without reference to social structural constraints. We cannot interpret social behaviour without acknowledging that it follows codes that it does not invent; at the same time, human invention creates a changing environment for every cultural code.[10]

---

[9]Paul Tillich, *Theology of culture*, ed Robert C Kimball (London, Oxford, and New York, 1959), 42.

[10]Jeffrey C Alexander, 'Analytic debates: understanding the relative autonomy of culture', in *Culture and society: contemporary debates*, edited by Jeffrey C Alexander & Steven Seidman (Cambridge, UK, and New York: Cambridge University Press, 1990), 25–26.

In the *pungwe,* the expectations of spiritual encounter, communal solidarity and liberative empowerment at night are expectations conveyed through the continuity of culture conditioning the traditions of SSR, the ideological innovations of the *Chimurenga* and the post-war renewal in the churches. At the same time, those culturally formed expectations take such radically different directions under the influence of ideology and religion that many participants consider the several phenomena to be totally discontinuous with one another.

The dynamics of continuity and change in the *pungwe* movement condition the relationship that the movement enacts between world religion and local religion. By definition, a world religion extends itself geographically over ethnically and culturally distinct groups of people, and it persists over relatively long periods of time. Such extension exposes a world religion to being changed by historical circumstances local to particular places and times. The inevitability of such large-scale change is illustrated by Ferdinand Saussure's semiotic discussion of the relatively small-scale transmutation of language:

> Time, which insures the continuity of language, wields another influence apparently contradictory to the first: the more or less rapid change of linguistic signs. In a certain sense, therefore, we can speak of both the immutability and mutability of the sign ... In the last analysis, the two facts are interdependent: the sign is exposed to alteration because it perpetuates itself. What predominates in all change is the persistence of the old substance; disregard for the past is only relative. That is why the principle of change is based on the principle of continuity.[11]

What is true of language is equally true of a social movement such as a world religion. It exists by virtue of continuity and shared identity projected over geography and over time, but this very extension and persistence exposes the religion to change. The dynamic of continuity and change can also be expressed in terms of the interaction of the old and the new, where the old is the pre-existing, local religious situation

---

[11] Ferdinand Saussure, 'Signs and language', in Alexander & Seidman, *Culture and society*, 62.

and the new is the immigrant world religion that encounters the local religion.[12]

The *pungwe* movement illustrates several general principles of the interaction between old and new. First, the new cannot be apprehended and appropriated except by means of the old, with the result that continuity persists in the midst of change. Shona people continue to appropriate the Christian gospel through the matrix of the *pungwe* with its long-standing, socially formed patterns of religious understanding and community life. Second, as the new is genuinely grasped, it is not merely captured by the old, but it transforms the old, so that elements of continuity experience significant change. Thus the *pungwe* in the churches not only borrows from the *pungwe* of SSR and of the *Chimurenga,* but it extends and transforms the forms of religious understanding and community life found in SSR and in the wartime rallies. Third, the mutually conditioning encounter of a world religion with a local religion in its cultural context is crucial to the world religion's continuing vitality. It is not merely a concession that the world religion must make in order to gain local acceptance. The current growth and renewal of Zimbabwean churches, especially in Manicaland, is due in large measure to the growth of the *pungwe* movement, which embodies complex cultural interactions between Christianity as a world religion and the local religion of SSR. Paradoxically, a world religion endures as a world religion not only by virtue of temporal and cross-cultural continuity, but also by virtue of its local discontinuity. Its unity endures by virtue of its diversity; its mutability and immutability are interdependent; its continuity depends on change; the old and the new are inextricably bound together.

The cultural dimension of the interaction between a world religion and local religions is illuminated by the crisis of the macrocosm postulated by Robin Horton to explain the development of Christianity and Islam in Africa. Horton puts religious change, and in particular the conversion of Africans to Christianity, in the social and political context of massive

---

[12]The typology of old and new is central to the title and content of Arthur Darby Nock's landmark study of conversion in the Hellenistic period, *Conversion: the old and the new in religion from Alexander the Great to Augustine of Hippo* (London and New York: Oxford University Press, 1933). Daneel has used the same typology for his three-part series on Shona AICs, *Old and new in Southern Shona Independent Churches.*

societal changes. He correlates the transition in allegiance from traditional to world religions with the transition from the microcosm of traditional society, with its limited social horizons, to the macrocosm of a wider world. In Africa, as elsewhere, the wider world was introduced by European colonialism as foreign powers dominated local authorities, incorporated local trade into national and global economies and made communication and travel accessible on a global scale. Religiously, this transition prompted a shift in allegiance from local spirits, relevant in the purely local setting, to an elaborated supreme being whose broad scope and following Africans thought was relevant to the new universe. In the moral dimension there was a shift from minimal moral strictures enforced by taboos to a universal moral code capable of sorting out issues among diverse groups of people in the wider world.

'The obvious inference' of the crisis of the macrocosm, says Horton, 'is that acceptance of Islam and Christianity is due as much to development of the traditional cosmology in response to other factors of the modern situation as it is to the activities of the missionaries.' The theory draws support from the fact that neither Islam nor Christianity made much headway in sub-Saharan Africa before the advent of Western colonialism and settlement, and this is true of Zimbabwe. In most African countries, including Zimbabwe, the rate of Christianity's growth has increased significantly since the end of colonialism at the same time that traditional religions have also experienced a revival. Independence both completes the incorporation of a people into the global macrocosm, sealing the legitimacy of a world religion, and provides a powerful impetus for the revival of the traditional views from which a people drew its identity. To some extent, the profile of Shona churches corroborates Horton's prediction that people with less exposure to the modern situation will be drawn toward AICs, which retain more of SSR's preoccupation with the functions of explanation, prediction and control, whereas people who are incorporated into modern education, economics and professional life may find MFCs more congenial, with their emphasis on 'other-worldly communion'.[13]

The *pungwe* movement demonstrates that, while Horton's intellectualist perspective offers important insights, it suffers from the excessive influence he attributes to macrocosmic developments as a tem-

---

[13]Robin Horton, 'African conversion', *Africa* 41, 2 (April 1971): 103, 96, 104.

plate setting the agenda for religion. African religious life has been affected profoundly by the developments Horton highlights, but there are also specifically religious impulses that prompt ecclesial affiliations and produce theological syntheses that defy categorisation in his typology. The *pungwe* movement affects a wide variety of church groups in parallel ways and nevertheless accommodates major theological and ecclesiological divergences, such as those between United Methodists and Marange Apostles. Church affiliations are often just as difficult to correlate with macrocosmic engagement as they are in a Western context, for example the Mutare optometrist who is a member of the PACG, an international businessman who is also a Marange Apostle, or the well-educated plantation manager who heads a Mugodhi congregation. With the increasing chronological distance between the present and the end of political and ecclesial colonialism, it becomes clear that the major theme of African Christianity both now and in the past, is not reaction to 'missionary Christianity', but African appropriation and transformation of the Christian gospel as Africans themselves understand it. This drama had many subplots, only one of which was the missionary factor. The *pungwe* movement exposes the fact that MFCs, such as the Methodists and Anglicans, are not creatures of missionary Christianity but are fully developed African churches with their own dynamic, contextual theologies. Similarly, the AICs are not simply protest reactions that retain elements of the African microcosm, but they are communities developing new theologies in dialogue with scripture and their understanding of the modern situation. Further, the relevant mission question now concerns not the Western impact but the *African* initiatives in mission that have brought Christianity to its rising crest in Africa. The *pungwe* movement is one such initiative.

In extending Horton's analysis to illuminate the global-local tension, Hefner observes that 'world religions are cultural adaptations to the problem of cultural communities being integrated into plural societies'. Reverse movement is also possible, for world religions can become parochialised, retreating from the universal to the local. In what Hefner calls 'the problem of Babel', the world religions' success poses the greatest threat to their integral unity, for by becoming transcultural they risk losing the homogeneity in which their identity consists.[14]

---

[14]Hefner, 'Anthropological study'.

The cultural dimension of the interaction between world religions and local religions makes it clear that the gospel-culture interaction in the *pungwe* movement is not peculiar to Christianity, nor is it exclusively an in-house theological phenomenon. Rather, it is an inevitable consequence of the diverse cultural contexts in which Christianity finds itself as a world religion. People in a local religious and cultural context work substantial transformations in the Christianity they have received and accepted, and yet they retain an essential continuity with that world religion that qualifies them as co-religionists with Christians around the world. Shona Christians have localised Christianity without parochialising it, for they have understood, embraced and held fast to gospel insights that their fellow Christians in other cultures recognise as universal.

The criteria that Shona Christians have applied in their localisation relate to the principal themes that the *pungwe* embodies, and the criteria may be phrased by way of several corresponding questions: 'We have embraced Mwari in the triune revelation of Christianity, but how can we meet this Mwari in ways that we experience profoundly as spiritual encounter? We recognise that the triune Mwari seeks to build a genuinely new and inclusive community among us, but how can we experience that in ways that will engage our own patterns of community? We welcome the triune Mwari's mission to liberate us from all that oppresses us and to empower us for new life, but how can that mission identify and confront the powers we experience as oppressive, and how can its liberating power become real in ways that we will recognise?' A central answer to these questions for Shona Christians has been the *pungwe* movement.

Democratisation of theological initiative

The appropriations and transformations that the *pungwe* movement has accomplished in relation to SSR and the wartime rallies suggest that communities within a variety of Christian churches are engaged in the task of constructive theology. The *pungwe* is the primary setting for this enterprise, and the principal actors are the leaders and members of local congregations. By offering to many or all members the opportunity to preach, the *pungwe* movement has democratised the theological enterprise and thus made it more open and creative than it was either in SSR or in the churches under missionary superintendence. The community distributes among its members authority to articulate publicly the meaning of Christian faith, its relationship to SSR and Shona culture, and its relevance to issues of family, poverty, gender and so on. The major emphasis on preaching in the churches means that during a typical *pungwe* the community hears from men and women, the elderly, youth and even boys and girls.[15]

Theologising in the churches is directed from within rather than from the outside. The *pungwe* movement has no outside directors in the form of church synods, hierarchs, trained theologians, textbooks or academic institutions, for most such sources of authority ignore the movement. Members of local communities do interact, however, with sources and structures of authority that are close to their situation. All *pungwe* communities regard the Bible as their authority for doctrine, spirituality, church structure and moral life. Received ecclesial traditions of worship and governance influence all communities, and founding documents have considerable authority in such groups as the Marange Apostles and the Mugodhi Church. Congregational leaders have more influence than ordinary members, although members can challenge and silence a leader, even among the authoritarian Marange Apostles. Leaders tend to assess trends according to the training they received – for instance, catechist school among Anglican leaders and extended nurture at the 'Regiment' in Gatsi for Jekenishen leaders – but, especially in the MFCs, they are open to having their centralised training challenged by developments at the grassroots. Ordained clergy in the MFCs have a great deal more training, but the lay-led nature of the movement and the fact that clergy can attend only a fraction of the *mapungwe* in their districts mean that their role, while influential, is not central. Personal experiences that people interpret as signs of the Holy Spirit are a strong source of authority. Finally, the community acknowledges the authority of people's life experience in the sense that anyone can receive a hearing on the nature of such realities as SSR, marriage, poverty or the war.

---

[15]As noted in chapter 6, some churches restrict preaching to men, either absolutely or more so than some other churches; included in this category are the AACJM, the SLAEJC, the ZAC and the FGCG. Two mitigating factors preserve the general point. First, wide participation among men itself constitutes a considerable sharing of authority beyond a single pastor or small group of leaders. Second, women join the debate, albeit more indirectly, through singing, prophecy and healing.

The construction of theology that is occurring in the *pungwe* movement is corporate, verbal, cumulative and long term. It occurs within the liturgical event, when all participants are present. Participants do not name their reflection as a 'theological enterprise', nor do they chart its progress. However, many people experience personal, pastoral and theological dilemmas in the relationships among Christianity, SSR and Shona culture, and they are aware of the historical and ecclesial options in the debate. They reflect on the issues using scripture, tradition and reason, with an intention to reach individual understanding and corporate consensus. This quality of reflection demonstrates that they are indeed engaged in a theological enterprise.[16] Individuals bring their dilemmas and reflections to the *pungwe,* and their fellow members are generous in enabling as many people as possible to be heard. The community trusts the interaction of the event itself to clarify the directions that the group can affirm. The process is verbal rather than written. People do not write out their sermons and prayers in advance, nor do leaders keep any record of the substance of the proceedings.[17]

In view of the corporate and verbal nature of the process, theological construction in the *pungwe* movement occurs cumulatively, advancing in a spiral progression of thought rather than along a straight line. What one person says may stimulate reflections in others, who further develop the concept and excite the community, and at the next *pungwe* people may focus on the idea again. On the other hand,

[16]This assessment differs from that of Adrian Hastings, who in discussing independent churches, writes: 'They have little of an explicit theology any more than has African traditional religion, but they have a praxis and a spirituality in which a theology is profoundly implicit.' Similarly, while this study sees theology in the future being shaped by reflection at the grassroots, Hastings comments, 'African theology in its present stage is shaping as something of a dialogue between the African Christian scholar and the perennial religions and spiritualities of Africa.' *African Christianity* (New York: Seabury Press, 1976), 54, 51. The difference between reflection in the academy and reflection in local communities signifies the distinction between *academic* theology and *popular* theology, not the distinction between theology and spirituality.

[17]The MU *mubatanidzwa* movement in the Tsonzo-Manica-Bonda area keeps a logbook of its gatherings that includes date, location, congregations present, presiding officers, theme scripture and funds collected. Summaries of sermons, prayers, or other events during the *mapungwe* are not recorded.

people may virtually forget it until some future time, or upon further reflection they may challenge it. Conversely, a concept that initially elicits little interest may be used by someone else months later with powerful effect. The process is inevitably long term when compared to the short time in which an individual might write an essay or a book to develop aspects of Shona theology. Because the process involves the entire community, however, thematic developments tend to endure and gather momentum. Over just a few decades of Shona religious life, the results are plain to see in the diverse theologies and liturgies of the churches. Significant changes have occurred within communities when they responded to deeply felt spiritual needs and reflected on them theologically: some MFCs have recovered drums in their worship; the PACG has focused increasingly on *zvikwambo*; some Methodists are reassessing the *pungwe* movement; pentecostalism is growing in some Anglican groups and so on.

Broad participation and shared authority mark the theological process as democratic. The post-war *pungwe* movement that leads the enterprise not only coincided with the establishment of a democratic republic, but it learned much from the wartime *mapungwe* that sought to prepare people for political self-determination. The rituals of SSR invited participation but not critical reflection. The limited practice of pre-war Christian *mapungwe* established a tradition of public discourse from which the guerrillas drew both for the form of their rallies and for the implications such discourse had for critical thinking. In making these implications explicit, the wartime rallies legitimised critical thinking and self-determination, and this was their most important legacy to the churches' *pungwe* movement. The guerrillas declared that all received authorities – chiefs, mediums, village heads, elders, males, clergy, government officials – were open to question and that local people had the opportunity and responsibility to ask questions, engage in debate and make decisions about where they stood. The consequence in the churches has been a post-war movement that arises from local congregations rather than from church bureaucracies, that celebrates lay leadership and that asserts its own authority over against the strictures of church institutions. Just as the war stimulated women to exercise initiative in relation to Shona patriarchy, the war stimulated Christians to exercise theological initiative in relation to inherited church structures. The result has been a democratisation of Shona Christianity.

The democratisation of Shona Christianity resembles the democratisation of Christianity Nathan Hatch describes occurring in the United States after that country's achievement of independence:

> The democratisation of Christianity ... has less to do with the specifics of polity and governance and more with the incarnation of the church into popular culture. In at least three respects the popular religious movements of the early republic (of the United States) articulated a profoundly democratic spirit. First, they denied the age-old distinction that set the clergy apart as a separate order of men and they refused to defer to learned theologians and traditional orthodoxies. All were democratic or populist in the way they instinctively associated virtue with ordinary people rather than with elites, exalted the vernacular in word and song as the hallowed channel for communicating with and about God and freely turned over the reins of power ...
>
> Second, these movements empowered ordinary people by taking their deepest spiritual impulses at face value rather than subjecting them to the scrutiny of orthodox doctrine and the frowns of respectable clergymen ...
>
> The early republic was also a democratic movement in a third sense. Religious outsiders, flushed with confidence about their prospects, had little sense of their limitations. They dreamed that a new age of religious and social harmony would naturally spring up out of their efforts to overthrow coercive and authoritarian structures. This upsurge of democratic hope, this passion for equality, led to a welter of diverse and competing forms, many of them structured in highly undemocratic ways ... Yet despite these authoritarian structures, the fundamental impetus of these movements was to make Christianity a liberating force; people were given the right to think and act for themselves rather than depending upon the mediations of an educated elite.[18]

The fact that the American movement produced new groups and occurred within established denominations parallels the Zimbabwean situation. The present study demonstrates that MFCs as well as AICs

---

[18]Nathan O Hatch, *The democratisation of American Christianity* (New Haven and London: Yale University Press, 1989), 9–11.

nurture creative initiative in the relationships among Christianity, SSR and Shona culture. Indeed, on the increasingly important issue of accepting leadership from women, MFCs tend to be more inclusive than most AICs.

The directions of influence between political innovation and religious innovation in these phenomena are complex. The Revolution was critically important in the American case:

> ... the Revolution dramatically expanded the circle of people who considered themselves capable of thinking for themselves about issues of freedom, equality, sovereignty and representation. Respect for authority, tradition, station and education eroded. Ordinary people moved toward these new horizons aided by a powerful new vocabulary, a rhetoric of liberty that would not have occurred to them were it not for the Revolution.[19]

The Zimbabwean experience was remarkably similar. Yet religion is not simply a dependent variable of politics, for it exercises its own power on other streams of social history.[20] In both the American and Zimbabwean situations, political democratisation received impetus from the religious sector as well as contributed to it. In the American case, people linked the Revolution's call for popular sovereignty with the earlier revival movement of George Whitefield.[21] In the Zimbabwean case, the guerrillas' rallies drew from both the *pungwe* of SSR and the pre-war *pungwe* of the churches, and the connection prompted the rediscovery and reappropriation of these traditions after the war. This dynamic demonstrates that political and religious move-

---

[19]Ibid, 6.

[20]Terence Ranger and Isaria Kimambo rightly criticise tendencies in African studies to treat religion as a dependent variable of politics, economics, colonialism, and the like, and they observe,'... if it is impossible to abstract *religious* history from political or economic or social history without distortion, so it should also be impossible to abstract *political* history without a similar distortion'. *The historical study of African religion: with special reference to East and Central Africa* (London, Nairobi, and Ibadan: Heinemann, 1972), 2.

[21]Hatch, 7. In general, however, Hatch's analysis takes insufficient account of the mutuality of religion and politics and conveys an impression that the democratising influence in America was unidirectional from politics to religion.

270

ments alike synthesise antecedents from diverse sources. In short, political democratisation catalysed but did not create the post-war *pungwe* movement in the Zimbabwean churches.

The democratisation of theological initiative invites comparison with Central and South American Christian base communities, which are defined as

> small lay-led communities, motivated by Christian faith, that see themselves as part of the church and that are committed to working together to improve their communities and to establish a more just society.[22]

The most celebrated feature of the base communities, often termed CEBs (for the Spanish *comunidades eclesiales de base*), is their mode of open discussion in which members explore biblical texts in relation to pressing community and national issues. A community's confidence that God's truth and intention for the group will become clearer through these discussions is very similar to the confidence that *pungwe* participants have in the corporate homiletic process, and in both contexts people's conception of the church is being altered as a consequence. In most other respects, however, differences between the two movements highlight the distinctiveness of the Shona case. CEBs developed, in part, as a response to political and economic repression, a feature that resembles the origins of the wartime *pungwe* in Zimbabwe; the present *pungwe* movement has been galvanised instead by political independence. Clergy were central in forming CEBs, whereas the *pungwe* movement is lay-initiated. CEBs are small cells of people committed to regular Bible study and Eucharist together, whereas most *mapungwe* are large occasional gatherings that are open to all.[23] CEB meetings are low-key and they focus on discussion, whereas *mapungwe* are celebratory, homiletic and liturgical. Participants in CEBs tend to be aware that they are involved in a theological transformation, perhaps on account of their educated leadership, whereas *pungwe* participants are preoccupied primarily with singing and preaching, and the theological transformation occurs along

---

[22]Philip Berryman, *Liberation theology* (Oak Park, Ill: Meyer Stone, 1987), 64.
[23]Ernesto Cardinale's transcriptions of discussions in Solentiname, Nicaragua, are a good example of CEB group process. *The Gospel in Solentiname*, translated by Donald Walsh (Maryknoll: Orbis, 1978).

the way. The political dimension of some CEBs prompts group members to carry out a specific liberative action in the wider community, whereas liberative empowerment in the *pungwe* occurs through a more general inspiration that participants apply as they see fit in their own situations. CEBs focus on individual growth in small groups, whereas Christian *mapungwe* constitute a revival movement that reaches out to wider and wider circles of people. CEBs represent a deliberate pastoral strategy, whereas *mapungwe* constitute a popular movement.

The vigil movement in mission perspective

The *pungwe* movement in its various dimensions serves as a historical and conceptual marker in missiology's interest in issues of gospel and culture. For much of the twentieth century, practitioners, historians, theologians and anthropologists of Christian mission have sought to understand the interaction of gospel and culture in mission's expansion to include diverse peoples and cultures. With concern for the continuing integrity of the Christian movement, missiologists have also sought to define appropriate parametres for the gospel-culture interaction. This study proposes that the role of the *pungwe* as an arbiter of social, cultural and religious discourse in Shona society suggests a missiological imperative that missionaries and indigenous Christians seek out and highlight such arbiters in their efforts to ground gospel proclamation in human cultures.

Mission thinkers early in the century tended to focus on theological conceptions of the interaction of gospel and culture rather than on anthropological models, and the insights of several continue to be important for understanding developments such as the *pungwe* movement. New 'revelations' from churches among recently evangelised peoples was the radical expectation of Roland Allen in his 1912 work, *Missionary methods: St Paul's or ours?* As he surveyed the state of mission-founded churches from the perspective of his Anglican experience in China, Allen could rejoice in much, saying, 'On all sides we see steady and increasing progress.' However, he emphasised his great reservation, that 'there are everywhere three very disquieting symptoms:'

(1) *Everywhere Christianity is still an exotic.* We have not yet succeeded in so planting it in any heathen land that it has

become indigenous ... it still remains true that Christianity in the lands of our missions is still a foreign religion. It has not yet really taken root in the country.

(2) *Everywhere our missions are dependent.* They look to us for leaders, for instructors, for rulers. They have as yet shown little sign of being able to supply their own needs ...

(3) *Everywhere we see the same types.* Our missions are in different countries amongst people of the most diverse characteristics, but all bear a most astonishing resemblance one to another. If we read the history of a mission in China we have only to change a few names and the same history will serve as the history of a mission in Zululand. There has been no new revelation. There has been no new discovery of new aspects of the Gospel, no new unfolding of new forms of Christian life.[24]

Paternalism and consequent dependency were problems in Christian mission that had received considerable attention during the nineteenth century, so Allen's regret over that dynamic in mission support and church administration was not unique.[25] Likewise, longing for the church in newly evangelised areas to become 'indigenous' was common in mission circles, although often this was understood to be the progress of the indigenous church in assimilating and managing the structures and lifeways introduced by Western missioners.

Allen's distinctive note was his intuition that when a culture welcomes the Christian gospel for the first time, in an embrace unfettered by

[24]Roland Allen, *Missionary methods: St Paul's or ours?* (Grand Rapids: Eerdmans, 1962), 141–142.

[25]What has come to be known as three-self mission theory was prominent in the writings of two prominent mid-nineteenth century mission thinkers, Henry Venn and Rufus Anderson, and in the policies of the major missionary societies that they led, the Church Missionary Society in the UK and the American Board of Commissioners for Foreign Missions. The theory emphasised the promotion of self-support, self-governance and self-propagation in the churches established among Christians in newly evangelised areas of the world. Max Warren, ed, *To apply the gospel: selections from the writings of Henry Venn* (Grand Rapids: William B Eerdmans, 1971), 60–71; R Pierce Beaver, ed. *To advance the gospel: selections from the writings of Rufus Anderson* (Grand Rapids: William B Eerdmans, 1967), 97–102.

foreign norms and expectations, people may apprehend and express the gospel in ways that reveal dimensions previously not exposed. Allen was arguing against a traditional understanding that the substance of the gospel is not only spiritually eternal but is temporally fixed in the message it conveys about the human condition, God's action and humanity's relationship with God. In this view, the role of culture, the lifeways of a people, is to provide what tourism promoters might call the 'local colour' and 'local flavour' of how the unchanging gospel is expressed in ever-changing local forms. The difference between Christianity in China and Zululand, the examples cited by Allen, would be readily apparent in modes of dress, music, architecture and, of course, language, but the *theological understanding* of the gospel would be – and, so the argument would run, *should* be – practically identical.

Allen believed that when a human group receives the gospel, the ways in which that people understand, live and express the gospel will constitute *a new revelation from God* about what the gospel actually is, what it means and what it entails for human life. Moreover, the ways in which a local culture expresses the gospel will be significant not only for the people of that local situation but for the universal church. It is no longer tenable, Allen would hold, for one part of the universal church to establish fixed norms of Christian belief and practice and judge other parts of the church in terms of how they conform to those standards. Instead, new insights into the gospel's nature and implications will issue from the encounter between gospel and culture. The argument asserts not that the essential meaning of the gospel changes but that any human apprehension of the gospel is partial and that it needs the perspective offered by other cultural groups. Insights emerging from particular situations illuminate the understanding of the global church.

The *pungwe* movement is an instance in which the missiological hope that Allen expressed has been fulfilled and the force of his three critiques has been answered. It is clear that Christianity is no longer an exotic foreign religion among the Shona people; the *pungwe* is an important means by which Christianity has become indigenous through integration with Shona culture. The movement stems so organically from local sources, initiative and leadership that the issue of dependence on foreign elements does not arise. Manifestly, the *pungwe* is a 'new unfolding of new forms of Christian life', and, as a movement shared among many churches, it is itself pluriform. Through it, there is a 'new discovery of new aspects of the Gospel', principally the movement's integration of Christian proclamation and celebration with communal confrontation with nocturnal evil. The *pungwe* movement constitutes a 'new revelation' that can enrich the life of the global church. Church life in China and in Zululand are no longer practically identical, but as the gospel has taken root in each context, unique insights and lifeways have emerged in gospel communities. The fact that the historical roots of the Christian *pungwe* appear very early in the missionary period suggests that new insights and new forms of community life were probably developing even while Allen wrote that they were not. They were developing in places and at times that were beyond the missionaries' normal oversight – in the more distant villages, in homes or in fields rather than in churches, or at unusual times. They developed in such circumstances because those were the only circumstances in which they *could* develop, in places and at times removed from watchful, judging eyes, where the people themselves could be the principal and authoritative actors in the drama of what shape the gospel would take in their culture.

E Stanley Jones, the American Methodist evangelist to India, shared Allen's emphasis on culturally local expressions of the gospel but developed the concept both more vividly and in terms of greater generality. In his 1925 'attempt to describe how Christ is becoming naturalised upon the Indian Road', he wrote:

> Every nation has its peculiar contribution to make to the interpretation of Christianity. The Son of man is too great to be expressed by any one portion of humanity. Those that differ from us most will probably contribute most to our expression of Christianity.

He recognised that Indian Christians thus far continued to think in Western terms, but he encouraged them to receive the gospel as Indians, with confidence that the result would be a uniquely eastern expression of Christianity:

> As that genius (of India) pours itself through Christian molds it will enrich the collective expression of Christianity. But in order to do that the Indian must remain Indian. He must stand in the stream of India's culture and life and let the force of that stream go

275

through his soul so that the expression of his Christianity will be essentially Eastern and not Western ... (Indian Christianity) must be particular before it can be universal. Only thus will it be creative – a voice, not an echo.

The *pungwe* movement is certainly particular to the Shona context, but it also has the capacity to enrich the collective understanding of the global church. Embracing the political dynamics of his time, Jones responded to the rising tide of Indian nationalism with the aphorism, 'Evangelise the inevitable.'[26] The post-war *pungwe* movement in the churches constitutes a similar response as Christians appropriated a communal mode that had proved powerful during the Liberation War and used it to evangelise many who were seeking religious community.

After Allen's 'new revelation' and Jones's 'Christ of the Indian Road', Hendrik Kraemer proposed the yet more radical theological model of 'new incarnation' to characterise the interaction of the gospel with cultures in Africa and Asia. His 1938 treatise *The Christian message in a non-Christian world* is better known for its neo-orthodox insistence on the radical discontinuity between Christianity and other religions. Advocating continued commitment to evangelism and mission, Kraemer wrote, 'To *decide* for Christ and the world He stands for implies a break with one's religious past ...' The church must be a community where faith, worship and life are not expressions of 'custom' but where the truth revealed in Christ is the criterion of faith and life, transcending all other criteria and authorities. While Kraemer thus defended the absolute uniqueness of Christianity as divine revelation, he believed that, at the practical level of Christian mission, 'adaptation' was imperative if Christianity was to overcome its 'foreign-ness' in many contexts: 'The problem of adaptation is that of the genuine translation of Christianity into indigenous terms so that its relevancy to their concrete situations becomes evident.' It was this urgency that prompted what was probably the first proposal of the incarnational model in the modern period. The New Testament's expression of the revelation of Christ through the thought forms of the Hellenistic world suggests, Kraemer wrote, that

---

[26]E Stanley Jones, *The Christ of the Indian Road* (Nashville: Abingdon, 1925), 1, 194, 193, 81.

276

... new incarnations and adaptations of Christianity in the concrete Asiatic and African settings are natural and legitimate. Christianity never fell and never can fall into a religious, cultural and social vacuum and therefore must find in its various environments an intellectual, emotional and institutional expression that in its psychological and social aspects can reasonably be called an expression and not an impediment or inhibition.[27]

Despite Kraemer's insistence on Christianity's discontinuity with other religions, his inclusion of religion in the vacuum that missionaries should not presume to exist indicates a recognition that religious interaction will be included in the cultural process that brings forth new incarnations of Christianity. More recently, Jesuit theologians have built on the practice of Francis Xavier, Roberto di Nobili and Matteo Ricci in their own tradition to advance incarnation as the model for inculturation.[28] Pedro Arrupe's definition of inculturation is representative:

Inculturation is the incarnation of Christian life and of the Christian message in a particular cultural context, in such a way that this experience not only finds expression through elements proper to the culture in question, but becomes a principle that

---

[27]Hendrik Kraemer, *The Christian message in a non-Christian world*, 2nd ed (New York: Harper; for the International Missionary Council, 1938; 1947), 291, 58, 314, 323, 313.

[28]Peter Schineller, 'A handbook on inculturation', (TMs, 1988), 32–50; Samuel Rayan, 'Flesh of India's flesh;' M Amaladoss, 'Inculturation: theological perspectives;' Paul Puthanangady, 'Inculturation in spirituality and worship;' *Jeevadhara* 33 (May-June 1976); 259–267, 293–301; 302–311. The text of the Second Vatican Council's Decree on the Missionary Activity of the Church is interpreted, albeit broadly, to encourage an incarnational approach: 'The seed which is the Word of God sprouts from the good ground watered by divine dew. From this ground the seed draws nourishing elements which it transforms and assimilates into itself. Finally it bears much fruit. Thus, in imitation of the plan of the Incarnation, the young Churches, rooted in Christ and built up on the foundation of the apostles, take to themselves in a wonderful exchange all the riches of the nations which were given to Christ as an inheritance.' Quoted by Kurien Kunnumpuram, 'Inculturation in Vatican II', *Jeevadhara* 33 (May–June 1976), 287.

animates, directs and unifies the culture, transforming and re-making it so as to bring about 'a new creation'.[29]

The model of incarnation connotes an organic integration of gospel and culture, with both elements undergoing transformation in the process of their mutual encounter. It suggests that the gospel is expressed not in spite of culture but through culture. The model suggests not only that every cultural expression is unique but that the gospel may be amplified and revealed anew through its encounter with culture. In all of these respects the *pungwe* is a case in point.

In the welter of interaction models that anthropological missiology has developed to analyse the reception of Christianity in human societies, some are more relevant to the *pungwe* movement than others, depending on how terms are interpreted. Accommodation and adaptation are the least suitable models for the process. Accommodation connotes a tone of concession on the part of either the missionary or the local society, with little substantial interaction or exchange between them.[30] Adaptation, perhaps the most common term in both casual and scholarly discourse on the subject, may denote more interchange, but the level of interaction is relatively superficial; like accommodation, it connotes concession in the interests of coexistence. Indigenisation is sometimes used in a full sense of the rooting of Christianity in all dimensions of the local situation, in which case the *pungwe* is certainly a case in point. Alternatively, indigenisation sometimes connotes a church's adoption of the externals of local custom, such as modes of dress and the like, without substantive engagement with local culture and religion. The term is also used to denote the handing over of ecclesial authority to local leaders; while this is no longer a significant *pungwe* issue with respect to Western missionaries, it continues to be an issue between some African leaders and their local congregations.

Inculturation is relevant to the pungwe phenomenon as 'the symbolic exchange between the faith being preached and the receiving

---

[29]'Letter to the whole society on inculturation', *Studies in the International Apostolate of Jesuits* 7 (June 1978): 2.

[30]Luzbetak, 67–68, notes that, although in theory accommodation affirmed wholeheartedly 'neutral' and 'naturally good' elements in non-Christian ways of life, its practice tended to focus on superficial features of the receiving culture rather than on deep structures of thought and feeling.

278

culture',[31] and the term is an appropriate shorthand characterisation of the *pungwe* movement. Inculturation highlights both the mode of reception by local people and the searching, listening and learning mode of gospel proclamation by missionaries. The *pungwe* movement exemplifies the double movement of inculturation that David Bosch stresses:

> Inculturation suggests a *double movement*: there is at once inculturation of Christianity and Christianisation of culture. The gospel must remain Good News while becoming, up to a certain point, a cultural phenomenon, while it takes into account the meaning systems already present in the context. On the one hand, it offers the cultures 'the knowledge of the divine mystery', while on the other it helps them 'to bring forth from their own living tradition original expressions of Christian life, celebration and thought'.[32]

Appropriation and transformation are the processes that this study highlights in inculturation. People of the receiving culture appropriate the Christian gospel authentically and so enter into fellowship with a global body of Christians. At the same time they transform the gospel into a living process within their culture through the distinctive emphases of the *pungwe*. Conversely, they appropriate insights and emphases from their culture that become transformed through integration with gospel experience.[33]

Contextualisation is a model relevant to the *pungwe* as a 'level of the faith, in which, to the cultic aspects and the intra-church power struggles is added a process of conscientisation about power struggles in the

---

[31]Ruy Costa, 'Inculturation, indigenisation, and contextualisation', in *One faith, many cultures: inculturation, indigenisation, and contextualisation*, edited by Ruy Costa (Maryknoll: Orbis Books; and Cambridge: Boston Theological Institute, 1988), xiii.

[32]David J Bosch, *Transforming mission: paradigm shifts in theology of mission* (Maryknoll: Orbis Books, 1991), 454.

[33]Thomas Christensen explores a similar process among the Gbaya people of Cameroon and the Central African Republic in *An African tree of life* (Maryknoll: Orbis Books, 1990), 153–154 and passim. The relationships between gospel and culture that H Richard Niebuhr describes in his famous *Christ and culture* are generally one-sided in focusing on Christian evaluations of culture, for Niebuhr did not have the benefit of cross-cultural mission experience. However, enculturation as conceived in this study resembles most the model of 'Christ the transformer of culture'. (New York: Harper & Row, 1951), 190–229.

world, in which the church participates either actively or passively'.[34] The *pungwe* movement's heritage in SSR's political involvement and in the mobilisation rallies of the Liberation War have marked the church vigils with a continuing engagement with the realities of power in society and in the spirit world. Alternatively, Luzbetak defines contextualisation more broadly as 'the various processes by which a local church integrates the Gospel message (the "text") with its local culture (the "context") and three levels of the process: cultural forms, incarnation and underlying psychology.'[35] This broader interpretation of contextualisation brings the full range and depth of the *pungwe* movement under the umbrella of one term.

Translation as a model of Christian proclamation and reception is a more recent proposal by Lamin Sanneh, who explains that linguistic translation itself is the most significant mission engagement with culture:

> Scriptural translation rested on the assumption that the vernacular has a primary affinity with the gospel, the point being conceded by the adoption of indigenous terms and concepts for the central categories of the Bible. As long as missionaries were committed to translation, so long would vernacular concepts and usage continue to determine the assimilation of Christianity, including the understanding of God by more inclusive criteria.[36]

Gospel expression in the categories of the receiving culture implicitly affirms that the culture is a vehicle capable of communicating divine revelation and this affirmation has empowered African peoples for religious renewal, social transformation and political liberation.[37] These large-scale consequences originate in the linguistic exchange in which

---

[34]Costa, xiii–xiv.

[35]Luzbetak, 69–78.

[36]Lamin Sanneh, *Translating the message: the missionary impact on culture* (Maryknoll: Orbis Books, 1989), 266. 'Two major consequences for the religious status of culture may be characterised as, first the "relativisation" of all cultural arrangements, and, second, the "destigmatisation" of all Gentile or taboo cultures. Thus would transcendent truth subsume cultures and mobilise them at the same time.' Sanneh, *Encountering the West: Christianity and the global cultural process: the African dimension* (Maryknoll: Orbis Books, 1993), 135.

[37]Sanneh, *Translating,* 53, 159.

a missionary asks a native speaker what his or her name for God is and then proceeds to use that name in sharing the gospel. It is clear that the earliest vernacular proclamations of the gospel in Zimbabwe set in motion a process by which Shona people received Christianity into their language and worldview, where it both affirmed and challenged existing theological and social norms. As they embraced the immigrant religion, they reappropriated materials from their traditions in ways that transformed what they received and what they had to offer. The *pungwe* movement intensifies and focuses the ongoing play of linguistic and theological resonances in this process, ranging from such matters as the connotations of the word *pfumo* (spear) in spiritual warfare to the meaning of *mweya* (spirit) in Shona cosmology. The vigils constitute a forum for theological discourse and growth around such issues, because they are the context where the realities are experienced most profoundly.

'Local theology' is the principal outcome of the *pungwe* movement. Robert Schreiter maintains that, pretensions to universality notwithstanding, all theologies are local theologies, for every theology reflects an interaction with local historical circumstances and cultural conditions. Using a semiotic model of cultures as networks of signs, Schreiter conceptualises the interaction of church tradition and local culture as a series of steps that begin with the 'opening' of church tradition, local culture, or both, and include modifications on either side that are then verified with reference to both tradition and culture.[38] The *pungwe* is what Schreiter terms a 'semiotically dense' entity in culture. It offers complex webs of signification that are, at the same time, flexible in forming links of meaning with new urgencies and new information, so that it becomes a contextualising agent during ongoing historical processes. Its combination of formative power and its flexible receptivity has enabled it to endure.

In the most general terms, the *pungwe* functions as a flexible arbiter in the social, political, economic and religious discourse of Shona society. The lively theological controversies of the churches seek out the *pungwe* as a setting where issues can be debated by the community gathered close to its cultural roots. In such discourse, the *pungwe*

---

[38]Robert J Schreiter, *Constructing local theologies* (Maryknoll: Orbis Books, 1986), 22–38. A diagram of the historical development of the *pungwe* along the lines of Schreiter's model appears as appendix 5.

both demands accountability and offers generosity. It exercises control as a forum of accountability as movements must express their urgencies through the *pungwe* and thereby through the lifeways and thought forms of SSR. It is likely that any initiative that seeks a major place in Shona life must, at some time or another, be in contact with the practice of *pungwe.* What new movements must be accountable for is ensuring that they remain close enough to Shona religio-cultural roots to maintain tradition's coherence and ensure the continuity of Shona identity. As they comply, the *pungwe* marks them with its distinctive themes: spiritual encounter, community solidarity and liberative empowerment. The *pungwe* is generous in its side of the bargain, for as new initiatives embrace the practice, the *pungwe* releases enormous reserves of hope, energy and commitment in the people. Thus, new initiatives are able to maintain their own integrity even as they receive the distinctive marks of the *pungwe* that offer them the power to develop into movements. As a ritual process in the churches, the *pungwe* not only bears messages, but it invites a community dialogue on personal, spiritual and community issues central to Christians.

The central importance of this phenomenon for evangelism, church growth and mission outreach suggests that missionaries and indigenous Christians in other contexts must be alert for such arbiters in cultural settings, for these phenomena may hold the key to effective vital church life and effective mission work. The *pungwe* movement suggests that, in practice, the natural process of authentic Christian community is likely to identify and develop such arbiters on its own. The movement thus fulfils much of Kwame Bediako's vision in his manifesto of the significance of modern African Christianity, especially his fifth thesis: 'The study of Christianity in Africa in its total religious and socio-political context will help point the way for the church to exist in a post-Christendom era.'[39]

The populist nature of the *pungwe* movement demonstrates that African grassroots Christians are creatively and dynamically directing the process by which the Christian gospel takes root in African cultures. The movement provides a liturgical, theological and missiological model of the cultural interaction of a world religion with a local

---

[39]Kwame Bediako, 'The significance of modern African Christianity – a manifesto', *Studies in world Christianity* 1, no 1 (1995), 61.

religion. For the churches, this process has rooted them in Africa's soil and catalysed a missional embodiment of the gospel in Shona society. In the *pungwe* movement we see that the relationship between Christian gospel and human culture includes both tension and embrace.

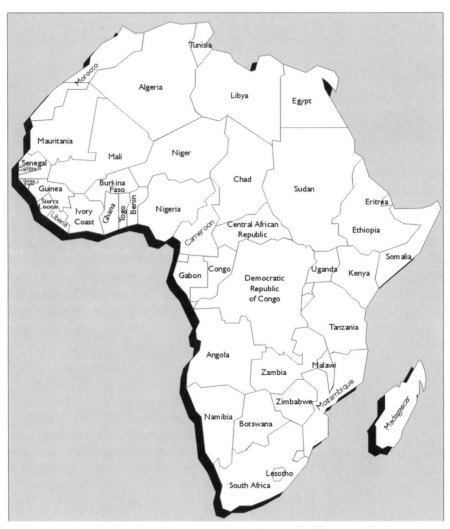

MAP 1 Zimbabwe on the African continent

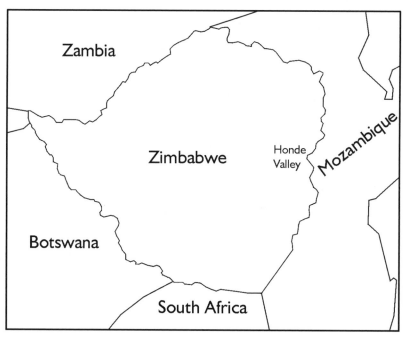

MAP 2 Zimbabwe

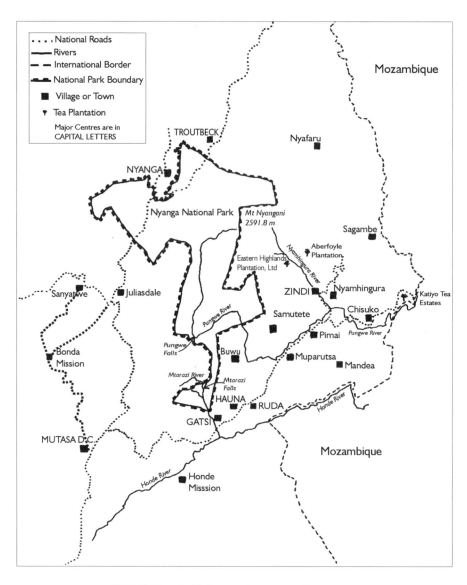

MAP 3 Honde Valley and surrounding areas

APPENDIX 2

Table of religious profession and affiliation

Table 1 Religious adherents in Africa, 1900–2000[1]

Religious group	1900	%	1980	%	2000	%
Christians	9 938 500	9,2	203 490 700	44,2	380 438 000	46,4
Roman Catholics	2 064 300	1,9	76 789 300	16,7	151 472 100	18,7
Protestants	2 533 600	2,3	54 403 500	11,8	100 557 200	12,4
Independents[2]	42 400	0,0	27 438 000	6,0	59 809 000	7,4
Orthodox	3 593 000	3,3	19 516 800	4,2	33 711 600	4,1
Anglicans	521 300	0,5	16 981 900	3,7	31 661 100	3,9
Marginal Christians[3]	1 200	0,0	1 832 700	0,4	4 812 200	0,6
Muslims	34 531 300	32,0	189 728 400	41,2	330 423 000	40,3
Ethnoreligionists[4]	62 685 300	58,1	63 872 800	13,9	73 351 500	11,9
Hindus	279 300	0,3	1 148 900	0,2	1 738 700	0,3
Baha'is	200	0,0	1 024 400	0,2	2 462 600	0,3
Non-religious	7 200	0,0	1 040 900	0,2	3 751 500	0,7
Jews	397 900	0,4	232 700	0,1	364 100	0,0
Africa Totals	**107 854 300**	**100**	**460 857 300**	**100**	**819 910 000**	**100**

---

[1]The table includes a selection of data from a more comprehensive table that appears in Barrett, *World Christian encyclopedia*, 782, supplemented by current figures supplied by Barrett in 1999. Barrett is the most widely recognised and cited statistician of global Christianity. The table focuses on statistics for professing Christians, defined as 'those publicly professing

(declaring, stating, confessing, self-identifying) their preference or adherence in a government census or public-opinion poll, hence known to the state or society or the public.' Barrett, 123. Affiliated Christians, by contrast, are 'church members; all persons belonging to or connected with organised churches; those on the churches' books or records, or with whom the churches are in touch, usually known by name and address to the churches at grass-roots or local parish level; ie those attached to or claimed by the institutional churches or organised Christianity and hence part of their corporate life, community and fellowship, including children, infants, adherents, catechumens, and members under discipline ...; total church membership, or total Christian community or inclusive membership; ... minus any doubly-affiliated, minus any disaffiliated.' Barrett, 125. Statistics of profession are selected for this table, in contrast to the aggregates cited for affiliation, because stated religious profession indicates the basic religious orientation that is the focus of this study.

[2]Independents, a term now preferred by Barrett over Non-White Indigenous Christians, designates what this study calls members of African-initiated churches. Barrett defines the term as follows: 'black/Third World indigenous Christians in denominations, churches or movements indigenous to black or non-white races originating in the Third World, locally founded and not foreign-based or Western-imported, begun since AD 1500, black/non-white-founded, black/non-white-led, forming autonomous bodies independent of Western and Eastern churches, with no Western ties, often schismatic, separatist, anti-establishment, sometimes anti-Western, anti-white or anti-European in reaction to Western influences.' Barrett, 836.

[3]'Marginal Protestants' designates 'followers of para-Christian or quasi-Christian Western movements or deviations out of mainline Protestantism (including pseudo-Christian 'New Age' cults), not professing mainstream Protestant christocentric doctrine but claiming a second or supplementary or ongoing source of divine revelation in addition to the Bible ...' Barrett, 832.

[4]Ethnoreligionists, a term now preferred by Barrett over Tribal Religionists, is 'a collective term for primal or primitive religionists, animists, spirit-worshippers, shamanists, ancestor-venerators, polytheists, pantheists, traditionalists (in Africa), local or tribal folk-religionists; including adherents of neo-paganism or non-Christian local or tribal syncretistic or nativistic movements, cargo cults, witchcraft eradication cults, possession healing movements, tribal messianic movements ...' Barrett, 846.

288

Table 2 Religious adherents in Zimbabwe, 1900-2000[5]

Religious Group	1900	%	1980	%	2000 (Est)	%
Christians	19 000	3,8	4 347 000	58,0	8 375 000	67,4
Protestants	6 000	1,2	1 547 700	20,6	1 500 000	12,1
Roman Catholics	6 000	1,2	1 079 000	14,4	1 150 000	9,3
African Indigen,	0	0	1 192 000	15,9	4 560 000	36,4
Anglicans	7 000	1,4	367 000	4,9	300 000	2,4
Tribal Religionists	479 800	96,0	3 034 300	40,5	3 744 000	30,1
Muslims	0	0	70 000	0,9	86 000	0,7
Baha'is	0	0	14 500	0,2	42 000	0,3
Country's Pop.	500 000	100	7 495 000	100	12 423 000	100

---

[5]The table includes a selection of data from a more comprehensive table that appears in Barrett, 768, supplemented by current statistics supplied by Barrett in 1999. Adherence denotes profession, not affiliation.

Table 3 Affiliation members of twenty Christian churches in Zimbabwe, AD 2000[6]

Church[7]	Year Begun	Congs	Adults	Affiliated	Percentage[8]
AACJM	1932	500	260 000	910 000	15,4
AME Ch	1900	120	32 000	40 000	0,7
Afr Reform	1891	756	36 109	60 000	1,0
AFM	1918	975	55 000	87 000	1,5
Anglican	1888	500	73 275	237 000	4,0
ZAOGA	1965	1 709	300 000	600 000	10,2
Bapt Conv	1950	503	70 000	150 000	2,6
Rom Cath	1561	170	300 700	940 000	16,0
CCAP	1912	70	6 350	23 000	0,4
DRC	1894	10	9 000	17 000	0,3
Evang Luth	1903	220	20 000	60 000	1,0
First Ethiop	1926	4	3 000	4 000	0,07
Full Gospel	c 1915	82	7 655	15 000	0,3
Jeh Witness	c 1910	700	12 456	56 000	1,0
Mai Chaza	1952	160	3 585	60 000	1,0
Meth (UK)	1890	1 116	39 870	101 000	1,7
Salv Army	1891	687	67 526	150 000	2,6
7 Day Adv	1894	395	166 000	278 000	4,7
UCC	1892	70	1 185	4 300	0,07
United Meth	1896	650	65 000	163 000	2,8
Ziwezano	c 1960	15	1 000	5 000	0,09
Ndaza Zion	1922	NA[9]	5 000	12 000[10]	0,2
Table totals		**9 412**	**1 534 441**	**3 972 000**	**67,63**
Total of all[11]		**15 610**	**2 308 000**	**5 877 000**	**100**

[6]The table is derived from data in Barrett, 770–771, supplemented by current statistics provided by Barrett in 1999.

290

7The twenty churches listed here represent 5,9 per cent of the 340 denominations known in 1999, 75 of them Protestant mission-founded and 250 African-initiated. However, the selection represents all of the largest churches and some of the smaller ones that apear in this book. Full names of the churches are as follows: African Apostolic Church of Johane Marange; African Methodist Episcopal Church; African Reformed Church in Zimbabwe, with origins in the Dutch Reformed Church of South Africa; Church of the Province of Central Africa, a province of the Anglican Communion; Apostolic Faith Mission of South Africa; Assemblies of God Africa, also called the Zimbabwe Assemblies of God, Africa; Baptist Convention of Zimbabwe; Roman Catholic Church in Zimbabwe; Church of Central Africa, Presbyterian; Dutch Reformed Church (Mother Church); Evangelical Lutheran Church in Zimbabwe; First Ethiopian Church; Full Gospel Church of God in Southern Africa; Jehovah's Witnesses; Mai Chaza Church; Methodist Church in Zimbabwe, often called the English Methodist Church; Salvation Army, Zimbabwe Territory; Seventh-day Adventst Church; United Church of Christ, with origins in the American Board of Commissioners for Foreign Missions; United Methodist Church; Ziwezano Church, the Church of Wisdom, a Honde Valley breakaway from the United Methodist Church; Zion Apostolic Church. The Jekenishen Church, the Pentecostal Apostolic Church of God, and the Unity of African Apostolic Faith Church (Mugodhi) do not appear in Barrett's work.

8This column sets forth the percentage each church represents of the total affiliated church members in Zimbabwe.

9In some cases, information is not available.

10This figure seems far too low and may reflect inadequate census figures from the church, even when allowance is made for the fact that affiliation refers to membership rolls rather than religious profession. In general, AICs and many MFCs are not concerned to count members with precision, and this may apply even to the Anglican figures. Rapid population growth, the post-war growth of the churches, and the logistical difficulty of compiling membership totals in rural areas make the task difficult. The table should be interpreted to indicate rough proportions rather than exact membership.

11Figures for all 340 Christian denominations in Zimbabwe, including those not listed.

APPENDIX 3

Terms of discourse

For the inquiring student and scholar, this appendix clarifies in detail a number of important terms used in this study.

Religion is the dimension of human individual and social experience concerned with relationships between human beings and reality experienced as supernatural or divine. These relationships are experienced in thought, emotion and morality, and they are pictured in an idealised way in ritual. This study characterises such relationships as they are experienced by people in a particular cultural context, describes the complex process by which loyalties shift among alternative sets of relationships with the supernatural and highlights the mutual influence of such sets of relationships in the midst of religious change. *A religion* – that is, a particular religion, as distinguished from the religious dimension of human experience – is the comprehensive religious pattern of thought and practice that a social group shares and develops over time.

In specifying that the supernatural distinguishes the religious dimension from other dimensions of life, this definition does not articulate aspects of the overall function of religion, its deep structure, or its theological significance. In this way it differs from other definitions, including the well-known definition offered by anthropologist Clifford Geertz:

> A system of symbols which acts to establish powerful, pervasive and long-lasting moods and motivations in men (sic) by formulating conceptions of a general order of existence and clothing these conceptions with such an aura of factuality that the moods and motivations seem uniquely realistic.[1]

Geertz's definition emphasises too much the systematisation of sym-

---

[1]Geertz, 'Religion as a cultural system', 90.

292

bols and not enough the relational dimension of human experience. A symbol system is credited with its own operation upon people and the creative interaction of people with symbols is not given sufficient weight. More important, contrary to Geertz's own commitment to 'thick description',[2] the definition appears to bleach religion of its unique and universal feature, which is concern with reality that is posited as supernatural or divine.

A *world religion* is a religious system which through a process of cultural adaptation and geographical diffusion develops an identity recognised and shared by adherents in diverse cultural and geographical contexts. A *local religion* is a religious system which has a frame of reference confined to a particular and relatively homogeneous cultural context. The two categories, world and local, are not mutually exclusive. World religions began as local religions and they retain some of their originally local features in their global extension. As world religions become extended, their life depends upon becoming contextually relevant in local areas. Moreover, the form in which a world religion is diffused is bound to be affected by the local context of those responsible for the diffusion. In becoming thus contextual, world religions always run the risk of reverting to the simply local and losing their universal frame of reference. On the other side, it is difficult today to locate a purely local religion, for in the modern period most local religions have assimilated aspects of world religions that have impinged on them through mass communications, world travel and the like.[3]

Culture is the socially patterned media with which people interact to express and organise themselves. Culture is the lifeways of a people, and it includes the whole range of social experience. Culture includes but is not limited to what contemporary Shona people call their 'customs', 'traditions', or 'culture', terms generally used to refer to crafts, dances, beliefs and living patterns of the Shona surviving (or not surviving) from their history before contact with European settlers. As a concept used in this study, culture embraces the full range of contemporary social and political realities, including urbanisation, recovery from the dislocations of war, changes in the status of women, rising

---

[2]Clifford Geertz, 'Thick description', in *The interpretation of cultures*, 10.
[3]This discussion is indebted to Robert Hefner, 'Anthropology of religion'.

educational levels, shortages of resources, controversy regarding a one-party state and so on. Culture thus includes what is rapidly changing as well as what seems relatively static.

The definition of culture offered here is an interactive definition, a feature crucial to this study's focus on interactions related to the *pungwe*. The phrase 'socially patterned' includes reception of historically transmitted material from the past, but acknowledges that the contemporary social patterning of this and other material is as active and powerful as what is received. Individuals and groups interpret the media in diverse ways, and patterning operates along a wide spectrum of conformity with the social patterning of such material in the past. The term 'media' includes artifacts, practices and symbols from the past, but it assumes that their meaning is not 'given' – that is, prefigured or predetermined – but arises out of the interaction of people with those media, whether the interaction is primarily intellectual, emotional, artistic, technical or ritualist. This view not only accounts for cultural change, but it incorporates change as one of the chief features of culture. Avoiding anachronism, culture becomes a robust concept thoroughly grounded in present reality, with all its creative innovation and variety.

Shona Spirit Religion is a neologism formulated to designate the religious system practiced today by many Shona people both in continuity with their ancient religion and in dynamic interaction with more recent religious and cultural currents. The term identifies the main element in the religion, which is a range of spirit beings, most of them ancestral,[4] and specifies the social context in which the religion is practiced. 'Shona Spirit Religion' is preferred over a number of other terminological options. 'African Traditional Religion' has long and honourable usage in the study of religion in Africa, but it has the disad-

---

[4]The term 'spirit' rather than 'ancestral' has been used in the term 'Shona Spirit Religion' for several reasons. First, Shona cosmology reserves a supreme place for the God, *Mwari,* who is not necessarily ancestral. Second, the religion stresses explicitly the spirits of the ancestors, not the ancestors themselves, although this distinction is frequently vague. The ancestors are termed *madzitateguru,* a term sometimes used interchangeably with *vadzimu,* which refers specifically to the *spirits* of the ancestors, *mweya yamadzitateguru.* It is the *vadzimu* who are generally invoked in prayer. Third, a few apparently non-ancestral spirits also make an appearance.

vantage that people may infer too much uniformity throughout Africa, for it does not designate the particular beliefs of any specific people.[5] The term 'traditional', whether appended to 'African' or 'Shona', can reinforce the erroneous impression that African religions are more traditional than others, remaining static and unchanging, not dynamic enough to engage with the modern world and thus – so the impression is elaborated – primitive and obsolete. Moreover, such designations obscure the fact that other religions such as Islam and Christianity value tradition as a locus of authority and have developed impressive African traditions of their own.

'Primal religion' may be a helpful term for characterising some aspects of the beliefs and practices of Shona people, but it does not offer sufficient scope for diversity.[6] With 'primal religion' there is a natural tendency to privilege as authentic the beliefs and practices of a people

---

[5] J M Schoffeleers writes, 'We need to escape from the old idea of African religions as fundamentally similar ...' *Guardians of the land: essays on Central African territorial cults*, ed by J M Schoffeleers (Gweru: Mambo, 1979), 29. 'African Traditional Religion' (ATR) has been used by major scholars of religion in Africa, and three have books with that title: Bolaji Idowu, *African Traditional Religion: a definition* (London: SCM Press, 1973); Geoffrey Parrinder, *African Traditional Religion*, 3rd ed (London: Sheldon Press, 1974); and O Oladimeji, *African Traditional Religion* (Olesa, Nigeria: Ilesanmi Press, 1980). The bibliography of African religious life exhibits a shift toward the expressions 'African religion' and 'African religions', which avoid characterising indigenous religions as a certain *kind* of religion at the outset. John Mbiti has always preferred such designations, eg, *African religions and philosophy* (Garden City, NJ: Anchor Books, 1970).

[6] 'The word *primal* connotes something basic, fundamental, prior. Primal religions are the non-universal religions of the world's preliterate peoples.' Robert Cameron Mitchell, *African primal religions* (Niles, Illinois: Argus Communications, 1977), 98. Even the term 'non-universal' may be problematic. Because adherents of primal religions have not been mission-oriented in the Christian and Muslim sense of appealing to other groups to share their beliefs and practices, they may be seen to be content with a more local circle of adherence. In the late twentieth century, however, Westerners often find primal religions attractive because they see apparently universal themes, such as the earth being sacred, ancestors being worthy of veneration, and the like. The case is sometimes made, moreover, that these themes are more universal and more accessible than what are argued to be the historically particularistic claims of Christianity and Islam. 'Universal' and 'non-universal', therefore, are contested terms, and as qualities they exist in the eye of the beholder.

295

prior to contact with European Christians or Arab Muslims and to bracket later changes as inauthentic. In fact, in almost any context in Africa, 'pre-contact' beliefs and practices were scarcely static, for there were significant influences from other African groups as a result of migration, trade and war. 'Shona religion' fails to account for the plurality of religious affiliations among Shona people. The term bifurcates the religious situation on the assumption that immigrant religions have not and cannot become genuinely Shona, an assumption that this study seeks to erode.[7] 'Animism' might be a useful term in that it focuses on spirits, the *animae* of the Latin root, but the term is often understood as referring to belief in the spirits of rocks, trees and the like, which are not the focus of SSR.[8] In addition, the term has long connoted primitive and lower-order status in an assumed hierarchy of religions.[9]

Indigenous religion is a term of convenience used in this study to refer to the pre-colonial provenance of SSR. It has a historical reference and is not intended to distinguish such religion from 'foreign' or 'alien' religious impulses. This point is made for two reasons. First, it is factually erroneous as well as personally dismissive to suggest to a Shona Christian that his or her religious affiliation is with a 'foreign' religion when the person was born into that affiliation and now believes pas-

---

[7]Responding both to the charge that the term 'religion' in Africa imposes an alien distinction between religious life and social experience and to the imputation of 'foreignness' to Christianity and Islam, Terence Ranger and Isaria Kimambo observe: 'There is no satisfactory definition of religion which allows us to separate it from political or economic or social life; nor can it be maintained seriously that Islam and Christianity have not become African religions in the fullest sense.' The *historical study of African religion: with special reference to East and Central Africa* (London, Nairobi, and Ibadan: Heinemann, 1972), 1.

[8]Mitchell, for instance, defines animism as 'Belief in spirits; in particular the attribution of an innate soul to natural phenomena or objects'. Mitchell, 96. In the past African religion was equated with animism, eg, *Jerusalem Meeting of the International Missionary Council*, 297.

[9]Edward B Tylor, often called 'the father of anthropology', defined religion as 'the belief in Spiritual Beings' and animism as 'the general belief in spiritual beings'. His statement, 'Animism characterizes tribes very low in the scale of humanity', articulated an understanding of animism that persists today. *Primitive culture: researches into the development of mythology, philosophy, religion, language, art, and custom*, 6th ed (London: John Murray, 1920), 424, 426.

sionately in it. Second, this study seeks to demonstrate that interaction with Shona religion and culture is confirming Christianity as a genuinely indigenous phenomenon in the Shona context. Thus the term 'indigenous', as used here, has no polemical or evaluative connotation. *Popular religion* is the religion of the greater part of the population, as distinguished from the religion of elites, whether those are the political, educational, social, economic, or ecclesiastical elites. Popular religion may be plural in a particular context, and it may include various admixtures of world religion and local religion.[10]

In this study *Christianity* as a world religion is considered as it interacts with local Shona Spirit Religion. Broadly speaking, the criterion of Christianity is Jesus Christ. This statement is intended not as a theological affirmation but as a way of highlighting a marker in human discourse. Thus, when 'Jesus' repeatedly appears in conversations, prayers, sermons and readings, there is good reason to assume that the people involved in the events observed identify themselves as Christian. Sociologically and anthropologically, this means that any individual or corporate expression of spirituality, theology, ethics, or social life in which participants profess that Jesus Christ is centrally normative for them has a claim to be considered a manifestation of Christianity.[11]

Church is used in this study to refer to any group of people who identify themselves as an organised Christian body. Beyond this criterion of self-identification, a church is a social grouping of Christian people whose shared membership is defined by certain identifiers estab-

---

[10]It is not helpful to limit the term 'popular religion' to the religious beliefs and practices of oppressed, marginalised, or minority groups, as do Jacques Van Nieuwenhove and Berma Klein Goldewijk, 'Popular religion, liberation and contextual theology: exploring some questions', in *Popular religion, liberation and contextual theology*, eds Jacques Van Nieuwenhove & Berma Klein Goldewijk (Kampen, Netherlands: Uitgeversmaatschapij J H Kok, 1991) 1–12.

[11]Similarly, Muhammed is the criterion of Islam, Buddha the criterion of Buddhism, *vadzimu* the criterion of SSR, and so on. The definition deliberately avoids any theological elaboration of what *kind* of understanding of Jesus Christ qualifies as authentically Christian. That question of theological normativity is debated very actively by Shona Christians, of course, but at the outset only the most basic definition of Christianity is helpful for the interreligious encounter.

lished by the group. The most obvious identifier is simply the name of the group and people's decision to identify themselves with that name, for example 'Ndiri muZioni' (I am a Zionist). Identifiers include distinctive practices, written materials, internal structure with differentiated roles and designated leadership, customary meeting places and ownership of buildings. Other identifiers involve perennial issues that are matters of interpretation, discussion and controversy, such as conformity with group norms of theology, ritual and behaviour. Related to this is willingness to accept the guidance of persons designated as group leaders.

Among Shona Christian groups, the term 'church' is universal, having been transliterated into Shona as *chechi*.[12] Most groups formally identify themselves by name as churches, and all groups speak of themselves theologically as churches. The important terminological distinction between *mission-founded churches* and *African Initiated Churches* highlights a church's founding conditions, with some churches established by Western-origin missionaries and others founded by African Christians, whom their followers often call prophets. This terminology has the advantage of focusing on historically established facts rather than on ecclesial features that can become anomalous over time. The common terms 'mission churches' and 'independent churches', for instance, encourage erroneous assumptions that an MFC is still directed by a Western mission society or that an AIC has no ties to other churches or to outside organisations.[13]

---

[12]*Chechi* is an entry in the dictionary of standard Shona, it being noted that the term refers (as does the English term) to both the body of people and the physical sanctuary. Another word that is not so common in Manicaland is *kereke*, which is derived from the Afrikaans *kerk*. The most common Shona-derived word is *sangano*, 'meeting' or 'fellowship', derived from the verb *kusangana*, 'to meet'. Hannan, sv. *Chita* is a word used for sub-groups within churches. Churches in the *Chipostori* tradition of 'apostolic' churches commonly call assemblies of their members simply *Vapostori*.

[13]Within their worldwide communions, MFCs in Zimbabwe vary in their degree of autonomy. The Church of Central Africa, Presbyterian, is an autonomous jurisdiction. In Anglican polity, each diocese has considerable autonomy, although subject to the legislation of the Province of Central Africa, which is autonomous within the non-juridical Anglican Communion. The United Methodist Church is more globally centralised, so that the Zimbabwe Conference is subject to the quadrennial General Conference. The Roman

Ritual is understood in terms of the definition offered by anthropologist Robert Hefner: 'the physical performance of more or less formalised sequences of communicative behaviour, the form of which is not directly created by the performer'. The religious rituals studied here are interaction rituals, which, as Hefner develops the concept, are 'rites concerned with the communication of attitudes and feelings of persons in a relationship'.[14] The rituals of SSR are concerned with communicating the attitudes and feelings of persons among themselves and with ancestral spirits and Mwari. The rituals of Christianity, including the *pungwe* of the churches, are concerned with communicating the attitudes and feelings of persons among themselves and with God, who is conceived along biblical lines with various degrees of continuity and discontinuity with the spirituality of SSR. Discerning just what is being communicated, by whom and to whom is a major objective of the study.

A *pungwe* is an event in which people intentionally stay up all night, more or less without sleep, for a form of social interaction, the purpose and tone of which may be primarily social, political or religious. The word is used in connection with both the all-night traditional dances of rural communities and the all-night social dances put on by popular bands in the cities. The night-time rituals of SSR have individual names depending on their purpose and content, but in their nocturnal aspect they are commonly designated *mapungwe*. During the Liberation War, freedom fighters popularised the word *pungwe* as the

---

Catholic Church continues to be very centralised, with major appointments and policies needing the consent of Rome. Some AICs that had no cooperative relationships with other Christian groups have joined *Fambidzano,* the first ecumenical movement of African Initiated Churches in Zimbabwe, and some are now members of the World Council of Churches. Others have become somewhat dependent on Western churches for funding development projects. Some AICs are international in scope – the Marange Apostles, the Mugodhi Church, and the Pentecostal Apostolic Church of God among them – so that local communities may face issues of centralised control across national borders, a thorny problem with which the MFCs have long experience. Thus the traditional distinction based on outside ties now requires too many qualifications to be useful. The World Council of Churches has begun using the term African Instituted Churches; see World Council of Churches, *Consultation with African Instituted Churches* (Geneva: World Council of Churches, 1996).

[14]Robert Hefner, 'Anthropological study of religion'.

name for their dusk-to-dawn mobilisation rallies with rural residents. Since the war, *pungwe* has become a standard term for dusk-to-dawn vigils in a wide range of Christian churches, both mission-founded and African-initiated.

Mission consists of the spiritual vision and the practical means through which people promote their religious faith and work and invite the adherence and participation of others.[15] Mission involves crossing boundaries with a message and the boundaries may be personal, familial, ethnic, geographical, linguistic, national, cultural, or a combination of these. In this study, the term refers primarily to mission initiatives by Shona Christians and secondarily to the efforts of Western missioners among them. The night rallies of the wartime guerrillas are also discussed as a mission initiative.[16]

Missiology as used in this study refers to the study of the history, theology and practice of Christian mission. Contemporary missiology has

---

[15]This formulation is intended to apply to the mission efforts of all religions. The term arose in the Christian context, however, on the basis of the Latin translation *mittere* of the Greek verb *apostellein*, used in the New Testament to refer to the sending of persons to proclaim the gospel, especially as in Jesus sending his disciples. An especially illustrative example is Mt 10:5: 'These twelve Jesus sent out (*apesteilen*), charging them ...' On the lexical history of the term 'missiology', the Dutch missiologist Johannes Verkuyl comments: '... since the beginning of church history many derivations appeared from the Latin translation of the Greek verb *apostellein: mittere, missio, missiones,* etc. The derivation *missio* only surfaces in the sixteenth century when both the Jesuit and Carmelite orders of monks sent out hundreds of missionaries. The publications of the *Sacra Congregatio de Propaganda Fide* dating from this century also use this term. Ignatius of Loyola and Jacob Loynes consistently employ the term *missio*.' Johannes Verkuyl, *Contemporary missiology: an introduction* (Grand Rapids: William B Eerdmans,1978), 2.

[16]The literature of Christian mission history and theology is enormous. Much of the theological literature is devoted to the effort to define the proper motives, directions, scope, goals and methods of Christian mission. Classic debates concern the relative importance of evangelisation and development, exemplary living and verbal witness, gospel uniqueness and the spirituality of other religions, social justice and church-planting, and so on. The definition of Christian mission offered here is historical, not theological. We see, however, that aspects of the classic debates are very real for Shona Christians both as they view mission history in Zimbabwe and as they address mission opportunities in their own ecclesial life.

a special interest in issues related to cross-cultural encounter, because such encounter is inherent in mission initiatives that cross ethnic, linguistic and national boundaries. As an academic discipline, missiology is also broadly concerned with the growth of the Christian movement. This study is missiological in several senses: it discusses the nature and impact of specific mission initiatives; it seeks to discern decisive factors in the growth of the Christian movement in a particular setting; it deals extensively with cross-cultural and interreligious encounter; and it explores the dynamics of Christian appropriation in a culture.

APPENDIX 4

Essay project on Christianity and tradition[1]

Your written responses will be very helpful in the research project on Christianity, tradition and the *Pungwe*. The blanks to fill out are followed by essay questions. If you wish to withhold your identity, you need not offer the information at the bottom of the page. Thank-you very much! – Rev T Presler

Your Age _____ Male or Female _____ Education _____

Marital Status _____ Number of Children _____

Present Church Membership _____ Years _____

Previous Church Affiliations _____

Here are the essay questions. Please use the paper provided with this question sheet. Either English or Shona is fine!

1 How and why did you become a Christian? What were you before?

2 In your view, what does it mean to be a Christian?

3 What spiritual experience do you enjoy and value most?

4 What role does the *Pungwe* play in your spiritual life?

5 What experiences did you have of *Mapungwe eChimurenga* (night vigils of the Liberation War)?

6 What is your attitude toward *Kuombera Vadzimu* (reverencing the ancestral spirits) and what customs do you practice in relation to the *Vadzimu*?

7 What influence have missionaries and mission churches had in your life?

8 Why do you prefer the practices of your present church over those of other churches?

OPTIONAL INFORMATION: Name _____

Local residence _____ *Musha* (Home Village) _____

EHTE Position _____Years with EHTE _____

Congregation _____ Position _____

I agree to have my responses used in the research project.

Signature _____ Date _____
_____

[1] A Shona version of this form was circulated to those who preferred it.

302

Historical relationships among the *pungwe* of SSR, the *pungwe* of the Liberation War, and the *pungwe* movement in the Christian Churches

Church tradition   Shona Spirit Religion and culture

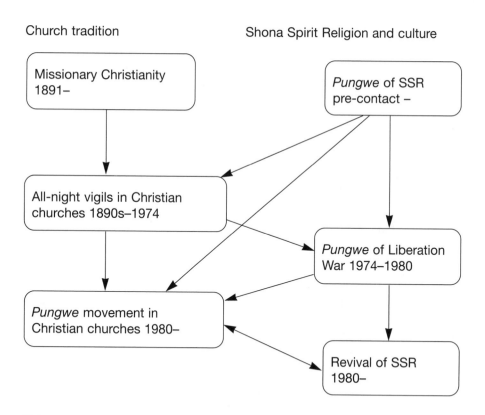

Missionary Christianity 1891–

Pungwe of SSR pre-contact –

All-night vigils in Christian churches 1890s–1974

Pungwe of Liberation War 1974–1980

Pungwe movement in Christian churches 1980–

Revival of SSR 1980–

Notes
* Arrows indicate ritual and theological influences between bodies of social practice.
* The two columns are adapted from the diagramme in Robert Schreiter, *Constructing local theologies*, 25.

APPENDIX 6

The Mothers' Union and the Fishermen in the mission-founded churches

The Mothers' Union and the Fishermen have such prominent roles in leading all-night vigils in the mission-founded churches that detailed historical background on these groups is important in understanding the movement as a whole.

Women in the MFCs associate as the Mothers' Union (MU), which Anglicans call the *Gungano reVadzimai* and Methodists call *Rukwadzano rweVadzimai*.[1] This group is very active in most congregational, district, conference or diocesan initiatives in such areas as group singing, Bible study, stewardship and evangelism. Its chapters organise numerous *mapungwe,* and its members are prominent in leading congregational vigils.

The MU was founded in the Church of England as part of a general renewal of British parish life that took place in the nineteenth century, when revivalism prompted interest in personal spirituality and fostered the founding of many age- and gender-based groups in congregations.[2] The foundation for the MU was laid by Mary Heywood Sumner in 1876, when she called together the women of her husband's parish church at Old Alresford in the diocese of Winchester. The general purposes seem to have been to connect women's faith with their mothering experiences, to provide opportunities for fellowship and to strengthen marriage in the face of rising divorce rates. At a church congress at Portsmouth in 1885 Sumner called for a national mothers' organisation to raise the general tone of English society.[3]

---

[1] Both *gungano* and *rukwadzano* refer to the gathering together of people.

[2] John R H Moorman, *A history of the Church in England* (London: Adam & Charles Black, 1953), 366.

[3] Olive Parker, *For the family's sake: a history of the Mothers' Union, 1876–1976* (London and Oxford: Mowbrays, 1975), 7–8, 13–14.

In the Anglican case, as the presence of the church was consolidated in other parts of the world through the mission outreach of the SPG and the Church Missionary Society, establishment of MU chapters became a routine part of Anglican mission strategy, and the group became an international organisation.[4] The place of the MU in Anglican thinking in Rhodesia can be gauged in the report of the archdeacon of Mashonaland to the 1932 missionary conference of that diocese: 'I would draw attention to the gradual increase in the branches of this Union. As I have travelled around the diocese nothing has been so full of promise as the keenness in which the women are anxious to be linked up together in the Mothers' Union. It is of great promise and of untold good. Nothing could be more healthy for the life of the church than a great union of African women banded together to uphold the sanctity of Christian marriage and pledged to bring up their children as true children of Christ. We need to take courage here.'[5]

A similar development took place in other MFCs, so that in Zimbabwe today there are MU chapters in most Methodist, Presbyterian, Congregational, DRC and Salvation Army congregations, and a similar organisation is active in RCC congregations. Ranger quotes the following oral testimony on the founding of the Methodist *Rukwadzano*: 'In 1930 at Old Umtali, men and women were filled with the Holy Spirit. They started going to the forest to pray. Mai (Mother) Wanetsama started going to pray in the forest ... She used to go to these places at night. At Gandanzara ... a group used to go in the forest to pray. Baba Katsidzira came and told the women to start the organisation since others had already started on it. After a very short time these women elders went to different places to do the Lord's work.' The group's constitution was drafted in 1938.[6] It is significant that the Methodist MU was itself born in the practice of *pungwe*.

---

[4]By 1890 the MU had branches in practically every English diocese and was found in many British colonies as well. Parker, 15. The 'Wave of prayer' printed inside the covers of the British *MU Service Book* solicits members' prayers for the many parts of the world where there are MU chapters. *Mothers' Union service book* (London: Mothers' Union, (1948)), ii–iii.

[5]Archdeacon of Mashonaland, Report to Diocesan Missionary Conference, September 1932, Zimbabwe National Archives.

[6]Ranger, 'Protestant missions in Africa: the dialectic of conversion in the American Methodist Episcopal Church in Eastern Zimbabwe, 1900–1950',

In the late twentieth century, the MU in Britain consists mostly of older women, and the vitality of the organisation is lower than it was formerly. The international headquarters of the Anglican MU continues to be located in London, at Mary Sumner House, where in late 1993 staff and operations were considerably reduced. In many African countries, by contrast, the organisation is growing among MFCs, and in many Anglican provinces and dioceses, the MU is commonly described by such terms as 'the mainstay of the Church'. Membership in 1993 was reported to be 170 000 in Britain and Ireland and 600 000 in the rest of the Anglican Communion.[7] The figure for the UK may be accurate, but the estimate for elsewhere in the Anglican Communion probably reflects outdated statistics and spotty reporting from other parts of the world. In 1980 the professed Anglicans of Uganda alone were estimated at 3,46 million and those with a documented affiliation numbered 2,14 million. Women's preponderance in church membership and the MU's popularity among them suggest that there are more that 600 000 MU members in that country alone.

It is striking that, at least in the case of the Anglicans, the mission export of the MU prompted a racial differentiation in women's work in areas where there were substantial numbers of white settler women, as in Rhodesia and South Africa. While missionary women and men promoted the MU of 'the Mother Church' among African women, white women, even those who may have been MU members in Britain, formed their own organisations, which had no institutional relationship with the MU in Britain.

This race-based separation freed the African MU from white control and freed it for the indigenous, liberative spirituality that the organisation has come to embody for many African women. This liberative dimension is especially pronounced in the Shona context, partly because *pasichigare* Shona society did not feature women's associations. In some other African countries, the MU functions as a Christian complement to traditional women's associations, with corresponding limitations of its scope. For Shona women, the MU was an innovation

---

in *Religion in Africa: experience and expression,* eds Thomas D Blakely, Walter E A van Beek, and Dennis L Thomson (London: James Curry; Portsmouth, NH: Heinemann, 1994), 306–307.

[7] *Church Times* 12 November 1993.

that provided a structure through which they could build solidarity and make their collective voice heard in church and community.[8]

MU life is highly structured and regulated. Members of local MU chapters in Manicaland wear uniforms (which vary among the denominations), pay dues to their congregational chapter, participate in district-wide or diocesan initiatives and attend weekly meetings almost as regularly as they do Sunday liturgy. The norms of the organisation include daily personal and family prayer, bringing up children in the church, forming a strong Christian marriage, avoiding alcohol and divorce and staying aloof from ancestral spirit veneration. Among the vows and intentions listed on the Shona MU membership card for Zimbabwean dioceses is the statement, 'I will try with God's power to protect my home from the danger of drunkenness, betting, throwing evil bones and other sinful acts.'[9] In addition to these qualifications, a woman must have been married in a church wedding service and must be a mother.[10] The various transactions involved in concluding a Shona marriage may consume many years in traditional custom. This fact and the reluctance of many Shona men to commit to a church wedding means that the typical local MU chapter has a number of women who are not full members but who attend meetings and participate in activities for years before their initiation. The initiation services for new MU members are therefore major events for the local MU chapter and congregation, with representatives attending from other congregations as well.

The Fishermen, or *Vabvuwi*, constitute the male counterpart to the MU.[11] Much smaller than the MU, its members are active in congregational leadership and in organising *mapungwe*, both among them-

---

8'There is little evidence of women's formal associations before the impact of the missions and, later, colonialism. These have developed from church and other associations and are today very widespread, but there is otherwise nothing comparable to the women's societies found elsewhere in Africa.' May, 31.

9'*Gungano re Vadzimaï*', (Mothers' Union membership card), (Harare: Diocese of Mashonaland, nd).

10Exceptions to the motherhood qualification are sometimes made. The wife of the pastor of the congregation is automatically the president of the local MU chapter and therefore must be a member. When a clergy couple have not been married long enough to have a child but have nevertheless entered upon parish duties, the priest's wife may be initiated into membership.

11The singular of the name is *mubvuwi*.

selves and for the parish or district. The *Vabvuwi* are found in a number of MFCs, and in each church they are organised and governed separately. *Vabvuwi* of various churches wear distinctive sashes and pin an identifying badge on their jacket lapels, with the inscription 'Anglican Wabvuwi' or 'Methodist Wabvuwi', as the case may be.

The origins of the *Vabvuwi* are obscure, but the movement likely arose early in this century at the initiative of Shona men who had become Methodists through UMC work at Old Mutare Mission. The idea took hold in other MFCs largely on account of the attractiveness of the *mapungwe* that the Methodist *Vabvuwi* led. The Anglican organisation functioned early at Penhalonga and at Bonda but did not receive episcopal recognition until 1962.

Ministries of *Vabvuwi* include preaching, healing, exorcising, visiting the sick and lapsed, preparing church members for the sacraments and helping in congregational administration. Like MU members, *Vabvuwi* must have been married in church in order to qualify for membership.[12] The organisation imposes a number of restrictive rules that result in relatively small membership: monogamy, no drinking of alcohol, no smoking of tobacco, no adultery, no betting on horses and no consultation with diviners or spirit mediums.[13] Among Anglicans, the insistence of the *Vabvuwi* on abstinence from alcohol and their promotion of *mapungwe* appeared to threaten schism and made establishing the organisation difficult:

> In the very beginning, Christians had difficulty trying to introduce the idea of *Vabvuwi*. The priests did not like it, because the *Vabvuwi* said that they did not like drinking beer. The priests said, 'Drink moderately', but if a person drinks, you cannot control yourself. So the priests said, 'You now want to establish your own church.' The *Vabvuwi* argued with the priests until it was agreed

---

[12]The reluctance of many Shona men to have their marriages solemnised in church is usually attributed to the churches' prohibition of polygyny. The power and attraction of the MU is such that for years after being married according to customary law a Christian wife will likely lobby her husband for a church wedding. When he finally agrees it is mainly in order to give his wife the opportunity to receive communion, become a full MU member, and have their children baptised.

[13]*Anglican Vabvuwi*: ((Harare: Diocese of Mashonaland) nd).

upon by the bishop (Cecil Alderson) ... that there would be the *Vabvuwi* and the Mothers' Union.[14]

The MU and *Vabvuwi* function in MFCs as lay orders of ministry with a strong sense of community and discipline. At the same time these organisations are rooted firmly in their local congregational setting and are subject to the clergy's authority. Their membership hierarchy, promotion of uniforms and frequent meetings foster a strong identity as pietist and activist groups within the churches. The restrictions placed on members are taken quite seriously, and infractions are dealt with by the leaders, often in consultation with the entire membership. At a congregation near Bonda in 1985, for instance, a *mubvuwi* who was a respected congregational leader decided to leave the Anglican Church and join the Apostles of Johane Marange, a transition handled quietly by church authorities. For his controversial departure from the *Vabvuwi*, however, the local chapter organised a *pungwe* that was attended by 400 people, including the departing member, who, as required, handed over his badge and sash with great ceremony during the night.

The large following of the MU includes most women in the local congregation, if aspirants as well as full members are taken into account. These high numbers and the strong discipline of both groups give them considerable authority in setting the tone and norms of local congregational life.[15] Many night vigils are organised by these groups and when vigils are organised under other auspices it is usually the MU members and *Vabvuwi* who are the leaders.

---

[14]Bernard Matseketsa, church members interview, 13 March 1991, EHTE.

[15]*Ngoma*, the Methodist worship book, includes among its worship resources liturgies for the initiation of members into the MU, the *Vabvuwi*, and the Methodist Youth Fellowship.

GLOSSARY OF SHONA WORDS

Note: The plurals of most Shona nouns, all forms of adjectives and the conjugations of all Shona verbs are formed by prefixes. Nominal and adjectival prefixes consist of one syllable, but verbal forms may include several prefixes, which conjugate the verb and indicate direct or indirect objects. Therefore, the reader should first attempt to isolate the word root when looking up a plural noun, any adjective, or a conjugated verb in this alphabetical listing. Nouns appear in the glossary in their singular form; plural forms, some of them identical with the singular form, are also noted. Verbs appear in their infinitive form, which carries the prefix *ku-*; thus, all verbs appear under *ku-*.

baba	Father. Customary title and term of address for any man who is a father; used with or without surname. When capitalised, refers to biblical account of God as Father. Plural: *vanababa*
badza	Hoe, common tool of agricultural cultivation, traditionally an important article of bride-wealth. Plural: *mapadza*
barika	Polygyny
bere	Hyena, considered to be a companion and symbol of witches. Plural: *mapere*
chechi	Church (term derived from English) Plural: *machechi*
chikwambo	Spirit to whom a debt is owed. In particular, spirit of a childless man who was murdered and who returns to claim a woman from the murderer's family so that she can bear children whom he can claim as descendants. Plural: *zvikwambo*
chimbwido	Female scout assisting guerrillas during Liberation War. Plural: *zvimbwido* or *vanachimbwido* (male: *mujiba*)

310

Chimurenga	Zimbabwe's Liberation War, which resulted in independence in 1980
chipoko	Ghost. Plural: *zvipoko*
chipostori	Apostolic theology, liturgy, church structure and social life in the tradition of Spirit-type African Initiated Churches, especially the AACJM
chiremba	Doctor. Refers to a practitioner of conventional Western medicine, a healing spirit, or a female diviner-healer. Plural: *zviremba*
chisi	Day of rest, mandated by the spirit elders, when fields must not be ploughed
chita	Organisation that provides continuing fellowship. Plural: *zvita*
chitsinga	Physical disorder caused by sorcery; also the material object that inflicts the disorder. Plural: *zvitsinga*
Chivanhu	Shona Spirit Religion. Language and customs of the people
chivanse	Cleared area around a house or in the centre of a *kraal*, usually with the earth packed down to a smooth surface
demoni	Demon, evil spirit (term derived from English). Plural: *mademoni*
dhiri	Congratulatory ceremony for married couple upon birth of first child, celebrated with a *pungwe* by Zion Apostolic Church
dima	Darkness
doro	Ritual beer
fodya	Tobacco; tobacco snuff, used by mediums to bring on spirit possession
gomo	Mountain. Plural: *makomo*
gona	Medium's collection of articles believed to invoke and direct the power of spirits. Often gathered in a basket. May consist of cloths, pieces of wood, hair,

fur and animal parts. Noun derived from verb *kugona*, to be able

gungano	Large meeting that includes groups from large geographical area. Used by United Methodists and Marange Apostles to refer to meetings that last several days. Plural: *magungano*
hama	Relative. Term used frequently as spiritual metaphor for new extended family of the church. Plural: *hama.*
high-density suburb	Post-independence administrative and journalistic term for quasi-municipal entities, formerly called 'African townships', established around Rhodesian cities reserved for white residents. Although residents of the high-density suburbs continue to be exclusively black Africans, the former white suburbs, currently termed 'low-density suburbs', that are closer to the city centres have increasing numbers of black residents
hondo	War
hosho	Rattle, usually made of dried gourd, used to accompany singing
imba	House, home. Plural: *dzimba*
ishe	Chief, usually referring to a sub-chief. Lord, with reference to God. Plural: *madzishe*
ivhu	Earth, dust
kopje	Small hill (Afrikaans term)
kraal	Homestead (term derived from Afrikaans), a fenced area that encloses a family's thatched dwellings
kubatwa	To be grasped, seized. Often used in connection with possession by spirits or inspiration of Holy Spirit
kudenga	Sky. Heaven
kufemerwa	To be breathed into, inspired; often used in connection with work of the Holy Spirit
kuimba	To sing
kumuka	To wake up, rise from sleep. To rise from the dead

312

kuparidza	To preach
kuprofita	To prophesy
kurapa	To heal
kurara	To sleep
kuroora	To marry (as a man)
kuroorwa	To be married (as a woman)
kuroya	To practise wizardry
kuseni	Early morning
kusvikirwa	To be possessed by a spirit
kutamba	To dance, play
kuyedza	To dawn
lobola	Brideprice. (Also *lobolo*)
madzitateguru	Forebears, ancestors
maharklos	Choir singers in the African Apostolic Church of Johane Marange
mai	Mother. Customary title and term of address for any woman who is a mother; used with or without surname. Plural: *vanamai*
mambakwedza	Pre-dawn period, between about 3 am and 5 am, or the beginning of light
mambo	King, usually referring to a major territorial chief. Plural: *madzimambo*
mangwanani	Morning, from dawn until about 11 am. Also a greeting, 'Good morning'
manheru	Evening, from about 4 pm to between 9 pm and 11 pm. Also a greeting, 'Good evening'
masikati	Midday and afternoon, from about 11 am until about 4 pm. Also a greeting, 'Good afternoon'
masowe	Wilderness; uninhabited area to which people retire for prayer, either individually or corporately

313

mbuya	Grandmother. Customary title and term of address for any woman who is a grandmother; used with or without surname. Plural: *vanambuya*
mharidzo	Sermon. Plural: *mharidzo*
mhondoro	Territorial spirit. Physical or visionary lion that embodies a territorial spirit. Medium possessed by a territorial spirit. Plural: *mhondoro*
mhuri	Family, both nuclear and extended. Plural: *mhuri*
moto	Fire
msasa	Name of common indigenous tree
mubapatidzi	Baptiser, a ministerial office in AICs. Plural: *Vabapatidzi*
mubatanidzwa	Meeting that brings together congregations from different Christian churches. Plural: *mibatanidzwa*
mudzimu	Ancestral spirit. Also generic term for spirit, hence used sometimes to refer to the Holy Spirit, *Mudzimu Mutsvene*. Plural: *vadzimu, midzimu*
mufundisi	Teacher, preacher, pastor, presiding elder in a church. In mission-founded churches, term refers to clergy. In AICs, term refers to pastors and elders subordinate to prophetic figures. Plural: *vafundisi*
mujiba	Male scout assisting guerrillas during Liberation War. Plural: *vanamujiba, vajiba*. (Female scout: *chimbwido*)
mukayi	Tea plucker. Plural: *vakayi*
mukomana	Boy. Plural: *vakomana*
mukuwasha	Son-in-law. Plural: *vakuwasha*
munamati	One who prays, worshipper, church member, especially with reference to members of the Unity of African Apostolic Faith Church. Plural: *vanamati*
munamato	Prayer. Use of the term is generally limited to Christian context. Plural: *minamato*
muparidzi	Preacher. Plural: *vaparidzi*

mupostori	Apostle (term derived from English and Greek), referring both to biblical apostles and to members of many Spirit-type AICs especially the AACJM. Plural: *vapostori*
mupristi	Priest (term derived from English). Generally refers to Roman and Anglican clergy. Plural: *vapristi*
muprofiti	Prophet (term derived from English). Generally refers to biblical figures and to AIC leaders who are believed to discern, heal, exorcise and direct by the power of the Holy Spirit. Plural: *vaprofiti*
murapi	Healer. Ministerial office in African Initiated Churches. Plural: *varapi*
muroora	Daughter-in-law. Plural: *varoora*
muroyi	Wizard. Term includes both female witches and male sorcerers. Plural: *varoyi*
musangano	Meeting of people. Plural: *misangano*
musasa	Shelter; temporary camp. Plural: *misasa*
musha	Home. May refer to a person's *kraal*, but generally refers to a person's home village, where extended family traditionally has lived. Plural: *misha*
mushonga	Medicine, including the material healing agents prescribed both by diviner-healers of SSR and by physicians of conventional Western medicine. Plural: *mishonga*
musikana	Girl. Plural: *vasikana*
mutambo	Dance. Drama. Game. Plural: *mitambo*
mutungamiriri	Leader. Plural: *vatungamiriri*
muvhangeri	Evangelist (term derived from English). A ministerial office in AICs. Plural: *vavhangeri*
mwana	Child, offspring. Plural: *vana*
Mwari	God. Territorial spirit with shrine in the Matopo Hills near Bulawayo

Mweya Mutsvene or *Mweya Unoyera*   Holy Spirit

mweya	Spirit. Plural: *mweya*
nganga	Diviner-healer. Plural: *nganga*
ngoma	Drum. Plural: *ngoma*
ngozi	Avenging spirit. Plural: *ngozi*
njuzu	Water spirit. Plural: *njuzu*
nyika	Land, country, territory. Plural: *nyika*
nyoka	Snake. Plural: *nyoka*
Paseka	Annual observance of the Lord's Supper in AICs, often around the time of Easter (term derived from Hebrew *pesakh*)
pasichigare	Pertaining to traditional Shona society prior to contact with Europeans
pungwe	A social, political or religious gathering that continues from dusk until dawn. Plural: *mapungwe*
Rabhauma	Highest rank in any order of ministry in the AACJM
rondavel	Round, thatched structure, typically devoted to a household or agricultural use such as sleeping quarters, cookhouse, granary and the like (term derived from Afrikaans.)
roora	Brideprice
ropa	Blood
rufo	Funeral
rufu	Death
runyaradzo	Community gathering to console bereaved family
Sa	Mister, a prefix to a man's surname
sadza	Stiff porridge made from white maize meal; staple food of Shona people in Zimbabwe
sekuru	Grandfather. Customary title and term of address for any man who is a grandfather, used with or without surname. Plural: *vanasekuru*
shavi	Alien spirit. Plural: *mashavi*

simba	Strength, power
svikiro	Spirit medium. Plural: *masvikiro*
tezvara	Father-in-law. Plural: *vanatezvara*
upfu	White maize meal from which *sadza* is cooked
usiku	Night, beginning between about 9 pm and 11 pm and continuing until *mambakwedza,* the period before dawn, or, more loosely, until dawn
vakomana	Boys. Term often used to refer to guerrillas of Zimbabwe's Liberation War
wakaipa	Bad, evil. (Prefix varies according to class of noun modified)
wakanaka	Good. (Prefix varies according to class of noun modified)

SOURCES

A: Liturgical events

Divination session. Mai Makwiana, *nganga* of SSR. 6 May 1991, Hilltop Village, EHTE. Tape recording, transcript and handwritten notes.

Easter *Paseka*. Pungwe Branch, Pentecostal Apostolic Church of God. 30 March 1994, Hamudikuwanda. Tape recording, transcript and typewritten journal.

Easter Sunday Service. United Methodist, EHTE congregation. 31 March 1991, school, Village No 3, EHTE. Tape recording, transcript and handwritten notes.

Easter Sunday Service. Zion Apostolic Church, EHTE congregation. 31 March 1991, field, Village No 3, EHTE. Tape recording, transcript and handwritten notes.

Funeral. Anglican service for Maxwell Gorogodo. 5 June 1985, Dziwa. Handwritten notes.

Funeral. Rites of Shona Spirit Religion for Leonard Mandioma. 26 January 1985, Manyore, near Sanyatwe. Handwritten notes.

Good Friday Liturgy. St Peter's Anglican Church, Mandea. 29 March 1991, St Peter's Church, Mandea. Tape recording, transcript and handwritten notes.

Household Prayers. St Luca's Apostolic Ejuwel Jekenishen Church, EHTE congregation. 13 May 1991, home of Silas and Lydia Sithole, Village No 3, EHTE. Tape recording and typewritten notes.

Night Service. *Mubatanidzwa* convened by Maronda Mashanu Anglican Church, EHTE. 5–6 April 1991, Village No 3 Hall, EHTE. Participating churches: African Methodist, Anglican, Church of Central Africa Presbyterian, Roman Catholic, Salvation Army, United Methodist, Unity of the African Apostolic Faith Church. Tape recording and transcript.

Night Service. *Rutandadzo* by members of Maronda Mashanu Anglican Church, EHTE. 20–21 January 1994, home of Shepstone and Veronica Muzvidzwa, EHTE. Tape recording and handwritten notes.

Night Service. *Rutandadzo* by members of Maronda Mashanu Anglican Church, EHTE. 21–22 April 1991, home of Shepstone and Veronica Muzvidzwa, EHTE. Tape recording, transcript and handwritten notes.

Night Service. St Luca's Apostolic Ejuwel Jekenishen Church, EHTE congregation. 5 April 1991, field, Village No 3, EHTE. Tape recording, transcript and handwritten notes.

Night Service. Zion Apostolic Church, EHTE congregation. 27 March 1991, field, Village No 3, EHTE. Typewritten notes.

Pungwe. Anglican *Vabvuwi*. 16–17 March 1985, St George's Anglican Church, Dziwa, in Bonda Church District. Handwritten notes.

Pungwe. Apostolic Faith Mission congregation. 25–26 May 1991, Pimai. Tape recording.

Pungwe. Bonda Church District Youth Rally. 6–7 September 1985, St David's Anglican Church, Bonda. Handwritten notes.

318

Pungwe. Dhiri. Zion Apostolic Church, EHTE congregation. 4–5 May 1991, village hall, Village No 3, EHTE. Tape recording, transcript and handwritten notes.

Pungwe. Dhiri. Zion Apostolic Church, EHTE congregation. 18–19 May 1991, pre-school building, Village No 9, EHTE. Tape recording, transcript and handwritten notes.

Pungwe. Easter revival. 30–31 March 1991, Hamudikuwanda congregation of Pungwe Branch of Pentecostal Apostolic Church of God. Tape recording, transcript, handwritten notes and typed journal.

Pungwe. Easter Vigil. 6–7 April 1985, St David's Church, Bonda. Handwritten notes.

Pungwe. Easter Vigil. 29–30 March 1986, St David's Church, Bonda. Handwritten notes.

Pungwe. Festival of Bernard Mizeki. 22–23 June 1985, St David's Anglican Church, Bonda. Handwritten notes.

Pungwe. Festival of Bernard Mizeki. 14–16 June 1996, Mizeki Shrine, Marondera. Video and audio recordings.

Pungwe. Festival of Shona Spirit Religion. 24–25 May 1991, kraal of medium Mai Muzanenhemo, Zindi Township. Tape recording and handwritten notes.

Pungwe. Funeral vigil for Lillian Nyazika. 17–18 June 1984, home of Kennesia and Frederick Nyazika, St David's Anglican Mission, Bonda.

Pungwe. Funeral vigil for Linda Mupambo. 27–28 August 1985, home of Betty Mupambo, Nyamazi. Handwritten notes.

Pungwe. Funeral vigil for Mai Zambezi. 29–30 January 1985, Anglican Church of the Holy Name, Sakubva. Handwritten notes.

Pungwe. Funeral vigil for Violet Feremba. 18 March 1985, Feremba, near Bonda. Handwritten notes.

Pungwe. Gungano of Chikomba congregation of African Apostolic Church of Johane Marange. 12–13 April 1991, Mutemangao. Tape recording, transcript and handwritten notes.

Pungwe. Gungano of Men of the United Methodist Church (Vabvuwi). 11–12 May 1991, Nyangombe. Tape recording, transcript and handwritten notes.

Pungwe. Gungano of Murara congregation of African Apostolic Church of Johane Marange. 19–20 April 1991, Murara. Tape recording, transcript and handwritten notes.

Pungwe. Home visit of Unity of the African Apostolic Faith Church congregation. 25–26 May 1991, Zindi. Tape recording.

Pungwe. Kusimbiso Panguva Dzokurwara (Strengthening in Time of Illness). Pastoral visit by members of Maronda Mashanu Anglican Church at EHTE and by members of Methodist, Baptist and Zimbabwe Assembly of God Africa churches. 10–11 May 1991, home of Mai Karadzandima, Zindi. Tape recording, transcript and handwritten notes.

Pungwe. Mothers' Union *mubatanidzwa.* 21–22 February 1986, St David's Anglican Church, Bonda. Handwritten notes.

Pungwe. Mubatanidzwa convened by Eastern Highlands United Methodist Church. 25–26 May 1991, Village No 3 Hall, EHTE. Participating churches: African Methodist, Anglican, Church of Central Africa Presbyterian, Jehovah's Witnesses, Roman Catholic, United Methodist, Unity of the African Apostolic Faith Church, Zimbabwe Assembly of God Africa. Tape recording, transcript and handwritten notes.

Pungwe. Mubatanidzwa convened by Maronda Mashanu Anglican Church, EHTE. 12–13

April 1991, Village No 3 Hall, EHTE. Participating churches: African Methodist, Anglican, Church of Central Africa Presbyterian, Roman Catholic, Salvation Army, United Methodist, Unity of the African Apostolic Faith Church. Tape recording, transcript and handwritten notes.

Pungwe. Paseka. Zion Apostolic Church, EHTE congregation. 20–21 April 1991, field, Village No 3, EHTE. Tape recording, transcript and handwritten notes.

Pungwe. Pastor's visit. 30 April–1 May 1986, outside site, Nyachibva Anglican congregation, Nyachibva, Manica Communal Area. Handwritten notes.

Pungwe. Pastor's visits. 4–5 March 1986, 20–21 May 1986, home of Elisha Manyau, St Bernard's Anglican Church, Manyau. Handwritten notes.

Pungwe. Pastor's visit. 18–19 February 1986, St Denys Anglican Church, Njerama. Handwritten notes.

Pungwe. Runyaradzo for Mai Mutsanya. 8–9 January 1994, Mutsanya kraal, Pimai. Tape recording, transcript and handwritten notes.

Pungwe. Runyaradzo for Maxwell Gorogodo. Congregation of St George's Anglican Church, Dziwa. 31 May–1 June 1986, home of Sylvester Gorogodo, Dziwa. Handwritten notes.

Pungwe. Samanga congregation of Unity of African Apostolic Faith Church. 28–29 April 1991, Chitambo. Tape recording, transcript and handwritten notes.

Pungwe. St Luca's Apostolic Ejuwel Jekenishen Church, EHTE congregation. 18–19 May 1991, Village No 6, EHTE. Tape recording, transcript and handwritten notes.

Pungwe. St Luca's Apostolic Ejuwel Jekenishen Church, EHTE congregation. 30 April–1 May 1991, Philip Sithole kraal, Buwu. Tape recording, transcript and handwritten notes.

Pungwe. Stewardship rally. 2 June 1984, St David's Anglican Church, Bonda. Handwritten notes.

Pungwe. Wilderness mountain vigil. Pungwe Branch, Pentecostal Apostolic Church of God. 8–9 May 1991, Dombomupunga Mountain. Tape recording, transcript and handwritten notes.

Pungwe. Wilderness mountain vigil. Zindi congregation of Unity of African Apostolic Faith Church. 11–12 January 1994, Nyanga Escarpment. Tape recording and transcript.

Pungwe. Youth rally. 15–16 January 1994, St James Anglican Church, Nyamhingura. Video recording, tape recording, transcript and handwritten notes.

Sunday Service, Easter Day. Eastern Highlands United Methodist Church. 31 March 1991, Village No 3 School, EHTE. Tape recording, transcript and handwritten notes.

Sunday Service, Morning Prayer. Maronda Mashanu Anglican Church, EHTE. 7 April 1991, EHTE. Tape recording, transcript and handwritten notes.

Sunday Service, Morning Prayer. Maronda Mashanu Anglican Church, EHTE. 16 January 1994, EHTE. Tape recording and handwritten notes.

Sunday Service. Apostolic Faith Mission, EHTE. 7 April 1991, Village No 3 School, EHTE. Typewritten notes.

Sunday Service. Church of Central Africa Presbyterian, EHTE. 16 January 1994. Village No 3 School, EHTE. Tape recording and handwritten notes.

Sunday Service. Pungwe Branch, Pentecostal Apostolic Church of God. 19 May 1991, Hamudikuwanda. Handwritten notes.

Sunday Service. Zone revival. Apostolic Faith Mission, Hauna. 14 April 1991, store, Hauna. Typewritten notes.

Sunday Services. Several hundred services in Anglican churches throughout Bonda and Nyanga Church Districts, October 1983-June 1986.

B: Interviews[1]

Chikomba, Chief. 10 April 1991, Chikomba. Typewritten notes.

Chimbidzo, Alice. Member, youth group of Banket Anglican Parish. 30 December 1993, Banket. Typed notes.

Chimonyo, Loveness. Member, Unity of the African Apostolic Faith Church. Tea plucker, EHTE. 23 May 1991, Village No 3, EHTE. Handwritten notes.

Chimuti, A. F. Officer, World Vision International. In English, 10 April 1991, Chisuko. Typewritten notes.

Chitare, Pearson. Church Council member, United Methodist Church, EHTE. Industrial Relations Officer, EHTE. In English and Shona, 10 April 1991, 20 May 1991, 4 January 1994, EHTE. Tape recording and transcript, typewritten notes.

Church leaders, forum on theology. In Shona and English, 18 May 1991, EHTE. Tape recording and transcript. Participants: Pearson Chitare, UMC; Shepstone Muavidzwa, Anglican Church; Noah Mushunje, Anglican Church and UMC; SaMuyambo and others.

Church leaders, Pentecostal Apostolic Church of God. 30 March 1991, Hamudikuwanda. Participants: Daniel Gukutikwa, Ezekiel Mhlambo, SaMukasi, SaNemutenzi. Tape recording and transcript.

Church leaders, St Columba's Roman Catholic Mission, Hauna. In Shona and English, 18 January 1994, Hauna. Participants: Phillip Kembo, seminarian; Francis Sanyanga, catechist; Tafirenyika Nyagope, church council chairperson. Tape recording and transcript.

Church leaders, St Gabriel's Anglican Church, Chirarwe. In Shona and English, August 1987, Chirarwe. Participants: Elisha Gunda and SaMakunike, church council members; Edward Mangwanda and the late Richard Masara, catechists. Tape recording and transcript.

Church leaders, Zion Apostolic Church, EHTE congregation. 19 May 1991, Village No 9, EHTE. Participants: Bp Titus Chinyama, Jean Lambert, Bp James H Maphosa, SaMutuhmani, Joseph Pickle. Tape recording, transcript and typewritten notes.

Church leaders. In English, 16 April 1991, EHTE. Participants: the Rev David Manyau (Anglican), Michael Mbona (Anglican), Lovemore Mupinda (Mugodhi). Typewritten notes.

Church members. 13 March 1991, EHTE. Participants: SaKwadingepi (United Church of Christ), Thomas Marira (Anglican; former guerrilla), Bernard Matseketsa (Anglican), David Mubaira (United Methodist). Tape recording and transcript.

DeWolfe, the Rev Shirley. United Methodist minister, Old Mutare Mission. In English, 2 May 1991, Old Mutare Mission. Handwritten and typed notes.

Dhliwayo, Roderick. Member, Apostolic Faith Mission; foreperson EHTE. In English, 5 April 1991, EHTE. Handwritten notes.

---

1 Interviews are in Shona, unless noted as being in English.

Diviner-healers of Shona Spirit Religion, Christian clergy and conventional medical personnel at workshop organised by Chitepo District Medical Officer. 12 November 1985, Chitepo District Headquarters. Handwritten notes.

Evangelists, African Apostolic Church of Johane Marange. 12–13 April 1991, *Pungwe* of Chikomba congregation of African Apostolic Church of Johane Marange, Mutemangao. Participants: Philip Moda, SaChimbuwa, SaGogodi, SaManhare, SaMvura, SaNyeredzo. Tape recording and transcript.

Evangelists, African Apostolic Church of Johane Marange. 14 January 1994, *Gungano* of Murara congregation of African Apostolic Church of Johane Marange, Nyamakatore. Participants: SaGoro, Stephen Matawa, Philip Moda, SaMuomba, Ernest Mutasa, SaMwareka. Tape recording and transcript.

Evangelists, African Apostolic Church of Johane Marange. 19–20 April 1991, *Pungwe* of Murara congregation of African Apostolic Church of Johane Marange, Murara. Participants: Ernest Mutasa, SaDuri, SaMajaro and others. Tape recording and transcript.

Ganza, Sa. Catechist, African Methodist Episcopal Church (AMEC). 19 May 1991, Surura River Branch AMEC congregation, Hamudikuwanda. Typewritten notes.

Hewgill, Anthony. Former general manager, EHTE. In English, 24 March, 25 March 1991, EHTE. Handwritten notes.

Holderness, Rev Richard. Retired Anglican priest. Former priest-in-charge, Bonda Church District. In English, 23 January 1994, Marondera. Typewritten notes.

Johns, David Machare. Husband of founder of Pentecostal Apostolic Church of God. In English, 22 January 1994, Mutare. Handwritten notes.

Kachali, Baba. Leader, Leader, Vabvuwi chapter, United Methodist Church, Tsonzo. 25 August 1987, Watsomba. Tape recording and transcript.

Kachali, Mai. Leader, Mother's Union chapter, United Methodist Church, Tsonzo. 25 August 1987, Watsomba. Tape recording and transcript.

Kahlari, the Rev Togarasei. United Methodist Pastor, Gatsi United Methodist Church. 30 April 1991, Gatsi; 12 May 1991, en route Nyangombe to Gatsi. Tape recording, transcript, handwritten and typed notes.

Makoni, Enos. Environmental health officer, Nyangombe. In English, 12 May 1991, Nyangombe. Handwritten notes.

Mangwarara, E Treasurer, Pentecostal Apostolic Church of God. In Shona and English, 22 April 1991, Mutare. Tape recording and transcript.

Manika, Mrs R C. Storekeeper. 22 May 1991, Manika Store, Gatsi. Typewritten notes.

Manyau, the Rev David. Priest, Anglican Church; priest-in-charge of Mandea Church District. In English, 16 April 1991, EHTE. Typewritten notes.

Marange, Sa. United Methodist lay leader. Paymaster, City of Mutare. 11 May 1991, Nyangombe. Typewritten notes.

Marohwa, Kingston. Church council member, Maronda Mashanu Anglican Church, EHTE. Carpenter, EHTE. 20 January 1994, EHTE. Handwritten notes.

Matsanzike, Samson. Diviner-healer, Chipinge. 1 January 1994, Magwizi bus between Kadoma and Masvingo. Handwritten notes.

Matseketsa, Bernard. Church council member, St James Anglican Church, Nyamhingura. Clerk, EHTE. 18 May 1991, EHTE. Tape recording and transcript.

Matunia, Costa. Pastor, Banket Apostolic Faith Mission. 24 April 1991, Banket. Handwritten notes.

Maunganidze, Mbuya (Beulah Mashita). Founder, Pentecostal Apostolic Church of God. 22 April 1991, Mutare. Tape recording and transcript.

Mawere, John. Orphanage coordinator, Beulah Jones Organisation, Pentecostal Apostolic Church of God. 22 January 1994, Mutare. Handwritten notes.

Mbigi, Lovemore. Former personnel manager, EHTE; former lay leader, St Peter's Anglican Church District, Mandea. In English, September 1990, Newton, Mass. Handwritten notes.

Mbona, Michael. Church council member, Mandea Anglican Church District. Assistant Head, Mandea Secondary School. 20 January 1994, EHTE. Handwritten notes.

Mhika, Baba. Catechist, Church of Central Africa Presbyterian congregation, EHTE. 16 January 1994, EHTE. Handwritten notes.

Mhlambo, Evelyn. Prophet, Pentecostal Apostolic Church of God. 9 May 1991, 19 January 1994, Pimai. Tape recording and transcript.

Mhlambo, Ezekiel. Elder, Pentecostal Apostolic Church of God. 30 March 1991, Hamudikuwanda; 8–9 May 1991, Dombomupunga. Tape recording and transcript.

Mubaira, David. Lay preacher, United Methodist Church. 20 March 1991, EHTE. Tape recording and transcript.

Mubure, Sa. Anglican *mubvuwi*, St James' Church, Nyamhingura. 18 May 1991, EHTE. Tape recording and transcript.

Mukadiwe, Sa. Member, Chikomba congregation of African Apostolic Church of Johane Marange. 13 April 1991, *Pungwe* of Chikomba congregation of African Apostolic Church of Johane Marange, Mutemangao. Tape recording and transcript.

Mukata, the Rev Samuel. Minister, Gatsi United Methodist Church. 12 January 1994, EHTE. Typewritten notes.

Mukwindisa, the Rev Kennedy. United Methodist minister, church headquarters, Harare. 11 May 1991, Nyangombe. Handwritten notes.

Munetsi, Chamutenga P. Former freedom fighter. Telephone operator, EHTE. Member, Maronda Mashanu Anglican Church, EHTE. 24 May 1991, EHTE. Tape recording and transcript.

Mupinda, Lovemore. Manager, Milimani Estate, EHTE. Evangelist of Unity of the African Apostolic Faith Church. In English and Shona, 25 March 1991, 26 March 1991, 1 April 1991, 2 April 1991, EHTE. Handwritten notes.

Mupinda, Sheadman. Member, Zion Apostolic Church. 2 April 1991, 17 April 1991, EHTE. Handwritten notes.

Mushunje, Noah. Member, Maronda Mashanu Anglican Church, EHTE. Mechanic, EHTE. 21 April 1991, EHTE. Typewritten notes.

Mushunje, Violet. Prophet, Pentecostal Apostolic Church of God. 22 April 1991, Mutare. Tape recording and transcript.

Muzanenhamo, Mai. Spirit medium, Zindi. 21 May 1991, 23 May 1991, Zindi. Tape recording and transcript.

Muzide, Naison. Tea plucker. 3 April 1991, EHTE. Handwritten notes.

Muzvidzwa, Shepstone. Accountant, EHTE. In English and Shona, 5 May 1991, 3 January 1994, 11 January 1994, EHTE. Typewritten notes.

Muzvidzwa, Wilma. Visitor, EHTE. Anglican. In English and Shona, 4 January 1994, EHTE. Typewritten notes.

Mwanza, Abraham. Manager, Zindi Tea Processing Factory, EHTE. In English, 24 May 1991, EHTE. Handwritten notes.

Nyagomo, Maxwell. Courier, EHTE. Anglican. 3 April 1991, EHTE. Handwritten notes.

Nyarota, the Rev Lloyd. United Methodist pastor, Chikore. 12 May 1991, Nyangombe. Handwritten notes.

Simanga, Luke. Member, Zion Apostolic Church, EHTE congregation. 4 May 1991, Village No 3, EHTE. Handwritten notes.

Sithole, Mai. Member, Hauna Apostolic Faith Mission; tea plucker, EHTE. 15 April 1991, EHTE. Typewritten notes.

Sithole, Silas. Prophet, St Luca's Apostolic Ejuwel Jekenishen Church, EHTE congregation. 13 May 1991, 18 January 1994, Village No 3, EHTE. Tape recording, transcripts and handwritten notes.

Tuff, Brian. Manager, EHTE. In English, 12 January 1994, EHTE. Handwritten notes.

Zindi, Chief. April 1991, Zindi. Handwritten notes.

ZIRRCON Staff (Zimbabwe Institute for Religious Research and Conservation of Nature) (in English and Shona), 3 January 1994, Masvingo. Participants: Anderson Aarsman, Marthinus Daneel, Farai, Leonard Gono, Bishop Ruben Marinda, Bishop Mutikizizi, Raviro, Clever Zunde, Solomon Zvanaka, and Tarisai Zvokuomba. Tape recording and transcript.

Zizhou, Webster. Personnel manager, EHTE. Apostolic Faith Mission member. In English and Shona, 17 May, 18 April 1991. EHTE. Typewritten notes.

C: Essay project participants

Chawati, Isaiah. Evangelist, FGCG. Foreperson, EHTE.

Chibvuma, Elias. Member, ZAOGA. Security Guard, EHTE.

Chitare, Pearson. Member, UMC. Industrial Relations Officer, EHTE.

Dhliwayo, Roderick. Youth Zone Secretary, AFM. Foreperson, EHTE.

Hamadziripi, Obvious. Member, AACJM. Electrician, EHTE.

Kahlari, the Rev Togarasei. Pastor, UMC.

Kavhuru, Daniel Patrick. Secretary, Anglican Church. Teacher, EHTE.

Madenya, Noah. Member, Family of God. Personnel Clerk, EHTE.

Makunike, Thomas. Elder, PACG. Farmer.

Makwenda, Mission. Member, CCAP. Tea plucker, EHTE.

Mapudzi, Shadreck. Member, Anglican Church. Personnel Secretary, EHTE.

Masiyakurima, Gilbert. Member, Anglican Church. Gardener, EHTE.

Matinenga, Peter. Secretary, UAAFC. Telephone Operator, EHTE.

Matsikira, Isaac. Member, SLAEJC. Cook, EHTE.

Matsikira, Mai. Member, SLAEJC. Farmer.

Mhlanga, Leonard. Member, ZAOGA. General Worker, EHTE.

Muchesa, Simon Dube. Member, UMC. Unemployed.

Muparutsa, Maxwell. Member, ZAOGA. School mentor, EHTE.

Mupinda, Lovemore. Evangelist, UAAFC. Estate Manager, EHTE.

Mushunje, Noah. Member, Anglican Church and UMC. Clerk, EHTE.

Mvumih, I. D. Preacher, PACG. Farmer.

Nyagomo, Maxwell. Member, Anglican Church. Factory Worker, EHTE.

Nyamuchengwe, Joseph. Youth Chairperson, Anglican Church. Secondary student.

Semu, Leon. Youth Vice-secretary, RCC. Research assistant, EHTE.

Sithole, Silas. Prophet, SLAEJC. Tea plucker, EHTE.

Taulo, Aneck. Sectional leader, ZAOGA. School mentor, EHTE.

Zizhou, Margaret Thando. Member, AFM and SDAC. Teacher, EHTE.

Zizhou, Webster. Member, AFM. Personnel manager, EHTE.

D: Archival and unpublished materials, circulars, pamphlets and maps

Archdeacon of Mashonaland and Director of Native Missions in the (Anglican) Diocese of Southern Rhodesia. Report to Diocesan Missionary Conference, St Augustine's Mission, (Penhalonga), September 1932. TD. File ANG 1/1. Zimbabwe National Archives, Harare.

Balfour, Francis T, Fort Salisbury, to Canon Balfour, (SPG, London), 15 September 1891. LS. File ANG 1/1. Zimbabwe National Archives, Harare.

Broderick, George E P. 'History of the Diocese of Southern Rhodesia (formerly the Diocese of Mashonaland)', (1953). TD. File BR 3/3/1. Zimbabwe National Archives, Harare.

Chikonzo, S E. 'MUMC South Convention Revival' (Schedule). (10–12 May 1991). TD, mimeographed.

Eastern Highlands Tea Estates (Private) Limited. 'Conditions of Service Manual Part I (Labour Manual), Amended 1st April 1991'. TD, mimeographed. 1991.

Edwards, Frank, Fort Salisbury, to J Edwards, 19 September 1892. ALS. File ED 1/1/1. Zimbabwe National Archives, Harare.

Evans, St John. Report of the Director of Missions, (Mashonaland Anglican) Diocesan Synod, 1950. Mimeographed. File ANG 1/1/9. Zimbabwe National Archives.

Federation of Rhodesia and Nyasaland, map, 'African Tribes and Languages of the Federation of Rhodesia and Nyasaland', 1964.

'Gungano reVadzimai'. (Mothers' Union membership card.) (Harare: Diocese of Mashonaland, nd.)

Hatendi, Peter. 'Ad Clerum: of offences'. Diocese of Harare. TD, mimeographed. 1990.

Hatendi, Peter. 'The bishop's charge – 1986'. Diocese of Harare. TD, mimeographed. 1986.

Hatendi, Peter. 'The path to God (Mwari): Christ or Midzimu'. Address to the Institute of Contemporary Christianity, 4 April 1984, Harare. TD, mimeographed.

Hatendi, Peter. (Untitled circular to youth.) Diocese of Harare. TD, mimeographed. 7 December 1989.

Hefner, Robert. 'The anthropological study of religion'. Lectures in Boston University, fall 1989. Class notes.

Kirby, Jon P. 'Changing strategies for problem solving: comparing Christian and Muslim converts in northern Ghana'. Paper presented at the Conference on Conversion in Africa, Centre for the Study of World Religions, Harvard University, 12–15 May 1988. TD, photocopied.

Kirwen, Michael C. 'How African Traditional Religions assimilate Christianity'. Paper presented at the Conference on Conversion in Africa, Centre for the Study of World Religions, Harvard University, 12–15 May 1988. TD, photocopied.

Machike, Langston S, St Mary's Mission, Salisbury, to Fr Smith, St Faith's Mission, Rusape, 11 February 1948. ALS. File ANG 16/1/1. Zimbabwe National Archives, Harare.

Manley, Marcelle. 'The pilgrimage to Matonjeni', *Annual Report: June 1992-July 1993*, of the Zimbabwean Institute of Religious Research and Ecological Conservation (ZIRRCON). Masvingo. TD, photocopied. 1983.

Masuko, Elijah M P. 'Gospel and culture'. Paper presented at Haggai Institute Regional Seminars, Accra, 1–7 September 1985. Anglican Diocese of Manicaland, Mutare, Zimbabwe. TD, mimeographed. 1985.

Munyame, I S, acting town clerk, City of Mutare, to Organising Secretary, Pentecostal Apostolic Church of God, 4 August 1993. TLS, photocopied. 1993.

Musiwacho, Vasco. '*Mavambo Ruziyo Rwechivanhu*'. [Beginnings of the story of the religion of the people]. [Mutare.] TD, mimeographed. [1985.]

Muzvidzwa, J O K. 'Research on contribution of early childhood centres to [Eastern Highlands Tea Estates] Company's production'. TD, photocopied. 1991.

Presler, Titus Leonard. 'The secularisation of Anglican missions in Zimbabwe'. TD. 1985.

Report of the [Anglican] Diocesan Translation Committee (Mashonaland) to the Synod of 1950. Signatories: Reginald Smith, CR, chairman; Peter Spencer, secretary. TD, mimeographed. File ANG 1/1/9. Zimbabwe National Archives, Harare.

Schineller, Peter. 'A handbook on inculturation'. TMs, photocopied. 1988.

Service Register, St David's Mission, Bonda, 1915–1918. St David's Church archives, Bonda.

'The formation of the Unity of African Apostolic Faith Church'. Ms copy by Lovemore Mupinda, May 1991. [Original a publication of the Unity of African Apostolic Faith Church.]

Vail, Heroy H. Lectures on modern history of Africa, Fall 1986, Harvard University. Class notes.

Vail, Heroy H. 'Spirits, women and resistance: a Central African case'. TMs, photocopied. 1987.

Zimbabwe National Evangelism Task Committee, *Target 2000*. Handbook for Target 2000 Congress, held 7–10 September 1992, Harare. TD, photocopied. 1992.

Zvanakaka, Solomon. 'Mountain vigil', *Annual Report: June 1992-July 1993*, of the Zimbabwean Institute of Religious Research and Ecological Conservation (ZIRRCON). Masvingo. TD, photocopied. 1993.

E: Published works

Aland, Kurt & Matthew Black, Carlo M Martini, Bruce M Metzger & Allen Wikgren. *Novum Testamentum Graece*. 26th edition. Stuttgart: Deutsche Bibelstiftung, 1979.

Alexander, Jeffrey C. 'Analytic debates: understanding the relative autonomy of culture'. In *Culture and society: contemporary debates*, edited by Jeffrey C Alexander & Steven Seidman, 1–27. Cambridge, UK and New York: Cambridge University Press, 1990.

Allen, Roland. *Missionary methods: St Paul's or ours?* Grand Rapids: William B Eerdmans, 1962.

Altman, Lawrence K. 'Parts of Africa Showing HIV in 1 in 4 adults'. *New York Times*, 24 June 1998, A1.

Amaladoss, M. 'Inculturation: theological perspectives'. *Jeevadhara: A Journal of Christian Interpretation* 33 (May–June 1976), 293–301.

Andrews, C F. *John White of Mashonaland.* London: Hodder & Stoughton, 1935.

Anglican Consultative Council. *Partners in mission.* London: Anglican Consultative Council, 1973.

Arnold, William Edward. *Here to stay: the story of the Anglican Church in Zimbabwe.* Lewes, Sussex: Book Guild, [1985].

Arrupe, Pedro. 'Letter to the whole society on inculturation'. *Studies in the International Apostolate of the Jesuits* 7 (June 1978), 1–15.

Aschwanden, Herbert. *Symbols of death: an analysis of the consciousness of the Karanga.* Translated by Ursula Cooper. Gweru: Mambo Press, 1987.

Aschwanden, Herbert. *Symbols of life: an analysis of the consciousness of the Karanga.* Translated by Ursula Cooper. Gweru: Mambo Press, 1982.

Atkinson, N D. 'The missionary contribution to early education in Rhodesia'. In *Christianity South of the Zambezi*, vol 1, edited by A J Dachs. Gweru: Mambo Press, 1973.

Auret, Diana. *Reaching for justice: the Catholic Commission for Justice and Peace, 1972–1992.* Gweru: Mambo Press, in Association with the Catholic Commission for Justice and Peace in Zimbabwe, 1992.

Barrett, David B. *Schism and renewal in Africa: an analysis of six thousand contemporary religious movements.* Nairobi: Oxford University Press, 1968.

Barrett, David B, ed. *World Christian encyclopedia: a comparative survey of churches and religions in the modern world, AD 1900–2000.* Nairobi, Oxford and New York: Oxford University Press, 1982.

Batson, C Daniel & W Larry Ventis, *The religious experience: a social-psychological perspective.* New York and Oxford: Oxford University Press, 1982.

Beach, D N 'The initial impact of Christianity on the Shona: The Protestants and the Southern Shona'. In *Christianity South of the Zambezi*, vol 1, ed A J Dachs. Gwelo, Rhodesia: Mambo Press, 1973.

Beaver, R. Pierce, ed. *To advance the gospel: selections from the writings of Rufus Anderson.* Grand Rapids: William B. Eerdmans, 1967.

Bediako, Kwame. 'The significance of modern African Christianity – a manifesto'. *Studies in world Christianity* 1, No 1 (1995), 51–67.

Bellah, Robert. 'Religious evolution'. *American Sociological Review*, 29 (1964), 358–374.

Bere-Chikara, Fidelis. 'Cattle: the life blood of Shona society'. In *Shona customs: essays by African writers*, pp. 20–23, eds Clive and Peggy Kileff. Gweru: Mambo Press, 1970.

Berger, Peter L. 'Some second thoughts on substantive versus functional definitions of religion'. *Journal for the Scientific Study of Religion* 13 (1974): 125–133.

Berryman, Phillip. *Liberation theology: essential facts about the revolutionary movement in Latin America and beyond.* Oak Park, Ill: Meyer Stone Books, 1987.

Bhaibheri rine Apokirifa. 2nd edition. [Harare]: Bible Society in Zimbabwe, 1984.

Bhaibheri: Magwaro Matsvene aMwari: Testamente Yekare neTestamente Itsva. Salisbury: Bible Society, 1949.

Bhebhe, Ngwabi. *Christianity and traditional religion in western Zimbabwe, 1859–1923.* London: Longman, 1979.

327

Booth, Newell S, Jr, ed. *African religions: a symposium.* New York: NOK Publishers, 1977.

Bosch, David J. *Transforming mission: paradigm shifts in theology of mission.* American Society of Missiology Series, No 16. Maryknoll: Orbis Books, 1991.

Boulaga, F Eboussi. *Christianity without fetishes: an African critique and recapture of Christianity.* Translated from the French by Robert R Barr. Maryknoll, NY: Orbis Books, 1984.

Bourdillon, Michael F C. *The Shona peoples: an ethnography of the contemporary Shona, with special reference to their religion.* 3rd edition. Shona Heritage Series, Vol 1. Gweru: Mambo Press, 1987.

Bourdillon, Michael F C. *The Shona peoples: an ethnography of the contemporary Shona, with special reference to their religion.* 2nd edition. Shona Heritage Series, Vol 1. Gweru, Zimbabwe: Mambo Press, 1982.

Bourdillon, Michael F C. 'Traditional religion in Shona society'. In *Christianity south of the Zambezi,* vol 1, ed A J Dachs. Gweru: Mambo Press, 1973.

Bourdillon, Michael F C, ed. *Christianity south of the Zambezi.* Vol 2. Gwelo: Mambo Press, 1977.

Bourdillon, Michael F C & Paul Gundani. 'Rural Christians and the Zimbabwe Liberation War: a case study. In *Church and state in Zimbabwe,* eds Carl Hallencreutz & Ambrose Moyo, 147–161. Gweru: Mambo Press, 1988.

Bozongwana, W. *Ndebele religion and customs.* Gweru: Mambo Press, 1983.

Bucher, Hubert. *Spirits and power: an analysis of Shona cosmology.* Cape Town: Oxford University Press, 1980.

Buku reMunamato weVese (Book of Common Prayer). Gweru: Mambo Press, 1983.

Cardenal, Ernesto. *The Gospel in Solentiname.* Translated by Donald D Walsh. Maryknoll: Orbis Books, 1978.

Chater, Patricia. *Crossing the boundary fence.* With illustrations by Helen Mills. A Quest Children's Novel. Harare: College Press, 1988.

Chater, Patricia. *Grass roots: the story of St Faith's Farm in Southern Rhodesia.* London: Hodder & Stoughton, 1962.

Chavunduka, G. *Traditional healers and the Shona patient.* Gweru: Mambo Press, 1978.

Chennells, Anthony. 'The image of the Ndebele and the nineteenth-century missionary tradition'. In *Christianity South of the Zambezi,* vol 2, ed M F C Bourdillon. Gwelo: Mambo Press, 1977.

Chigwedere, Aeneas. *From Mutapa to Rhodes: 1000 to 1890 AD* London, UK, and Salisbury, Zimbabwe: Macmillan, 1980.

Christelow, S J. 'The Bonda years, parts 1–5'. *The Link.* January, February, March, April, May 1969.

Christensen, Thomas G. *An African tree of life.* American Society of Missiology Series, No 14. Maryknoll: Orbis Books, 1990.

Christensen, Torben & William R Hutchison, eds. *Missionary ideologies in the imperialist era: 1880–1920: papers from the Durham Consultation.* Aarhus C, Denmark: Forlaget Aros, 1982.

Christian Audio Visual Action. *Bhaibheri Rinopindura Mibvunzo Yako* (The Bible answers your questions). Harare: CAVA, nd.

Church of the Province of Central Africa. *The Holy Eucharist, morning and evening prayer, 1975; Chisanganirano Chinoera, 1975, Murongerwo Womunamato Wamangwanani Namanheru.* Cincinnati: Forward Movement Publications, 1989.

Clarke, D. G. *Agricultural and plantation workers in Rhodesia: a report on conditions of labour and subsistence.* Mambo Occasional Papers: Socio-Economic Series No 6. Gweru: Mambo Press, 1977.

Clooney, Francis X. 'Christ as the divine guru in the theology of Roberto de Nobili'. In *One faith, many cultures: inculturation, indigenisation and contextualisation,* pp 25–40, ed Ruy O Costa. Boston Theological Institute, Annual Volume 2. Maryknoll, NY: Orbis Books; and Cambridge: Boston Theological Institute, 1988.

Costa, Ruy. 'Introduction: Inculturation, Indigenisation and contextualisation'. In *One faith, many cultures: inculturation, indigenisation and contextualisation,* ed Ruy Costa, pp. ix–xvii. Boston Theological Institute Annual Series, vol 2. Maryknoll: Orbis; and Cambridge: Boston Theological Institute, 1988.

Cox, Harvey. *Fire from heaven: the rise of pentecostal spirituality and the reshaping of religion in the twenty-first century.* Reading, Mass: Addison-Wesley, 1994.

Cox, Harvey. 'Healers and ecologists: Pentecostalism in Africa'. *Christian Century* 111.32 (9 November 1994): 1042–1046.

Crane, Julia G. & Michael V Angrosino. *Field projects in anthropology: a student handbook.* 2nd edition. Prospect Heights, Ill: Waveland Press, 1984.

Crowther, Samuel & John Christopher Taylor. *The gospel on the banks of the Niger: journals and notices of the native missionaries accompanying the Niger expedition of 1857–1859.* Np, 1859; reprint, London: Dawsons of Pall Mall, 1968.

Dachs, Anthony J, ed. *Christianity South of the Zambezi.* vol 1. Gweru: Mambo Press, 1973.

Dachs, Anthony J. & W F Rea. *The Catholic Church in Zimbabwe, 1879–1979.* Gweru: Mambo Press, 1979.

Daly, Ron Reid, as told to Peter Stiff. *Selous Scouts: top secret war.* Cape Town: Galago, 1983.

Daneel, Marthinus L. *Fambidzano: ecumenical movement of Zimbabwean Independent Churches.* Gweru: Mambo Press, 1989.

Daneel, Marthinus L. *Old and new in Southern Shona Independent Churches.* Vol 1, *Background and rise of the major movements.* The Hague and Paris: Mouton, 1971.

Daneel, Marthinus L. *Old and new in Southern Shona Independent Churches.* Vol 2, *Church growth: causative factors and recruitment techniques.* The Hague: Mouton, 1974.

Daneel, Marthinus L. *Old and new in Southern Shona Independent Churches.* Vol 3, *Leadership and fission dynamics.* Gweru: Mambo Press, 1988.

Daneel, Marthinus L. *The God of the Matopo Hills: an essay on the Mwari Cult in Rhodesia.* The Hague: Mouton, 1970.

Daneel, Marthinus L. *Quest for belonging: introduction to a study of African Independent Churches.* Gweru, Zimbabwe: Mambo Press, 1987.

Daneel, Marthinus L. *Zionism and faith-healing in Rhodesia: aspects of African Independent Churches.* Translated from the Dutch by V A February. The Hague and Paris: Mouton, 1970.

de Rosny, Eric. *Healers in the night.* Translated from French by Robert R. Barr. Maryknoll: Orbis Books, 1985.

Dickson, Kwesi A. 'Mission in African Countries'. In *Christian Mission-Jewish Mission,* eds Martin A Cohen & Helga Croner, 187–206. New York: Paulist Press, 1982.

329

Dickson, Kwesi A. *Theology in Africa*. Maryknoll, NY: Orbis Books, 1984.

Dickson, Kwesi & Paul Ellingworth, eds. *Biblical revelation and African beliefs*. London: Lutterworth Press, 1969.

Donovan, Vincent. *Christianity rediscovered*. 2nd edition. Maryknoll, NY: Orbis Books, 1982.

Douglas, Mary. *Natural symbols: explorations in cosmology*. With a new introduction by the author. New York: Pantheon Books, 1982.

Etherington, Norman. 'South African missionary ideologies, 1880–1920: retrospect and prospect'. In *Missionary ideologies in the imperialist era: 1880–1920; papers from the Durham consultation*, eds. Torben Christensen & William R Hutchinson, 191–199. Aarhus C, Denmark: Forlaget Aros, 1982.

Evans, H St John T. *The Church in Southern Rhodesia*. London: Society for the Propagation of the Gospel in Foreign Parts, 1945.

Farrant, Jean. *Mashonaland martyr: Bernard Mizeki and the pioneer church*. London, UK and Salisbury, Rhodesia: Oxford University Press, 1966.

Fashole-Luke, Edward, Richard Gray, Adrian Hastings & Godwin Taisie, eds. *Christianity in Independent Africa*. Bloomington, Ind: Indiana University Press, 1978.

Fernandez, James W. *Bwiti: an ethnography of the religious imagination in Africa*. Princeton: Princeton University Press, 1982.

Fernandez, James W. 'The precincts of the prophet: a day with Johannes Galilee Shembe'. *Journal of Religion in Africa* 5, 1 (1973), 32–53.

Frederikse, J. *None but ourselves: masses vs mass media in the making of Zimbabwe*. Harare: Zimbabwe Publishing House, 1982.

Gann, Lewis H & Thomas H Henriksen. *The struggle for Zimbabwe: battle in the bush*. New York: Praeger, 1981.

Geertz, Clifford. 'Ethos, World view and the analysis of sacred symbols'. In *The interpretation of cultures*, 126–141. New York: Basic Books, 1973.

Geertz, Clifford. 'Religion as a cultural system'. In *The interpretation of cultures*, 87–125. New York: Basic Books, 1973.

Geertz, Clifford. 'Thick description: toward an interpretive theory of culture'. In *The interpretation of cultures*, 3–30. New York: Basic Books, 1973.

Gelfand, Michael, ed. *Gubulawayo and beyond: letters and journals of the early Jesuit missionaries to Zambesia (1897–1887)*. London: Geoffrey Chapman, 1968.

Gelfand, Michael. *African crucible: an ethico-religious study with specific reference to the Shona-speaking people*. Cape Town: Juta & Co, 1968.

Gelfand, Michael. *Growing up in Shona society*. Gweru: Mambo Press, 1979.

Gelfand, Michael. *Shona religion, with special reference to the Makorekore*. Cape Town: Juta & Co, 1962.

Gelfand, Michael. *The genuine Shona: survival values of an African culture*. Gweru: Mambo Press, 1973.

Gelfand, Michael. *The spiritual beliefs of the Shona*. Gweru: Mambo Press, 1977.

Gelfand, Michael. *The traditional medical practitioner in Zimbabwe: his principles of practise and pharmacopoeia*. Gweru: Mambo Press, 1985.

Gelfand, Michael. *Ukama: reflections on Shona and Western cultures in Zimbabwe*. Gweru: Mambo Press, 1981.

Gelfand, Michael. *Witch doctor: traditional medicine man of Rhodesia*. London: Harvill Press, 1964.

330

Gibbon, Geoffrey. *Paget of Rhodesia: a memoir of Edward, 5th Bishop of Mashonaland.* Bulawayo: Books of Rhodesia, 1973.

Godwin, Peter. *Mukiwa: a white boy in Africa.* New York: Atlantic Monthly Press, 1996.

Gray, Richard. *Black Christians and white missionaries.* New Haven: Yale University Press, 1990.

Guttierez, Gustavo. *A theology of liberation: history, politics and salvation.* Translated and edited by Caridad Inda & John Eagleson. Maryknoll: Orbis Press, 1973.

Hallencreutz, Carl F. 'A council in crossfire: ZCC 1964–1980'. In *Church and state in Zimbabwe,* eds Carl Hallencreutz & Ambrose Moyo, 51–113. Gweru: Mambo Press, 1988.

Hallencreutz, Carl F & Ambrose Moyo, eds. *Church and state in Zimbabwe.* Gweru: Mambo Press, 1988.

Hannan, M. *Standard Shona dictionary.* 2nd edition, with Addendum. Harare: College Press, 1981.

Harnack, Adolf. *The mission and expansion of Christianity in the first three centuries.* Translated and edited by James Moffatt. New York: GP Putnam's Sons; London: Williams & Norgate, 1908.

Hastings, Adrian. *A history of African Christianity, 1950–1975.* Cambridge, UK: Cambridge University Press, 1979.

Hastings, Adrian. *African Christianity.* New York: Seabury Press, 1976.

Hefner, Robert W. *Hindu Javanese: Tengger tradition and Islam.* Princeton: Princeton University Press, 1985.

Hefner, Robert W, ed. *Conversion to Christianity: historical and anthropological perspectives on a great transformation.* Berkeley, Los Angeles: University of California Press, 1993.

Horton, Robin. 'African Conversion'. *Africa* 41, 2 (April 1971): 85–108.

Hove, Masotsha Mike. *Confessions of a wizard.* Gweru: Mambo Press, 1985.

Hymns ancient & modern: revised Full Score Edition. (London): Hymns Ancient & Modern, Ltd., 1981.

Idowu, E. Bolaji. *African Traditional religion: a definition.* Maryknoll: Orbis, 1973.

James, William. *The varieties of religious experience: a study in human nature.* The Gifford Lectures on Natural Religion delivered at Edinburgh in 1901–1902. New York: Longmans, Green & Co, 1902.

Jenkins, David & Dorothy Stebbing. *They led the way: Christian pioneers of central Africa.* Cape Town, South Africa: Oxford University Press, 1966.

Jones, E. Stanley. *The Christ of the Indian Road.* New York: Abingdon Press, 1925.

Joyce L. Kazembe. 'The women issue'. In *Zimbabwe: the political economy of transition, 1980–1986,* ed Ibbo Mandaza, 377–404. Dakar: Codesria, 1986.

Jules-Rosette, Benetta. *African apostles: ritual and conversion in the Church of John Maranke.* Ithaca, NY: Cornell University Press, 1975.

Jules-Rosette, Benetta. 'Women as ceremonial leaders in an African Church: the apostles of John Maranke'. In *The new religions of Africa,* ed Benetta Jules-Rosette, pp. 127–144. Norwood, N. J.: Ablex, 1979.

Jules-Rosette, Benetta, ed. *The new religions of Africa.* Norwood, NJ: Ablex, 1979.

Kabweza, O M, L M Hatugari, M A. Habutyinei & C Hove. *Pasichigare: essays on Shona culture in retrospect.* Gweru: Mambo Press, 1979.

Kanengoni, Alexander. *Effortless tears.* Harare: Baobab, 1993.

331

Kato, Byang H. *Theological pitfalls in Africa*. Kisumu, Kenya: Evange, 1975.

Katz, Richard. *Boiling energy: community healing among the Kalahari Kung*. Cambridge, Mass: Harvard University Press, 1982.

Kee, Howard Clark. 'From the Jesus movement toward institutional Church'. In *Conversion to Christianity: historical and anthropological perspectives on a great transformation*, ed Robert W Hefner, 47–63. Berkeley, Los Angeles: University of California Press, 1993.

Kileff, Clive & Peggy, eds. *Shona customs: essays by African writers*. Gweru, Zimbabwe: Mambo Press, 1970.

Kirby, Jon. 'The non-conversion of the Anofu of Northern Ghana'. *Mission Studies* 2, 2 (1985), 15–25.

Kirwen, Michael C. *The missionary and the diviner: contending theologies of Christian and African religions*. Maryknoll: Orbis, 1987.

Knight-Bruce, George Wyndham Hamilton. *Journals of the Mashonaland Mission, 1888 to 1892*. London: Society for the Propagation of the Gospel in Foreign Parts, 1892.

Knight-Bruce, George Wyndham Hamilton. *Memories of Mashonaland*. London and New York: Edward Arnold, 1895.

Kraemer, Hendrik. *The Christian message in the non-Christian world*. 2nd ed. New York: Harper; for the International Missionary Council, 1938; 1947.

Kriger, Norma. *Zimbabwe's guerrilla war: peasant voices*. African Studies Series, No 70. Cambridge: Cambridge University, Press, 1992.

Kunnumpuram, Kurien. 'Inculturation in Vatican II'. *Jeevadhara: a journal of Christian interpretation* 33 (May–June 1976), 283–292.

Lagerwerf, Leny. *Witchcraft, sorcery and spirit possession: pastoral responses in Africa*. Mambo Occasional Papers: Missio Pastoral Series, No 19. Gweru: Mambo, 1992.

Lan, David. *Guns and rain: guerrillas and spirit mediums in Zimbabwe*. Harare: Zimbabwe Publishing House, 1985.

Langham-Carter, R R. *Knight-Bruce*. Borrowdale, Rhodesia: Christ Church, nd.

Lapsley, Michael, S S M. *Neutrality or co-option? Anglican Church and state from 1964 until the independence of Zimbabwe*. Mambo Occasional Papers: Missio-Pastoral Series No 16. Gweru: Mambo Press, 1986.

Lindbeck, George A. *The nature of doctrine: religion and theology in a postliberal age*. Philadelphia: Westminster Press, 1984.

Lugira, A. M. *African Religion*. Nyangwe, Zaire and Roxbury, Mass: Omenana, 1981.

Luzbetak, Louis J. *The church and cultures: new perspectives in missiological anthropology*. Maryknoll, NY: Orbis, 1988.

Madziyire, Salathiel K. 'Heathen practises in the urban and rural parts of Marandellas area and their effects on Christianity'. In *Themes in the Christian History of Central Africa*, ed T O Ranger & John Weller, 76–82. Berkeley: University of California Press, 1975.

Mafu, Hezekiel. 'The 1991–92 Zimbabwean drought and some religious reactions'. *Journal of religion in Africa* 25, No 3 (August 1995): 288–308.

Mahamba, Irena Ropa Rinopfuka. *Woman in struggle*. 2nd edition. Gweru: Mambo Press, 1986.

Maitland, Sara. *Ancestral truths*. New York: Henry Holt, 1993.

Mandaza, Dominic M. 'Traditional ceremonies which persist'. In *Shona customs: essays by African writers*, pp. 54–60. Edited by Clive & Peggy Kileff. Gweru: Mambo Press, 1970.

Manungo, Kenneth Dzutsumwa. 'The role peasants played in the Zimbabwe War of Liberation, with special emphasis on Chiweshe district'. PhD dissertation, Ohio University, 1991.

Marange, Johane. *Humboo Hutsva hwavaPostori* (The new Revelation of the Apostles). Np.

Martin, David and Phyllis Johnson. *The struggle for Zimbabwe: The Chimurenga War*. Harare: Zimbabwe Publishing House, 1981.

Martin, Luther H. *Hellenistic religions: an introduction*. New York: Oxford University Press, 1987.

Massachusetts Companion Diocese Committee. 'A venture in partnership: an evaluation of the companionship between the diocese of Massachusetts in the USA and the Dioceses of Harare, Lundi and Manicaland in Zimbabwe, 1984–89'. In *1989 Diocesan Journal of the Two Hundred Fourth Annual Session of the Diocesan Convention, November 3–4. 1989: Minutes and Papers of the Convention, Reports of Commissions, Committees, Staff and Related Organisations*, 193–210. Boston: Diocese of Massachusetts, (1990).

Maxwell, David. 'Witches, prophets and avenging spirits: the second Christian movement in North-east Zimbabwe'. *Journal of Religion in Africa* 25, No 3 (August 1995), 309–337.

May, Joan. *Zimbabwean women in customary and colonial law*. Zambeziana, Vol 14. Gweru, Mambo; Edinburgh: Holmes McDougall, 1983.

Mbiti, John. *African religions and philosophy*. Garden City, NJ: Anchor Books, 1970.

Mbiti, John. *An introduction to African religion*. London: Heinemann, 1975.

Mbiti, John. *Concepts of God in Africa*. London: SPCK, 1970.

Mbiti, John. *The prayers of African religion*. Maryknoll, NY: Orbis, 1975.

McLaughlin, Janice. 'We did it for love': refugees and religion in the camps in Mozambique and Zambia during Zimbabwe's Liberation Struggle'. In *Church and state in Zimbabwe*, eds Carl Hallencreutz & Ambrose Moyo, 127–145. Gweru: Mambo Press, 1988.

Meekers, Dominique. 'The noble custom of *Roora*: the marriage practises of the Shona of Zimbabwe'. *Ethololology* 32, 1 (Winter 1993), 35–54.

Milingo, E. *The world in between: Christian healing and the struggle for spiritual survival*. Gweru: Mambo Press, 1985.

Mitchell, Robert Cameron. *African primal religions*. Major World Religions Series, edited by Donald K Swearer. Niles, Ill: Argus Communications, 1977.

Molland, Frank Hulme. In *witch-bound Africa: an account of the primitive Kaonde tribe and their beliefs*. London: Seeley, Service & Co., 1923.

Moorcraft, Paul L & Peter McLaughlin. *Chimurenga! The war in Rhodesia, 1965–1980*. Marshalltown, South Africa: Sygma Books & Collins Vaal, 1982.

Moorman, John R H. *A history of the Church in England*. London: Adam & Charles Black, 1953.

Mothers' Union. *The Mothers' Union Service Book*. Rev ed. London: Mothers' Union, (1948).

Moyana, Henry V. *The political economy of land in Zimbabwe*. Gweru: Mambo Press, 1984.

Moyana, Henry V. *The Victory of Chief Rekayi Tangwena*. Makers of Zimbabwean History. Harare: Longman Zimbabwe, 1987.

Mukandi, Jonathon J. *Zvousiku* (Things of Night). Gweru: Mambo Press, 1983.

Murphree, Marshall W. *Christianity and the Shona*. New York: Humanities Press, 1969.

Mutasa, Garikai. *The contact*. Mambo Writers Series, English Section, Vol 20. Gweru: Mambo Press, 1985.

Muzorewa, Abel T. *Rise up and walk*. Nashville: Abingdon, 1978.

Muzorewa, Gwinyai H. *The origins and development of African theology*. Maryknoll: Orbis, 1985.

Ndwiyo Dzechechi Dzevu: Buku Rekutanga. (Hymns of the Churches of the Earth.) Np: Church Music Service, nd.

Ndwiyo Dzomuchechi. (Hymns for Church Use.) Revised edition. London: SPCK, 1966.

Neill, Stephen. *A history of Christian missions*. 2nd ed rev by Owen Chadwick. Harmondsworth, UK: Penguin, 1986.

Neill, Stephen. *Colonialism and Christian mission*. New York: McGraw-Hill, 1966.

Ngoma dzeUnited Methodist Church yeZimbabwe (Drums of the United Methodist Church of Zimbabwe). Mutare: Conference Board of Publications and Communications, 1964.

Nida, Eugene A. *Customs and cultures: anthropology for Christian missions*. (New York:) Harper & Brothers, 1954; reprint ed, Pasadena: William Carey Library, 1975.

Nida, Eugene A & William D Reyburn. *Meaning across cultures*. Maryknoll, NY: Orbis, 1981.

Niebuhr, H Richard. *Christ and culture*. New York: Harper & Row, 1951.

Nock, Arthur Darby. *Conversion: the old and the new in religion from Alexander the Great to Augustine of Hippo*. London and New York: Oxford University Press, 1933.

Nyamiti, C. *Christ as our ancestor: christology from an African perspective*. Mambo Occasional Papers: Missio-Pastoral Series, No 11. Gweru: Mambo Press, 1984.

Nyika, Tambayi O. *A rat on her back: a play*. Translated from the Shona *Ndinodawo Mwana* (I also want a child). Mambo Writers Series: English Section, Vol 24. Gweru: Mambo Press, 1986.

Oduyoye, Modupe. *The sons of the gods and the daughters of men: an Afro-Asiatic interpretation of Genesis 1–11*. Maryknoll, NY: Orbis, 1984.

Okorocha, Cyril. *The meaning of religious conversion in Africa: the case of the Igbo in Nigeria*. Aldershot, UK and Brockfield, Vt: Avebury, 1987.

Oladimeji, O. *African Traditional Religion*. Olesa, Oyo State, Nigeria: Ilesanmi Press, 1980.

Oosthuizen, G C *Post-Christianity in Africa: a theological and anthropological study*. Grand Rapids: William B. Eerdmans Publishing Co, 1968.

Parker, Olive. *For the family's sake: a history of the Mothers' Union, 1876–1976*. London and Oxford: Mowbrays, 1975.

Parrinder, Geoffrey. *Africa's three religions*. London: Sheldon Press, 1976.

Parrinder, Geoffrey. *African traditional religion*. 3rd ed. London: Sheldon Press, 1974.

Parrinder, Geoffrey. *Religion in Africa*. New York: Praeger, 1969.

Parsons, Robert T, ed. *Windows on Africa: a symposium*. Leiden: EJ Brill, 1971.

Peadon, W. R. . *Missionary attitudes to Shona culture, 1890–1923*. Salisbury, Rhodesia: Central Africa Historical Association, 1970.

Pobee, John. *Toward an African theology*. Nashville: Abingdon, 1979.

Poewe, Karla, ed. *Charismatic Christianity as a global culture*. Studies in Comparative Religion. Columbia: University of South Carolina Press, 1994.

Presler, Henry H. *Primitive religions in India: a textbook on the primitive religious type among India's tribals*. Indian Theological Library No 6. Bangalore: Christian Literature Society, for the Senate of Serampore College, 1971.

Presler, Titus Leonard. 'An immersion in Africans' living experience of Christ in community'. *Cowley* 20, No 4 (Spring 1995), 8–12.

Presler, Titus Leonard. 'From Boston to Zimbabwe: young pilgrims find the "heart of God".' *Episcopal Life* 7, No 8 (September 1996), 1, 3.

Presler, Titus Leonard. 'Missionary Anglicanism meets an African religion: a retrospect on the centenary of Bishop Knight-Bruce's entry into Zimbabwe'. *Missionalia* 17, 3 (November 1989), 162–175.

Presler, Titus Leonard. 'Mizeki Pilgrims "See God with new eyes".' *Episcopal Times* 19, No 5 (September 1996), 20–21.

Presler, Titus Leonard. 'Wilderness nights: the cultural interaction of Christian gospel and Shona Spirit Religion in the *pungwe* movement among Manicaland Christians in Zimbabwe'. ThD dissertation, Boston University, 1994.

Presler, Titus Leonard. 'Zimbabwe'. *Encyclopedia of politics and religion*, edited by Robert Wuthnow, sv. Washington: Congressional Quarterly Books, 1998.

Puthanangady, Paul. 'Inculturation in spirituality and worship'. *Jeevadhara: A Journal of Christian Interpretation* 33 (May–June 1976), 302–311.

Punch, Maurice. *The politics and ethics of fieldwork*. Qualitative Research Methods, 3. Beverly Hills, London and New Delhi: Sage, 1986.

Radcliffe-Brown, A. R. *Taboo*. The Frazer Lecture. Cambridge, UK: Cambridge University Press, 1939.

Ranger, Terence O. 'Holy men and rural communities in Zimbabwe, 1970–1980'. In *The Church and War*, ed W J Sheils, 443–461. Papers read at the Twenty-first Summer Meeting and the Twenty-second Winter Meeting of the Ecclesiastical History Society. Studies in Church History, vol 20. Oxford: Basil Blackwell, for the Ecclesiastical History Society, 1983.

Ranger, Terence O. 'Medical science and Pentecost: the dilemma of Anglicanism in Africa'. In *The Church and healing: papers read at the Twentieth Summer Meeting and the Twenty-first Winter Meeting of the Ecclesiastical History Society*, ed W J Sheils, 333–365. Oxford: Basil Blackwell, for the Ecclesiastical History Society, 1982.

Ranger, Terence O. *Peasant consciousness and guerrilla war in Zimbabwe: a comparative study*. Harare: Zimbabwe Publishing House, 1985.

Ranger, Terence O. 'Protestant Missions in Africa: the dialectic of conversion in the American Methodist Episcopal Church in Eastern Zimbabwe, 1900–1950'. In *Religion in Africa: experience and expression*, eds Thomas D. Blakely, Walter E A van Beek & Dennis L Thomson, 275–313. Monograph Series of David M Kennedy Centre for International Studies, Brigham Young University. London: James Curry; Portsmouth, NH: Heinemann, 1994.

Ranger, Terence O. 'Religious pluralism in Zimbabwe: a report on the Britain-Zimbabwe Society Research Day, St Antony's College, Oxford, 23 April 1994'. *Journal of Religion in Africa* 25, No 3 (August 1995), 226–251.

Ranger, Terence O. *Revolt in Southern Rhodesia, 1896–97: a study in African resistance*. Evanston: Northwestern University Press, 1967.

Ranger, Terence O. 'The death of Chaminuka: spirit mediums, nationalism and the guerilla war in Zimbabwe'. *African Affairs* (June 1982), 349–69.

335

Ranger, Terence O. *The invention of tribalism in Zimbabwe*. Mambo Occasional Papers: Socio-Economic Series, No 19. Gweru: Mambo, 1985.

Ranger, Terence O and Isaria N Kimambo, eds. *The historical study of African religion: with special reference to East and Central Africa*. London, Nairobi: Heinemann, 1972.

Rayan, Samuel. 'Flesh of India's flesh'. *Jeevadhara: a journal of Christian interpretation* 33 (May–June 1976), 259–267.

Rea, W. F. *The missionary factor in Southern Rhodesia*. Salisbury, Rhodesia: Central Africa Historical Association, 1962.

Rosny, Eric de. *Healers in the night*. Translated from the French by Robert R Barr. Maryknoll, NY; Orbis, 1985.

Sanneh, Lamin. 'Christian missions and the western guilt complex'. *Christian Century* (8 April 1987), 330–334.

Sanneh, Lamin. *Encountering the West: Christianity and the global cultural process: the African dimension*. Maryknoll: Orbis, 1993.

Sanneh, Lamin. *Translating the message: the missionary impact on culture*. American Society of Missiology Series, 13. Maryknoll, NY: Orbis, 1989.

Sanneh, Lamin. *West African Christianity: the religious impact*. Maryknoll, NY: Orbis, 1983.

Saussure, Ferdinand. 'Signs and Language'. In *Culture and society: contemporary debates*, edited by Jeffrey C. Alexander & Steven Seidman, 55–63. Cambridge, UK: Cambridge University Press, 1990.

Schoffeleers, J M. 'Introduction'. In *Guardians of the land: essays on Central African territorial cults*, pp 1–46, ed J M Schoffeleers. Gweru: Mambo Press, 1979.

Schreiter, Robert J. *Constructing local theologies*. Maryknoll, NY: Orbis, 1986.

Schweder, Richard A. & Robert A LeVine, eds. *Culture theory: essays on mind, self and emotion*. Cambridge, UK: Cambridge University Press, 1984.

Shona Ritual: Kuchenura munhu, kana kuti, kurova guva, kana kugadzira mufi (Purifying the person, or beating the grave, or preparing the dead). Gweru: Mambo Press, 1982.

Shona Ritual: Minamato Yokukomborera (Prayers of Blessing). Gweru: Mambo Press, 1981.

Shorter, Aylward. *African Christian theology: adaptation or incarnation?* Maryknoll: Orbis, 1977.

Shorter, Aylward. *Jesus and the witchdoctor: an approach to healing and wholeness*. London: Geoffrey Chapman & Maryknoll: Orbis, 1985.

Shorter, Aylward. *Prayer in the religious traditions of Africa*. Nairobi: Oxford University Press, 1975.

Shuro, G. '*Chisingaperi Chinoshura*' (Eternal Bad Luck). In *Hondo yeChimurenga: nyaya dzeHondo dzakaunganidzwa neLiterature Bureau* (The Liberation War: stories of the war, collected by the Literature Bureau), pp. 196–200. Gweru: Mambo Press, 1984.

Shweder, Richard A. & Robert A LeVine, eds. *Culture theory: essays on mind, self and emotion*. Cambridge, UK: Cambridge University Press, 1984.

Skelton, Kenneth. *Bishop in Smith's Rhodesia: notes from a turbulent octave 1962–1970*. Mambo occasional papers: Missio-Pastoral Series No 12. Gweru: Mambo Press, 1985.

336

Society for Promoting Christian Knowledge. *Rwendo rwomuKristu: tsamba yeminamato yamazuva ese norudzidziso rweChechi Katorike.* (The journey of the Christian: lessons for daily prayers and an explanation of the Church Catholic). Rev. ed. London: SPCK, 1969.

Spottiswood, George A., ed. *Official report of the missionary conference of the Anglican communion on May 28, 29, 30, 31 and June 1, 1894.* London: Society for Promoting Christian Knowledge, 1894.

Stackhouse, Max L. 'Contextualisation, contextuality and contextualism'. In *One faith, many cultures: inculturation, indigenisation and contextualisation,* ed Ruy O Costa, 3–13. Cambridge, Mass: Boston Theological Institute; Maryknoll, NY: Orbis, 1988.

'Streamlining Mother's Union means lost jobs'. *Church Times,* 12 November 1993, 1.

Sundkler, Bengt G. M. *Bantu prophets in South Africa.* 2nd edition. London, New York: Oxford University Press, for the International African Institute, 1961.

Tambiah, Stanley J. 'The form and meaning of magical acts: a point of view'. In *Modes of thought,* eds R Horton & R. Finnegan, 199–229. London: Faber & Faber, 1973.

Taylor, John V. *The primal vision: Christian presence amid African religion.* London: SCM, 1963.

Testamente Itsva yaShe wedu Jesu Kristu. (The New Testament of Our Lord Jesus Christ.) (Harare): (Bible Society in Zimbabwe), 1980.

The Jerusalem meeting of the International Missionary Council, March 24-April 8, 1928, vol 1: The Christian life and message in relation to non-Christian systems of thought and life. New York: Internatonal Missionary Council, 1928.

Tillich, Paul. *Theology of culture.* Edited by Robert C. Kimball. New York: Oxford University Press, 1959.

Turner, Harold W. *Religious innovation in Africa: collected essays on new religious movements.* Boston: G. K. Hall, 1979.

Turner, Philip. 'The wisdom of the fathers and the gospel of Christ: some notes on Christian adaptation in Africa'. *Journal of religion in Africa* 4 (1971), 45–68.

Turner, Victor 'Liminality and community'. In *Culture and society: contemporary debates,* edited by Jeffrey C. Alexander & Steven Seidman. Cambridge, UK: Cambridge University Press, 1990.

Edward B. Tylor. *Primitive culture: researches into the development of mythology, philosophy, religion, language, art and custom.* 6th ed. London: John Murray, 1920.

Vail, H. Leroy. 'Religion, language and the tribal myth: the Tumbuka and Chewa of Malawi'. In *Guardians of the land: essays on Central African territorial cults,* ed J M Schoffeleers, 209–233. Gweru: Mambo Press, 1979.

Verkuyl, Johannes. *Contemporary missiology: an introduction.* Translated from the Dutch and edited by Dale Cooper. Grand Rapids: William B Eerdmans Publishing Co, 1978.

Walker, Sheila S. *The religious revolution in the Ivory Coast: the prophet Harris and the Harrist Church.* Chapel Hill: University of North Carolina Press, 1983.

Warren, Max, ed. *To apply the gospel: selections from the writings of Henry Venn.* Grand Rapids: William B Eerdmans, 1971.

Watt, W Montgomery. *Religion in Africa.* Edinburgh: University of Edinburgh Centre of African Studies, 1964.

Weinrich, A K H. *African marriage in Zimbabwe and the impact of Christianity.*

Zambeziana, Vol 13. Gweru, Mambo Press; Edinburgh: Holmes McDougall, 1983.

Weller, John & Jane Linden. *Mainstream Christianity to 1980 in Malawi, Zambia and Zimbabwe*. Gweru: Mambo Press, 1984.

Werner, D. 'Miao spirit shrines in the religious history of the Southern Lake Tanganyika Region'. In *Guardians of the land: essays on Central African territorial cults*, ed J M Schoffeleers, 89–130. Gweru: Mambo Press, 1979.

Westermann, Diedrich. *Africa and Christianity*. New York: AMS Press, 1977, c 1937.

Whiteside, J. *History of the Wesleyan Methodist Church of South Africa*. London: E Stock, 1906.

World Council of Churches. *Consultation with African Instituted Churches: Ogere, Nigeria, 9–14 January 1996*. Geneva: World Council of Churches, (1996).

Zuesse, Evan M. *Ritual cosmos: the sanctification of life in African religions*. Athens, Ohio: Ohio University Press, 1979.

Zvarevashe, Ignatius M. 'Witches and witchcraft'. In *Shona customs: essays by African writers*, eds. Clive & Peggy Kileff, 48–50. Gweru: Mambo Press, 1970.

Zvobgo, Chengetai J. 'The African franchise question: an aspect of church-state relations in colonial Zimbabwe, 1921–1972'. In *Church and state in Zimbabwe*, eds Carl F Hallencreutz & Ambrose Moyo, 29–50. Gweru: Mambo, 1988.

Zvobgo, Chengetai J M. 'Shona and Ndebele responses to Christianity in Southern Rhodesia'. *Journal of Religion in Africa* 8, 1 (1976), 41–51.

Zvobgo, Chengetai J M. 'The influence of the Wesleyan Methodist Missions in Southern Rhodesia, 1891–1923'. In *Christianity South of the Zambezi*, vol 1, ed A J Dachs. Gweru: Mambo Press, 1973.

Zimbabwe Census 1992: Preliminary Report. Harare: Central Statistical Office, 1992.

Zimbabwe: Country Profile, 1997–98. London: Economist Intelligence Unit, 1997.

INDEX

References to photos are printed in
boldface
References to footnotes include the
page number and note number

339

barrenness. *See* fertility
base communities (CEBs), 271, 272
Battle of Chinoyi, 67n2
Bediako, Kwame, 282
betting, 307, 308
Bible, 246, 266, 271
    reading at *mapungwe*, 110, 126,
        127, 205
Bible study, 163, 200, 304
Board of Commissioners for Foreign
    Missions, 273n25
Bonda Church District, 21, 22, 219
Bonda Mission, 21, 22, 23, 93, 105,
    107, 110, 114, 149, 219, 308
Bosch, David, 279
Botswana, 161
bride-price (*lobola or roora*), 136,
    138, 193, 194
British South Africa Company
    (BSAC), 28
Broderick, George, 105, 107
Burrough, Paul, 93n62
Bwiti religion, 255n7, 256n7

Cahill, Tony, 152
camp meetings
    of Marange Apostles (*gungano*),
        162, 163
    of Methodists (*gungano*), 108,
        111, 219, 255
cannibalism, 60, 61
capitalism, 73
CCAP. *See* Church of Central Africa –
    Presbyterian
Chavunduka, Gordon, 224n14
chiefs, 26, 27, 37, 39, 40, 51, 52,
    56, 101, 102, 106. *See also*
    Mutasa, Chief; Mangwende,
    Chief
chikwambo. See avenging spirit
    (*chikwambo*)
child abuse, 231
child care, 33
child custody, 194, 247
child-bearing, 137, 159, 182, 193,
    195, 196, 197. *See also* fertili-
    ty

China, 68, 272
chisi. See day of rest
Chitambo, David, 204, 206
Chitungu, Fabian, 105
Chivanhu 43. *See also* Shona Spirit
    Religion
Christian Council of Rhodesia, 92
Christianity
    affirmed by *guerrillas*, 96
    African, 11, 16, 20, 100, 282
    associated with whites, 91, 92,
        95, 218
    confrontation with SSR, 258
    cultural dimensions, 18
    debate with SSR, 222–232
    definition, 297
    denounced by guerrillas, 14, 87,
        90, 92, 97, 106, 217, 252
    encounter with indigenous reli-
        gion, 16, 18, 19
    growth of, 10–13, 15, 263
    indigenization of, 274, 276
    interaction with SSR, 222, 262
    localization of, 228, 265
    'mass movement', 100, 104, 106
    missionary, 19, 20, 264
    opposition to SSR, 150
    relation to colonialism, 87
    relationship with African religions,
        10
    relationship with other religions,
        276
    relationship with SSR, 232, 267,
        270
    Shona, 255
    world, 11, 12, 250
Christmas, 149, 151
church, definition, 297
church affiliation, 264
church authorities, 148
church buildings, 162, 189, 191,
    200
church councils, 161
church festivals, 22, 107, 142, 149,
    184, 200
church growth, 12, 13, 15, 35, 149,
    156, 216, 220, 242, 262, 282

340

341

342

Mozambique (FRELIMO), 30, 67
Full Gospel Church of God, 33, 155, 214
funerals. *See* death rituals

Gbaya people, 279n33
Geertz, Clifford, 250, 251, 252, 254
gender-based groups, 142, 144–147, 163, 304. *See also* Fishermen; Mothers' Union
Gethsemane, 119, 120, 172
Ghana, 161
glossolalia, 148, 159, 186, 192, 201, 204, 245, 249
God Bless Africa, 165n21, 192
gomo, kuenda ku-. See mountain, going to
gona. See medicine bundle
Gorogodo, Sylvester, 143
gospel-culture interaction, 100, 104, 222, 249–281
gourd rattles. *See* rattles
Great Vigil of Easter, 23, 149
growth, church, 12, 13, 15, 35, 149, 156, 216, 220, 242, 262, 282
guerrillas, 14, 30, 65, 66, 69, 70–76, 78
   promotion of SSR, 35, 65
   suppression og Christianity, 90–96
gungano. See camp meetings

Harare, Anglican Diocese of, 148
harvest, 42, 56
Hastings, Adrian, 267n16
Hatch, Nathan, 269
Hatendi, Peter, 148
healing, 13, 38, 42, 55, 108, 128, 141, 156, 158, 159–160, 168, 172, 179, 182, 183, 186, 192, 210, 229, 235, 236, 245, 249, 308
Hefner, Robert, 253, 254, 264
Hellenistic period, 17n7
Hinduism, 17n7, 255n7
HIV. *See* Aids

Holy Spirit, 14, 122, 123, 131, 133, 141, 148, 155, 156, 158, 163, 174, 176, 178, 192, 197, 198, 208, 209, 235, 236, 237, 245, 254, 266
Honde Valley, 23–31, 25
Horton, Robin, 262, 263, 264
Hwange National Park, 67n2
hyenas, 60, 206, 208
hymns, 75, 96, 240

ideology, 251, 252
illness, 37, 42, 49, 54, 59, 130, 150, 159, 181, 223, 227, 230, 233, 244
incest, 49, 60
incorporation, 15
inculturation, 277, 278, 279
independence, political, 13, 15, 21, 216, 217
independent churches, 298. *See* African Initiated Churches
India, 275
indigenisation, 273, 274, 276, 278
indigenous religion, 296. *See* Shona Spirit Religion
initiation of spirit mediums, 13, 38, 55, 56, 257
inspiration, 209
inter-religious encounter, 18, 35, 127, 250
Islam, 10, 11, 262, 263

Jekenishen Church. See St Luca's Apostolic Ejuwel Jekenishen Church
Jesus, 117, 126, 129, 131, 134, 136, 137, 140, 149, 172, 176, 188, 192
Jones, E Stanley, 275, 276
Judas, 117

Kahlari, Togarasei, 128, 129, 130, 131, 132, 139, **146**, 147
Kanengoni, Alexander, 80, 81
Katiyo Tea Estates, 29
kingdom of God, 127, 135

Mhlaudzi, Silas, 120
mhondoro. See clan spirit
ministry groups, 163, 172
Ministry of Community Development and Women's Affairs, 247
miracles, 158, 184
misfortune, 42, 49, 63, 150, 167, 176, 178, 196, 231, 233, 244
missiology, 20
    definition, 300
mission, 19, 158, 161, 165, 182, 184, 200, 211–213, 250, 272–283
    African initiative, 12, 20, 104, 155, 211, 264
    by guerrillas, 14, 35, 65, 79, 96–98
    definition, 10, 96, 300
    Euro-American, 11
    growth and, 11, 13
    in AICs, 156
    pungwe as, 97
    vision, 162, 167, 182, 206
mission churches, 298. *See* mission-founded churches
    mission-founded churches (MFCs)
    attitude toward Liberation War, 94
    attitude toward SSR, 227
    critique of AICs, 228
    drums used in, 237, 268
    Eucharist in, 238
    leadership in, 270
    leadership training in, 266
    missionary legacy, 264
    prayer in, 238
    role in African Christianity, 20
    school and hospital institutions, 224
    western cultural influence on, 19
    wilderness in, 257
missionaries, 200, 263, 272, 275, 277, 279, 280, 281, 282
    Euro-American, 19, 20, 101, 250, 255, 278
    opposition to *pungwe*, 107
Mizeki, Bernard, 103–104, 150
monogamy, 308

morality. *See* ethics
Moses, 174, 188
Mothers' Union (MU), 22, 91, 110, 114, 128, 144, 227, 304
mountain, going to (*gomo, kuenda ku-*), 163, 188
mountains, 108, 131, 162, 189
Mozambican civil war, 24, 30, 183, 196
Mozambique, 23, 24, 29, 30, 67, 68, 70, 78, 85, 161, 182
Mozambique National Resistance (MNR or RENAMO), 30
mubatanidzwa. See ecumenical *pungwe*
Muchakata Church. *See* Methodist Church
Mugodhi Church. *See* Unity of African Apostolic Faith Church
Mugodhi, Elijah, 198
murder, 39, 82, 179, 187, 190, 192, 195, 196, 231
Mutasa, Chief, 26
Mutasa, Garikai, 72
Muzorewa, Abel, 92, 93
Mwari, 97, 103, 223, 234
    cult of, 40, 58
    in Christianity, 94, 102, 235, 238, 254
    in SSR, 39, 40, 41, 52, 58, 59, 89, 90, 102, 106, 235, 244

Native Purchase Area, 30
Native Reserves, 28, 29. *See also* Tribal Trust Lands
Ndaza Zionists. *See* Zion Apostolic Church
Ndebele people, 26
Niebuhr, H Richard 279n33
night, 215, 222, 232, 234, 256, 257
    controversy over meeting time, 154
    in Christianity, 119, 123, 132, 142, 143, 144, 147, 159, 172–174, 178, 187, 197, 213, 232, 241, 242, 250, 254
    in Liberation War, 65
    in Shona culture, 152, 153, 154,

245, 247, 248, 258
  in SSR, 46, 49, 50, 52, 55–59,
    63–64, 243, 253
  in witchcraft, 59–63
  in wizardry, 48
norms, 17, 18, 19, 20, 199
Nyabereka, Mai, 134, 135, 137

Old Mutare Mission, 108, 114, 154,
    219, 308
orders of ministry, among Marange
    Apostles, 160
orphans, 183, 199, 201

PACG. *See* Pentecostal Apostolic
    Church of God
Paget, Edward, 29
pastoral care, 149–151, 202
patriarchy, 63
patrilineage, 193, 195, 197
Penhalonga, 21, 29, 93, 110
Pentecostal Apostolic Church of God
    (PACG), 33, 156, 179–197,
    180, 264, 268
Pentecostal movement, 236n36
pentecostalism, 110, 111, 148,
    152, 154, 168, 192, 268
planting, 42
poison, 59, 60
political talks, 66, 72, 73, 80, 96
polygyny, 138, 160, 161, 201, 210,
    308n12
popular religion, 297. See Shona
    Spirit Religion
possession, 13, 41, 46, 50, 52–57,
    89, 109, 186, 195
potshelf, 50, 51
poverty, 33, 49, 231, 266
power, negotiation of, 208–211
prayer litanies, 191
prayerbook worship, 238n37
praying, 13, 35, 94, 108, 109, 116,
    117–120, 121–124, 125, 126,
    127, 128, 129, 130, 131, 132,
    141, 142, 143, 147, 148, 150,
    159, 161, 162, 163, 165, 172,
    173, 174, 182, 183, 188,

190–192, 197, 202, 204, 205,
    209, 210, 235, 236, 238, 245,
    305, 307
preaching, 13, 22, 108, 127–33,
    137, 139–141, 142, 145, **146**,
    148, 149, 165, 172, 190, **203**,
    204, 205, 236, 245, 265, 266,
    308. See also political talks
pre-dawn (*mambakwedza*), 13, 55,
    56, 57, 109, 147, 149, 192,
    234
Presbyterian Church. *See* Church of
    Central Africa, Presbyterian
primal religion, 295. *See* Shona
    Spirit Religion
primal religions, 250
promiscuity, 139, 231
prophecy, 148, 158, 179, 181, 208,
    210, 235, 236, 245
prophets, 163, 189, 199, 201, 206
  founding, 179
prostitution, 83, 231
Protected Villages (PVs), 30, 76, 77,
    114
pungwe
  definition, 299
  etymology, 43–46
Pungwe Falls, 44n17

rain, 52, 56
rape, 231
rattles (percussion instruments)
    (*hosho*), 127, 164
Rebellion of 1896. *See* Shona
    Rebellion of 1896
refugee camps, 78n29
religion
  definition, 18, 297
  in Africa, 10
  interaction wth culture, 19
religious change, 19, 261, 262
revelation, 274–276, 280
Rhodesia Front (RF) forces, 30, 66,
    67, 70, 79, 83
Rhodesian government, 29
Ricci, Matteo, 277
rites of passage, 256, 257